Two Points to Remember

(1) Moustachial, Submoustachial and Malar Stripes: Do not confuse these terms. The moustachial stripe is the dark line from the bill below the eye, along the lower border of the ear-coverts. The pale line below this is the submoustachial, and the dark line below that, down the sides of the chin and throat, is the malar. (Many observers confuse the moustachial and malar stripes.)

(2) Tertials These are the elongated inner-most secondaries that cloak the primaries at rest (the secondaries are often hidden or mostly hidden).

THE MACMILLAN
BIRDER'S GUIDE
TO EUROPEAN AND MIDDLE EASTERN BIRDS

INCLUDING NORTH AFRICA

ILLUSTRATIONS BY ALAN HARRIS
TEXT BY HADORAM SHIRIHAI
AND DAVID A. CHRISTIE

MACMILLAN

First published 1996 by Macmillan
an imprint of Macmillan General Books
25 Eccleston Place, London SW1W 9NF
and Basingstoke

Associated companies throughout the world

ISBN 0 333 58940 8

1 3 5 7 9 8 6 4 2

A CIP catalogue record for this book is available from
the British Library.

Typeset by Parker Typesetting Service, Leicester
Printed and bound in Great Britain by
BPC Hazell Books Ltd
A member of The British Printing Company Ltd

Contents

Introduction

This book is the natural sequel to the widely acclaimed *Macmillan Field Guide to Bird Identification* (Harris *et al.* 1989), which dealt in some depth with identification of 'difficult' species and groups. Whereas that volume (for convenience, referred to hereafter as 'vol. 1') was restricted largely to species on the British and Irish List, however, the present work covers the rest of Europe, together with most of the Middle East and North Africa. The two volumes together therefore cover the major pitfalls likely to be encountered in the West Palearctic.

Here we discuss about 70 subjects (species pairs or groups), in each case in the form of a 'brief identification paper'. These are confined to those where real problems exist, or where a species is frequently confused with others.

Because of the much larger region covered, however, the difficulties are often much more complex. Good examples are the brown *Aquila* eagles, the orange-billed terns, wheatears, *Sylvia* warblers and buntings, among many others. At times there may appear to be some overlap between the two books (e.g. Honey Buzzard, *Hippolais* warblers), but this was inevitable and the present text, far from repeating points made in vol. 1, instead adds significantly to the discussion from a much wider West Palearctic point of view. For instance, in Britain, the Honey Buzzard, although variable, needs to be distinguished only from Common and Rough-legged Buzzards; on passage in the Middle East, however, it shows an extraordinary variety of plumages, confusing the unwary, and also needs to be told from the Steppe form of Common Buzzard and from Long-legged Buzzard.

Choice of subjects was far from simple and required much thought. We believe that we have selected those which most often cause problems, or are particularly difficult, but limitations of space have meant that we had unfortunately to omit a number of other, perhaps equally problematic species. For these, the reader is recommended to consult the identification papers that now appear regularly in a number of journals, in particular *British Birds, Birding World, Dutch Birding* and *Limicola*.

Acknowledgements

A number of identification consultants commented on various sections of text. We greatly appreciate their expertise on the following subjects: egrets (P. Dubois, P. Yésou), eiders (P. Lehman, R. Millington, D. Sibley), goldeneyes (S. Gantlett, P. Lehman, D. Sibley), various raptors (W.S. Clark, I.J. Ferguson-Lees, D. Forsman, B. Génsbøl, R.F. Porter, D. Zetterström), partridges, Spotless Starling, choughs and ravens (S. Madge), sand plovers (D. Fisher, E. Hirschfeld), Oriental Turtle Dove (E. Hirschfeld, H. Jännes), *Calidris* waders (R.J. Chandler, J. Dunn, L. Jonsson, P. Lehman), gulls (T. Hoogendoorn), terns (K. Mullarney, K. Malling Olsen), scops owls (H. Delin), nightjars (N. Cleere), larks (R. Hargreaves, K. Mild, C.S. Roselaar, M. Ullman), pipits (P. Alström), wheatears (H. Jännes, K. Mullarney, M. Ullman, A.B. van den Berg), small *Acrocephalus* (C.S. Roselaar, L. Svensson), *Hippolais* (S. Harrap), *Sylvia* (K. Baker, G. Gargallo), *Phylloscopus* (P. Alström), flycatchers (C. Bradshaw, K. Mild, N.J. Riddiford), sparrows (P. Clement), redpolls (H. Jännes, P.J. Nikander), Rustic, Little and Black-headed Buntings (C. Bradshaw). Vocalisations: L. Svensson and K. Mild.

We are all particularly grateful to Peter Colston at the Natural History Museum, Tring, whose helpfulness and patience during our visits to the skin collection are very much appreciated. We also acknowledge the role of the publishers, Macmillan, and especially Julian Ashby, who realised the importance of publishing this 'second volume'. We thank *British Birds* magazine and its Executive Editor, Tim Sharrock, for encouraging us in this work, and similarly the staff of the magazines *Birding World* and *Dutch Birding*.

We wish also to thank the many people who have accompanied us in the field over the years and with whom we have had much fruitful and exhilarating discussion, or who have helped us in similar ways: in addition to those mentioned above, these include, in particular, Yaron Baser, David M. Cottridge, Paul Doherty, Ehud Dovrat, Philip Fawkes, the late Peter Grant, James Hancock, Bill Laird, Rami Mizrachi, John Morgan, Dave Nurney, Neil Pinder, Hans Schekkerman, and André van Loon.

Finally, we are indebted to C.S. Roselaar and the rest of the *BWP* team, particularly Duncan J. Brooks, for many years of encouragement and for providing important information on taxonomy.

AH wishes to thank Mike Harris, Jim Redwood, Paul Roper and Paul Tout for making their sound knowledge and extensive libraries available.

Ian Dawson kindly read the proofs and made a number of useful comments and suggestions.

How to use this book

There is no strict format, but each article starts with a brief section 'Where and When', outlining in very general terms where the observer may expect to find the species and, where relevant, at what times of year. In many cases, references are given at the end; these indicate where the reader may find additional or more detailed information in the generally available literature, primarily the magazines *British Birds*, *Dutch Birding*, *Birding World*, *Limicola*, some Scandinavian and Finnish journals and published books.

Approach to Identification

It goes without saying that gaining experience in the field is vital if one is to improve one's knowledge and skills. Studying the commoner birds at all times of year, in all plumages and in as many different sets of conditions as possible (e.g. in various habitat types, different lighting, singly and when accompanied by other birds) will lead to a far greater ability to pick out a scarce or difficult-to-identify species. It is more practical to identify an Upcher's Warbler if you have spent a lot of time looking in detail at Olivaceous Warblers.

Rather than jumping to conclusions, the birder should, when faced with 'something different', consider all options. All species vary individually to a greater or lesser extent: with closely similar species, this should always be borne in mind. Seasonal and age differences can also be considerable, and species which look very different in breeding plumage can be much more alike in other plumages. Aberrant individuals also occur.

Even some common birds can, when seen far from one's 'local patch', look very unfamiliar. This may be because different subspecies are involved, or because of different light conditions (e.g. in deserts some species can look larger but sleeker, and may show more plumage contrasts).

With all species that are difficult to identify or are confusable with others, it is always exceedingly important to take the fullest possible notes, including details on size and shape, structure, plumage, voice, behaviour etc, not forgetting habitat, general circumstances, lighting and so on. Only then will you, and others, be in a position to confirm an identity without any lingering doubts.

Effects on appearance of plumage condition and other factors

Shape and structure are often important in identification. It must be stressed, however, that in many cases judging these calls for great caution, objectivity and experience. Moreover, the bird's posture and whether its plumage is sleeked or fluffed up can alter its shape and thus modify its apparent structure.

Size is best evaluated by comparison with known birds alongside or nearby, but beware of the effects of size illusion (seen through magnifying equipment, the farther of two objects looks larger than it actually is in comparison with the nearer one; this factor increases the higher the magnification and the closer the observer is to the objects). In reality, however, it is impossible to make any meaningful estimate of size except at close quarters and when *relative* size can be compared against that of another species nearby. Nevertheless, size can sometimes be estimated using one's experience of species in different conditions and from different angles; ways of judging size/shape vary for each species group, and these are often detailed in the individual texts.

Light conditions and angle of view influence the appearance of colours and feather patterns. Normal colour contrasts can be masked by strong sunlight (dark colours tend to appear paler, grey looks white etc), or produce simply a dark silhouette (e.g. birds over the sea), while many underpart markings are obscured on a bird backlit against the sky (but backlighting enhances any translucency in the wings/tail). On the other hand, strong underlighting (e.g. from desert sand or rocks, or from snow) sharpens any contrasting markings. True colours and more subtle markings are normally seen best in cloudy or duller weather. Raptors overhead, however, are best observed against a blue sky; in a cloudy sky they look colourless and lacking in contrast, and in 'soft afternoon light' appear extremely different in colour and pattern.

Colours are also affected by habitat. Strong or bright colours tend to reflect on a bird's plumage, and even green foliage can lend a variably strong greenish tint to a bird's plumage.

Many features that are influenced by angle of view and/or by a bird's posture (e.g. gape line on eagles, wing structure of raptors and other soaring birds) require much experience for accurate assessment to be made, and may at times be properly judged only on photographs. Certain markings, such as dark feather centres or fringes, are best seen from behind or head-on. Diffuse pale fringes to tertials, when seen from the side, can, misleadingly, look rather sharply defined (see Ménétries's Warbler).

Voice

This is often very important in bird identification. Expressing songs and calls in words, however, is extremely difficult and no two people will agree on what best represents the sounds heard. Only practice in the field (listening and locating the bird responsible

for the vocalisation) will enable the observer properly to learn these aspects, but sound recordings can go a long way to helping this process.

Ageing and Sexing

Correct determination of the age and sex of a bird is often an essential first step in identification. Even some modern field guides, however, are inadequate in their depictions of plumages, and this can easily lead to confusion or misidentification. For some of the relatively commoner species, such as the *Sylvia* warblers or the harriers, it may be vital to determine the age and sex of an individual if mistakes are to be avoided. Yet most of the 'in-between' plumages are not (or, worse, are inaccurately) illustrated in some guides. In this book we have given due emphasis to these factors where they are important.

Moults and Ageing Terminology A thorough understanding of these aspects will prevent many errors being made in the field. Most adult birds moult twice a year, having a partial (body) moult in late winter/spring and a compete moult in late summer, but there are important exceptions to this general rule.

The first plumage after leaving the nest is the *juvenile plumage*. For most species, this is usually held until late summer/autumn, when a body moult produces *1st-winter plumage*, often similar to adult but with juvenile flight and tail feathers and some coverts (but note that many large non-passerines remain in more or less full juvenile plumage for a year or so). In the subsequent spring the body feathers are moulted again, giving *1st-summer plumage*, followed in late summer/autumn by complete moult (i.e. body, wings and tail) which results in *2nd-winter plumage*. At this stage most birds resemble adults, but there are some notable and important exceptions (see below).

Describing a bird's age by using calendar-year terminology is often useful, especially for species whose plumage development from juvenile to adult progresses slowly, with lengthy transitional plumage stages. 1st calendar-year is the period from hatching to 31 December of the same year; 2nd calendar-year is from 1 January to 31 December of the following year; and so on.

Complete moult includes all contour feathers. Partial moult involves a variable number of head and body feathers, wing-coverts, tertials and rectrices. The main moult strategies are: a single annual post-breeding moult (complete); a complete post-breeding and a partial pre-breeding moult; partial post-breeding and complete pre-breeding; and a complete post-breeding and a complete pre-breeding moult. Some passerines have a single complete moult, but the tips of the feathers wear off in spring to reveal a brighter spring/summer appearance.

Post-juvenile moult is normally partial, but in a few species (pratincoles and Moustached Warbler, among others) is complete.

Complete moult usually starts with the primaries (innermost and its covert first) or with some body feathers. Primaries are usually moulted from innermost to outermost (descendently). In falcons, however, primary moult starts with the 4th primary (counted from innermost) and continues in both directions. Large raptors and other large birds, as well as many terns and others, have a serial moult of primaries, the feathers being moulted in several consecutive series or waves: one series begins, but moult terminates before reaching the end of the primaries (= arrested moult, see below); in the next moult season it is resumed from where it finished, but a further moult starts again from the beginning. Up to three generations of feathers may be present at any time, and some large birds (e.g. large gulls, large eagles) may take several years before the last juvenile primary is replaced. Secondaries are usually moulted from outermost to innermost (ascendantly), but moult may start from several points and continue in either or both directions. In many large raptors, and others, there may be serial moults from these centres, producing a variable mix of worn and fresh feathers. Tertials are moulted separately,

often starting with the central one. Tail feathers are usually moulted in pairs from the centre outwards or from the outers inwards. Primary coverts are normally moulted with their respective primaries, secondary coverts being replaced in a more irregular order. Head and body feathers are moulted in several places simultaneously, the moult generally finishing before that of the remiges.

Two terms should be understood. *Arrested moult* is the replacing of only part of a tract of feathers (usually the remiges) during a moult period, some or all remaining feathers being renewed in the next moult period (when moult may also start again from the original point). *Suspended moult* is when moult of primaries/secondaries is temporarily halted (e.g. during migration), before being resumed later from the point of cessation.

Timing and Duration of Moult There is often little or no overlap in timing between moult and breeding or moult and migration. Some birds, however, start moulting while still nesting (some female raptors while still incubating), and immatures and failed breeders start earlier than breeding adults. Moult takes longer the larger the bird. A small passerine can complete its moult in 2-3 months, a large gull may take six months to complete a moult cycle, and a large raptor may take several years. Northern populations moult faster than southern ones.

Practical Applications In the field, many birds can be aged by their moult status. Large raptors and 1st-summer waders are good examples. Passerines showing moult contrasts among the secondary coverts and tertials in autumn can be aged as 1st-winters (in a few species adults show such moult contrasts, but much more pronounced as the old feathers are much more heavily worn than in 1st-years); same applies to 1st-summers, which show more heavily worn (unmoulted) feathers (chiefly remiges) than adults at same time. Birds moulting remiges in autumn are adults (excluding those few species with a complete post-juvenile moult: grouse, phasianids, coursers, pratincoles, sandgrouse, pigeons, and a few passerines). Moult can sometimes help greatly in identification, e.g. when very similar species have different moult strategies.

The moult status of any individual bird can be judged by the different feather generations in its plumage. These generations normally differ in colour, pattern, shape, length and degree of wear.

Pelicans

Where and When White *Pelecanus onocrotalus* and Dalmatian Pelicans *P. crispus* both breed in isolated colonies locally in southeast of region, on large reed- or marsh-fringed lakes (some on small islands in open lakes); at other times found also on smaller or more open waters and sometimes on sheltered coasts. White is widespread on passage through Levant (include Russian migrants) and Nile valley; Hula valley in N Israel a main stopover site and important wintering ground. Dalmatian is rare/endangered; a partial or short-distance migrant. Pink-backed *P. rufescens* is vagrant from sub-Saharan Africa/SW Arabia, rather regular Egypt.

General Features All three are huge pale-coloured birds with long, very broad wings and massive bill and throat-sac (pouch). They differ mainly in wing pattern and bare-part colours. Usually show considerable individual variation, both in plumage (largely age-related) and in size (female smaller than male, juvenile usually smaller than respective adult), but principal features for species identification do not change with age. Adult plumage acquired slowly, complete by about 4th-5th calendar-year; younger birds show vestiges of immature markings. Note that Pink-backed shows less obvious age differences (including underwing pattern).

White and Dalmatian Pelicans

At Rest *Adults* Dalmatian is somewhat bigger than White (apparent only when the two seen together), with plumage less clean white, more grey-tinted than that of White (which often has orangey tinge to body). Dalmatian always has curly, bushy nape crest (longer in breeding season) and less 'tidy' plumage, whereas White looks neater and has drooping nape crest (in breeding season only). On Dalmatian, feathering of forehead abuts upper mandible in a broad, slightly concave line; this feathering much narrower on White and tapers to a point at

bill base. BARE PARTS Huge throat-sac is dull yellow-grey on adult Dalmatian, becoming positively orange to red when breeding, much redder than White's in spring (which at other times is yellow). Bare facial skin around eye on Dalmatian restricted and dull yellow, becoming purple for short time in spring, while on White it is more extensive and yellow, turning pinky to orange in spring. Dalmatian in all plumages has grey legs (fleshy on White, turning orangey-pink in spring), and a pale yellowish eye (deep red on White, appearing black). *Juveniles* Fairly distinct. Juvenile White is dark brown above and dingy below, whereas Dalmatian is much paler with just a tinge of brownish to upperparts. Colours of facial skin and throat-sac very similar on both, but note Dalmatian's dark grey legs. Immature White is less dark and more like juvenile Dalmatian (apart from latter's grey legs). Patterns of forehead feathering differ in same way as for adults. Otherwise, compare flight characters (see below).

Pink-backed Pelican

Slightly smaller than the other two (noticeably so when seen with Dalmatian) and generally drabber and greyer than adults of either (but beware juveniles of latter), with inconspicuous 'frizzy' darkish nape crest (not curly, nor drooping). Breeding adult has variable pinky tinge above, particularly on rump and wing-coverts, and on undertail-coverts, this colour absent at other times. Forehead feathering much as Dalmatian. Bill and throat-sac paler than on White or Dalmatian, pale yellowish-flesh, becoming yellower when breeding; at close range, dark 'ribbing' effect visible. Legs pale, fleshy-grey to orangey, turning pinky-red in spring. Very small area of bare skin around eye is yellow, orange or (non-breeding) pinky with variable blackish outer ring, eye very dark and lores blackish, all giving characteristic 'fixed-stare' expression. Juvenile Pink-backed (browner

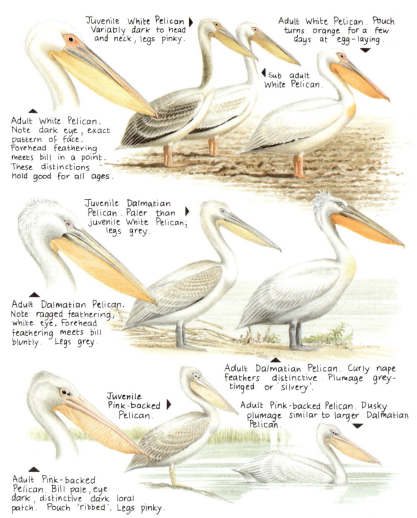

Juvenile White Pelican ▶
Variably dark to head
and neck, legs pinky.

Adult White Pelican. Pouch
turns orange for a few
days at egg-laying.

◀ Sub adult
White Pelican.

▲ Adult White Pelican.
Note dark eye, exact
pattern of face.
Forehead feathering
meets bill in a point.
These distinctions
hold good for all ages.

Juvenile Dalmatian
Pelican. Paler than ▶
juvenile White Pelican;
legs grey.

▲ Adult Dalmatian Pelican.
Note ragged feathering,
white eye. Forehead
feathering meets bill
bluntly. Legs grey.

▲ Adult Dalmatian Pelican. Curly nape
feathers distinctive. Plumage grey-
tinged or 'silvery'.

Juvenile ▶
Pink-backed
Pelican.

Adult Pink-backed Pelican. Dusky
plumage similar to larger Dalmatian
Pelican ▼

▲ Adult Pink-backed
Pelican. Bill pale, eye
dark, distinctive dark loral
patch. Pouch 'ribbed'. Legs pinky.

above) rather similar to non-breeding adult
(and to juvenile Dalmatian) but with less
distinctive facial pattern, lacks black ring
around facial skin and has dusky (not black)
lores (but eye still dark); also has dark brown
tail, and bill and throat-sac subdued in colour
with no hint of yellow (look very pale and
washed out). Immature as juvenile, but with

less brownish, more grey, cast above (and see
also flight).

Flight identification

All pelicans in flight look massive-bodied,
very short-tailed, front-heavy, with broad,
'fingered' wings and huge bill. With reasonable views (i.e. when patterns/colours can be

discerned), should be separable using wing pattern and (if visible) bare-part colours. *Underwing* White Pelican always shows the most contrastingly patterned underwing: all-dark flight feathers, with rest of underwing (and underparts) contrastingly white (adult) or with variably dark forewing (lesser and part of median coverts) and broad whitish central band (juvenile); immature becomes progressively whiter on coverts and blacker on flight feathers and can at certain stages recall juvenile/non-breeding Pink-backed (see below). Dalmatian's underwing is always much more uniform, pale greyish, becoming somewhat darker along tips of primaries and secondaries, and with paler greater coverts forming long, indistinct, paler central band (and look for the dark grey legs). Pink-backed in breeding plumage has underwing pattern somewhat reminiscent (in distant view) of juvenile/immature White, but much less contrastingly marked, having dusky greyish flight feathers and cinnamon-grey coverts with broad paler central band; juveniles and

non-breeding adults with greyish-white coverts may recall adult White, but flight feathers are not quite so dark and total effect is less contrasting (note also that juvenile's remiges, as opposed to adult's, are more variegated with contrasting dark inner webs, while immatures are intermediate; such bicoloured remiges are never found on any White, but not that unlike Dalmatian's. In good views of Pink-backed overhead, outermost visible primary finger is much shorter than longest ones, while bill/throat-sac and legs always appear very much paler and washed out. *Upperwing* Adult White's upperwing pattern mirrors that of its underwing, but with secondaries pale-edged (less solidly black), while juvenile almost entirely brown above apart from contrasting pale rump/back (and often with paler areas on mantle and lesser/greater coverts). Adult Dalmatian rather dusky-looking above, with blackish on primaries and less so on secondaries, while juvenile is also tinged brown on mantle, tail and wing-coverts. Pink-backed has similar

Adult Pink-backed Pelican.

Adult Dalmatian Pelican.

Adult underwing patterns distinctive. Dalmatian Pelican shows diffuse dark tip and rear edge, with white translucent mid-wing. White Pelican has distinct dark primaries and secondaries. Note leg colours.

Of the pelicans, only immature White Pelicans show dark marks to underwing-coverts.

Adult Pink-backed Pelican. Small, underwing pattern midway between those of larger species.

Juvenile White Pelican. Underwing variegated.

Adult Dalmatian Pelican.

Adult White Pelican.

Adult Pink-backed Pelican. Dusky above, white rump area, pale bill, outermost primary falls short of wingtip.

Adult White Pelican above. Similar to Dalmatian Pelican but 'crisper'.

upperwing pattern to young Dalmatian, but pale pinkish-grey (adult) or brownish-grey (juvenile) coverts with darker grey flight feathers (at all times showing less contrast than either White or Dalmatian); at all ages, but particularly juvenile, tends to have rather marked whitish uppertail-coverts/rump with deep extension onto back and mantle and contrasting with darker scapulars and tail.

References Harrison (1983), Hollom *et al.* (1988), Madge (1991).

White Egrets

Where and When Little Egret *Egretta garzetta* is fairly widespread in W Palearctic, though breeding locally, mainly in south; on passage throughout and south of breeding range and in winter found principally from Mediterranean southwards (good numbers now winter NW Europe). Western Reef Egret *E. gularis* occurs on coasts from Red Sea to Sri Lanka (race *schistacea*) and W Africa (nominate *gularis*), with increasing records from Mediterranean. Great White Egret *E. alba* is a scarce, local breeder at scattered sites from Austria eastwards (a few nest Netherlands and France), wintering Camargue and eastern Mediterranean; vagrants increasingly recorded farther north. Cattle Egret *Bubulcus ibis* is very local resident in Iberia, N Africa, France and E Mediterranean, and a surprisingly rare, erratic vagrant north to Britain and Scandinavia.

Habitat All occur at wetlands, but Cattle Egret more likely to be found on pasture and other fields, where associates with cattle or other large mammals (note that Little may occasionally occur in same situation). Western Reef is found essentially at/near salt water, while Little and Great White just as likely to frequent freshwater habitats (though commonly at salt water outside breeding season).

Identification All species have all-white plumage, but Western Reef (frequently) and Little (very rarely) also occur in a dark morph and breeding-plumaged Cattle shows much buff. Main points to look for are size and structure, and colour of bare parts (latter change with age and seasonally, being brightest for brief period during courtship, prior to breeding). Elongated plumes are developed in breeding season (not always coinciding with colour changes of bare parts), but

individuals outside range at this time of year may sometimes show bare-part changes without acquiring breeding plumes; also, plumes are easily lost or damaged during breeding. Note that differences given below apply only in W Palearctic.

Little and Western Reef Egrets

Both are considerably smaller than Great White, and at all times distinguished from Cattle Egret by much longer bill. Little is the most familiar species, and in most cases should not cause any problems (bill typically black/blackish), but some Western Reef can be very close to Little in structure. Both species acquire long breeding plumes on nape, breast and mantle/scapulars, and also brighter bare-part colours in spring (courtship). Following text concentrates on Western Reef and its separation from Little Egret.

Size and Structure In direct comparison with Little, Western Reef is very slightly larger, and less neat and elegant (more stocky). Race *schistacea* variable, but those seen in W Palearctic (Near East) generally have thicker-looking legs but with relatively slightly shorter tarsus (can look clearly shorter-legged), thicker-looking neck (often held in more snake-like posture), and more angular head profile, with much shallower forehead and steeper rear crown/nape (forehead and crown more gently rounded on Little); differences in head shape, however, depend much on posture/behaviour, and often not at all apparent. Bill distinctly deeper-based with slightly (but always noticeably) curved culmen (outer third), so less sharply pointed than Little's; averages slightly longer than on Little, but this not always obvious. Note that invidual variation

Note sizes of these non-breeding herons. ▶

◀ Grey Heron

◀ Great White Egret

◀ Little Egret

Careful observation of bill structure useful. The gape line of Great White Egret extends back beyond eye. Note blunter bill tip of Western Reef Egret. ▼

◀ Cattle Egret

Great White Egret ▲

Little Egret ▲

Western Reef Egret ▲

Cattle Egret ▲

Non-breeding Little Egret. Lores greyish, sharp bill blackish. Legs black, feet yellow. ▼

Note bill and leg colours. ◀

Breeding Little Egret grows plumes on nape, breast and scapulars. Lores blue-grey except for a brief courtship period, when lores and feet turn pink or reddish. ▲ ◀

Juvenile Little Egret may show paler bill base, greener legs and feet. Sharp bill. ▶

Breeding Western Reef Egret. Thick blunt-tipped bill, short tarsus. ▲

Non-breeding Western Reef Egret. Note bill shape, short greenish tarsus. ▶

Breeding Western Reef Egret of race 'gularis'. Bill black, lores yellow. Legs black, feet yellower. ▶

occurs, as well as much biometrical overlap with Little. On W African race *gularis*, structural differences usually less marked (some white morphs can be virtually identical to Little, including in bill shape and size).

Bare-part Colours Vary seasonally; also much individual variation. Adult Little has black bill and legs and yellow feet (in winter bill can be paler at base and feet may show greenish tinge); lores usually greyish or blue-grey (rarely green-grey). In courtship, feet and lower tarsus briefly turn orange/red and lores bright red, orange or bluish-pink, soon returning to non-breeding colours (lores first colourless before turning greyish). Apparent Little Egrets with pale, yellowish to greenish-grey, legs (reported rarely both in winter and in breeding colonies) or with yellowish lores (possibly effect of sunlight on colourless lores or of hybridisation?) require further investigation. Juveniles and immatures have paler (dark brown) bill, often pinkish at base of lower mandible, and a few have one or both mandibles fleshy-horn to straw-yellow (thus young Little can have bill colour similar to Western Reef); legs often tinged paler (green/brown), and very occasionally pale-legged (light green/brown-green/yellowish), recalling some Western Reef. Bare parts of Western Reef are as follows. *Non-breeding and immature* Race *schistacea* has bill basically brownish-yellow or even yellowish (with darker tip), can appear rather patchily marked; lores yellowish or greyish-yellow; and legs and feet generally brownish (rarely blackish-brown), brown-green or brown-yellow with yellower (but less contrasting than on Little) soles. Nominate *gularis* has bill brown or brownish-horn (sometimes yellower or pinkish at base), lores yellow or pale greenish (but often blue-grey or greyish, as Little), and legs blackish-brown or brown (variably spotted yellowish/greenish) with yellow soles and lower tarsus. *Breeding* Bill of *schistacea* yellow (rarely black), of nominate black. Bare-part colours brighter and deeper, more brown or orange-brown, and legs often black with bright yellow feet. For brief period during courtship, bill (base) flushes reddish, lores turn pale

yellow or more briefly red and feet/lower tarsus orange/red, colours becoming less bright as breeding commences.

Plumage Little is normally all white (but see below). Western Reef polymorphic. *White-morph* Very rare in nominate *gularis* (at least in north of range); much commoner in *schistacea* and often predominant in north of range. All white, as typical Little Egret, though can show a very few scattered dark feathers (especially on wings, conspicuous in flight). *Dark-morph* Nominate *gularis* is dark slate-grey, often tinged bluish (but can look blackish in field); in some lights head and breast may show a glossy blue or greenish tinge and underparts a slightly brown tinge, but such tonal differences subtle and visible only in favourable conditions. Juveniles brown or dark grey-brown; immatures a shade paler than adults, duller (lack gloss) and usually with browner wings (retained juvenile feathers). At all ages, chin (and to variable extent upper throat and lower ear-coverts) white; also often has white patch on one or both wings (white primary coverts and more rarely alula) and a few white feathers may occur on any part of body (mostly head and wings). Dark *schistacea* normally ash-grey, often with lavender tinge (paler than dark nominate), or occasionally dark grey; white areas as on nominate (on Asiatic populations, white on wing can extend to primaries). *Intermediates* Variable 'mixed' plumages occur. Race *schistacea* not uncommonly has upperparts very pale ash-grey, neck and body sides pale (variably mottled grey and white) and lower breast and belly whitish; and occasionally has grey back, white head with pale grey/whitish neck and underparts and extensive white on outer wing. Both these plumages rare in nominate, but latter sometimes has head, neck and body mostly white, often with a few dark flecks on back and flanks, and wings mostly grey, often with a few white feathers. Some immature *schistacea* have body washed/mottled grey, but underparts clean white. (Note that confusion exists over whether intermediate birds are always immatures or whether adults can show such plumage variation; suggestion that some intermediate immatures turn into dark adults needs confirmation.)

Dark Little Egrets Very rare (?) and little known. A few dark birds identical to Little in shape and structure have been seen in recent years in S Europe: some uniform or almost wholly pale grey, others as some *schistacea* (wings and back pale grey, neck and head paler grey/white, belly off-white to white); one such 'pied' bird bred near Camargue in 1992. A very small minority of light grey to almost black birds (varying from uniform to irregular dark patches) occur regularly in a Little Egret colony in N Israel, and very dark, almost blackish 'Little' also seen in E Africa. Research urgently needed on such individuals (particularly at breeding colonies), true identity of which still disputed.

In Flight Western Reef has rather longer wingspan than Little (latter's approximates to that of Herring Gull *Larus argentatus*) and wings may appear slightly larger and more rounded, but sometimes much as Little; feet normally appear bigger and more 'floppy' (can be striking in direct comparison), and

show less colour contrast with legs. Can show a few scattered dark feathers on tail, wing-coverts and especially flight feathers (secondaries), lacking on Little Egret. Flight may appear stronger, less buoyant (heavier-bodied), and may (especially *schistacea*) recall small Grey Heron *Ardea cinerea*, but largely dependent on wind conditions.

Hybrids In Camargue, nominate *gularis* of dark morph has apparently interbred with Little, producing three 'white-looking' young, and hybridisation may have occurred elsewhere in S Europe. In other parts of its range, notably in India and E Africa, interbreeding between Little and dark-morph *schistacea* has been claimed, resulting in individuals that are piebald or mostly white with some dark feathers and have highly variable bare-part colours.

Habitat and Behaviour Western Reef mainly coastal (but also penetrates well inland in Africa), while Little generally a freshwater bird but commonly found in salt-water habitats (especially in winter), and the two occur side by side in places. Western Reef often adopts a more horizontal stance than

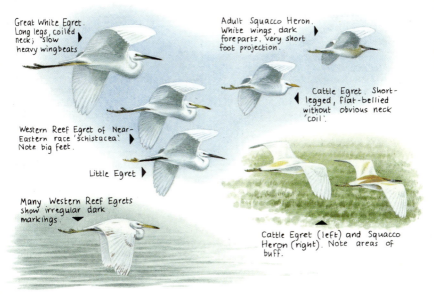

Great White Egret. Long legs, coiled neck; slow heavy wingbeats

Western Reef Egret of Near-Eastern race 'schistacea'. Note big feet.

Little Egret

Many Western Reef Egrets show irregular dark markings.

Adult Squacco Heron. White wings, dark foreparts, very short foot projection.

Cattle Egret. Short-legged, flat-bellied without obvious neck 'coil'.

Cattle Egret (left) and Squacco Heron (right). Note areas of buff.

Little when resting or feeding, and not uncommonly performs 'canopy feeding' (but Little sometimes does this, too). Both may feed solitarily or gregariously, depending on conditions and food availability.

Great White Egret

Large size and very long neck normally obvious and sufficient for identification (but see below). Much bigger than other white egrets, size of Grey Heron, and at all times plumage entirely white. Has long, clear bright yellow bill, yellowish-green lores, and blackish-brown legs with yellower tibia and soles (latter never so obvious as on Little). During courtship, bill becomes reddish with shiny black culmen, lores turn bright green, and legs black with reddish tibia and soles (often joined by red line down sides of tarsus); legs and lores quickly revert to non-breeding colours, while bill changes back more gradually to yellow (starting from base). In eastern race *modesta* (could occur as vagrant), bill is entirely black and both tibia and whole tarsus red during courtship. Diagnostic of all races at all times is that gape line extends beyond level of eye (on other egrets always stops short of eye). *In flight* In flight, especially at distance or at some height, size difficult to assess, but always appears heavy, less buoyant than smaller species, with prominent 'neck pouch' and longer legs, and wingbeats are much slower (recall Grey Heron).

Cattle Egret

Should not present any problems. Slightly smaller than Little, and in general shape much more stocky and squat-looking (characteristic hunched posture when at rest): has shorter neck, larger, more rounded head with obvious forward extension of feathering bulging onto lower mandible, and much shorter and deeper bill (curved upper mandible) which is wholly yellow, though juveniles not uncommonly retain wholly or partially black bill to at least late summer; has pale yellow lores, and also shorter legs which are dark greenish-brown (usually with paler tibia), with feet same colour. During courtship, bill, lores and legs become deep red, later turning deep yellow (changes from tip inwards) and then reverting to non-breeding colours; around this period also develops diagnostic bright buff feathering on head, breast and mantle/scapulars (on some, this coloration rather pale, can appear all white from distance). In flight, gives impression of being 'more rounded', with legs/feet projecting less beyond tail and with faster wingbeats than Little.

Similar Species Squacco Heron *Ardeola ralloides* (breeds patchily southern part of region, winters Africa; vagrant elsewhere) is at all times unmistakable on ground (shows relatively little white). In flight, however, very different, with fully white wings, tail and rump: note Squacco's darker mantle and scapulars, and much shorter projection of feet beyond tail compared with all other species.

References Dubois & Yésou (1995), Hancock (1984), Hume (1992).

Eclipse Male, Female and Immature Eiders

Where and When Common Eider *Somateria mollissima* is a circumpolar breeder by shallow inshore waters south to northern Britain and NW France, in winter mainly in south of range but also on C European lakes, with vagrants south to Mediterranean and Black Seas. King Eider *S. spectabilis* has similar but even more northerly (high-arctic tundra) distribution, wintering mainly arctic Norway and rare vagrant further south, but regular winterer N Scotland. Both are abundant, particularly in north of ranges. Spectacled Eider *S. fischeri* is an exceptional vagrant (fewer than five records in W Palearctic) from NE Siberia/Alaska. All three winter mainly along or off sea coasts. Steller's Eider *Polysticta stelleri*, a non-breeding visitor to coasts of extreme N Scandinavia (occasionally breeds) and the Baltic and rare vagrant south to France and Britain, is very different from the others, and is not treated here.

Moult Drakes of all *Somateria* species have almost continuous moult from juvenile through to 2nd winter, by when generally recognisable by variable amount of adult-like features (full male plumage acquired 3rd/4th calendar-year); before then rate of progress of moult varies greatly among individuals, hence a wide variety of plumages. Juveniles retain wing, tail, belly and rump feathers until late spring/summer (females) or autumn (males) of 2nd calendar-year.

General Adult males in full plumage unmistakable, and not discussed here; eclipse males also reasonably easy to identify (bill features obvious, retain full upperwing-coverts). Other plumages (female and 1st-winter) can be confusing, but with reasonable views identification fairly straightforward. Main points on which to concentrate are head-and-

bill shape and coloration, bill feathering and flank/upperpart pattern. Following text deals only with those features enabling correct species identification.

Common and King Eiders

Size In direct comparison, King somewhat smaller than Common (which is largest of all eiders), with shorter bill and slightly shorter neck.

Head-and-bill Shape King's shorter bill and slightly (sometimes markedly) bulging forehead give impression of more rounded or even more square head than Common's (Common's long head and bill produce distinctive triangular profile, bill and forehead often appearing as straight line). Bill feathering also very different: on King, feathering of loral region extends only short way towards nostril, ending in rounded profile (on

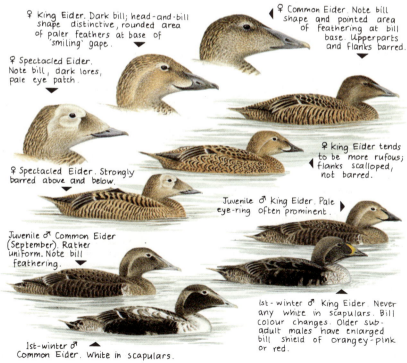

♀ King Eider. Dark bill; head-and-bill shape distinctive, rounded area of paler feathers at base of 'smiling' gape.

◄ ♀ Common Eider. Note bill shape and pointed area of feathering at bill base. Upperparts and flanks barred.

♀ Spectacled Eider. Note bill, dark lores, pale eye patch.

♀ king Eider tends to be more rufous; ◄ flanks scalloped, not barred.

♀ Spectacled Eider. Strongly barred above and below.

Juvenile ♂ King Eider. Pale eye-ring often prominent. ►

Juvenile ♂ Common Eider (September). Rather uniform. Note bill feathering. ▼

1st-winter ♂ King Eider. Never any white in scapulars. Bill colour changes. Older subadult males have enlarged bill shield of orangey-pink or red.

1st-winter ♂ ▲ Common Eider. White in scapulars.

Common, cheek feathering protracted into long pointed wedge to just below rear edge of nostril), but forehead feathering reaches well down on culmen to almost level with rear edge of nostril (on Common does not reach so far and less obvious, especially in profile). An additional, often surprisingly useful feature is King's gape line, which curves up across (often pale) cheeks, producing 'grinning' expression (Common looks more 'morose'; lower edge of bill and chin seem to run together, obscuring gape line).

Plumage *Female* King generally has rustier plumage tone than Common, but much individual variation in both. Note that King's two raised feather points (rear inner scapulars) usually difficult to see. Note following features of King. **1** HEAD Usually rather plain, but generally fore cheeks and chin paler than rest, at times contrastingly so, though whole head sometimes very pale (and normally paler than Common's, though some female King, especially 1st-winters, can be dark-headed); usually shows pale eye-ring with pale line extending from rear edge back and then downwards, separating nape from ear region (Common may have pale ring or short supercilium, but lacks pale line, though latter shown by some 1st-year males). **2** FLANKS King shows well-pronounced dark scallop, crescent or arrowhead markings (feathers with black subterminal crescents), instead of Common's straighter, more vertical bold stripes (but note that younger King shows more vermiculated pattern, closer to that of Common). **3** BILL COLOUR Bill darker than Common's, dark grey to slaty and contrasting with paler adjacent feathering, but may be somewhat paler behind tip and usually (always?) has small black nail (Common has larger and very pale, whitish nail, obvious in head-on view). *Juvenile* until about September (timing varies), juveniles of both species rather uniform dull grey-brown, with body markings obscure (but often with variable paler eye-ring and adjoining line, more prominent on King). Head-and-bill features important differences. *1st-winter male* Males have partial moult from late summer/

autumn into even more uniform sooty-black/blackish-brown plumage with white on breast; with further moult additional white areas gradually develop on upperparts, flanks and head, but huge individual variation in extent of white feathering at any particular date (some may remain virtually blackish apart from white breast). Head-and-bill shape and bill feathering (see above), however, still best features for separation. Other important differences are that King never shows any white in scapulars (white variably present on Common), and its initially dark bill soon acquires some yellowish to pale orange/pinkish colour (usually fairly obvious pale orange shield and greyish to reddish bill) before 2nd calendar-year (Common's bill greyish, perhaps with paler patches). By 1st summer usually more white visible on upperparts, and bill features should be sufficient to prevent confusion. *Eclipse male* Plumage sooty-brown but for retained white upperwing-coverts, and with variable amount of white on breast and sometimes upperparts (note that King never shows any white in scapulars). King's bill shield reduced in size (still noticeable) but bill remains bright red. Neither species should cause any major problems in this plumage.

In Flight Common appears heavy and deep-bodied, with heavy wingbeats but remarkably fast speed. In direct comparison, King's somewhat smaller size, shorter neck, more compact build and slightly quicker wingbeats fairly obvious, and female also shows whiter underwing with dark leading edge (on female Common, whitish axillaries the palest part of underwing).

Spectacled Eider

Somewhat smaller than Common, which it most resembles. At all times, shows highly distinctive broad pale eye-rings (aptly termed 'goggles') and broad cloak of feathering extends from forehead over upper culmen to about level with nostrils.

Plumage *Female* Differs from other two in more obvious, regular dark barring above and on flanks (ground colour generally more rufous in tone), but mainly in diagnostic head pattern: very large, very pale (light buff-brown) circular eye patch isolating dark eye and (equally) pale chin and throat, contrasting with dark (though paler than upperparts) rear crown/hindneck and with even darker forehead and loral area. Bill darker than on Common, blue-grey, almost as dark as on female King, but with small pale nail. Young female paler, with less obvious (narrower) barring/mottling on breast, and spectacles less obvious (though still visible enough). *1st-winter male* Juvenile basically as female, but with closer barring below; spectacles greyish, less marked, but still distinctive. Foreneck shows some white from about 1st autumn

(but white apparently never extends over breast as it does on Common and King), and white feathering gradually appears on mantle/scapulars. Probably shows at least a hint of yellow or orange on bill from 1st autumn/winter. *Eclipse male* Dark grey-brown or sooty overall, breast perhaps somewhat paler/brighter; upperwing-coverts remain white. Eye patches duller and greyer, but still fairly conspicuous (contrast with darker loral region).

In Flight Dark front of head (lores etc) contrasting with pale eye patches striking, even at distance.

References Alström *et al.* (1991a), Madge & Burn (1988), Skakuj (1990).

Eclipse Male, Female and Immature Goldeneyes

Where and When Common Goldeneye *Bucephala clangula* breeds rather commonly in northern Holarctic forests south of tundra, south to Scotland, Germany and Czech Republic, wintering on fresh waters, estuaries and sheltered coasts from S Iceland and S Scandinavia to northern Mediterranean (straggling further south). Barrow's Goldeneye *B. islandica* breeds at lakes and rivers in NW and NE Nearctic (partly overlaps with Common) but also in Iceland; Iceland population largely resident, moving to ice-free waters in winter, and occasional birds further south (south to France, Germany) likely to be of Canadian origin (or escapes).

Identification

Main problem is distinguishing female or immature Barrow's from similar-plumaged Common Goldeneyes (full-adult males, adequately treated in good field guides, should cause no problems, but eclipse males may confuse the unwary). Accurate determination of head shape essential at all times (much overlap in other features).

Size and Structure Barrow's is rather larger than Common (fairly obvious in direct comparison, and with experience possibly assessable with lone individuals). Most important is head shape: Barrow's has very steep (even

vertical), clearly 'swollen' forehead, with crown peaking more before or above eye and then sloping back and turning down into markedly full, bushy lower nape (head rather oblong in shape); Common has more sloping (still fairly steep) forehead rising evenly into more rounded crown (peaking above or often behind eye) and curving immediately down into rather less bushy nape (giving more triangular head shape). Differences usually fairly distinct on birds resting, swimming past or in alert posture, and can be striking when the two seen together, but often obscured by changes in posture (e.g. actively feeding Common can appear flatter-crowned); prolonged views from various angles normally needed for confirmation.

Bill Shape Barrow's usually has slightly deeper-based, more stubby-looking bill with steeper upper mandible (hint of convex shape to upper half of culmen), but overlap occurs and this feature (marginal and difficult to judge) not wholly reliable.

Adult Females Females of the two species are very similar, but the following features are shown by most Barrow's. **1 HEAD COLOUR** Somewhat darker chocolate-brown and reaching a little onto uppermost neck, leaving narrow whitish collar (on Common, brown extends only to lower edge of throat, with

Adult ♀ Common Goldeneye.

Adult ♀ Barrow's Goldeneye.

1st-winter Common Goldeneye.

Adult ♀ Common Goldeneye. Compare bill shapes, head shapes, extent of brown down neck. Differences in bill colour and shape not constant.

Adult ♀ Barrow's Goldeneye. Note head shape and larger size.

Adult ♀ Common Goldeneye.

Note subtle differences in wing patterns.

Head shape is not useful on birds actively feeding.

Adult ♀ Barrow's Goldeneye.

1st-winter Common Goldeneye.

1st-winter ♂ Common Goldeneye frequently moults in the face spot from the front, giving a Barrow's Goldeneye-like crescent.

1st-winter Barrow's Goldeneye.

very slightly broader collar, but difference minimal and very hard to judge). In summer both species duller, with grey-tinged head and no obvious collar. 2 UPPERWING Barrow's has plain forewing or at best only narrow whitish tips to median coverts (not forming band, or only broken one), with most of greater coverts white with broad black tips, and inner 4–6 secondaries white; Common differs in having upper median coverts white (forming solid band extending to alula region) and lower ones black, black tips to white greater coverts slightly smaller (especially in central area), and more white on secondaries (inner 7–8). Thus, inner wing of Barrow's shows slightly narrower panel of white with one uniformly broad black bar and dark leading edge (but beware young female Common, see below), whereas Com-

mon's inner wing looks mostly white with two narrow black bars. 3 BILL PATTERN On Barrow's, usually yellowish with blackish at base and on nail (latter often larger and more conspicuous than on Common), but bill all yellow in Nearctic and on some individuals of other populations; on Common, generally blackish with yellow near tip, but can rarely be all yellow. Overlap in bill coloration thus makes this feature unreliable. Both have bill all dark in summer.

Eclipse Males As adult females, but retain full male upperwing pattern: Barrow's has inner wing white with black bar across base of greater coverts and black leading edge; Common lacks covert bar (concealed by white medians; occasionally trace of black shows). Bill generally all dark.

1st-winters Basically similar to summer

females (i.e. dull grey-brown on head, no collar etc), but both species have more uniform forewing (markings on lesser/median coverts much reduced or absent, especially on females). 1st-winter (and adult female) Barrow's thus extremely close to 1st-winter Common, but with slightly broader greater-covert bar (though covert tips tend to be somewhat smaller than on adults, and on both species can disappear with wear by summer of 2nd calendar-year). Both acquire adult features (including bill coloration) gradually, more obviously from late winter/

spring (2nd calendar-year). Head shape remains best criterion, but note that differences somewhat less marked on younger birds (skulls still developing). (Note that 1st-winter male Common moulting in face spot from the front can appear to show hint of pale crescent behind bill, recalling adult male Barrow's, but generally shows much less white than Barrow's and head shape and other features should help distinguish it.)
References Garner (1991), Madge & Burn (1988).

Black and Red Kites

Where and When Black Kite *Milvus migrans* is widespread in the Old World. In much of Palearctic migratory (only partially in south). Three races in W Palearctic: nominate *migrans* in Europe and N Africa, intergrading in W Siberia/C Asia with *lineatus* (individuals reminiscent of which noted on passage/in winter in Middle East); *aegyptius* resident in Egypt and W Africa. Species is rather abundant in parts of S Europe and Levant, and regular vagrant to N and W Europe. Usually in open country with tall trees, often near water and often in close proximity to humans (e.g. refuse tips). Red Kite *M. milvus* breeds central W Palearctic, mainly C and SW Europe; mainly migratory in north, becoming resident and dispersive further south; accidental N Europe and Middle East. Generally prefers low-lying hilly country with woods in vicinity of water, but often in drier more mountainous areas, and less associated with man. Outside breeding season, the species may feed and roost together.

Identification

The two are rather distinct (some overlap). Following main features should be established. **1 SHAPE AND MODE OF FLIGHT** Red is characteristically long-winged and long-tailed, giving elegant, slender appearance with distinctly slimmer, longer body than Black (more barrel-shaped, with proportionately shorter/broader wings and usually

shorter, thicker tail). Red usually has clearly narrower hands (only 5 prominent fingers) and diagnostically shows deeply forked and triangular tail, compared with Black's ample hands (6 prominent fingers) and generally poorly forked tail. Beware, however, that often broken central feather pairs on Black produce confusingly deep fork; see also *aegyptius*, below. Red's flight is characteristically leisurely, rather slow and agile with easy (but elastic) tern-like wingbeats and with constant obvious twisting (and often fanning) of tail, whereas same manoeuvres by Black are usually more 'floppy', much less flexible and elegant. Red often soars with arm slightly raised and hand flattish or with tip raised (generally flatter or often slightly arched in Black), and glides with wing (mainly carpals) held slightly forwards from body and with generally flexed and arched (but less angled/drooped than Black) hands, but aerial conditions may cause both to adopt similar flight attitude (see also *aegyptius*). **2 UPPERPARTS/UPPERWING** Red shows distinct pale sandy-brown panel along median coverts which usually contrasts well with rest of wing (less so with pale mantle/scapulars), whereas Black has browner diffuse and less contrasting panel and also more uniformly browner upper body. Upper primary patch wider and paler on Red than on most Black; beware that juvenile Black (with broad whitish covert tips) or faded adult (but chiefly 1st-summers) may appear to show more pronounced paler panel at distance, so check other features (see also plumage variations of both species, below). **3** UNDERPARTS/UNDERWING Red shows obvious large, white, square-shaped patch across inner and base of outer primaries, which are also less barred. On Black this feature highly variable with race and age (see below), from obscure patch to rather conspicuous one (in latter case, especially in strong underlighting, can be confusingly similar to Red). Red's underbody is typically rich rufous and buff (darker on adult) and brighter/paler than inner underwing, lacking adult Black's browner or more sooty-red appearance or juvenile Black's more contrasting pale rear body and more obvious whitish streaks on front/sides of body. **4** TAIL COLOUR Red Kite's tail is redder (even orange), particularly above (and more brightly translucent from below), usually more so even than most brightly coloured Black, on which often accentuated by strong underlighting (see also plumage variation). **5** HEAD Always appears whiter (even whitish-faced) on Red, which tends to lack Black's variable dark eye patch/mask. (Other features largely related to species variation, but overall impression of Red is of a more contrastingly patterned and paler bird than Black.)

Plumage Variation of Red Kite Juvenile differs from adult in having rather distinct whitish tips to upper greater coverts forming narrow but (when fresh) clear wingbar; from below, greater and often median coverts tipped narrowly white and bordering more obvious solidly blackish greater-covert band, so wings more variegated; underbody typically paler rufous (also in relation to inner wing) and streaked yellowish-buff centrally on breast and upper belly, leaving paler/plainer buffish-rufous rear body, including undertail-coverts (adult's body generally more evenly and clear reddish-chestnut with broad blackish shaft streaks, showing less contrast with inner wing but instead clearest contrast with undertail). Often juvenile's tail is slightly less deeply forked (or even shorter), somewhat less reddish and tends to have

rather clearer (visible when spread) subterminal band. When fresh, juvenile upper lesser/median coverts rather obviously tipped/edged whitish-buff, while head generally less white, with buffish streaks on crown and nape and whitish streaks largely confined to forehead, ear-coverts and throat. Juvenile has dark eye and fully black culmen; on adult, eye dark and culmen yellow with darkish tip. Adult plumage acquired at about two years.

Geographical and Plumage Variation of Black Kite Juvenile differs from adult in having on average shorter 6th primary finger (sometimes even as short as adult Red) and often shallower or even non-existent (when tail spread or partly folded) tail fork; also has distinct (but wear off during winter) whitish streaks/spots below and fringes on upperwing-coverts (often forming wide pale panel above), and while still fresh shows narrow whitish tips on secondaries, tail and greater coverts on both surfaces; secondaries solidly blackish, contrast highly with whiter/wider primary patch and with underbody (which often appears rather buffish-brown) and greyish-brown tail (which also more heavily barred), and has more pronounced dark eye patch, a feature retained even in transitional plumages when approaching adult. Both juvenile and early immatures generally lack adult's whitish (streaked) head and rather uniform dark sooty-red underparts with very narrow black shaft streaks; tail is browner, often with small buffish-white uppertail-covert tips, and eye is darker. Caution is important when separating Red and Black Kites, since two further races of Black can complicate matters. Race *lineatus* is longer-winged (approaching Red) and typically has rather uniform head (dark brown feather centres with fringes rufous-buff, not whitish as nominate) with fairly distinct dark ear-coverts: adult browner than nominate, particularly below (less sooty rufous-brown), with much broader dark feather centres (instead of shaft streaks) on chest, while lower underparts usually distinctly browner-buff with no streaks (most nominate adults streaked) and tail less rufous, but has much larger white

Juvenile Red Kite. Warm rufous wing panel and obvious forked rufous tail.

Juvenile Red Kite. Large white patches on underwing, pale rufous underparts, tail pale and deeply forked.

Juvenile Black Kite. Paler than adult, but less contrasting than Red Kite.

Juvenile Black Kite above. Warm brown with paler coverts, dark mask, shallow tail fork.

Black kite of race 'lineatus'.

Black Kite of race 'aegyptius'.

In Middle East, beware paler and more reddish nominate Black Kite from east and races 'lineatus' and 'aegyptius'. These show pale under primaries like Red Kite; small 'aegyptius' has tail deeply forked.

Adult Black Kite. More uniform than juvenile.

Adult Black Kite of race 'aegyptius'. Bill all yellow.

Juvenile Black Kite of race 'aegyptius'. Boldly spotted cream.

Juvenile Black Kite. Dark mask, warm brown body streaked darker, cream covert fringes

Marsh Harrier similar to Black Kite in gliding flight.

Black Kite

Juvenile Red Kite. Warmer rufous than Black Kite, paler-headed; fresh scapulars and mantle brightly fringed, as on Turtle Dove.

Dark Booted Eagle. Inner primaries and tail pale. Heavy eagle head, otherwise similar to Black Kite.

primary patch below (though still more clearly barred inside); juveniles of both races rather similar. Intermediates between nominate and *lineatus* occur in E Europe and eastwards, some having large white area on primaries as *lineatus*, but overall reddish (see plate); commonly seen on passage in Middle East, where strong lighting exaggerates these features and can lead to misidentification as Red Kite. Race *aegyptius* slightly smaller and lighter in build, generally paler with more rufous in plumage, and adult's bill fully yellow; also has more pointed silhouette and more deeply cleft tail; juvenile also differs from those of preceding races in having buff apical spots on head feathers (instead of whitish/buff feather centres = streaks) and more diffuse and broad buff feather centres below (instead of sharply defined and white). **Distinctions When Perched** Red is warmer buff-rufous overall, with predominantly whitish head lacking obvious dark eye mask, brighter upperparts with blackish centres and clear-cut rufous-buff fringes to mantle/scapulars and upperwing-coverts (pattern diffuse and browner on most Black). On Red, wingtips fall well short of tip of redder-orange tail (on Black, reach close to tip of brownish tail). **Confusion Risks** Black often appears surprisingly large and eagle-like at various distances. At moderate distances, commonest confusion may arise with superficially similar (at least in size and sometimes in shape, especially if tail fork obscure) Marsh Harrier· in non-adult-male plumage or with dark/rufous morphs of Booted Eagle. Separated from former by

following features: **1** seen head-on, always appears to show some arching of wings, lacking Marsh's raised wings when soaring or hunting; **2** splayed primary fingers distinctly longer than on Marsh; **3** most (not all) Black Kites tend to show some tail fork (diagnostic), pale panel on upper median coverts (never on Marsh, but adult female Marsh often shows whitish upper forewing-coverts), and distinctly paler patch across inner and base of outer primaries; **4** most (not all) Marsh have narrower and slightly rounded tail, solid white markings on head, and show indistinct/no pale primary patch, blackish wingtip or barring on remiges/rectrices (see also Harris *et al.* 1989). From dark/rufous morphs of Booted: **1** Black's tail may, if fork obscured (through damage or moult), appear square-ended as Booted, but latter usually shows more rounded body and bull-headed eagle-like appearance, and less of kite's downward-angled hands or projecting carpals when gliding or even soaring (for other flight modes of Booted, see latter); **2** although both show pale upper median-covert panel, Black lacks Booted's diagnostic white patch at base of leading edge and clear-cut whitish uppertail-coverts; **3** outer tail feathers always well barred on Black, unbarred (and paler) on Booted. At longer distances or with birds gliding high overhead, separation very difficult if above features not discernible (see plate), though often possible with telescope and previous experience (differences in outline and wing position); even so, a few often left undetermined.

Lappet-faced, Black and Griffon Vultures

Where and When The most widespread is Griffon Vulture *Gyps fulvus*, breeding patchily over S Europe, N Africa and east to SC Asia. Black *Aegypius monachus* is rather widespread but sporadic in SW and SE Europe and Asia Minor/Levant eastwards. Lappet-faced *Torgos tracheliotus* is essentially a subtropical/tropical African bird, penetrating in small numbers into N Africa, Arabia and Israel. All show preference for precipitous nesting sites

in varied mountain landscapes, Griffon in colonies on cliff ledges, the other two usually on isolated tree. All are generally resident or partially migratory. Griffon overlaps in range separately with Black and Lappet-faced; latter two may meet only in winter in range of Lappet-faced.

Identification and Ageing All three are usually seen in poor circumstances (long distance, inadequate lighting), so silhouette (both perched and in flight) and wing position and shape of great use in most observations. Effects of different lighting on plumage appearance are greater than expected, and some experience needed to evaluate features correctly: e.g. underparts of Griffon when in shadow or in cloudy sky may appear darker and even reminiscent of those of Lappet-faced, or latter's underparts may resemble Griffon's in side lighting (early morning, late afternoon), so awareness of real and illusory effects of light important. Wind and other factors also influence wing position and jizz. In most of region Griffon likely to be confused with Black Vulture, but in Middle East existence of Lappet-faced can complicate matters. Ageing of little importance in species separation.

Black and Griffon Vultures

Wingspan 250–295 and 240–280 cm, respectively. Considerable difference in plumage between the two. Both on ground and in flight, Griffon's marked contrast between remiges and wing-coverts (and body) should be clearly detectable, whereas Black is rather uniform and very dark (at close quarters may show paler but complex head pattern, paler feet and browner/blacker underwing-coverts), and at distance appears just black. Beware, however, Griffon with patches of dry blood and other discoloration (can cover whole upper body, including species' diagnostic whitish head, neck and ruff), which can appear much darker from distance. In flight, under most conditions, Griffon soars with wings in shallow V and bulging remiges (marked S-curve to trailing edge formed by huge outer primaries jutting out noticeably from short inner ones, and long outer/short inner secondaries), as opposed to Black's invariably flat wings when soaring and almost parallel and straighter edges. Black Vulture, particularly when soaring at distance, may be confused with all-dark *Aquila*, e.g. adult Imperial Eagle (but latter has proportionately narrower wings, more square-ended and longer tail, well protruding head, paler undertail-coverts and conspicu-

ously pale crown and nape); shape and size similarly rule out distant adult Steppe and Spotted Eagles, both of which show various whitish markings above on primary bases and uppertail-coverts/rump. Some characters (wing and tail shape and proportions) may invite confusion with darkish immature White-tailed Eagle, but even if latter's whitish axillary patch and rectrix centres and pale-streaked breast cannot be seen it should be recognised by markedly protruding neck and head.

Variations *Griffon* 1st-years differ from adult in having darker bill and eye (yellowish-horn in adult), pale brownish-buff ruff (cleaner and whiter on adult), in being darker with greater contrast between blacker remiges and warmer rest of plumage (which has some rich ginger-tawny pigments; adult predominantly sandy and duller in tone); also in having profusely whitish-streaked underbody, and paler and less variegated underwing-coverts (created by wider solidly whitish-sandy median-covert band). Immature retains sharp contrast between wing-coverts and remiges for 2 years, and full plumage acquired at age of 5–6 years. *Black* 1st-years differ from adult in being blacker (almost sooty-black, less brown) and with darker wing-coverts and body contrasting more with remiges, also in having plainer underwing-coverts almost lacking adult's broken narrow whitish bars on lesser and central coverts (usually noticeable at close range); head dark brown (paler with blackish eye mask on adult). Full plumage gradually acquired at about 6 years.

Lappet-faced Vulture

Wingspan 255–290 cm. From distance not easily separable from Black and Griffon, as more variable in plumage and shares features of both. Given reasonable view, however, identifiable by following characters. Averages larger and heavier than Griffon and nearer to Black, though always appears more powerful and huge, with more massive bill and broader head (protruding downwards and forwards in flight). Soars on flat or slightly downward-arched wings (nearer Black, but never in V as

Adult Griffon Vulture below. Patchily paler coverts, dark remiges.

Griffon Vulture from above, showing pale wing coverts.

Adult Black Vulture below. Dark coverts, slightly paler remiges.

Juvenile Griffon Vulture. Underwing-coverts paler and plainer than adult.

Adult Lappet-faced Vulture below. Variable pale line along coverts, pale thighs.

Only Griffon Vulture soars on raised wings.

Black Vulture

Lappet-faced Vulture. Upperwing-coverts silvery-brown, midway between Griffon and Black Vultures.

Griffon Vulture. Upperparts pale.

Juvenile Black Vulture. Uniformly black beneath.

Juvenile Lappet-Faced Vulture is darker and more uniform below than adult.

Adult Black Vulture. All dark, pale head.

Lappet-faced Vulture. Pale head, isolated eye, pale thighs.

Head patterns distinctive in close views.

Griffon Vulture

Lappet-faced Vulture

Juvenile

Black Vultures

Adult

18

Griffon), and wings comparatively longer with clearly defined longer secondaries than the shorter inner primaries, giving bulging trailing edge (recalls broad-winged effect of Black and, superficially, the S-shape of Griffon). Tail distinctly shorter than on latter two, more rounded and occasionally wedge-shaped, but with (as remiges) very pointed tips, appearing serrated.

Plumage *Underparts* As Black, differs rather markedly from Griffon in having darker (but less solid) underwing-coverts than much of greyish-toned remiges; forewing ends abruptly in pale broken bar formed by pale mottling in middle of lesser coverts, which, along with greyish greaters, usually contrast with darker median-covert band. Beware, however, darker and less marked (usually immature) Lappet-faced or heavily marked adult Black, which can look rather alike; use structural and upperpart features. Also differs in having non-uniform underbody: belly smooth and darkish, breast creamy-white with broad dark stripes, flanks and tibia feathers usually pale creamy-brown, and nape surrounded by a light creamy-brown ruff. *Upperparts* Paler than Black, but not so pale as Griffon: shows a certain contrast between the paler wing-coverts and mantle to tail-coverts and the darker remiges (recalling Griffon, but with less contrast); adult often has whitish marks on back.

Variations Little difference between young and adults in Middle East race *negevensis*, but African races show clear differences: adults have whitish underparts with obvious lanceolate black feathers and well-developed bar on underwing-coverts, as well as coarse and numerous skin folds, large lappets extensively coloured darker red; young are reminiscent of average *negevensis* form. Typical head of *negevensis* shows thick pale greyish-brown down (again a feature shown mainly on young of African races, decreasing in extent on adults), and small skin folds with red restricted to back of head and upper neck and with inconspicuous (almost invisible) lappets. Acquires full plumage at 5–7 years.

Hen, Montagu's and Pallid Harriers

Where and When Hen Harrier *Circus cyaneus* breeds in Holarctic, including most of Europe (not Asia Minor), and is mostly migratory, wintering C and S Holarctic (where also resident) and, in small numbers, Middle East and N Africa; in open low-lying country such as heathland, grassland and rather damp areas, but also adapted to agriculture. Montagu's Harrier *C. pygargus* breeds NW Africa, C and S Europe, locally Turkey and east to C Asia and is highly migratory, wintering south of Sahara and in India; prefers open plains, heathland or wetlands (broad river valleys, marshes, lake margins, bogs, moorland), but also adapted to cultivated areas, on passage in drier areas and in winter chiefly grasslands. Pallid Harrier *C. macrourus* breeds from C Asia west to SE Europe, wintering C and E Africa, Middle East and S Asia; habitat as for Montagu's, but stronger preference for entirely open terrain, especially dry grassy steppe (and usually adapts to open agricultural areas), tending to avoid wetlands. In W Palearctic, Hen overlaps widely in range with either Montagu's (almost anywhere) or Pallid (eastwards), while latter two often overlap on Asian breeding grounds or on passage in Middle East, where Hen and Pallid winter in same areas. In much of Europe Pallid is rare or a vagrant.

Identification of females and juveniles

General Although separating 'ringtail' harriers can be exceedingly difficult, it is made easier if age is assessed correctly (see characters detailed below under each species and age groups). As a rule, Hen differs from Montagu's and Pallid in wing shape and in lacking distinct juvenile plumage, but confusion potential does exist (mainly between adult females or 1st-summer birds, in particular with regard to Pallid).

SEPARATING HEN FROM MONTAGU'S AND PALLID

Juvenile Hen is very close to adult female, but has warmer plumage, with underparts deep buff-yellow and lightly streaked (whiter and boldly streaked on adult female) and upperwing-coverts saturated rufous-brown (more brownish-grey on females); also has darker secondaries with greyer pale bands and diffuse and broader, often blackish bars (whiter with sharply set-off blackish bars and broader intervening ones on females), undertail-coverts and leg feathering generally streaked (not blob-marked), and more prominent dark ear-covert patch and pale-tipped greater upperwing-coverts. 1st-summers much as adult female, but remiges evenly worn (lacking arrested-moult effect of female) and secondaries still show juvenile pattern. Adult female, juvenile and 1st-summer Hen separable from all plumages of Montagu's and Pallid by having noticeably *Accipiter*-like wings with broader arm and inner hand and broadly rounded ample wingtip (five fingers), whereas Montagu's and Pallid have much slimmer wings (straighter rear edge) and more pointed hands (four fingers; 5th very short). 'Ringtail' Hen differs further from those of Pallid (which can appear rather heavy-bodied and broad-winged) and Montagu's in following characters. **Perched** Hen has longer wing-and-tail projection and relatively shorter legs; averages more heavily streaked on head/neck, with rather faint collar, creating less conspicuous facial pattern (usually lacks pronounced whitish collar and darker/solid ear-covert patch of Montagu's/ Pallid, but some older females of latter, particularly Pallid, can have very similar pattern), and usually poorly developed whitish nape patch (but variable). These and other characters (e.g. primary spacing, nature of rear underpart streaking, upperwing-coverts, etc) are subtle, and for all three species individual variation, abrasion and moult activity render them of little practical use. *In flight* Hen shows odd combination of underwing features: on adult females, hand reminiscent of adult female Montagu's (more

evenly spaced bars on primaries almost from bases to tips, and prominent trailing edge), but secondaries intermediate between Montagu's and Pallid but tending towards Pallid (terminal band usually broader towards wing base and the two dark inner bars narrower, but pale bands whiter and almost reach body); juveniles/1st-years show converse pattern, hand recalling that of juvenile Pallid (mostly unbarred primary bases and well-barred paler fingers) but secondaries rather characteristic, with equally very broad dark bars. Other field characters subtle and variable in distinctiveness, e.g. at close quarters facial pattern may aid identification, and pale forewing panel above usually less distinct than on other two species. Otherwise, tail pattern similar to adult Pallid but more contrasting (bolder, wider bands) and uppertail-covert patch usually larger than on other two. Bear in mind possible vagrancy of N American race *hudsonicus* of Hen (see Harris *et al.* 1989), juveniles of which (rarely, approached by nominate) can be tricky: mainly rufous below with streaking almost restricted to upper breast and with rather pronounced Pallid-like facial pattern, but shape/size and other plumage features (e.g. wing and tail patterns, lack of solid dark neck-side patches) still typical of Hen.

SEPARATING MONTAGU'S AND PALLID

Once age determined (see below), combination of *underwing pattern* (all remiges for adult female, only primaries for juvenile), *facial pattern* (some individual variation and overlap), *axillary pattern*, *body streaking*, *tail features*, general *proportions* and *mode of flight* (adults) will enable identification.

Adult Females In autumn/early winter, differ from juveniles in lacking rich rusty-ochre underparts and blackish-brown upperparts. In spring, easily separated from less advanced 1st-summers as latter much as juveniles (chiefly in Pallid) but duller, though some 1st-summer females (chiefly Montagu's) well towards adult and ageable largely by remiges: adult females usually have cleaner secondary pattern, with whiter pale bands and sharply set-off blackish bars (less so on

Adult ♀ Hen Harrier

Juvenile ♀ Hen Harrier. Warm fresh plumage, underparts without club-like spots typical of adult ♀.

Adult ♀ Hen Harrier. Wings broad and heavy, some wing barring. Five-fingered wingtip, four long primaries.

Adult ♀ Hen Harrier. Clearer banded secondaries, boldly streaked body.

Juvenile ♀ Hen Harrier. Plain remiges, pale wing-coverts. Large white rump.

Adult ♀ Pallid Harrier. Clean white collar, face mask reaches bill. Tail longer than wingtip.

Juvenile Pallid Harrier. Note face pattern, clear buff 'ruff', dark collar. Face mask reaches bill, thin weak supercilium.

Adult ♀ Pallid Harrier. Plain upperwing, clear collar, usually dark breasted. Lacks barring to axillaries.

Pale stripe to secondaries reduced to spots by body. Compare to ♀ Montagu's Harrier.

Juvenile Montagu's Harrier (left) lacks strong head pattern of juvenile Pallid Harrier (right). Compare underwing patterns.

Juvenile ♀ Montagu's Harrier Wide supercilium, whiter around eye, restricted dark mask.

Adult ♀ Montagu's Harrier. Wide pale bar on secondaries, coverts barred.

Adult ♀ Montagu's Harrier. Note dark bar on upperwing.

Adult ♀ Montagu's Harrier. Pale faced, eye crescent joins wide supercilium.

21

Pallid), and primary pattern usually characteristic of their species (and also different from respective juvenile/1st-summer: see below), and, with experience, arrested-moult effect discernible (through telescope); 1st-summers have generally dark secondaries (contrasting greatly with primaries) and typical juvenile pattern, with broad and diffuse blackish bars and more greyish pale bands. If such a 1st-summer is dismissed as adult, there is high risk of misidentification. Main characters in order of importance as follows. 1 HAND PATTERN Pallid's under primaries usually markedly paler than secondaries, and show reduced and more 'hook-shaped' barring confined to central area, leaving fingers and bases unbarred; primary bases create wide pale wedge (or boomerang-like shape) bordering primary coverts; dark trailing edge indistinct/diffuse. On Montagu's, primaries typically show evenly spaced complete barring from bases well onto fingers; dark trailing edge sharply demarcated. 2 SECONDARIES A major difference between the two in underwing pattern is that Pallid's secondary region (including greater coverts) looks contrastingly darker than primaries, with only one rather prominent pale, greyish band across distal arm (on Montagu's, pale area/bands wider/cleaner and match pale ground colour of primaries). At close quarters, however, Pallid's pale bands clearest/broadest on outer arm, tapering and darkening inwards and vanishing towards body, while rearmost pale band narrower than dark trailing band (on Montagu's, evenly thick/pale right up to body, so dark bars well separated throughout, while rearmost pale band generally broader than dark trailing band). In addition, Pallid has three dark bars fairly equally spaced, but rather diffuse, with inner two poorly developed and clearly narrower than trailing edge, which usually broader towards wing base; on Montagu's, dark bars widely spaced and well defined, inner two closer together (producing broader rearmost pale band) and central bar most prominent and blacker than trailing band, which is browner and evenly narrower

throughout (secondary pattern recalls adult male). 3 UNDERWING-COVERTS AND AXILLARIES Pattern detectable at close quarters: on Pallid, greater coverts and axillaries densely but finely pale-spotted (distinctly barred on Montagu's) on much darker ground colour which usually contrasts with paler lesser coverts (contrast indistinct on most Montagu's). 4 UNDERPART STREAKING Although variation considerable, most Pallid tend to have denser and bolder streaking on upper breast but lower breast and belly finely streaked, creating demarcated impression (Montagu's more evenly and finely streaked on all underparts), and brown/rufous markings on trousers and undertail-coverts are usually in form of 'double-spots', i.e. broad subterminal spot joining with dark narrow centre and broad base, but often diffuse (unlike more lanceolate streaks of Montagu's). 5 FACIAL PATTERN In reasonable views, Pallid's typical (but highly variable) pattern usually pronounced: rather sharply defined neck-collar (less obvious on very old females) which often crosses throat (typical Montagu's has indistinct and extremely streaked pale half-collar never extending to throat); black streak through eye separating very narrow white supercilium from narrow white cheek, and dark ear-covert crescent usually better developed, extending farther forwards to loral region and bordered by whitish collar connecting with supercilium (Montagu's broader supercilium usually joins whitish cheek to form rather extensive pale area around eye and reaching farther onto loral region, thus face side typically whiter except for isolated ear-covert patch, giving open-faced impression and generally with poorer contrast). 6 UPPERWING Most Pallid show rather plain upperwing (no or very indistinct barring, and usually only on primaries), but often some contrast between darker secondaries and paler primaries. On Montagu's, especially older birds, less contrast between arm and hand and usually slightly suffused greyish, with barring rather visible (particularly blackish bar across secondaries), but beware that many 2nd-winter/

summer birds still have darker remiges, chiefly secondaries, and hardly any barring, just as Pallid. 7 TAIL On Pallid, bars on outer feathers are dark brown or blackish (rufous on typical Montagu's) and entire undertail pattern more like that of Hen, with much broader/darker terminal band, inner (second) one closer to centre and third bar less visible behind tail-coverts (unlike many Montagu's, but much variation and overlap render this feature of little use). 8 SUBSIDIARY FEATURES Pallid averages slightly heavier in build (usually lacks Montagu's small-bodied proportions), with marginally shorter but fuller tail and more ample and straighter hand, flight thus appearing slightly more powerful (light and graceful in Montagu's). Pallid has 5th primary proportionately longer and hand more regularly fingered, producing impression of straighter trailing edge and fuller hand than Montagu's (which has hand noticeably longer and more pointed, with three longest primaries closer together and more protruding). Markings on uppertail-coverts more barlike on most Pallid, streak-like on Montagu's. When perched, Pallid's legs slightly longer and wingtips fall a bit short of tail tip (reach tip on Montagu's). *Cautionary note:* Incorrect age assessment is the root cause of many misidentifications: e.g. 2nd-summer female Montagu's often have heavier breast streaking, lack upper secondary bar and have retained, rather uniformly dark juvenile secondaries, and often show distinct pale collar; can easily be taken for adult female Pallid.

Juveniles Easily aged by being darker above, largely unstreaked chestnut below, with particularly dark secondaries and strong facial pattern. Main distinguishing features in order of importance as follows. 1 PRIMARY PATTERN Pallid shows diagnostic unbarred primary bases creating distinct boomerang-shaped wedges around primary coverts and sometimes to about halfway down on arm, while fingers variably barred (on pale/greyish background, sometimes darker) and trailing edge diffusely greyish. Montagu's hand shows *Buteo*-like pattern, with unbarred dark grey/blackish fingers as well as broader and

sharply set-off trailing edge; most also show indistinctly barred or unbarred bases to central and/or outer (but usually longest) primaries. Beware, however, that sexual dimorphism creates some individual variation, extreme being juvenile female Montagu's with greyer/paler fingers and even one or two small bars or spots on base/centre of four outer fingers, and with somewhat indistinct trailing edge. 2 FACIAL PATTERN Typical Pallid shows most striking facial markings: diagnostic broad unspotted whitish collar emphasised by rather solid dark brown neck side, extensive dark ear-covert area typically reaches farther towards throat sides (leaving only small white area on central throat or merely chin) and towards bill base to create distinct dark loral area, and white area around eye usually greatly reduced; in extremes, collar completely encircles head and front of face is solidly blackish (facial-disc impression). Montagu's has much more white around eye, including deeper supercilium, broader white on cheek and loral region, and in front view face appears largely white; dark ear-covert patch usually confined to area behind (and very slightly in front of) eye; half-collar generally less clearly defined and shorter, with more rusty tone and various markings, and usually tapers or becomes diffuse towards nape and merges with pale throat; dark neck-side patches smaller and poorly developed. 3 UNDERPART STREAKING Pallid usually lacks discernible streaks on breast or body sides; Montagu's normally shows rather prominent streaking on breast (sides) which usually extends to upper flanks. 4 TAIL PATTERN Underside of Pallid's outer feathers usually look plain, almost unmarked very pale buff (pale bands whiter) and sometimes only dark subterminal band prominent; Montagu's shows distinctly more rusty colour on both sides of the same feathers, which variably but more evenly banded below, and usually has rather diffusely barred upper central tail feathers. 5 SUBSIDIARY FEATURES Perched juveniles of the two differ somewhat in leg length and wing/tail-tip projection (see under females). Most (not all) Pallid tend to

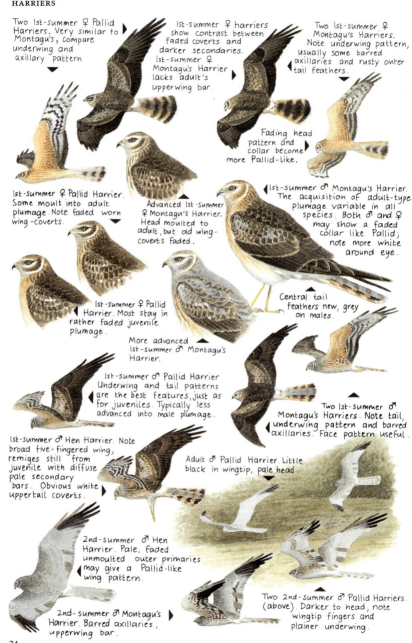

Two 1st-summer ♀ Pallid Harriers. Very similar to Montagu's. Compare underwing and axillary pattern

1st-summer ♀ harriers show contrast between faded coverts and darker secondaries. 1st-summer ♀ Montagu's Harrier lacks adult's upperwing bar.

Two 1st-summer ♀ Montagu's Harriers. Note underwing pattern, usually some barred axillaries and rusty outer tail feathers.

Fading head pattern and collar become more Pallid-like.

1st-summer ♀ Pallid Harrier. Some moult into adult plumage. Note faded worn wing-coverts.

Advanced 1st-summer ♀ Montagu's Harrier. Head moulted to adult, but old wing-coverts faded.

1st-summer ♂ Montagu's Harrier. The acquisition of adult-type plumage variable in all species. Both ♂ and ♀ may show a faded collar like Pallid; note more white around eye.

1st-summer ♀ Pallid Harrier. Most stay in rather faded juvenile plumage.

More advanced 1st-summer ♂ Montagu's Harrier.

Central tail feathers new, grey on males.

1st-summer ♂ Pallid Harrier Underwing and tail patterns are the best features, just as for juveniles. Typically less advanced into male plumage.

Two 1st-summer ♂ Montagu's Harriers. Note tail, underwing pattern and barred axillaries. Face pattern useful.

1st-summer ♂ Hen Harrier. Note broad five-fingered wing, remiges still from juvenile with diffuse pale secondary bars. Obvious white uppertail coverts.

Adult ♂ Pallid Harrier. Little black in wingtip, pale head

2nd-summer ♂ Hen Harrier. Pale, faded unmoulted outer primaries may give a Pallid-like wing pattern.

2nd-summer ♂ Montagu's Harrier. Barred axillaries, upperwing bar.

Two 2nd-summer ♂ Pallid Harriers (above). Darker to head, note wingtip fingers and plainer underwing.

have unstreaked median and lesser under-wing-coverts (on most Montagu's, only les-sers unstreaked), and as a rule streaking on greater (and median) coverts is better devel-oped on Montagu's, but much overlap ren-ders this of little use. All Pallid lack barring on (outer) axillaries shown by some (not all) juvenile Montagu's. Pallid tends to show more constantly chestnut-toned underparts (usually rather deep yellowish-rufous/ochre); Montagu's more variable, with extremes of very deep rufous-brown (hardly ever occurs on Pallid) to warm yellowish-rufous (as many Pallid).

1st-summer Females From late winter and spring of 2nd year, variation both in amount of moulted/unmoulted feathers and in plu-mage patterning considerable (though Pallid on average moult less in partial 1st-winter moult and are more constant in characters). Some may retain juvenile plumage (faded and worn), while some acquire almost adult-like plumage. Accurate ageing essential (since adult females similar). Characters in general order of importance as follows. 1 PRIMARY PATTERN Retained primaries differ as for juveniles, but prominence of features reduced through bleaching. 2 AXILLARY PATTERN Pallid lacks Montagu's diagnostic barred axillaries (rarely, reduced or lacking on less advanced birds), instead having streaks/spots just as adult female. 3 TAIL PATTERN As for juveniles. 4 HEAD AND UNDERPARTS Pallid, unlike many Montagu's, tends to moult less of head, body and underwing-coverts during 1st winter, so in late winter and spring still more or less juvenile-like (many Montagu's more female-like) but worn and strongly bleached. Note that more advanced Pallid show strong similarity to Montagu's (especially when latter have more distinct collar) and both can have rather similar (heavier) breast streaking. Moreover, the rare Pallid that moults much of body shows a more intermediate plumage, unlike 1st-immature feathers of Montagu's (which have more adult-like pattern); unfortunately, Pallid showing this transitional body-feather pattern are more like Montagu's (adult or

well-advanced 1st-summer) and the two are closer in underpart pattern. Note also that less advanced 1st-summer Montagu's with retained juvenile head but strongly bleached/worn can show more marked head pattern (rather more Pallid-like); and those which have moulted only part of head-and-breast region, having unmoulted belly area with rather plain juvenile-like pattern, can some-what recall adult Pallid. So, in spring, correct ageing followed by examination of remex pattern below is the key to identification. 5 LEG LENGTH AND WING/TAIL PROJECTION May be useful on perched birds, as with adult females (which see).

Identification of males

Adult Males Identification usually straightforward. *Hen* the largest, broadest-winged and generally heaviest in build (nota-ble in flight), with broad arm and rather rounded ample hand with long 5th primary: when perched, easily distinguished by darker bluish-grey head and upper breast contrast-ing with paler, unmarked underparts; in flight, diagnostic large black wingtip (outer-most primaries) and large white uppertail-covert patch. *Montagu's* distinctive, with variable amount of rust-coloured streaking on underparts (reduced with age, may be lacking on very old males) and with black secondary bars (see Harris *et al.* 1989). *Pallid* very similar in size and shape to Montagu's, though slightly larger and broader-winged, but reliably separated by plumage features: 1 distinctly paler whitish-grey, lacking darker head and chest, and with less black in wingtip; 2 unstreaked below and unmottled above; 3 folded wings fall slightly short of tail tip, and legs distinctly longer; 4 in flight, shows sharply defined narrow black wedge on hands both above and below (black confined to 2nd-5th/6th primaries), and with very pale overall plumage can give tern-like impression (but bear in mind 2nd-year Hen, or sometimes Montagu's, with paler unmoulted outermost primaries forming rather similar black wingtip pattern: see below); 5 lacks clear-cut whitish patch on uppertail-coverts. At very long range, and with some experience, the slimmer build and generally more buoyant and tern-like flight of Montagu's and Pallid can be detected (Hen has typically slower flight with slightly heavier wingbeats, somewhat recalling Marsh Harrier *C. aeruginosus*). Remember also, however, that poorly marked (usually very old) male Montagu's could sometimes be mistaken for Pallid at long range.

Immature Males From (partial) post-juvenile moult in 1st winter and until about 1 year old, *1st-summer males* of all three are paler and worn, with whiter belly, a few new grey (slightly brownish-tinged) upperpart feathers and new greyish central tail feathers, while darker-looking secondaries contrast with surrounding area, and whole effect rather variegated. Some acquire more grey feathers, including head to breast (chiefly Montagu's, on which grey typically darker and more demarcated). Much of plumage nevertheless still juvenile, and they should be identified accordingly (see above), but beware that these early transitional plumages can be very tricky: e.g. less advanced 1st-summer Montagu's but with well-developed half-collar and distinct dark ear-covert patch (typical of many 1st-summer Montagu's) could be misidentified as 1st-summer/adult female Pallid. Correct ageing thus essential before identifying species. With 1st-summer males (uniform primaries and distinctly darker secondaries), primary pattern is diagnostic for Pallid and Montagu's, while the most useful feature for Hen is its much broader and round-tipped wings as well as its underwing pattern (same criteria separate the three in juvenile plumage: see above); other plumage characters, especially on birds well advanced towards adult, should be regarded as no more than subsidiary, as they are potentially misleading in early transitional stages. Following first complete moult, at end of summer of 2nd calendar-year, *2nd-winter males* more or less resemble adults, though moult highly variable and usually the two outermost primaries and some secondaries are unmoulted and some of body plumage has 'transitional-

patterned' feathers, which can produce mixed characters of two species in one bird; extreme caution demanded when dealing with such birds. For example, 2nd-winter Hen usually shows unmoulted (worn and faded) outermost two primaries next to 4/5 new black central primaries, creating black wedge shape not unlike pattern of adult male Pallid; same applies, rarely, with 2nd-winter Montagu's when also its upper secondary bar is ill-defined owing to only partially moulted secondaries; 2nd-winter Pallid can give field impression (chiefly at distance) of Hen or Montagu's, owing to rather darker grey new upperparts and some head feathers plus clear-cut rusty-streaked breast against whitish belly creating dark-hooded impression. In spring/summer of 3rd year (after suspended winter moult), when all/most juvenile plumage replaced by adult-like feathering, the three species are easily identified as if adults (some near-adults have more dirty grey and some brown feathers on head/neck and upperparts, as well as some faint streaks below). Final, complete adult plumage usually acquired in post-breeding moult of 3rd year.

Odd plumages

Melanistic Montagu's Montagu's occurs in a melanistic form, which is rare but needs to be distinguished from superficially similar melanistic Marsh. Size and shape should easily identify them, while Montagu's barred wing and tail feathers (adult female and juvenile) or black primaries and sooty-grey secondaries (adult male) are never found on melanistic Marsh, which has unbarred tail and varying amount of basal white on under primaries (males) or all remiges (females and juveniles).

Hybridisation Frequency of hybridisation among all three and resultant plumages poorly known. Recent pairing of Pallid and Montagu's in Finland produced young almost identical to juvenile Pallid, including head pattern, though body streaking somewhat approaching Montagu's; hybrid adult female would probably be dismissed in field as one of the two, while hybrid adult male, with obvious mixed characters, should not be, but such plumages not recorded. *References* Delin & Svensson (1988), Forsman (1984, 1993a, 1995), Harris *et al.* (1989), Lontkowski & Skakvj (1995), Porter *et al.* (1981), Svensson (1971).

Levant and Eurasian Sparrowhawks

Where and When Eurasian Sparrowhawk *Accipiter nisus* is one of commonest raptors across W Palearctic, largely sedentary or partially migratory except in Fennoscandia and N Russia, where a true migrant; in open country alternating with woodland, and only on passage/in winter in subtropics and desert (few). Levant Sparrowhawk *A. brevipes* breeds in broadleaved woodland in Balkans and countries around Black Sea east to Caspian area, migrating through Levant to winter E Africa, with contracted passage mostly in dense flocks of hundreds/thousands very characteristic (e.g. peak of 20,000+ at Eilat in spring, usually around 20–25 April).

General Levant shows slightly reduced sexual dimorphism in plumage and mainly in size (female Eurasian clearly larger than male), but more distinctive juvenile plumage. Both have complete post-juvenile moult in summer of 2nd year (at same time as adults' complete post-breeding moult); only Levant juveniles (most) moult much of body, and even some rectrices/remiges, to adult plumage in winter, but still ageable during 1st spring and (unlike Eurasian) easier to sex by plumage.

Structure and Flight With experience, Levant often identified by shape and flight: may appear to have somewhat falcon-like jizz when gliding, but in most situations action and shape truly hawk-like. Differs from Eurasian in proportionately longer and slimmer wings and shorter tail. Most distinctive features are straighter rear wing edge (only slightly bulging secondaries), and more pointed hand (wingpoint formed of two primaries (counted inwards) with shorter but distinctly sloping fingers and no protruding 6th primary; Eurasian's wing appears rather shorter and rounded, with distinct curved trailing edge and ample hand (wingpoint of three primaries, fingers longer with longer 4th/5th and distinctly protruding 6th primaries). Levant's flight appears less stiff, with shallower but more rapid beats (effortless and easy manoeuvrability), relieved by longer soaring and/or gliding.

Adults *Males* Male Levant distinguished from any Eurasian plumage by dark eye within diffuse broad grey ear-coverts (detectable in close view), lacking Eurasian's yellow/orange eye and well-demarcated grey crown reaching a little below eye and leaving wide buff ear-coverts. At all ranges, Levant's dark primaries and particularly their tips, well pronounced on both surfaces, are the most distinct features (not marked in other plumages, and altogether lacking in all Eurasian): from above clearly defined from grey upperparts (both perched and in flight), from below solidly black tips well set off from whitish and more or less unbarred flight feathers. Otherwise, ochre bars on underbody and underwing-coverts cleaner and deeper, with reduced pale intervening bars, notably on chest, and tail usually shows about 6 more closely spaced bars (5 or fewer on Eurasian), with barring reduced or lacking on outermost and central pairs. *Females* Female Levant differs from male in pronounced and complete underwing barring but strongly reduced dark wingtip, generally broader and more complete tail bars (often at least partial on central pair), and better-defined, broader and darker barring on body and underwing-coverts (unlike many adult males, bars are browner, edged blackish); also has much better-developed dark central throat line. Dark wingtip, although reduced in prominence (due partly to strongly marked anterior underwing), still clearly darkish grey and giving more or less same effect as on male (but not in 1st-summer females, which see),

Adult ♀ Eurasian Sparrowhawk. Greyish above, note pale throat, supercilium, few tail bars, yellow eye.

Adult ♀ Levant Sparrowhawk. Brown, uniform face, dark eye, finer breast barring.

Adult ♀ Eurasian Sparrowhawk. Broad rounded wingtip and bulging rear edge of wing. Fewer, broader tail bars, pale throat.

◄ Adult ♀ Levant Sparrowhawk.

Adult ♂ Eurasian Sparrowhawk. Dark above, orange cheeks, pale eyes.

Adult ♂ Levant Sparrowhawk. Very pale below, dark wingtips.

Levant Sparrowhawks migrate in flocks.

Adult ♂ Levant Sparrowhawk. Pale above, grey cheeks, dark eyes, breast barring very fine.

1st-summer ♀ Levant Sparrowhawk. Juvenile wings and tail, often mainly adult-type body feathers below.

Adult ♂ Eurasian Sparrowhawk. Broad wings, heavily barred underparts, lacks obvious dark wingtips.

Juvenile Eurasian Sparrowhawk. Heavily barred beneath.

Juvenile Levant Sparrowhawk. Wingpoint made up of 2 primary tips. (3 in Eurasian Sparrowhawk, right).

Juvenile Eurasian Sparrowhawk. Note pale eyes, supercilium, gingery breast barring.

Juvenile Levant Sparrowhawk. Uniform head, dark eyes, dark mesial streak, breast spotted (not barred).

this usually separating it at distance from female Eurasian. Other male features (grey ear-coverts, tail barring) but also throat line also valid for separating female from superficially similar plumages (i.e. including young males) of Eurasian. Since in this plumage the two species more closely resemble each other (e.g. almost identical underpart barring), it is advisable to look for wing shape and flight action or other features which require more precise appreciation, e.g. adult female Levant lacks varying degree of whitish supercilium shown by Eurasian female (and many males) of all ages and has dark (not yellow/orange) eye and dark central throat line. (See also 1st-summers for variation in head pattern, which sometimes applies also to adult female.)

Juveniles Levant generally unmistakable: underparts with striking drop-shaped streaking (never found on any Eurasian), otherwise flight feathers barred below much as Eurasian, but unlike latter still have central throat line, more bars on tail and dark (instead of yellow) eye, and lack Eurasian's whitish supercilium. Besides smaller size, many juvenile males can be sexed by having on average narrower, greyer, more diffuse barring on flight feathers (including trailing edge) and largely greyish fingers with indistinct/no bars (whiter and darker-barred on females). Note that juvenile Eurasian often have some streaks/spots/heart-shaped marks on throat

and upper breast, but pattern never so obvious or so extensive as on juvenile Levant. **1st-summers** 1st-spring/summer Levant tends to show varying amount of adult-like plumage, though nearly always with retained juvenile feathering on mainly chest (drop-shaped streaks) and upperparts (old brownish feathers). Such mixed plumage unique to Levant, but beware many 1st-summer Eurasian with odd non-bar-shaped markings on upper chest that at quick glance may appear confusingly similar. These 1st-year Levant can in fact be very tricky: a few may have entire underparts adult-like (barred) but retain juvenile flight feathers (well barred, no darker wingtip), and such individuals (especially females) are much more like Eurasian. Best identified by differences in mode of flight, wing shape/formula, and by grey hood with dark eyes, more tail bars, central throat line, presence of at least some mixed old (brown) and new (grey) upperpart feathers, and lack of supercilium; many 1st-summer males also tend to have unbarred greyish fingers. Note that some young Eurasian (also some adult females) have extensive grey-brown on ear-coverts which may give effect of 'full-hooded Levant', but should also have pronounced supercilium; conversely, moulting young Levant may show some whitish lateral crown streaks, but never complete supercilium.

Long-legged and Steppe Buzzards

Where and When Long-legged Buzzard *Buteo rufinus* breeds N Africa and SE Europe through Middle East to C Asia, being mostly resident or a partial migrant, but mainly migratory in north/east of range; its dark morph largely confined to Asia west to Levant and its small and more rusty race *cirtensis* breeds mainly N Africa/Arabia. Common Buzzard *B. buteo* is generally the most widely distributed, mainly in two distinct populations: *B. b. vulpinus*, so-called Steppe Buzzard, breeds from NE Europe to c. 96°E in Siberia, migrating twice yearly through Middle East (where meets confus-

ingly similar Long-legged Buzzard); nominate *buteo* inhabits most of western and central parts of W Palearctic, overlapping in north with Rough-legged Buzzard *B. lagopus*, and is resident or a short-distance migrant; an extensive zone of intergradation between the races exists from Finland to Balkans.

General Separation on plumage complex. For simplification, the following presents the main identification pitfalls, which largely confined to their equivalent rufous and blackish morphs. Note that Steppe's grey-brown morph (which has a little rusty colour) is the most like nominate Common Buzzard and usually presents no difficulty. Combination of feather and moult patterns usually permits ageing: general tendency is for adults to have mixed-generation remiges (acquired by serially descendent and arrested moult, mainly post-breeding), clearer/broader blackish trailing edge to wing and subterminal tail band contrasting sharply with bases, and more uniform or bold pattern below, depending on species and individual variation (which see); juveniles/1st-years have uniformly fresh/worn narrower hand and more bulging secondaries (though may replace one or two inner primaries/outer secondaries in 1st winter), reduced subterminal tail band (may be lacking), but tail usually more barred, narrower/more diffuse trailing edge to wing, and less clearly patterned, also often streaked below.

Structure/Flight Shape, jizz and flight action the most useful features for nominate Long-legged, but their correct use requires care and practice. Flight mode the best character (and usually detectable long before confusingly similar plumage characters can be examined); active flight heavier, with slower and more majestic wingbeats in Long-legged; may therefore resemble Rough-legged, but heavier than latter or any Steppe. Seen gliding head-on, arm slightly raised and hand held horizontal (in Steppe, arm slightly more horizontal and hand often slightly lowered); when soaring, wings held in deeper V than in Steppe (even recalling Golden Eagle). Otherwise, Long-legged larger but more compact (broader and stouter body) than Steppe and has more conspicuous head on well protruding neck, thus appearing longer-necked; wings typically longer and broader and more rounded, can resemble an eagle's; tail fuller, and appears proportionately longer compared with rounded wings.

Plumage In adult Steppe, three main plumage types recognisable: 'fox-red morph', 'grey-brown morph' and 'blackish (dark) morph'. In Long-legged, four main types: 'pale morph' (often sandy birds, generally not found among adult Steppe), 'intermediate morph', 'rufous morph' and 'blackish (dark) morph'. It should be stressed that these

morphs refer to 'average typical birds', and wide variety of intermediates occurs: e.g. many Steppe intermediate between grey-brown and fox-red morphs, and many of Long-legged's pale and intermediate morphs show high degree of overlap; even intermediates between uniform fox-red and blackish morphs occur (some of latter are more slaty-brown and/or deep rusty-brown). Juveniles/1st-years of both species generally approach their respective adult morph type, are more difficult to separate, and often (mainly grey-brown and fox-red Steppe and pale and intermediate Long-legged) cannot be assigned to a category. *Distinctions between fox-red Steppe and pale/intermediate/rufous Long-legged* 1 UNDERPARTS Most Long-legged have pale head with usually more pronounced dark moustache and eye-stripe; pale head, throat and upper breast contrast strongly with sharply demarcated dark brown lower breast, belly and flanks/trousers. Equivalent Steppe morphs usually show mostly dark body sides and head/breast, moderately dark central belly/chest, and paler lower breast band and often trousers. Many Steppe (largely adults) also have varying amount of barring and/or (often in young) drop-shaped marks on breast/belly and flanks/trousers, usually indistinct or lacking on Long-legged. These tonal patterns rather constant for most birds, from palest to rustiest of both species. Note that some young Steppe (chiefly bleached spring birds) are very pale overall, especially on head/breast (where usually narrowly striped), with indistinct pale breast band, being generally reminiscent of pale Long-legged, but because of age still have dark eye (pale in Long-legged), while features such as underwing and tail patterns and shape often help to separate such tricky individuals; conversely, some rufous or any strongly patterned Long-legged (often young birds) tend to show rather pale breast band, and other strongly coloured and/or uniformly patterned birds tend to show rusty-brown on head/breast, which only slightly paler and merging into belly (see also below under N African race). Such birds usually very hard to assign to species, and other features must be looked for (as following). At least in nominate Long-legged, uniformly orangey-rufous individuals occur very rarely (as the classic uniform fox-red morph of Steppe), and then usually strongly saturated deep rufous-brown. 2 UNDERWING Classic Long-legged has rather uniformly rusty or evenly patterned underwing-coverts, while Steppe shows more marked difference between darkish (and usually faintly barred) greater coverts, pale medians and rusty lessers. Long-legged's carpal patch is solidly black or nearly so, i.e. with reduced or no white between median and greater primary coverts but at most a trace of diffuse paler greyish on exposed bases of outer greater primary coverts (but may show whiter bases to innermost coverts, which, if more exposed, reveal very diffuse scallop marks, and invariably unbarred), and carpal contrasts with remaining underwing-coverts; on Steppe, black in carpal area usually more limited to greater primary coverts (occasionally also on medians/lessers, when invariably a whitish and barred division on greater primary-covert bases up to leading edge to produce black 'comma'). Rest of underwing largely identical on both, but with tendency for Long-legged to have cleaner whitish-buff primary bases (with less strongly barred inners), whereas on Steppe these whiter and more strongly barred. 3 UPPERPARTS AND UPPER-WING Most Long-legged have paler and often more rufous and/or sandy (fringed) forewing and mantle/scapulars, larger or more prominent greyish-white primary-base patch and at least hint of dark carpal patch, as opposed to darker and non-contrasting coverts/mantle/ scapulars, reduced pale primary patch and indistinct/absent darker carpal patch of most Steppe; Steppe therefore more uniform above, with less pronounced darker remiges (notably at tips; generally more obvious dark wingtip on Long-legged), but leading edge often rather darker. Above-mentioned features, however, vary individually in both species, and can be confusingly similar. 4 TAIL Adult Long-legged's uppertail tends to appear clear pale

orange, usually unbarred or with only few dark bars distally (usually on inner webs and with rearmost widest), or sometimes un-barred but with hint of narrow dark subterm-inal band, and can often appear whitish, especially on bleached bird at distance, but note that most tend to have whiter tail (chiefly from below) since usually wider and contrast-ing whiter inner webs to 2nd-6th rectrices (counted inwards) and larger white base to shafts/centres of central pair. On adult Steppe, tail usually more densely and dis-tinctly barred, on both webs, with broader subterminal band, but beware that uniform fox-red morph often shows uniform rufous tail with only narrow subterminal band (but inner webs still mostly rufous nearer the outer webs). Juvenile tails of the two species often confusingly similar, as both largely barred throughout and often lack rufous, but Long-legged tends more frequently to show largely whitish base to central tail and to have 2nd-6th rectrices whiter on inner webs with stronger bars and darker on outer webs with indistinct/no barring (juvenile Steppe's tail more evenly coloured, barred on both webs). In both species, subterminal bar usually only slightly broader than the others on juvenile tails, but less apparent on Long-legged, on which sometimes broader or barring concen-trated distally (creating darker tail end). As variation in both species is huge and differ-ences in pattern of webs visible only when tail fanned, tail features of little use and require great care and practice. *Distinctions between blackish morphs of Steppe and Long-legged* Separation in this morph the most difficult of all, relying on size, shape/proportions and flight (see above). The only major plumage difference (with some overlap) seems to be the coarse and prominent, often also irregular or diffuse, dark barring of under remiges and (chiefly upper) tail seen on most Long-legged, especially 1st-years; on the other hand, Steppe seems always to show typical underwing barring common to all its morphs, with wider subterminal band (black and clear-cut on adults) and fine regular barring basally on secondaries and (chiefly upper) tail. If age

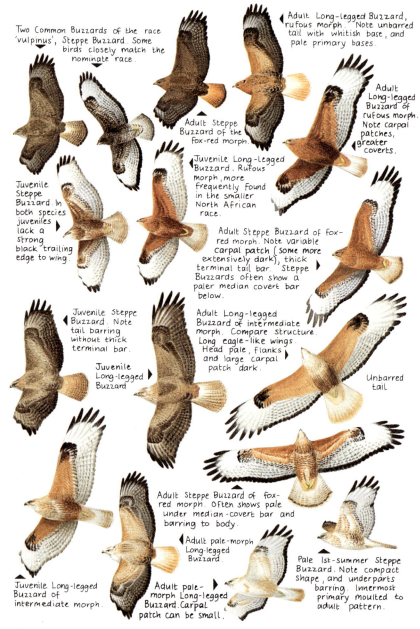

Two Common Buzzards of the race 'vulpinus', Steppe Buzzard. Some birds closely match the nominate race.

Adult Long-legged Buzzard, rufous morph. Note unbarred tail with whitish base, and pale primary bases.

Adult Steppe Buzzard of the fox-red morph.

Adult Long-legged Buzzard of rufous morph. Note carpal patches, greater coverts.

Juvenile Steppe Buzzard. In both species juveniles lack a strong black trailing edge to wing.

Juvenile Long-legged Buzzard. Rufous morph, more frequently found in the smaller North African race.

Adult Steppe Buzzard of fox-red morph. Note variable carpal patch (some more extensively dark), thick terminal tail bar. Steppe Buzzards often show a paler median covert bar below.

Juvenile Steppe Buzzard. Note tail barring without thick terminal bar.

Juvenile Long-legged Buzzard

Adult Long-legged Buzzard of intermediate morph. Compare structure. Long eagle-like wings. Head pale, flanks and large carpal patch dark.

Unbarred tail

Adult Steppe Buzzard of fox-red morph. Often shows pale under median-covert bar and barring to body.

Adult pale-morph Long-legged Buzzard.

Pale 1st-summer Steppe Buzzard. Note compact shape, and underparts barring. Innermost primary moulted to adult pattern.

Juvenile Long-legged Buzzard of intermediate morph.

Adult pale-morph Long-legged Buzzard. Carpal patch can be small.

Pale adult Long-legged Buzzard. Note lack of barring on underparts.

Juvenile intermediate Long-legged Buzzard. Note pale eye, barred tail tip.

Two adult fox-red Steppe Buzzards. Note tail pattern. Barred birds (left) are typical, plain rufous types (below) may be difficult.

Adult rufous Long-legged Buzzard. Streaked rather than barred; note plain tail.

Pale 1st-summer Steppe Buzzards may resemble pale Long-legged Buzzard. Note barred 'trousers'.

This plumage also typical of some small North African birds, race 'cirtensis'.

Adult blackish morph Long-legged Buzzard. Note coarse tail bars. Rarely, the tail is plain.

Adult blackish morph Steppe Buzzard. Only plumage difference may be the tail, finely barred with broad terminal band.

Juvenile blackish-morph Long-legged Buzzard. Secondaries often boldly barred.

Juvenile blackish-morph Long-legged Buzzard. Uppertail typically has broad dark bars.

Adult blackish-morph Long-legged Buzzards. Note coarse tail and underwing barring typical of most birds.

Shape and structure remain the best identification features.

Juvenile Blackish-morph Steppe Buzzard. Uppertail typically has fine, even bars. Secondaries evenly barred, greater coverts often barred.

33

determined, following features exhibit least overlap between the species. *Adult* Many (most) adult Long-legged with regular and finer barring and broad subterminal/trailing bands to tail and secondaries are indistinguishable in plumage from normal-patterned Steppe, but some have very whitish-buff and generally unbarred tail with only broad subterminal bar or just hint (spots, streaks) of this, a pattern generally not found in Steppe; some extreme blackish individuals (unlike any Steppe) have very bold black and white secondary bars of almost equal width (and, very rarely, same pattern on tail). Beware, however, that on some distant Steppe, especially in bright underlighting and mainly when observed from below, only the dark (sub)terminal band on tail is visible, so closer view (including of upperparts) important. *Juvenile* Many (most) juvenile Long-legged tend to have dark secondary and tail bars broader than intervening pale lines and rather broader (sub)terminal secondary and tail bands, with secondary bars and trailing edge often diffuse, and on extreme dark birds the dark area covers most of inner flight feathers, leaving distinct white primary bases: all unlike juvenile Steppe (which see, above). *Subsidiary differences* In very close views, both species show pale division in carpal patch below, formed by exposed pale bases to greater primary coverts, but this division (crescent) usually whiter/larger on Steppe and often with just a little barring (on Long-legged, exposed bases usually diffusely grey, but at most a trace of paler diffuse fringes or scallop marks and still more concealed); if no pale crescent, bird is usually Long-legged, but all look like this from distance! *N African/Arabian Long-legged* Existence of race *cirtensis* causes further problems. It is much smaller than Eurasian nominate, more compact and overlaps in size with Steppe; apart from smaller size and hence lighter impression in flight, however, all other characters given above for nominate apply also to *cirtensis*, which, fortunately, lacks blackish morph. Beware, however, that many *cirtensis* approach fox-red morph of Steppe in showing

no/less contrast between chest and belly (head to chest mainly paler rufous and belly deep rufous, or, rarely, uniform rufous overall), generally richer rufous (fringed) upperparts and more heavily barred tail, and even reduced or absent blackish carpal patches below: extremes with this combination of features must often be left undetermined. Unlike both nominate Long-legged and Steppe, juvenile *cirtensis* usually has cere pale bluish-grey (instead of yellow) and feet/tarsus yellow with brownish hue, and even darker/browner iris (instead of pale whitish-buff) in early stages. *Likelihood of confusion between Long-legged and Rough-legged Buzzards* Although the two overlap little in range (in winter, e.g. Bulgaria) and rarely show similar pattern, some young birds (paler/creamy Rough-legged and browner, less rufous Long-legged, mainly in distant view) can be confusingly similar in plumage, as well as in shape and size. Flight also not dissimilar, but at times Long-legged soars (or even glides) on slightly more raised wings, while Rough-legged tends to glide with carpal more markedly bent. Long-legged's tail can lack rufous/buff and have barring concentrated distally with broader (sub)terminal bar, but tail still lacks Rough-legged's diagnostic white base and wide black (adult) or dark greyish (juvenile) (sub)terminal band. Note that differences much more obvious on uppertail, and also if age determined: tail of adult Long-legged usually unbarred or with only hint of (sub)-terminal band (on Rough-legged, broad solid band and 1–4 extra bars on outermost feathers), while juvenile tends to have more evenly barred tail with less obvious broad terminal bar (instead of juvenile Rough-legged's much-reduced barring but still rather obvious broad (sub)terminal bar). Pale individuals of the two often almost identical below, including underwing-coverts, but Rough-legged's trousers longer and cover entire tarsus, and it tends to retain species' darker throat and whitish 'U' on lower breast, as well as (in this case diagnostic) whitish uppertail-coverts.

References Porter *et al.* (1981), Shirihai & Doherty (1990), Shirihai & Forsman (1991).

Honey Buzzard

Where and When Honey Buzzard *Pernis apivorus* is a summer visitor (mainly May-September) to much of forested areas of W Palearctic and east to C Siberia, all wintering Africa (where large number of immatures oversummer). Migrants typically concentrate in vast numbers at two major bottlenecks at each end of Mediterranean: at Strait of Gibraltar, but mainly Levant (NE Turkey and Israel), often in huge flocks/streams and in contracted period, peaking end August to mid September and end April to mid May.

Structure and Flight Most individuals show following features. Slimmer than similar-sized Common Buzzard and typically shows longer (about equal to wing breadth), narrower tail with slightly convex sides and rounded corners, and from close quarters shorter outermost rectrices detectable; neck slimmer and well protruding, with Cuckoo-like head and slender forward-pointing bill. Wings proportionately longer, with typically long but still relatively broad arm and also very long but rather ample and rounded hand (insignificant fingering); body narrow, elongated and appears suspended beneath plane of wings (which appear narrower than in nominate Common, less markedly so than those of Steppe, though differences often insignificant). Wings often appear parallel-edged, though in most flight postures shows smoothly bulging secondaries with sharply protruding carpal and narrower hand, all giving very light impression in air. Juveniles, however, often appear to have comparatively shorter and narrower wings, with proportionately broad and more bulging secondaries and obvious narrower hand, while tail averages shorter, and can even appear shorter-necked; such extremes may approach Common Buzzard, particularly Steppe form. Active flight characteristically elastic, with regular and even wingbeats which at times rather deep but mostly lifted higher with emphasis on upstroke (unlike Common's shallower, quicker and stiffer beats moved equally above and below horizontal). Diagnostically, soars on flat wings or with slightly lowered hands (though in strong thermals or side winds hand can be raised slightly); when gliding slowly, usually holds wings typically angled and slightly arched, with carpals well forwards and long hand pressed well back; in more open-winged gliding, head-on silhouette as that of other buzzards, with hands drooping, but more obvious bend between arm and hand (and rear edge of arm forms almost straight line and hand shows more frayed effect at tip). Very flexible wings sometimes twisted when soaring.

Plumage Variation Highly variable: from uniform blackish to almost completely white, with varying amount and combination of barring, blotching, streaking etc. The most characteristic are: uniform blackish, dark brown with reduced pale barring, uniform pale rufous-ochre/buff, whitish or buff with dense, even, bold barring/blotching, whitish with reduced or sparse bold barring, and almost completely white. These may be found in any age or sex, which show following basic characters. *Adult male* From below, flight feathers average more translucent than in female, with blacker or more sharply defined trailing edge and wingtip and more contrastingly black and usually broader (two) bars basally, which are usually closer together and concentrated towards underwing-coverts (and partly hidden by inners), thus leaving broader, cleaner space distally; distinctly darker and broader (sub)terminal tail band with huge white area between this and narrower and very close bars at tail base, innermost bar hidden for most part by undertail-coverts. Predominantly ash-grey head and clearly greyish cast to upperparts, which tend to show rather pronounced dark markings on upperwing (including dark trailing edge, one or two bars at remex bases and along greater coverts, as well as primary tips), and with tail pattern much as below. Otherwise, shows greater tendency towards neater

Adult ♂ Honey Buzzard. Note yellow eye, tiny bill and dull cere. Long tail and weak feet. Typical males have greyish face and secondaries with broad black tips.

Adult ♂ Honey Buzzard. Note tail pattern and sharp black trailing edge to wing.

Adult ♂ Honey Buzzard, rufous type.

Adult ♂ Honey Buzzard, barred type.

Adult ♂ Honey Buzzard, dark type. Tail pattern distinctive.

Adult ♂ Honey Buzzard, pale type. All males show sharp black trailing edge to wing and wide pale area to secondary bases.

Adult ♀ Honey Buzzard. Note wing and tail patterns.

Adult ♀ Honey Buzzard. Compare tail and underwing with male.

Adult ♀ Honey Buzzard. Typically browner than males.

Juvenile Honey Buzzard.

Juvenile Honey Buzzard. Note long tail, dark eye and yellow cere.

Juvenile Honey Buzzard, dark type. Dark secondaries evenly barred, fewer (but broader) bars than on Common Buzzard.

Juvenile Honey Buzzard of rufous type. May resemble Common Buzzard, but note long tail, barred body sides and axillaries, and extensive black to the fingers.

Juvenile Honey Buzzard, pale type.

and more clear-cut barring overall, and commonest type is white below with distinct dark barring on flanks, breast and underwing-coverts, (others almost uniformly white with restricted barring, yet others uniformly dark). *Adult female* Differs from male in less translucent flight feathers (with rather obvious effect of darker secondaries and paler primaries) on which dark trailing edge and wingtip more diffuse and the two (often three) inner bars greyer, narrower and less close together and thus more evenly spread, leaving narrower white interspace distally, while wingbars reach across bases of innermost secondaries to body and also well across primaries (level with emargination); tail bars narrower, with less distinct broader terminal band, and inner bars (often three) less close together and the second from tip well out from undertail-coverts (on male, usually contacts coverts). Above, predominantly brown, with strongly reduced grey on head and reduced dark wing markings. Underparts on average less distinctly patterned, and most appear rather uniformly brownish or richly mottled, more infrequently whitish with sparse, distinct barring. *Juvenile* Differs slightly in shape from adult, and usually distinguished by having 4 or 5 evenly spaced and uniformly wide bars on tail and flight feathers (bars generally narrower and more ragged than on adult); flight feathers far less translucent, with usually darker secondaries (often obscuring bars) demarcated from lighter primaries, and with much more extensive dark wingtip (all fingers), and body usually (in pale to medium morphs) heavily streaked and almost lacking adult's cross-bars. Upperparts generally dark brown with dark secondaries and obvious pale (often raggedly barred) primary patch and thin white tips to trailing edges of wing and tail and greater upperwing-coverts, while upper-tail-covert area often whitish; on pale birds lesser and median upperwing-coverts pale and mottled. White-headed juveniles also typically show black eye patch. Cere and basal portion of bill yellow and eye dark (grey and yellow, respectively, in adults).

Juvenile Plumages and Likelihood of Confusion Note that ratio of colour morphs among adults is not reflected in juveniles, most of which appear dark brown and less variable (blackish and white, or rufous, birds generally scarce). Some can look surprisingly like Common Buzzard (e.g. in mixed passage flocks or at distance). Basic structure and flight mode (see above) should be assessed objectively, and 'good' plumage features usually also detectable in favourable conditions. 1 DARK BIRDS Predominantly but variably dark/blackish-brown, often resembling dark nominate Common or blackish-morph Steppe, but should be distinguishable by diagnostic whitish (on very dark birds, greyish) band on greater underwing-coverts which appears to separate remaining coverts from darker secondaries (on dark *buteo/vulpinus*, basal secondaries are palest part of wing, so light area is farther back on wing; sometimes also paler median coverts leave narrow dark triangle at leading edge); also has fewer but broader dark bars on remiges and rectrices (denser, fainter and more numerous on Common, and with typically broader dark trailing edge to secondaries), and generally lacks nominate Common's pale mottling across lower breast. On less uniformly blackish-brown birds, underwing-coverts but mostly body sides and axillaries are boldly barred and dark carpal area more oval-shaped (not rounded like most *Buteo*); frequently whitish U-shaped uppertail-coverts (never found on *Buteo*), and has yellow on basal part of bill. Although tail may appear confusingly shorter than adult's, the protruding and clearly slimmer head/neck usually helps in such cases, and experienced observers should be able to note other silhouette differences and mode of flight. 2 REDDISH-OCHRE/BUFF BIRDS Correspond to adult of same morph, except for dark eye region. Sometimes misidentified as juvenile fox-red morph of Steppe Buzzard (which also rather similar in shape), but should be separable by more or less same features as for dark form of juvenile Honey. 3 VARIEGATED BIRDS Cover wide range of the variation spectrum but usually unmistakable, containing fairly pale plumages with variety of patterns; streaks, patches/blotches and sometimes a few cross-bars largely confined to rear body. Some are heavily streaked. **4 WHITISH BIRDS** Also a quite distinct form, predominantly white or buffish-white, often with varying amount of fine streaking on breast and body sides, and usually with distinct blackish eye patch. (Note that, although most juveniles over-summer in Africa, or a few reach just into

southern part of breeding area, some 1st-summers may be seen in Europe: often have partially moulted adult-like body and underwing-coverts with bold barring, but retain juvenile remiges and rectrices, which much bleached; cere should be at least mostly yellow, but eyes not yet pure yellow as full adult.)

References Forsman (1984), Forsman & Shir-ihai (in press), Harris *et al.* (1989), Svensson (1981).

Greater Spotted, Lesser Spotted, Steppe and Tawny Eagles

Where and When In W Palearctic, all four are found essentially in eastern and southern parts; occurrence of first three together on passage in Middle East, often in large num-bers, is a unique phenomenon. Lesser Spotted *A. pomarina* is summer visitor to eastern European and W Russian forests, usually broken and near water and damp areas; migrates through Levant (chiefly end March to mid April, end September to mid October; up to 141,000 in autumn W Israel), wintering mostly E Africa. Greater Spotted *A. clanga* breeds from north-central parts of eastern Europe across Asia, where largely summer visitor to lowland undulating forests (more frequently around swampy/riverine habitat than Lesser Spotted); much less numerous or gregarious on passage and in winter, mainly in Middle East and S Asia, usually in rather wet areas. Steppe Eagle *A. nipalensis* is primarily an Asiatic steppe breeder, entire population of race *orientalis* migrating through Middle East, chiefly mid October to mid November and end February to mid March (up to 76,000 at Suez and Djibouti in autumn and at Eilat in spring) and wintering mostly E Africa. Tawny Eagle *A. rapax* is a Paleotropical species; race *belisarius* breeds NW Africa and vagrant Egypt, Tunisia and Israel.

Approach to Identification Separation of these eagles, in all plumages, is one of the most complex identification challenges, invol-ving sets of many characters. Slow and lengthy progression from juvenile to adult

plumage, hence identification further compli-cated by age-class variations (tremendous individual variation), and effects of wear and bleaching. Much experience is called for and caution always essential. Nevertheless, some features are fairly constant for all plumages. Special attention should be paid to structure, shape and flight action (including head-on silhouette, relative proportions; note also that juveniles as a rule have narrower wings). Although identification best made on plu-mage, this is subject to many individual and age differences, so knowing the age-related plumage variations is exceptionally impor-tant. Note in particular *whitish carpal crescents* below, pale *primary patch* above, and *remex barring* (each species usually has characteristic pattern of bars, more pronounced on rela-tively paler inner-primary wedges, observa-ble from close quarters or from photographs). **Moult and Ageing** Understanding of moult strategies and duration is an essential starting point in clarifying typical and atypical plu-mage features of a particular age. Full adult plumage usually reached in autumn of about 5th year by Lesser Spotted, not until 5th-6th autumn by Greater Spotted and Steppe (latter sometimes 7th); all have complete moult (generally serial, but from about 3rd/4th summer becomes seemingly 'jumbled' owing to arrested and variably suspended moult waves) mostly in summer quarters, except Lesser Spotted (tends to moult relatively more on winter grounds, so plumage in more constant change during age progression);

Adult Lesser Spotted Eagle. Small buzzard-like head and small bill with round nostril and short gape. 'Trousers' tight, legs long.

Typical juvenile Lesser Spotted Eagle. Pale nape patch, compare spot pattern with juvenile Greater Spotted Eagle.

Dark juvenile Lesser Spotted Eagle. Note structure.

Pale juvenile Lesser Spotted Eagle.

Adult Greater Spotted Eagle. Looks large-headed with shaggy nape. Typically uniform dark brown. Gape ends below mid-eye.

Typical juvenile Greater Spotted Eagle.

Paler juvenile Greater Spotted Eagle.

Adult Steppe Eagle. Robust. Note long gape line reaching rear edge of eye, nostril clearly elongated.

Adult Tawny Eagle. Colour variable. Note nostril shape and gape line like the spotted Eagles. Eye pale.

Typical adults have pale nape and chin, bushy 'trousers'. Usually rather patchy overall.

Juvenile Steppe Eagle. Note structural features. Pale wing bars distinctive.

1st-spring Steppe Eagle. Pale wingbars worn and ragged, sometimes lost altogether.

39

birds tend to appear fresher in autumn than in spring. Note that innermost primaries, being lighter in colour and softer, appear more worn than they really are; also, 3rd-7th primaries (counted inwards) show much more wear than others of same generation. *Juvenile* Remiges and rectrices of same age, with tendency for bulging of secondaries; greater coverts (both surfaces) and trailing edges of wing and tail maximally tipped white, but in 1st spring heavily worn (less so under greaters). *2nd-winter/2nd-summer* Close to juvenile (less so in Greater and especially Lesser Spotted), but moulted remiges (renewed mainly in 1st summer) can give a good clue: new, longer inner primaries and several outer secondaries, chiefly 3rd/4th/5th (and sometimes some inners), and central pair of tail feathers show white tips, but narrower than on juvenile at same time; rest of plumage with mixed old juvenile and freshly moulted feathers, and white markings/tips reduced as retained juvenile feathers heavily bleached and new ones have smaller amount of white. *3rd-winter/3rd-summer* Generally approaching adult in overall pattern (less so in Steppe), with whitish tips/edges reduced, and diagnostically 0-5 (spotted eagles) or (0)2-7 (Steppe) outer primaries and a few secondaries very worn (retained from juvenile). Thus three main generations of flight feathers (caused by arrested moult, though clarification of age may be deflected by some suspension of moult and its resumption in winter): unmoulted very worn juvenile, first series of post-juvenile moult and arrested second series, and even a fourth may be present (recommencing in inner primaries), all creating ragged trailing edge, often with broken feathers and/or moult gaps, especially in spring. *4th-winter/4th-summer* Much as adult (apart from quite a few Steppe), with only few/narrow whitish markings on fresh remiges and coverts. After third moult completed (in autumn of 4th and spring of 5th calendar-year), most Greater Spotted and many Steppe have more or less finished their descendent moult (many Steppe retain 2-3

outermost juvenile primaries), but suspended moult prominently recommencing, so entire plumage mainly of mixed immature and adult-like feathers and pattern. *5th/6th-winter and 5th/6th-summer* Both spotted eagles mainly adult; Steppe still shows obvious immaturity, e.g. traces of white central underwing-bar, and has unevenly fresh and worn remiges including 2-3 outermost new primaries, which finally replace juvenile feathers in fourth moult. *Adult* Moult rather variable in duration (suspended and arrested). Note that variable amount of white on rump/uppertail-coverts shown by all non-adults decreases with age, but often prominent on older immatures and to some degree on adults; this feature is mentioned only if valuable for identification or ageing.

Lesser Spotted Eagle

Essential Features *Structure and flight* Wingspan 140-170 cm. Confusingly like Greater Spotted, though marginally less bulky. Wingbeats quicker than in following two species, and flight appears altogether lighter; wings gently arched (soaring) or more gently bowed (gliding), lacking Greater's almost heron-like attitude with deeper-hanging hand or sharper carpal kink. Some characteristic features in silhouette: wings comparatively short (particularly arm), more or less parallel-edged and gently rounded, with 7th primary tip (counted inwards) very short on adult and almost minute on juvenile (wingtip more square on Greater), in distant soaring flight appearing compact and buzzard-like with spread primary fingers neither long nor deep and never prominently splayed, and at same time gives a certain humpbacked appearance barely pronounced in other species; body looks big in relation to wing, which also appears relatively narrow, but wing shape of adult Lesser tends to approach that of juvenile Greater. Narrower wings give somewhat longer-tailed appearance, but wear may cause tail to look shorter. Head/neck relatively big/rounded and buzzard-like, with smallish bill for an eagle. *Plumage* At all ages, underwing-coverts vary from as dark as to (often diagnostically) paler than flight feathers; upperwing-coverts contrastingly paler than remiges (see below and cf. Greater Spotted). Almost invariably shows whitish double carpal crescent on underwing: narrow one at primary bases (usually longer than on Greater), and a second, rather distinct, on bases of greater primary coverts (largely absent on Greater) and not uncommonly extending to inner edge of primary coverts. Upper primary patch white and contrasting at all ages, though differs from Greater Spotted's only when adult/subadult, being more extensive: concentrate on bases of inner primaries. Remex barring largely invisible at distance (a few are completely unbarred), but at close quarters most show dense dark bars (at least as wide as intervening paler bars) right to tip: see below and cf. Greater.

Long-range Identification In far distance, look for relatively short, parallel-edged and round-tipped wings and longish tail; distinct individuals also show contrasting pale body and wing-coverts (both surfaces). Against blue sky, strongly marked individuals may reveal diagnostic whitish carpal crescents and/or primary patch.

Perched Length 60-65 cm. With experience, best told by more upright posture, with long legs, long narrow neck with buzzard-like head, small bill/short gape, and short and tight trousers (less bushy than on most Greater and especially Steppe). Juvenile's white markings differ from those of same-age Greater; differences between immatures less obvious, though most tend to lack Greater's more uniform and darker brown coloration, but usually have rather distinct pale lesser/median coverts and lower mantle and back contrasting with darker greater coverts, upper mantle/scapulars and, notably, flight feathers.

Age Variations and Comparisons *Juvenile* Fairly easily distinguished from juvenile Greater Spotted by paler mid brown lesser and median upperwing-coverts, sharply contrasting with blackish greater coverts and secondaries, and when fresh a clear band of

spots visible along greater coverts; some also have (chiefly outer) medians tipped whitish, but often discontinuously and/or invisible in field. Rufous-golden nape patch usually prominent and well defined (diffuse on Greater Spotted). Upper primary patch is the most extensive of all (but not much different from juvenile Greater Spotted's). In 1st spring, aside from some indistinct worn whitish tips to upper greater coverts/remiges/tail, appears almost adult-like (but evenly worn juvenile remiges and rectrices and notably pale, faded upperparts and head); with wear, primary patch changes as pale primary-covert tips worn away. From below, juvenile and 1st-spring/summer birds show two basic patterns: one has almost sandy-brown ground colour to underbody and coverts, usually visibly paler than remiges, and body rather distinctly streaked and mottled (such individuals, when fresh, are also palest-marked and frequently heavily tipped/streaked white above); second type has underbody and coverts darker or browner and less mottled, in tone more or less as flight feathers (these usually the least whitish-patterned above when fresh). Remex barring, though detectable only at close quarters, is more visible than on Greater Spotted. *Immature/subadult* 2nd-autumn/winter birds rather like juvenile, but whitish spots on greater upperwing-coverts reduced in size (as older juvenile: whitish tips worn off and newly moulted coverts have narrower tips), while some heavily marked birds show at least as much whitish tipping on median and lesser coverts as dark juvenile (see above), so check greater coverts and moult. From 2nd to 4th spring (summer), ageing difficult (can even be hard to tell from adult or heavily worn juvenile). Otherwise, separation from Greater Spotted should rely on same characters as for adult (see below) and the Essential Features listed above. Beware that, in these variable transitional plumages (and adult plumage as well), it is considerably more difficult or even impossible to separate from subadult Steppe Eagle solely by upperside colour/pattern (including primary patch):

one must therefore turn to structural and underpart features (but note that whitish line on greater coverts can be quite confusingly conspicuous on Lesser Spotted), and problems increase even more with distance or poor lighting. Concentrate on underpart colour and pattern of remiges, also pattern of greater coverts (see under Steppe). **Adult** Above, has no obvious white tips to remiges and rectrices or to greater coverts, and usually recognised by faded greyish-yellow area on head, back and wing-coverts, which can vary considerably in lightness or darkness according to degree of wear and state of moult: most also show darker mantle/scapulars, which can give 'saddle' effect (though not so pronounced as often seen on early immatures), but a few have entire upperparts almost uniformly coloured (rarely, rather evenly darker, with reduced contrast against remiges, thus indistinguishable from Greater Spotted by this feature); some have pale area on head, others darker, and so on. Aside from contrastingly patterned upperparts, the prominent primary patch is nearly always a useful distinguishing character. As with preceding ages, typical individuals showing paler underwing-coverts and body (milky-brown, against much darker remiges and tail) readily identified; on some, however, these areas hardly paler and in this respect matching adult Greater Spotted, such tricky birds (and also many 'normal' ones) being best identified from below by structural features, carpal crescents and remex barring. Note that a pale variant of adult Lesser Spotted exists, with pale rusty-brown body and lesser/median coverts, but usually normal-coloured above.

Greater Spotted Eagle

Essential Features *Structure and flight* Wingspan 155-180 cm. Rather robust but compact, often looking much bigger than it actually is, though heavier body appears suspended beneath plane of wings. Looks very broad-winged with short tail (about three-fifths width of wings), usually longer-winged than Lesser Spotted (but some broad-winged birds appear short-winged) and usually with slightly more pronounced bulging of secondaries; often more bull-headed, but head may look relatively small in relation to wing width. In active flight, appears subtly heavier and clumsier than Lesser Spotted but lighter than Steppe; wingbeats rather quick and flat, but usually with rather pronounced amplitude on downstroke. Soars with wings almost level, often with slightly downcurved hand approaching gentle arch of Lesser Spotted; when gliding, wings typically bowed (more deeply than Lesser Spotted) and with obvious angle between hand and arm, reinforcing short-winged impression. Great variation in proportions usually age-related, and slimmer juvenile (narrower wings, longer tail) often closely approaches older Lesser Spotted. Wing shape somewhere between Lesser Spotted's and Steppe's, so, when soaring, looks rather compact with ample hand, primaries evenly and distinctly spread to form more obvious fingering compared with Lesser Spotted, but again age differences render this of limited use in separation from Lesser Spotted, as juvenile's wingtip more rounded/narrower (blunter on adult); 7th primary clearly projects on adult, shorter on juvenile (approaching adult Lesser Spotted). *Plumage* On juvenile underwing-coverts blacker than secondaries, on adult dark to medium brown and similar to or slightly paler than secondaries; upperwing-coverts dark brown to mid brown, tinged greyish. Note existence of paler variant *'fulvescens'*, as well as various intermediates (see below). Almost always has only single white carpal crescent below, normally clearly demarcated at base of outermost 3 primaries. Primary patch above formed mainly by white bases to primary shafts and partially paler outer webs: on juvenile often large, not unlike that of Lesser Spotted; less developed on immatures; on adult much reduced/diffuse, more greyish, and often confined almost to base of inner primaries. Remex barring largely invisible at distance (a few are completely unbarred); close to, most show dense narrow dark bars (narrower than intervening pale bars), generally becoming fainter towards tips.

Long-range Identification Confusion most likely with Lesser Spotted, but adult also strikingly similar to adult Steppe. Adults and subadults rather uniformly dark, while juveniles show variable (depending on amount of pale spots) whitish patterning on covert panel above. Best identified by compact structure (broad wings and shorter tail). More square-cut hand with longish 7th primary also detectable, as well as single carpal crescent; in good light against blue sky, typical individuals may show darker underwing-coverts. See below for pale variants.

Perched Length 60-70 cm. Juvenile's pattern of white markings diagnostic. Plumage differences from both Lesser Spotted and Steppe in immature/adult plumages (especially worn) less obvious; those in 'brown plumage' are more uniform/darker than Lesser Spotted, but best identified by usually bulkier shape, with bull-head and broad neck (for other structural and plumage differences, see Lesser Spotted). Steppe is larger, more robust, with deep chest and very prominent shoulders, narrower drawn-out head on longer neck, big bill with long gape reaching far below eye (also oval-shaped nostril, but rarely visible in field), and more bushy trousers. Both spotted eagles lack Steppe's tendency for some barring on inner secondaries/greater coverts and tail, and Steppe has larger (at times quite visible) rusty nape patch, often reaching crown.

Age Variations and Comparisons *Juvenile* Variable, but usually blackish-brown with rows of whitish drop-shaped spots along upperwing-coverts (some birds may have a spot on more or less every body feather; others only on scapulars/tertials/wing-coverts with fewer on belly and trousers, approaching exceptionally well-spotted juvenile Lesser). Variable underparts show buffish rear body and obscure paler ochre body streaking (dark birds), but palest birds (though not *fulvescens*) often rather distinctly streaked. Very full-feathered head shows contrasting bright yellow gape. Unlike juvenile Lesser Spotted (which see), broader white tips to upperwing-coverts still present in 1st spring/summer, forming rather faded wing-bars. In flight, shows typical contrast below, with black coverts and paler remiges (latter vary between blackish-grey and almost black-looking depending on angle of light). Presence of only single, well-defined white crescent (at base of outermost primaries) of greatest use, but note that a few may also show indistinct diffuse whitish/greyish crescent at base of greater primary coverts. *Immature/subadult* 2nd-autumn/winter birds approach juvenile, but whitish upperwing spotting generally reduced as tips of old juvenile feathers mostly worn off and new feathers have smaller/more diffuse whitish tips. From 2nd summer (even spring) to 4th/5th spring-summer ageing rather difficult, though often, with practice, moult-related plumage type can provide useful guide (see Moult and Ageing and plate). With increasing age tends to appear more uniform and browner, with usually an indistinct/broken row of whitish tips to greater coverts and with primary patch becoming more adult-like (pale primary-covert tips worn off and feathers replaced by ones with reduced tips, inner primaries replaced by new, darker ones); with time, upperwing-coverts become distinctly browner/paler (but still darker and more evenly tinged reddish-brown, largely lacking contrasting yellow-brown covert area of most Lesser Spotted) and underwing contrast reduced as coverts become browner (apart from lesser and primary coverts, which often remain the blackest). These mainly adult-like plumages are best separated from Lesser Spotted by same characters as for adult (see below). Beware, however, that near-adult or adult Greater Spotted often appear confusingly similar to same-age (but especially unusually dark) Steppe, particularly at distance and in unfavourable light, when both look dark and uniform; differences in shape/proportions can be slight, mainly if bird not soaring. If underpart colours discernible (against blue sky or with strong underlighting), remiges of older Greater Spotted almost

Adult Lesser Spotted Eagle. Round wingtip with short fingers. 7th primary tip short. Pale wing-coverts and distinct pale primary bases.

Dark adult Lesser Spotted Eagle.

Adult Lesser Spotted Eagle. Two carpal crescents, paler coverts and body.

Dark adult Lesser Spotted Eagle lacks underparts contrast. Note structure and double carpal crescents.

Dark juvenile Lesser Spotted Eagles. Short arm and fingers, small-headed.

Two juvenile Lesser Spotted Eagles. Pale upperwing-coverts contrast with blacker greater coverts and secondaries. Clear cream spots along greater coverts. Double carpal crescent below, rufous nape usually prominent above.

2nd-winter Lesser Spotted Eagle. Similar to juvenile, pale spotting reduced.

Worn 1st-spring Lesser Spotted Eagle. Pale feather tips worn off and appears rather adult-like.

Ragged sub adult (3-year plus) Lesser Spotted Eagle, appears rather Steppe Eagle-like. Note structural differences and, typically, dark chin, double carpal crescent and unbarred outer primary bases.

Lesser Spotted Eagle (top) is humpbacked, with small fingers. Greater Spotted Eagle (below) glides on more arched wings with flat back and longer, wider-spaced fingers.

Two adult Greater Spotted Eagles. Uniformly dark, single carpal crescent below, little white in primary bases above. Short tail, broad wings, splayed fingers and long 7th primary.

Two paler adult Greater Spotted Eagles. Single carpal crescent on underwing.

Adult Greater Spotted Eagle.

Subadult (3rd year plus) Greater Spotted Eagle. Some close to Steppe Eagle. Note dark primaries without barring and finely barred secondaries; throat dark.

Pale adult Greater Spotted Eagle. Note structure/proportions and still reduced primary patch (white confined to primary shafts). Such pale birds similar to dark Lesser Spotted Eagle.

Two juvenile Greater Spotted Eagles. Very dark with pale double wingbar above, dark head contrasts with pale gape. Below, shows dark body and wing-coverts, greyer secondaries and single carpal crescent.

2nd-winter Greater Spotted Eagle above. Similar to juvenile, but spotting reduced, partially moulted coverts creating broken greater-covert bar. More squarish-shaped wing than juvenile, with uneven trailing edge.

By spring juvenile spotting can be considerably worn on Greater Spotted Eagle, but greater covert bar usually still apparent.

uniformly black (lack barring on bases of fingers), while on older Steppe they always have grey ground colour and diagnostically bicoloured primaries (black fingers with grey, coarsely barred bases right up to leading edge) and secondaries (more sparsely barred on much paler greyish ground and with broad dark trailing edge); Steppe also lacks distinct isolated carpal crescent, but unlike most Greater Spotted usually has clearly darker body and paler throat. Although both can be uniformly dark above, older Greater Spotted lack Steppe's usual rusty nape (and crown) patch and distinct primary patch

45

(usually large but diffuse on primary bases, not uncommonly a second patch on primary coverts), but on unusually dark Steppe both these features, as well as grey tinge on secondaries and tail and darker solid greater-covert bar, are often absent, producing almost identical upperparts. *Adult* As with preceding age-class, looks rather uniformly dark blackish-brown at moderate distance and can be difficult to separate from subadult/near-adult Steppe (but see above), and also from adult Lesser Spotted (especially unusually dark birds). These should always be identified using as many as possible of the Essential Features listed above, and see also under adult Lesser Spotted. Otherwise, most adult Greater Spotted (though less so than Steppe) have body slightly darker than underwing-coverts, a feature seldom shown by Lesser Spotted.

'Fulvescens' and Other Variants Greater Spotted has a pale morph, *'fulvescens'*, and intermediates, not only as juvenile/immature but also (and contrary to earlier opinion) as adult. With regard to separation from Lesser Spotted (chiefly when juvenile), an aberrant form exists which is less dark (mainly darkish mid brown) and is partly or extensively spotted/striped with yellowish rufous-brown on all body feathers, including lesser and median upperwing-coverts (underwing-coverts as normal, distinctly darker than flight feathers), but usually characterised by strongly and regularly variegated pattern (not so uniformly brown-coloured) and identified by structure, carpal crescent and primary patch. Another variant, superficially recalling juvenile Imperial Eagle, is rusty yellow-brown with irregular dark breast streaking, mottled/spotted brown above with brightly variegated wing-coverts, and often with broad pale bars along covert tips, but besides various plumage differences (e.g. narrower pale inner-primary wedges) it is smaller and lacks Imperial's long and square-cut wing and tail. A further rare variant is a mix of the last two: yellow-brown or pale mottling on dull greyish black-brown underwing-coverts, which are darker than or same colour as body,

but with normal upper surface. The form *'fulvescens'* (rare in Europe, commoner further east) is so distinctively bicoloured, generally buff and black, that it could be misidentified as pale or bleached juvenile Imperial or juvenile Spanish Imperial, but usually separated by clear structural differences, by e.g. reduced pale inner-primary wedge, and by lacking Imperial's upper-/underpart streaking (pectoral band), while Spanish Imperial has far more rusty-buff uppertail-coverts to lower back and usually unmarked lesser and median under primary coverts (from below, but mainly from above, blackish greater-covert bar more solidly black on *fulvescens*); could also be taken for exceptionally pale immature/subadult Steppe, but lacks latter's trace or more of pale central underwing band and barred remiges and rectrices. Main confusion risk, however, is with pale morph of Tawny Eagle (which see): at all ages *'fulvescens'* has body and wing-coverts (apart from normal-coloured greaters both above and below) rather uniformly pale rusty-yellow or pale golden-buff (wearing to whitish-buff), but usually with some darkening around bill/eye, often throat, breast and/or body sides and on forewing (both surfaces). Most *'fulvescens'* and intermediates can usually be identified as Greater Spotted by coloration and pattern of underwing, which retains that species' distinctive crescent and remex pattern, and by poorly developed primary patch (see plate).

Steppe Eagle

Essential Features *Structure and flight* Wingspan 175-230 cm. The largest in this group, comparable in size to Imperial Eagle. Compared with the spotted eagles, usually looks much more robust and powerful, with broad, heavier body (though usually appears suspended beneath plane of wings), and broader and longer wing with proportionately longer arm, which considerably increases wing area (even in juveniles, which have narrower wing, especially between 1st and 2nd springs when secondary tips worn away). Active flight distinctly heavy, with

Adult Steppe Eagle. Remiges coarsely barred, with broad terminal band.

Adult Steppe Eagle above. Pale nape, diffuse pale primary bases.

Dark adult Steppe Eagle. May recall Greater Spotted Eagle. Note long tail and large, diffuse primary patch.

Pale adult Steppe Eagle may recall Lesser Spotted Eagle. Note lack of carpal crescents, bicoloured primary bases (which are barred), dark trailing edge, dark body and carpal, pale chin.

Note deep fingers, parallel wing edges.

1st-spring Steppe Eagle. Pale feather tips worn (but still prominent on secondaries).

Juvenile Steppe Eagle. Strong contrast above, wide cream wingbars and pale inner-primary wedges.

Two juvenile Steppe Eagles showing variation. Broad underwing stripe distinctive. In rare variant bar is slightly greyer.

3rd-summer Steppe Eagle. Underwing bar reduced.

Steppe Eagle.

Tawny Eagle.

Note big 'bushy' hand of Steppe Eagle.

Subadult Steppe Eagle can recall Lesser Spotted Eagle of same age. Check bicoloured primaries (barring to base), new black-tipped secondaries, darker body and pale chin.

2nd-winter Steppe Eagle. New remiges white-tipped and protruding, largely worn back by 2nd-summer (right).

4th/5th-summer Steppe Eagle. Underwing bar further reduced, adult-type remiges moulting in. The dark bar of the trailing edge broadens with each moult to adulthood.

47

slower, clumsier beats than in both spotted eagles and wing stretched to its maximum on upstroke; when soaring, wings held flatter but with tendency to be slightly bowed, with lowered hand; gliding posture approaches that of Greater Spotted, with arm typically horizontal and angle between arm and noticeably drooping hand distinct but not so striking as on latter species. Extended wings fairly parallel-edged, though slight S-curve to rear (chiefly on juveniles), with long and ample hands and rather square wingtip with distinctly longer and more pointed 7th primary (especially compared with Lesser Spotted); long primary tips deeply spread to form the most obvious and well-spaced fingering of all four species. Tail varies in length and shape, usually somewhat longer than on spotted eagles (about three-quarters width of wing) but only a little shorter than Imperial's, and usually a rounded wedge shape (instead of square-cut). Neck rather broad but well protruding, looks proportionately longer owing to larger/longer head and bill; very close view may reveal diagnostic long gape line reaching to rear edge of eye (ends level with mid-eye on both spotted eagles), oval-shaped (instead of rounded) nostrils, and more deeply set eye with stronger shadow effect giving fiercer expression, especially when soaring and head drooped almost vulture-like (often slight humpbacked appearance at front). Race *orientalis* treated here; larger nominate eastern race (probably vagrant to Middle East) shows slight differences seen head-on, with proportionately even longer arm and with impression of larger wing area. *Plumage* Ground colour of underwing-coverts extremely variable with age but also individually, from light greyish buff-brown through mid brown (usually non-adults, with coverts paler than remiges) to dark brown (dark forms at all ages, tending to have coverts rather similar in colour to remiges); usually some sort of whitish central underwing band (lacking on some old birds), with carpals and trailing edge and/or wingtip nearly always darker than rest of underwing. Upperwing-coverts vary in accordance

with underpart tone, but most (even dark birds) tend to have coverts paler than flight feathers. Carpal crescent below almost always very poorly developed, usually diffuse but highly variable individually and dependent on age. Primary patch usually the most developed (compared with spotted eagles), nearly always big, greyish and diffuse, on non-adults covering almost entire hand, and often with second patch at base of greater primary coverts; on older birds usually smaller and often incomplete, and sometimes, on darker birds, very small and even recalling that of Greater Spotted. Splayed primaries diagnostically bicoloured, with blackish fingers and grey-and-barred bases (unbarred throughout on both spotted eagles); barring on secondaries more visible, always prominent at close quarters, with 7-8 well-spaced bars (9-11 closer bars on spotted eagles).

Long-range Identification If colours discernible, juveniles and most young immatures not easily mistaken (see below). At moderate/long distances, confusion most likely between older-immatures/adults of Steppe and spotted eagles, but distinguished (with difficulty) by size, proportions and often head-on silhouette, and maybe detailed plumage differences (see Immature/subadult of this and both spotted eagles). Many years' experience in Levant (where most eagles seen on high-altitude passage), at sites where up to 99% of *Aquila* eagles are Lesser Spotted or Steppe, has shown that small numbers of adult/near-adult Steppe (or Greater Spotted) in the enormous Lesser Spotted passage create fewer problems than occasional odd-plumaged Lesser (and vice versa at sites with huge numbers of Steppe but very few spotted eagles); where sometimes equal numbers of Lesser Spotted and Steppe observed (e.g. Suez, Dead Sea), identifying high-flying birds becomes extremely difficult, especially since immature Lesser Spotted with no covert/remex contrast can show effect of dark wingtip and trailing edge (or even indication of pale central band), just as on Steppe. Great care and much previous experience therefore called for: arm and hand proportions, degree and length of primary fingering, and relationships of wing breadth to tail length and wing plane to body are important pointers.

Perched Length 65-80 cm. Fresh juvenile readily distinguished by strikingly different whitish markings on wing-coverts. In all mainly brown, adult-like plumages, however (even 1st-spring birds with covert tips worn away), separation from immature/adult spotted eagles very difficult. More detailed distinctions given under latter two species.

Age Variations and Comparisons *Juvenile* Diagnostic broad white band across middle of underwing, formed by white greater primary and secondary coverts (though with variable dark centres); beware, however, that some have greyer greater coverts, reducing prominence of band, and juvenile and younger immature Lesser Spotted can have pale band (but much narrower, ill-defined, consisting mainly of drop-shaped whitish spots). Moreover, rare pale extremes of juvenile Steppe exist (probably corresponding to *'fulvescens'* Greater Spotted) which can have very pale buff/isabelline lesser and median underwing-coverts, not much different in shade from whiter greater coverts (some may even lack tonal differences, especially when bleached); such rare individuals also have better-developed pale inner-primary wedges, but otherwise mainly normal in colour and pattern (including remex barring) and are separable by these features plus shape from superficially similar bleached juvenile Imperial Eagle, which should also retain its diagnostic underpart streaking (see also Tawny Eagle). Fresh upperparts, including coverts, usually grey-brown with prominent broadly white-tipped black greater coverts, also often narrower white bar on median-covert tips; rear edge of wings and tail broadly white. At this age, white uppertail-coverts usually the most distinctive, and primary patch strongly developed (at least equal to juvenile Lesser Spotted) owing to much paler inner primaries, where wing mostly translucent with more clearly discernible barring. Otherwise, always shows distinct black wingtip on both surfaces, but with clear pale basal area on

primaries ('palm'). Surprisingly, even in early spring of 2nd calendar-year white tips of secondaries and their upper coverts and of tail are strongly bleached/narrower. *Immature/subadult* In 2nd autumn to 2nd spring much as juvenile, except most of retained juvenile remiges and their coverts much worn (very thin whitish tips) and the few moulted feathers distinctly longer with broad whitish-buffish tips (but not so broad as on fresh juvenile). Differences obvious in 2nd autumn; in 2nd spring all feathers become worn (sometimes no white tips left on old juvenile ones), though differences still recognisable, and especially if, exceptionally, up to three new remiges (chiefly secondaries) acquired in winter. 3rd-autumn to 3rd-spring birds usually readily aged, as the first plumage in which most of greater underwing-coverts moulted and replaced with prominently dark-centred ones (forming almost ragged dark bar in buffish-white coverts), but a few birds sometimes moult very few or none of these coverts, which then distinctly worn and bleached; most important therefore to age birds according to remiges, the wing being the most variegated with mixed generations of feathers in the still overall young-immature plumage. 4th-autumn to 4th-spring the first real 'old immature', in many respects approaching adult plumage (see also Moult and Ageing), though still with indication of immaturity in coverts: as with preceding age, greater underwing-coverts and rear secondary area tend to contain feathers with, respectively, larger dark centres and subterminal bands as age progresses, generally corresponding with reduced whitish tips on new secondaries and greater upperwing-coverts (when still fresh, in autumn) as well as with age-related remex pattern (i.e. combined generations: see Moult and Ageing) and overall coloration/pattern. These old immatures/subadults (4th-autumn to 5th/6th-spring), which have moulted their white underwing band (though fragments often remain) and have pale medium-brown wing-coverts above and below, are very like older Lesser Spotted; moreover, upperside characters, including primary patch, can be virtually identical (apart from Steppe's tendency towards more visible barring on remiges and rectrices). So, identification should be based primarily on coloration of flight feathers: usually shows first hint of a broad black trailing edge, a feature typical of adult Steppe, on both paler and barred rectrices and remiges, and also has diagnostically bicoloured primaries with blackish fingers and grey-and-barred bases. Additional adult-like features may help separate subadult Steppe from Lesser Spotted (see below), e.g. carpal area darker than underwing-coverts and chin and throat paler; subsidiary features include Steppe's more uniform coverts-scapulars-mantle (Lesser Spotted tends to show contrastingly darker mantle/scapulars than coverts) and usually more obvious whitish patch on back, but variation in both species reduces value of these features. Besides plumage, however, one can use relative features such as wing shape and formula, gliding posture etc, which, with experience, differ fairly obviously. *Adult* For separation of adult/subadult Steppe from trickiest plumages of Lesser Spotted, see preceding age-group; from Lesser Spotted at distance, see Long-range Identification above; from adult/subadult Greater Spotted, see Immature/subadult of latter. Aside from structural and flight features, most important indications of adult Steppe are as follows. Shade variable, but mostly dark and relatively uniform in colour on both surfaces: most (but not extreme pale birds) are dark brown to mid brown above with only slightly paler wing-coverts and mantle/back, with variable amount of whitish feathering (patches) on back and uppertail-coverts (features also found in the spotted eagles, but often vestigial in all three); despite variation, primary patch reasonably developed, even covering much of base of hand, but chiefly on inner primaries to create ill-defined translucent wedges; other features of remex patterning/contrast/barring are as on undersurface but generally obscured, though some individuals have in addition a distinct grey tinge to secondaries and tail so that

upperside pattern overall is reminiscent of underside; usually has clearly defined rusty yellow-brown nape (and crown) patch of variable size, difficult to see in flight. From below, flight feathers grey with black fingers and trailing edge and diagnostic, prominent coarse and sparse bars which extend onto primary bases (bicoloured primaries); carpal crescent largely obscure; underwing-coverts usually concolorous with or paler than remiges (and often still with trace of a few whiter tips and edges to greater coverts creating obscure central band), but usually paler than the blackish or dark brown body and undertail-coverts and the usual prominent dark carpal. Long gape line usually clearly separated from well-demarcated pale throat by dark line.

Tawny Eagle

Essential Features *Structure and flight* Wingspan 165-190 cm. Slightly smaller than Steppe, marginally larger than Greater Spotted. Active flight less powerful than Steppe's, wingbeats quite fast, usually with greater amplitude, and classic aquiline wing kink as well as protruding head very obvious; when soaring, wings very slightly raised so that bow shape sometimes approaches that of a spotted eagle, but almost always less drooped during most phases of both soaring and gliding (mainly in comparison with Steppe or Greater Spotted) and, particularly when gliding, more gently arched. Less 'migratory-shaped outline' than Steppe: more chunky but rather puny, with longer head-and-neck projection, big body/deep chest, but relatively shorter/broader wing and blunter hand; tail shorter and more square-ended (about two-thirds width of wing). Splayed primary fingers slightly shorter than Steppe's (but fingering at least as noticeable as on Greater Spotted); outermost and 6th primaries usually appear marginally shorter than wingtip, so prominent long 7th primary (comparable to Steppe's) closer in length to 6th. Hand proportionately slightly shorter than on Steppe, and more often shows marked difference between

Adult Tawny Eagle. Note gape length similar to the spotted eagles; nostril oval, like Steppe Eagle. Dark mantle and scapulars contrast with paler wing-coverts. Iris pale.

Adult Tawny Eagle. Note pale of tail-coverts extends to back.

Adult Tawny Eagle. Body contrasts with remiges; dark primary-covert crescent, moderate pale inner-primary wedges. Darkish throat.

Adult Tawny Eagle, pale morph.

Pale 1st-winter Steppe Eagle. Note facial characteristics. Typically heavily bleached.

Juvenile Spanish Imperial Eagle. Uniform rusty plumage, pale inner-primary wedges and trailing edge to wing.

Juvenile Imperial Eagle. Obvious streaks on breast.

Very pale 2nd-winter Steppe Eagle. Note coarse underwing barring.

Juvenile Greater Spotted Eagle of 'fulvescens' form. Pale salmon-cream body and coverts. Note dark greater coverts on both wing surfaces and poor under primary wedge. Tail short.

Juvenile Greater Spotted Eagle of rufous intermediate form. Face dark, underparts pale. Upperparts as typical juvenile.

Underwing typical but for paler coverts.

Juvenile Greater Spotted Eagle of 'fulvescens' form.

distinctly broader arm and narrower hand.
Plumage Unlike Steppe, colours generally
change little with age. Main morph or plumage type of sole race in region (*belisarius*)
shows contrasting pale tawny/buffish (rarely,
very pale foxy/rufous) wing-coverts above
and below, at all ages strongly demarcated
from darker remiges. Below, lacks striking
white greater-covert band shown by Steppe
in first three years, as well as subadult/adult
Steppe's solid dark carpal, but importantly
has paler lesser and median primary coverts
and solid dark, well-developed crescent on
greater primary coverts; often shows indication of white crescent (sometimes well demarcated), usually confined to about 3 outermost
primaries (less obvious than on Greater
Spotted). Above, wing-coverts usually diffusely dark-centred, giving less uniform overall
impression, while medians usually slightly
paler than lessers but contrastingly paler than
blackish greaters; primary patch insignificant
compared with Steppe, but usually better
developed than on most Greater Spotted.
Remiges usually finely and densely barred
(8-9 bars on most but variable, often almost
unbarred); barred bases to spread primaries,
as on Steppe.
Long-range Identification Unique shape
and proportions, notably the long neck, short
head and short tail, combined with flight and
striking coloration, often discernible at long
range, but closer inspection advisable, since
easily confused with species mentioned
below.
Perched Length 60-70 cm. Looks smaller and
rather weak compared with Steppe, and
tends to stand more erect. Gape line normally
a little shorter, ends level with centre of eye
(unlike Steppe, but nearer the two spotted
eagles); adult's iris yellowish-brown (dark
brown on Steppe); nostril mainly oval, as
Steppe.
Age Variations and Comparisons Plumage,
while changing little with age, is tremen-
dously variable within age-classes, with distinct morphs (and many intermediates) that
vary in frequency regionally: race *belisarius*,
treated here, usually predominantly tawny/

buffish-yellow (rarely, pale foxy). Since darker morphs 'more unmistakable' and apparently do not occur (or very rarely do) in N
Africa, following concentrates on pale morph,
also the most relevant in terms of possible
confusion with preceding three species. *Juvenile* Most characteristic features of juvenile
and all other ages are: shape (see Essential
Features); pale whitish/creamy-buff on
uppertail-coverts extending well onto back;
remiges and rectrices usually finely/densely
barred, or appear almost unbarred; conspicuous sandy-greyish wedges on inner primaries; body and coverts on both surfaces
mostly tawny or buff, contrasting greatly
with blackish remiges; and wing-covert pattern usually not found on other species (see
above). All ages differ from any Steppe in
shape, notably relative proportions of wing,
head/neck, body and tail, lack Steppe's distinctly barred remiges and rectrices, and
usually have more prominent inner-primary
wedges. Dark greater primary and secondary
coverts below rule out any juvenile or young-
immature Steppe, including rare '*fulvescens*'-
like type, which always has whitish greater
coverts; also lacks older Steppe's paler throat
and solid dark trailing edge, body and
carpals, but note that some young-immature
Steppe may already have rather dark greater
primary coverts and yet paler lesser and
median ones, though still with rather prominent white on (chiefly inner) greater secondary coverts. Above, most *belisarius* have pale
buff (less white) uppertail-coverts extending
onto back and lack Steppe's prominent white
primary patch and isolated small white patch
on upper back, instead being more variegated
(including diffusely dark-centred mantle/
scapular feathers and wing-coverts); under-
tail-coverts/vent usually more concolorous
with rest of underbody than on most Steppe.
Pale *belisarius* at all ages superficially resembles juvenile Imperial Eagle (both have prominent whitish uppertail-coverts to back, and
pale body, wing-coverts and inner-primary
wedges contrasting with blackish remiges
and rectrices), but is much smaller, with
proportionately shorter tail and hand, and

lacks Imperial's diagnostic brown-streaked chest, mantle and wing-coverts, while these and other characters should also be conclusive for heavily bleached birds. Same differences rule out juvenile Spanish Imperial, but confusion more likely since latter largely unstreaked below and has more buffish rufous-brown ground colour, more like foxy morph of Tawny. Aside from distinct size and shape differences, *belisarius* separable (with difficulty) by plumage. From above, usually lacks both imperials' (if latter not too worn) broader and more obvious whitish tips to remiges and greater and median coverts and at least some drop-shaped tips/streaks on lesser coverts, scapulars/mantle, and their tendency for paler basal uppertail feathers, but has generally whitish and mottled uppertail-covert area extending less far onto back than on Imperial (this area is never uniform rusty-buff as on Spanish Imperial), and dark-centred scapulars and tertials often create 'horseshoe effect' contrasting with paler upperwing-coverts (a feature usually not shown by either imperial); both imperials also lack white primary patch and rather extensive blackish carpal area above that are typical of most Tawny. From below, has less solidly blackish greater coverts and more uniform body than juvenile Spanish Imperial, which normally has more obvious contrasting paler undertail-coverts and vent and at least some dark streaks on breast. Perched *belisarius* lacks the quite clear tail/wingtip projection shown by both imperials. Since some *belisarius* and some '*fulvescens*' Greater Spotted are superficially very similar, caution is demanded: at all ages, *belisarius* should be separated by its more Steppe-like shape/structure (longer 7th primary and more square-cut wingtip, longer fingers and hand, longer and more square-cornered tail); most '*fulvescens*' show diagnostic solidly blackish greater coverts below (somewhat more

ragged on *belisarius*, with pale fringes/tips to individual feathers) that contrast strongly with whitish median-covert band, this band being usually well demarcated from buffish lesser coverts, a combination not found on the more uniform forewing of *belisarius*; most *belisarius* also have slightly more obviously barred remiges, including primary bases up to the blackish fingers (latter unbarred on '*fulvescens*', whose remiges usually appear plain blackish or blackish-grey), and comparatively indistinct carpal crescent; median primary coverts solidly blackish or blackish-centred on '*fulvescens*', whereas on *belisarius* they are same as lesser coverts. From above, the two can be nearly identical in pattern, apart from *belisarius*'s larger primary patch, barely more clearly barred remiges and rectrices, usually slightly larger/more complete black carpal, and greater contrast between mantle/scapulars and paler coverts, often with paler median-covert band (on '*fulvescens*', less contrast between latter areas but can be overall mottled). ***Immature/subadult*** Generally very like juvenile; best aged by moult study (see Moult and Ageing). Gradual body moult produces characteristic blotching from dark-centred new feathering, giving non-uniform appearance to body and wing-coverts; often some darker (browner) feathering on head and/or forebody, leaving buffish rear, and sometimes slightly more patterned lesser and median underwing-coverts. A little reduction in whitish upperwing bars and uppertail-coverts to back. ***Adult*** As preceding ages; best aged by moult study. As immature/subadult, shows a little increase in prominence of wing and tail barring.

References Brooke *et al.* (1972), Clark (1992), Forsman (1984, 1991b), Forsman & Shirihai (in prep.), Porter *et al.* (1981), Shirihai (1994a), Shirihai & Christie (1992), Svensson (1975, 1987).

Golden and Imperial Eagles

Where and When Golden Eagle *Aquila chrysaetos* is the most widespread eagle (Holarctic): in W Palearctic in wide range of open habitats from temperate north to desolate regions of south (to N Africa and Middle East), essentially in wild/remote mountain and upland areas (less so in lowland forest, chiefly in north); generally resident and dispersive. Imperial Eagle *A. (h.) heliaca* has much narrower distribution, from EC Europe (Slovakia/Hungary) across C Asia, breeding in more low-lying park-forest (e.g. wooded valleys alternating with wet patches), with no more than a few hundred pairs left in W Palearctic; resident in some southern areas, otherwise largely migratory, wintering NE Africa, Middle East and S Asia in open grasslands, semi-deserts and cultivated fields. Spanish Imperial Eagle *A. (h.) adalberti* breeds in similar habitats but confined to Iberia; resident (100 or so breeding pairs).

Golden Eagle

General Features Huge (wingspan 190-228 cm) yet elegant eagle with well-proportioned flight silhouette: long wings and tail (tail about equal to breadth of inner wing), noticeably protruding head/neck (though still obviously shorter than tail), and usually obvious bulging trailing edge (most pronounced on young; may be obscure on older birds and through wear and moult) and shallowly raised and slightly forward-pressed wings. Tail usually appears ample and evenly rounded. Active flight very powerful with slow, deep beats. Often seen soaring high up, or slowly patrolling mountain slopes with somewhat drooped head. Note that V-shaped wings when soaring, less so when gliding, not always obvious (at times held somewhat flatter); seen soaring head-on, the long hands show deeply curved fingers. *Plumage* Most plumages show yellow-gold crown and nape-shawl (on southern race *homeyeri*, paler/sandier and contrasts more with upperparts); paler panel on upper median and inner greater coverts, conspicuous on younger immature and subsequent plumages and more pronounced through bleaching and wear (on fresh northern juveniles shows as slightly different-toned rufous-brown panel, but can be paler and a little more obvious on fresh juvenile *homeyeri*). Remiges/rectrices generally bicoloured on both surfaces, varying considerably with age but also geographically.

Adult At close quarters, flight and tail feathers grey-brown basally with variable dark barring and broad trailing edges; from below, central underwing-coverts darker (though always mottled whitish), at least as dark as broad wingtip and trailing edges, while basal two-thirds of tail often the palest region. Upper surface similar in pattern, but with distinct paler middle-covert panel. Looks huge when perched, with long rear and legs, and generally pale brownish with obvious sandier wing panel; bull-necked and large-headed, usually with rather obvious golden shawl.

Juvenile Uniform-age remiges have the strongest S-curve to rear edge; also darkest overall, but with characteristic large white patches at bases of flight and tail feathers. Some have restricted white primary patch, this more frequent in southern populations, while white on primaries may be considerably reduced or lacking on a few juvenile *homeyeri*, but white tail base still as normal.

Immature/subadult Considerable individual (and geographical: *homeyeri*) variation; ageing achieved by combining moult pattern with age-related plumage variation. Younger immature (2nd-winter/summer) very like juvenile, but with upperwing panel more pronounced (bleached) and some new remiges and rectrices; after second and third moults (in 3rd winter to 4th summer) has three/four generations of remiges and rectrices, with clear differences between very worn retained juvenile feathers and fresh ones (general pattern still juvenile-like,

Adult Golden Eagle. Pale nape, patchy plumage forming a strong upperwing-covert bar in flight.

Adult ▶ Golden Eagle

◀ Golden Eagles. Wings held forward and raised in soaring flight. Adult dark, large tail.

1st-year Golden Eagle shows white bases to primaries and tail, above and below. This gradually lost with age. ▼

Adult Imperial Eagle. Pale nape, white 'epaulets'. Otherwise blackish with grey tail base.

◀ Adult Golden Eagle.

◀ Sub adult

All dark, pale shawl and ◀ tail base.

▲ 1st-year Golden Eagle of race 'homeyeri' has white in wing reduced or lacking.

Adult Imperial Eagle. Wings held flat, lacks bulge in rear of wing. ▶

Sub adult Imperial Eagle. Patchy, pale shawl. Pale inner-primary wedges. ▼

◀ 1st-year Imperial Eagle. Pale streaked breast and spotted above.

Adult Imperial Eagle. Very dark below.

◀ Adult Spanish Imperial Eagle. Broader winged, pale leading edge to wing. ▶

1st-year Imperial Eagle. Pale body, white inner-primary wedges, rump and wingbars.

▲ 1st-year Spanish Imperial Eagle. Uniform reddish-brown body. (For underparts, see previous plate) ▶

1st-year Imperial Eagle. Pale inner-primary wedge and streaked body.

though much paler overall). Older immatures or subadults (after fourth/fifth moults in 4th winter and onwards) characteristic, having varying amount of adult-type grey-brown and barred remiges (result of recommencing suspended moult, already started during third moult) among more juvenile-type, but white-based tail feathers retained longer and often still present when wings and body more adult-like. Some (mostly older) immatures can look extremely adult-like, though because of protracted, chiefly suspended, moult (mainly one or two moult waves at any time) have more uneven ragged trailing edge, often with broken feathers and moult gaps; adults' flight feathers appear more uniform in age (several moult waves at same time allow renewal of all feathers in less than two years, with less obvious differences in wear between groups of feathers).

Likelihood of Confusion Fairly easily separated from other *Aquila* by distinctive silhouette and by raised wing when soaring. Similar-sized Imperial and Spanish Imperial Eagles have relatively long wing, tail and head, and in subadult/adult somewhat similar plumage, too, but they soar on flattish wings and have more parallel-edged wings, narrower and squarer tail with sharper corners (tail also paler with clearer dense bars at base), and more uniform, blacker plumage with better-defined paler crown and shawl and diagnostic (but variable) white markings on shoulder and fore wing-coverts; both also lack Golden's distinct paler upperwing-covert panel. Distinctive shape and raised wings should readily eliminate Steppe and both spotted eagles, older birds of which also differ in plumage (given reasonable views): all lack Golden's two-toned tail and paler crown and shawl, and have different pale pattern on upperwing-coverts; Steppe also has paler underwing with obvious barring on remiges and variable whitish markings on upperparts, while both spotted eagles (mainly Lesser) have other clear differences in wing pattern. In reasonable conditions, separation from young White-tailed *Haliaeetus albicilla* fairly straightforward. Beware that Golden's rather

effortless flight and well-proportioned silhouette can lead to its size being underestimated; moreover, some buzzards (e.g. Rough-legged and dark-morph Long-legged) can give effect of whitish basal tail and flight feathers, but besides considerable size differences they differ markedly in shape, flight and many plumage features.

Imperial Eagle

General Features Averages smaller than Golden (wingspan 180-210 cm), but still very large and proportionately even heavier. Typically very broad-bodied, with well protruding thick neck and huge head (and bill), long wings and relatively longish tail (only slightly shorter than inner-wing breadth). Wings of adult almost parallel-edged, which with well-extended wing (mainly arm) and square hand (but incredibly deep-cut fingers) gives rectangular appearance; juvenile rather similar, but longer secondaries produce rather obvious broader inner wing and S-curved trailing edge (appears heavier and less agile than adult). Commonly soars with tail folded and square-shaped (typically sharper corners) and wings held flattish or sometimes very slightly raised and pressed forwards; in slow gliding, wing still tends to be held level at right angles to body. Active flight heavy, with well-executed, deep and powerful beats; clumsy on take-off, taking some time before really airborne. *Plumage* Moult generally as for Golden, but with sharper plumage differences between juvenile or subsequent immatures and full adult.

Adult Mostly blackish-brown, with rather well-demarcated yellowish-white crown and nape-shawl and bicoloured tail (inner tail greyish, finely and densely barred, creates pale rear region which often strengthened by pale undertail-coverts and accentuated by broad blackish terminal band); diagnostic small white shoulder patch, but often difficult to see. Underside, including throat and fore wing-coverts, very black-looking, with remiges paler greyish-black and diffusely barred (appear rather solid), with blacker wingtip and diffuse narrow trailing edge.

Upperwing similar, though less contrast between remiges and coverts (only indistinct paler basal primary patch, coverts sometimes with inconspicuous paler medians); mantle and forewing appear the blackest, sometimes with little contrast with paler lower back.

Juvenile In reasonable views, totally unmistakable: coarsely streaked brown-and-yellow underbody (but not rear), underwing-coverts (except greaters) and head/mantle; above, prominent yellowish tips to scapulars and lesser coverts, with boldly white-tipped median and (blackish) greater coverts and secondaries/inner primaries (creating obvious wingbars, at least when moderately fresh). In flight, shows characteristic paler inner 3 primaries (both surfaces) and wide pale area from back to uppertail-coverts (where only diffusely marked on lower back/rump). Greatly affected by bleaching and wear during 1st winter, and by 1st spring pattern often faded and plumage mainly sandy-coloured (brown fringes to individual feathers reduced or even worn off); in extremes, pale wingbars and trailing edge of (browner) flight and tail feathers greatly reduced, and may even create misleading pale central underwing-covert band (see below). We would stress that, on distant or moderately bleached birds, the most conspicuous features are the contrasts between the darker streaked breast (often shows as pectoral band) and mantle and the generally unmarked much paler rear body and lower back/rump, as well as between the dark hand and solid (rectangular) secondaries and the sandy inner-primary wedges.

Immature/subadult Although full adult plumage acquired over 5 or 6 years, a fairly clear division exists between younger immatures (up to about 3rd year), more or less reminiscent of juvenile, and older immatures, with a very patchy mix of older-immature and more adult-like feathers. In these two stages, ageing usually best gauged by combination of moult pattern with age-related plumage variation, e.g.: 2nd-autumn/spring birds differ from similar juvenile mainly in non-uniform age of flight feathers, with some primaries (mainly inner) renewed and the first new

secondaries of the moult waves, while below may appear at close range rather blotchy, and pale trailing edges of tail/wing and wingbars generally less conspicuous or worn off; in 3rd autumn/spring, as moult accelerated, more blackish-brown feathers gained and, since many remiges and rectrices renewed, trailing edges are rather ragged. In 4th-5th autumn (subadult), ragged trailing edges involve even more complex moult pattern (recommencing suspended moult rather dominant), and plumage rather variegated and patchy as more darker feathers (variably more adult-like) grow: latter show first mainly on throat, upper breast and lesser underwing-coverts ('younger characters' retained longest on rear body and both surfaces of central wing-coverts, as well as pale inner primaries), though flight and tail feathers already more or less adult-like.

Likelihood of Confusion At moderate distance, confusion most likely between older-immature or subadult Imperial and those of Steppe Eagle; differences in proportions and wing position far from striking, so distinguishing some of these tricky forms should be based on careful study of plumage. Unlike almost all Steppe, Imperial in older transitional plumages has rather contrasting (patchy) blacker forebody (typically throat to chest) than the obviously paler rear body to tail base (both surfaces pale, including frequently still large pale back/rump patch); usually already has large cream crown (typically extends to hindneck) contrasting with blackish head sides and throat, though retains at least in part the pale, indistinctly barred inner primaries and more clearly bicoloured tail (all inconspicuous and/or differently patterned on Steppe, which see); Steppe's characteristic barred flight and tail feathers and pale upper primary patch never shown to same degree by any Imperial. Conversely, Imperial at such ages may exceptionally show hint of light median-covert band below, recalling immature Steppe (but latter's band is on greater coverts), though other characters, and those which distinguish adults, should be conclusive. Confusion between adults/subadults of Imperial and Golden and between juvenile Imperial and *'fulvescens'* Greater Spotted is discussed under Golden and Greater Spotted; see also Black Vulture, and compare Spanish Imperial Eagle.

Spanish Imperial Eagle

General Features Very similar to Imperial Eagle, though to experienced observer appears to have proportionately shorter and broader-based wings, longer and somewhat less square-cut tail, and more protruding and rather thicker neck and head with distinctly heavier bill, all giving impression of 'heavier fore parts' and more compact shape (except longer tail). Somewhat more clumsy than Imperial, with even deeper beats and longer flight before really airborne. *Plumage* Moult and plumage development as Imperial, from which differs as follows.

Adult Larger, purer white patches ('braces') on scapulars extend clearly onto leading edge of upperwing (never so on Imperial), and in extreme cases may also be visible from below; otherwise much as adult Imperial.

Juvenile Distinctive rufous (not sandy-yellow) ground colour. Generally unstreaked below or with only few indistinct marks on breast (lacks clear streaking of juvenile Imperial, though latter when very worn/bleached can look almost unstreaked, especially in distant view); above, pale streaks/spots greatly reduced compared with Imperial.

Immature/subadult Little known, but younger immature (up to 2-3 years) and subadult (from about 5 years) should show conclusive characters of juvenile and adult respectively, thus differing from corresponding plumages of Imperial. Note that worn younger-immature Imperial shows much less obvious streaks (but still paler sandy-buff) and can look rather similar at distance, while reduced white shoulder and leading-edge patches of subadult Spanish Imperial can be misleading. Intermediate transitional plumages often inseparable from those of Imperial.

Likelihood of Confusion Very like Imperial, but well separated geographically. Distinctions from other confusion species (mainly *Aquila*) as given under Imperial, but note that rusty, almost unstreaked juvenile Spanish Imperial may more readily be confused with various plumages of Tawny and *'fulvescens'* Greater Spotted; see those species.
Reference Porter *et al.* (1981).

Bonelli's and Booted Eagles

Where and When Bonelli's Eagle *Hieraaetus fasciatus* is a scarce breeder in S Europe and parts of N Africa and Middle East (and S Asia); basically resident and dispersive, and highly territorial, in open mountainous regions with steep valleys (in winter, often in more open or lower areas). Booted Eagle *H. pennatus* is a summer visitor (generally March-October, a few winter Mediterranean area), in W Palearctic breeding largely in open undulating (or mountainous) woodland regions of S and EC Europe, Turkey and NW Africa; solitary on passage (occasionally up to three together). Populations of both generally decreasing.

General Although congeneric, the two differ considerably in size, shape, flight mode and plumage and are rarely confused in field: Booted much smaller, with plumage varying only with different morphs; Bonelli's distinctly larger, with plumage variation related to age. In poor view, however, both are often confused with other species.

Bonelli's Eagle

Structure and Flight Relatively large to medium-sized and powerful eagle, though proportions often give Honey-Buzzard-like elegant impression. Head and tail noticeably protruding, and latter distinctly broad and square-ended and often conspicuously long (about equal to inner-wing breadth). Wings most characteristic: square-shaped, broad and almost parallel-edged (though often shallow S-curve to trailing edge on young), which in combination with flat-winged position when

Adult Bonelli's Eagle. Dark above, pale below, variable amount of white to mantle/back. Base of tail paler, grey.

Adult Bonelli's Eagle. Pale body and forewing, contrastingly dark coverts, wings parallel-edged.

Adult Bonelli's Eagle. Variable white mantle/back patch, pale tail base.

Juvenile Bonelli's Eagle. Rufous beneath.

Paler bases to primaries.

Juvenile Bonelli's Eagle. Tail long and evenly barred, white back patch and uppertail-coverts.

Younger immature Bonelli's Eagle. Dark underwing coverts and body.

Juvenile Bonelli's Eagle. Pale orange underparts, hint of bar across underwing, dark ear-coverts.

Long-legged Buzzard. Note dark carpal patch.

Adult Booted Eagle. Pale birds have light underparts, lower scapulars and upperwing-coverts.

Pale Booted Eagle. Pied appearance distinctive.

Rufous Booted Eagle. Dark underwing-covert bar, paler primary window and tail.

Note pale shoulder spots in head-on view.

Dark Booted Eagle. As pale bird above, dark head and upper body below, becoming paler to undertail-coverts.

Booted Eagle. Patchy above.

Dark Booted Eagle. Dark body and underwing coverts, paler primary window and tail.

soaring gives appearance of 'flying table'; fingered primaries rather developed, though still appears to have square-cut hands. In slow gliding, wings tend to be flat with still rather straight trailing edge; carpals also pressed forwards (but this typically very obvious when stooping or displaying).

Plumage *Adult* Rather variable, but always shows following features below: whitish body and lesser coverts with varying degree of blackish drop-shaped and streak markings; prominent blackish central wing band and trailing edges of tail and wing; bases of remiges (chiefly outers) and rectrices rather pale and almost unbarred. Head usually distinctly dark with prominent whitish throat. From above, variable white mantle/back patch and rather uniform greyish-brown upperwing (though often with paler forewing, slightly paler remex bases, and darker rear edge and primary tips), and paler tail base with broad blackish terminal band. Head-on, usually shows prominent whitish marginal coverts. *Juvenile* From below, apart from prominent dark wingtip, predominantly pale warm buff with streaked chest and often (not always) narrow dark greater-covert bar, and tail and secondaries narrowly barred greyish, with whiter inner and basal outer primaries; no dark trailing edges. Dark earcoverts prominent. From above, much more uniform, with only indistinctly darker wingtip, greater-covert band and carpals, and whitish-cream uppertail-coverts and back (not mantle) patch. *Subsequent immatures* Full juvenile plumage retained to early summer of 2nd year, but worn (first moult at about 1 year old), and during next 3–4 years of serially descendent moult and varying degree of body moult gradually acquires adult plumage. Young immatures usually differ only slightly from juvenile in having patches of new buff-brown and more heavily streaked feathers below and few new secondaries/rectrices with wide subterminal band; broadly dark centred greater coverts may accentuate darkish middle underwing band. Older immatures (from 3rd winter) rather variable and variegated overall, with gener-

ally rather pronounced blackish central underwing band and somewhat ragged but distinct dark terminal tail and wing bands, and body whiter – generally as adult.

Possible Confusion Adult normally unmistakable. At distance, however, some Honey Buzzards may pose confusion risk (if their much smaller size not obvious), having rather similar proportions and wing position and somewhat similar black-and-white plumage, but Honey has slimmer head and prominent bars basally on remiges/rectrices and lacks Bonelli's prominent central underwing band and white mantle/back patch. With juvenile Bonelli's confusion again unlikely, but beware distant pale sandy Long-legged Buzzard, which also looks relatively large and eagle-like; latter's obvious raised wings when soaring, its lighter build with less broad wings (and less obvious fingered primaries) and shorter narrower tail, as well as its prominent dark carpal patches and trailing edges, should prevent such misidentification.

Booted Eagle

Structure and Flight Small(est) and compact eagle, not really larger than any *Buteo*, but still gives eagle impression: wings generally broad and parallel (only gentle curve to trailing edge, chiefly on young in autumn) but with prominent ample hand and rather deep-fingered primaries; bull-headed, with long tail (only slightly shorter than wing breadth) usually appearing straight and square-cut. Soars with wings flat or slightly drooped and pressed forwards, tail often fanned and flexed; active flight fast, straight and agile, with quick beats, and long glides with wings angled forwards and slightly lowered. Typically stoops from great heights.

Plumage Juvenile differs only slightly from adult in having remiges and rectrices of uniform age, broadly tipped white when fresh (all subsequent plumages having feathers of mixed generations, obvious white tips only when very fresh), and slightly less pronounced barring on flight and central tail feathers; when fresh, often somewhat more warm-buff/rufous on head and on more heavily streaked body, but overlap and bleaching render this feature of little use. Occurs in three morphs, all of which share following diagnostic features: UNDERTAIL has greyish, generally unbarred (and often suffused buff/rufous) outer rectrices, or appears fully so when folded, and also darker and barred centre and darker (sub)terminal band, but indistinct; UPPERPARTS with distinctly pale sandy median-covert panel, small but very sharply set-off pure white patch at base of leading wing edge (visible both from above and when seen head-on), variably prominent whitish uppertail-coverts, and pale scapulars. *Pale morph* Distinct pattern below: basically whitish-cream (often buff-suffused) body/wing-coverts, with varying degree of darkish spots/streaks chiefly on rear, inner and primary coverts, and darkening on head sides; pale innermost primaries. *Dark morph* Dark to medium brown, variably tinged rufous and streaked on underbody and lesser coverts, contrasting with blackish-brown or grey median and greater coverts and barred dark grey (not predominantly blackish as pale morph) secondaries; pale area on hand wider, usually rather sharply contrasting with black primary fingers. *Rufous morph* Generally a pale/rufous variant of dark morph with more pronounced blackish central underwing band, barred remiges and body streaking.

Possible Confusion Dark and rufous morphs can in certain situations be difficult to distinguish from Black Kite (which see). If upperpart features not visible, they may also at distance appear similar to female-like Marsh Harrier, but unlike latter soar and glide on flat or slightly lowered wings (not raised in shallow 'V') and have broader wings with deep-cut fingers, shorter/fuller tail and heavier body; Marsh also lacks darker mid-wing panel and paler forewing. Pale morph, owing to general underpart pattern, can at distance be confused with adult Egyptian Vulture; latter, however, much larger, with broader, wedge-shaped tail, and unlike Booted has about same black-and-white above as below and very different head. Under unfavourable conditions, pale morph may also be confused with both extreme whitish Common Buzzard and Honey Buzzard, but both these lack Booted's pale upper median-covert band and have shorter and only 5 (instead of 6) primary fingers. Note that Booted's white patch on basal leading edge often not visible at distance, and conversely something similar may rarely be shown by Honey Buzzard. Further features indicating whitish *Buteo/Pernis* and ruling out pale Booted include: 1 carpal patch below usually large and prominent, though variable (on extremely pale Common comma-shaped, or exceptionally rather obscure on Honey); 2 remiges and rectrices of varied tones (most dark in secondaries of juvenile Honey) and always barred; 3 head predominantly white, with variable dark markings in eye region (chiefly Honey); 4 most Honey have more distinct body streaks, and nearly all Common Buzzards have some dark markings on body sides; 5 with experience, overall shape, proportions and mode of flight different. Otherwise, tarsi fully feathered on Booted, not on Common or Honey Buzzards.

Common and Lesser Kestrels

Where and When Common Kestrel *Falco tinnunculus* is very common and widespread over W Palearctic, resident or partially migratory, but migratory in some northern parts; uses wide variety of habitats in open, flat or mountainous areas, and frequent near or within settlements, but main requirements (except in deserts) are small woods surrounded by open country. Lesser Kestrel *F. naumanni* is summer visitor, in W Palearctic chiefly to Mediterranean countries, EC Europe and N Middle East (vagrant N and W Europe), typically in open arid country, and noticeably more sociable than Common; colonies (up to 150 pairs, but may nest solitarily) usually in small towns, steep cliffs, ruins etc, and forms large roosts post-breeding and on passage.

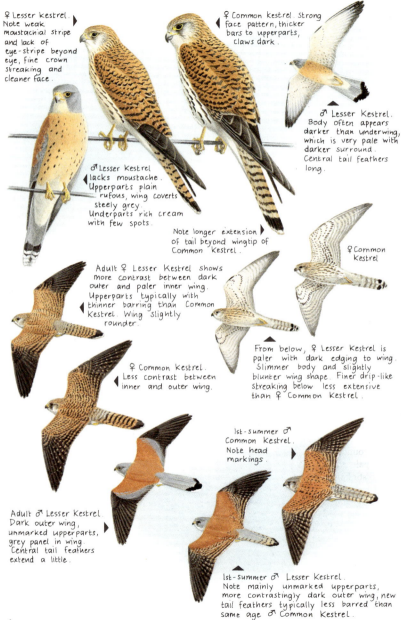

♀ Lesser kestrel. Note weak moustachial stripe and lack of eye-stripe beyond eye, fine crown streaking and cleaner face. ▶

♂ Lesser kestrel lacks moustache. Upperparts plain rufous, wing coverts steely grey. Underparts rich cream with few spots.

◀ ♀ Common kestrel. Strong face pattern, thicker bars to upperparts, claws dark.

♂ Lesser Kestrel. Body often appears darker than underwing, which is very pale with darker surround. Central tail feathers long.

Note longer extension of tail beyond wingtip of Common Kestrel. ▶

♀ Common Kestrel

Adult ♀ Lesser Kestrel shows more contrast between dark outer and paler inner wing. Upperparts typically with thinner barring than Common Kestrel. Wing slightly rounder. ◀

♀ Common Kestrel. Less contrast between inner and outer wing. ◀

From below, ♀ Lesser Kestrel is paler with dark edging to wing. Slimmer body and slightly blunter wing shape. Finer drip-like streaking below less extensive than ♀ Common Kestrel.

1st-summer ♂ Common Kestrel. Note head markings. ▶

Adult ♂ Lesser Kestrel. Dark outer wing, unmarked upperparts, grey panel in wing. Central tail feathers extend a little. ▶

1st-summer ♂ Lesser Kestrel. Note mainly unmarked upperparts, more contrastingly dark outer wing, new tail feathers typically less barred than same age ♂ Common Kestrel.

General, Structure and Flight Separating the two kestrels, particularly in female-like plumage, is often extremely difficult, and they cannot always be distinguished by plumage alone; identification, however, normally safely based on combination of plumage differences (usually at close quarters), structure and flight action. Use of last two aspects requires much experience, but, once learned, can be a major aid to identification. Lesser differs in following ways: slightly smaller, more delicate, appearing slimmer and showing rather rounded/chunky head on more tapered body, with proportionately shorter wings and tail; when perched, wingtips reach dark subterminal tail band (not so on Common); and in flight its narrower but, most importantly, slightly more rounded and shorter hands (as well as thinner tail) usually produce much lighter flight, with characteristic shallower but rather stiffer and flappy beats, frequently giving 'winnowing' impression. Lesser's tail (chiefly males) often somewhat more wedge-shaped owing to marginally longer (projecting) central feathers, but exceptionally Common shows this, too.

Adult Males Perched Lesser should be readily separated by wingtip position (see above) and by its unmarked rufous upperparts (heavily barred/spotted on Common), bluer and cleaner head (lacking Common's obvious moustache and whitish cheeks on rather finely but prominently streaked head), bluish-grey greater-covert panel (lacking on Common), and almost unmarked vinous-tinged rufous-buff underparts with only few smaller/rounder spots (heavily marked on buff to pale warm brown on Common). In flight, distinguished from Common by cleaner/whiter underwing contrasting with darkish tip (and often diffuse trailing edge) and almost plain buff body; from above, unmarked rufous back/mantle and forewing and blue-grey panel between latter and dark flight feathers diagnostic. Whiter underwing effect created by very pale creamy-white coverts, either densely spotted (sometimes heavily, approaching Common) or often almost completely unspotted, and by whiter

flight feathers (very faint/thin greyish bars) which enhanced by darker primary tips. Some of these flight features not easy to detect, but at close quarters other plumage features discernible, and general proportions and flight action always useful.

Immature Males Juveniles undergo partial post-juvenile moult from about mid autumn (Lesser usually after migration) which includes body feathers and usually central pair of tail feathers, but rest of tail, wing-coverts, tertials and remiges retained. So, 1st-summer male Lesser very like Common (with spotted/barred upperwing-coverts and tertials, and no blue-grey wing panel), but often distinguished by new unspotted chestnut feathers on mantle, cleaner bluish-grey head (or, if head still mainly female-like, usually has only faint moustache and lacks Common's dark rear eye-stripe), and also by wingtip position, as well as flight and proportions.

Adult Females and Juveniles In both species, adult females and juveniles very similar (though juvenile's flight and tail feathers all evenly fresh, and markings tend to be stronger/heavier, but much variation and in practice ageing often impossible in field), and the two age-classes share same field characters. Although the two species exhibit a number of rather constant distinguishing features (albeit with degree of overlap), there will always be difficult individuals which may not be identifiable, but majority, given good views, should be. A combination of most of following features essential for safe identification. 1 STRUCTURE, PROPORTIONS AND FLIGHT Involves position of folded wing when perched (diagnostic) and flight action: see above. 2 HEAD PATTERN Lesser has on average finer and diffuser (less heavily marked) moustachial stripe than Common, and lacks latter's small eye-stripe behind eye. Most also tend to have cleaner/paler grey-white cheeks with much fainter streaks, pale area often extending widely to throat and forehead to form more greyish face. Crown streaks (dark centres) usually finer than on Common. 3 UPPERPART MARKINGS Barring on chestnut mantle/scapulars and lesser coverts generally very similar on both species. On Lesser bars tend to be more V-shaped, with deeper inner curve and straighter outer line which protrudes centrally in a sharp point to feather tip (on Common Kestrel more triangular or bar-like, or sometimes with shallow inner curve and slightly rounder outer outline), but this must be used with extra care because of variation in both species. **4 TAIL BARS** On Lesser, bars usually average slightly narrower, less straight and less symmetric as bars broken at shafts (usually broader, slightly bolder and more straight/symmetric on Common), but variation in both species renders this feature of little use in field. **5 UPPERTAIL-COVERTS** Chestnut grey-brown on juveniles of both species, but often washed pale greyish on adult Lesser, a feature seen rarely on Common (largely older females), and because of this overlap best regarded as subsidiary feature. **6 UNDERPARTS** Extremely similar on both species, but on adult female Lesser (against corresponding Common) streaking below on average slightly less developed (somewhat more sparse) and finer, more drip-like, giving general effect of more neatly and less densely marked underparts; this character, however, individually variable, and useful only with extreme birds. Juveniles of the two species even more similar, but, as with females, streaks penetrate somewhat less onto rear body on Lesser, flank streaking usually reaching to a point level with middle of under secondaries (on Common, more often to level with trailing edge); on Lesser, markings tend to be denser on upper breast sides (usually more evenly spread throughout on Common). **7 UNDERWING** Lesser has somewhat whiter/cleaner and less marked underwing: flight-feather bars less dark and mainly on outer webs, with inner webs plainish, while primary bases unbarred or diffusely barred on wide area; less densely and more thinly/faintly spotted underwing-coverts, particularly primary coverts. Whiter and cleaner primary coverts and primary bases form rather extensive pale carpal region; on Common Kestrel, pale area on primary bases usually smaller and primary coverts more heavily marked with 3–5 rows of dark spots (thin 'crescents). Lesser's whiter/cleaner primaries usually enhanced by relatively dark primary tips, and paler carpal region usually contrasts more with exposed darkish alula (when hovering), giving slightly more contrasty appearance. Beware, however, that underwing features are sometimes less useful in separation of juveniles, which are more variable and show greater overlap between the species. Moreover, it must be stressed that extreme caution is called for when assessing female-like underwings: they often vary individually, and differing viewing angles and light conditions can easily lead to misidentification.

Call, and Claw Coloration Claw colour diagnostic: invariably whitish on Lesser, blackish on Common. Some calls of Lesser recall Common's, though much faster and more chattering in general, and often (chiefly in colonies) gives high-pitched, hoarse trisyllabic contact call, a rasping 'kee-chee-chee' or 'chet-che-che', less piercing and more feeble and slurred than in Common.

Eleonora's, Sooty and Allied Falcons

Where and When Both Eleonora's *Falco eleonorae* and Sooty Falcons *F. concolor* are late-summer visitors (May-November) uniquely adapted to a seasonal food supply (largely autumn migrants) when feeding nestlings: former breeds colonially mainly on Mediterranean islands and coastal cliffs, Sooty in desert mountains or coastal cliffs and coral islands in S Israel, S Jordan, Arabia, Sinai and Egypt; seen together on passage in Middle East, and Eleonora's vagrant north to Britain and Scandinavia and Sooty as far as Malta. Hobby *F. subbuteo* and Red-footed Falcon *F. vespertinus* are widespread summer visitors (April-October), former to most of Europe (in forests/wooded areas with open ground) and latter mainly from C Europe eastwards (in more open terrain, e.g. wooded steppe with meadows or open crops, often in lower mountains or river valleys): the two often migrate in same areas (also on passage with Sooty and/or Eleonora's in Middle East/N Africa), and frequently seen at same stopover sites, e.g. open fields; Red-footed generally rare/vagrant to most of W Europe.

General Sooty does not have pale and dark morphs as previously thought, its dark plumage being related to age (occurs in older/adult birds), whereas Eleonora's shows distinct dark and pale morphs in adult plumage; in Red-footed all-dark plumage related to both age and sex (shown by older/adult male only), but lacking altogether in Hobby. All have complete adult post-breeding moult (largely in winter quarters); post-juvenile moult mostly partial, including many/most body feathers, and retain most/all flight and tail feathers (pale tips lost) into 2nd winter.

Structure and Flight All four appear more or less slim, long-winged and long-tailed. Eleonora's, however, averages larger, with proportionately even longer tail and wings and distinctly broader and longer arm, and narrow body appears suspended beneath; characteristic slow foraging flight with relaxed soft wingbeats (reminiscent of distant skua), and typically spends much time gliding and soaring on flattish wings over sea and coastal cliffs, but agile and fast in pursuit flight. Sooty is intermediate between Eleonora's and Red-footed, generally a smaller version of Eleonora's, but wings proportionately narrower and tail slimmer and slightly shorter (and often looks slightly more wedge-tipped with marginally more protruding central feathers); pursuit flight swift and direct, with strong, regular, often rather deep beats. Red-footed, although more closely related to this species group, resembles a kestrel in outline and flight action: about size of Hobby, but averages smaller and more finely built, with narrow but less pointed wings and distinctly longer tail, and may thus approach Sooty and Eleonora's (especially when soaring); active pursuit often with

regular, loose kestrel-like wingbeats, but still more agile and stiffer-winged, approaching Hobby, and catches insects in similar patrolling flight, but also regularly hovers in kestrel-like fashion. Hobby distinctly smaller than Eleonora's but only marginally smaller than Sooty: characteristic in having somewhat shorter wings (arm) but scythe-like pointed hand and relatively shorter and often more square-cut tail, while at times may appear blunter-winged as Red-foot though arm and tail still average shorter; typical silhouette is with long primaries smoothly curved and flexed back; generally agile and active, with quick and stiff energetic wingbeats, also commonly seen in low powerful flight or in patrolling insect-catching flight (insects eaten during brief glide), but also flies with more rapid stiff winnowing flicks and typical long direct stoops with almost closed wings when after birds.

Note that size varies with sex (smaller male of larger species about same size as larger female of smaller species), and shape differs slightly with wear (e.g. tail appears shorter on worn birds) or with age (e.g. juvenile wings average more rounded at tip). All species have more or less same wing position when soaring (wings flattish and often fully outstretched) or when gliding, though in Sooty and Eleonora's wings usually nearly horizontal, whereas more tendency to be lowered in Hobby and Red-footed.

Separation of Dark Plumages Aside from shape/size, Sooty differs from dark-morph Eleonora's in having predominantly sooty lead-grey or paler bluish-grey body and coverts (deep sooty or blackish-brown on Eleonora's) and appears rather uniformly coloured, though below with darker body, wingtip and rear tail which at times appear blackish (lacking Eleonora's contrast of paler/silvery remex bases and solidly black underwing-coverts and body), while from above shows darker/blackish hands (contrast less pronounced on Eleonora's) and rear tail (more uniform on Eleonora's). Sooty's yellow cere often more prominent, chiefly on male on which more orange-yellow; when perched, blacker primaries appear much darker than blue-grey wing-coverts. Adult male Red-footed has silvery-grey flight feathers, contrasting with slate-blackish coverts, head and tail below and with dark slate-grey remaining plumage above; diagnostic dull red undertail-coverts and trousers visible at closer range. Although 1st-summers of all three species retain juvenile's barred remiges and rectrices and varying amount of body and covert feathers, resultant plumages are very different: Eleonora's and Sooty resemble respective adults (though ageable by vestiges of immaturity, and same sometimes applies with 2nd-autumn birds); Red-footed unique in having pale translucent flight and (most of) tail feathers with prominent dark barring, oddly patterned underwing-coverts (partially moulted or fully retained juvenile), and head and body usually show mixed sooty/blackish, grey and rufous feathers, with often buff on breast and collar, as well as slate-grey (new) mantle to uppertail-coverts but old bleached upperwing-coverts. 2nd-autumn male Red-footed even more variegated, with blackish-grey (new) central primaries and central secondaries against much paler remaining remiges, almost producing black-and-white pattern.

Adult Pale-morph Eleonora's Differs from all similar plumages of other falcons (Hobby, and juveniles of Sooty and Red-footed) in being rufous/deep buff and variably narrow-streaked below (often leaving paler and/or almost unstreaked undertail-coverts and trousers), with diagnostic blackish underwing-coverts which contrast with paler (largely greyish) remiges and whitish cheek/throat patch; remiges typically unbarred (at least outer ones) and have darker tips (palest parts are primary bases, and often basal greater primary coverts); and whitish-cream cheek patch is conspicuous against rather broad but long and well-defined moustache, but although relatively wide extends only little onto neck sides. Tail unbarred above and indistinctly barred below. With upperparts uniformly brownish-black to bluish-black (slightly darker flight feathers), and darkish

impression below, appears overall darker than any Hobby or juvenile Sooty or Red-footed.

Juvenile Eleonora's Reminiscent of adult pale morph, but contrast between underwing-coverts and body may be obscure and remiges/rectrices are strongly barred, so more likely to be confused with Hobby (chiefly juvenile) and juvenile Sooty and Red-footed. Apart from size/shape and flight action (see above), following plumage characters should, used with caution, reveal its correct identity. Underwing-coverts, although copiously barred and mottled, look dark brown and rather uniform (especially in extreme lighting or when wings in shadow), and since the pale bars of remiges are generally whiter, especially at base of primaries, there is often effect of pale outer wing panel bordered by very dark wingtip, trailing edge and underwing-coverts and by moderately darkish secondaries; note that paler bases of greater primary coverts create rather distinct comma effect at tips. All unlike other species, which generally appear to have more evenly patterned underwing or even with impression of slightly paler underwing-coverts; beware, however, that slightly darker coverts often found on juvenile Red-footed, and in very high overhead view, if other features not seen, the two can appear confusingly similar. Another character of juvenile Eleonora's is its usually indistinct pale area (patches) across nape (other species show variable obvious pale collar or at least obvious nape patches); although shares with Hobby almost uniform-looking upperparts (but browner, and has sharp arrowhead-shaped instead of rounded centres to individual feathers, mainly lower rear scapulars), has distinctly longer tail and larger wings (see also above); from similar-shaped juvenile Sooty it also differs in lacking latter's tendency of darker remiges and paler coverts, both dorsally (where Sooty also greyer) and beneath, as well as its broader subterminal tail band and distinct projecting central tail feathers; and from juvenile Red-footed differs in uniformly dark upperparts/uppertail

Juvenile Hobby. Dark brown above, heavy streaking extends to flanks, wings longer than tail.

Juvenile Red-Footed Falcon. Warm-Fringed upperparts, note head pattern.

Adult pale-morph Eleonora's Falcon. Dark brown above, pale orange below, with minimal shaft streaking.

Adult pale-morph Eleonora's Falcon. In flight, dark wing-coverts contrast with pale bases to remiges.

Strongly barred tail.

Juvenile Red-Footed Falcon. Dark wingtip and trailing edge. Underwing barring obvious. Underpart streaking thin but obvious.

Juvenile Sooty Falcon. Slate above with cream fringing. Underparts streaking grey and diffuse. Note head pattern. Tail longer than Hobby, unbarred.

Juvenile Hobby. Dark below, heavy body streaking.

Juvenile Eleonora's Falcon. Note tail length, body streaking strongest on breast. Barred outer tail feathers.

Juvenile Sooty Falcon. Dark below, body streaking obscure. Note tail shape with wide terminal bar.

Juvenile Red-Footed Falcon. Dense tail barring with thicker terminal bar, paler upperwing coverts contrast with remiges.

Juvenile Hobby. Uniformly dark above, short tail.

Juvenile Eleonora's Falcon. Dense, dark wing-covert bars contrast with primary bases and body.

Juvenile Sooty Falcon. Note grey body and darker remiges. Tail darkens to pointed tip.

Juvenile Eleonora's Falcon. Very dark above, pale collar often obscure.

Adult ♂ Red-footed Falcon. Slate grey, reddish bare parts, chestnut undertail coverts. Pale wings.

Adult Sooty Falcon. Grey, becoming darker to wings and tail, chin whitish.

Dark-morph Eleonora's Falcon. Paler bases to remiges contrast with body and coverts. Note tail shape.

Adult Sooty Falcon. No contrast beneath except wing and tail extremities.

Dark-morph Eleonora's Falcon. Uniform above.

Adult ♂ Red-footed Falcon. Blunter-winged, dark body and wing-coverts.

Adult Sooty Falcon. Darker outer wing and tail tip. Note tail shape.

Dark-morph Eleonora's Falcon. Uniform dark slate, becomes browner with time.

Adult ♂ Red-footed Falcon. Darker body, paler 'silvery' outer wing.

(instead of well barred, with distinctly paler upperwing-coverts) and more complete black head pattern (lacking Red-foot's whitish forehead, paler/streaked crown, and distinctly darker rear crown bordered by obvious pale collar). Juveniles of all have rather variable and similar underpart streaking, though on Eleonora's typically finer (but close-spaced on breast as well as body sides, where bolder arrow-shaped or some bar-like markings; also on undertail-coverts) and all on deeper buffy ground colour: together giving darker body plus darker overall impression than Hobby (on which underparts evenly, densely and boldly streaked), Red-footed (streaks the most fine and both evenly and widely spaced), or Sooty (variable streaking diffuse, with greyish-buff fringes, and tends to be denser on upper breast and flanks, giving duskier overall impression, often with dark 'breast-shield').

Juvenile Sooty Characteristic in being small/slim, with dark remiges (notably primaries) contrasting with paler sooty-grey upperparts and upperwing-coverts (on which buffy fringes narrow and indistinct), and below predominantly 'dirty' yellow-brown on body (diffusely streaked) and underwing-coverts and with flight-feather bases paler than, and contrasting with, dark hands and trailing edge; the diffuse streaking often creates duskier appearance, notably on upper body sides, and heavier/denser streaking on upper breast may appear almost as breast band. Throat and cheeks typically deep buff. Uppertail is uniform and almost concolorous with rest of upperparts, while undertail (except central feathers) fine-barred and with fairly wide blackish subterminal band (juveniles of all species have white-tipped tail); darker and projecting central feathers noticeable from below. Head pattern, with dark crown extending below eye as dark moustachial stripe and dark mark on rear ear-coverts, is similar to that of juvenile Hobby (but pale area on throat/cheek is warmer buff than the normally whiter area on Hobby) and to that of juvenile Eleonora's (though latter's dark rear ear-covert mark poorly developed and extension of pale area onto nape reduced); differs in head pattern from juvenile Red-footed as latter differs from juvenile Eleonora's (which see). Differs rather markedly from juvenile Eleonora's in smaller size, in pattern of upper- and underwings and in rear tail features (see above). From juvenile Hobby also in shape (notably has longer tail; see also above) and in having two-toned upper- and underwings and broad dark subterminal band to undertail (all evenly patterned on Hobby) and is deep buff below, including throat/cheek (whitish on Hobby). Separated from juvenile Red-footed by more uniform upperparts and tail (Red-footed has well-barred tail and obvious darker subterminal markings on upperparts) and by more complete head markings (see above); ground colour and streaking below, as well as shape and flight, also differ. Note that projecting central tail feathers most distinct on Sooty, but may be indicated by fresh-plumaged individuals (mainly juveniles) of congeners.

Separating Juveniles of Hobby and Red-footed Falcon If reasonable view obtained, juvenile Red-footed usually easily separated by wide pale forehead and neck-collar (crown more complete and partly connected with upperparts on Hobby), well-barred uppertail (uniform on Hobby) and richly patterned upperparts with dark subterminal markings and clear contrast between paler coverts and darker remiges (Hobby more uniform, darker, with only indistinct pale fringes). From below, should be distinguished by yellower underparts/underwing with typically wider dark hands and trailing edge, whiter/wider bars on flight feathers and finer, paler body streaking (on Hobby, underwing appears darker/unpatterned, with dark trailing edge confined to hand, and body much more densely and boldly streaked; tail barring less complete, virtually restricted to inner webs). The two also differ in shape and flight action.

References Clark *et al.* (1990), Forsman (1995a), Porter *et al.* (1981), Small (1995).

Large Falcons

Where and When Five large falcons *Falco* occur in the region. Gyr Falcon *F. rusticolus* is a rare breeder largely confined to tundra, barren uplands or rocky coasts (often in partly wooded areas) in the Arctic/Subarctic; resident to partially migratory, rarely extending south of 60°N in winter, and vagrant W Europe. The widespread Peregrine Falcon *F. peregrinus* is rare to locally common in wide range of (usually open) habitats, from arctic/alpine to semi-desert; resident, dispersive or migratory (race *calidus* of northern tundra winters as far south as S Africa). Saker Falcon *F. cherrug* is rather widely distributed but uncommon in warm-temperate zones from C Asiatic steppes west to SE Europe (mainly Hungary) and Turkey; winters regularly Middle East, with few records from rest of Europe and N Africa. Lanner Falcon *F. biarmicus* generally replaces Saker in Mediterranean and Africa, typically in dry areas (especially semi-desert/desert in east and south); three races in W Palearctic, all largely resident, overlapping with Saker only in winter/passage months. Barbary Falcon *F. pelegrinoides* inhabits deserts of N Africa, Middle East and C Asia; mostly resident and dispersive.

Main Problems Main problems are: separating Gyr and Peregrine, chiefly in N (even C and NW) Europe, especially darkish Scandinavian/NW Russian Gyr and non-adult Peregrine (particularly large female *calidus*); pale juvenile grey-morph Gyr and immature European Saker, in countries where either could occur as vagrant; Lanner and Saker, mainly non-adults, in areas where they meet (winter/passage) or could occur as vagrants; while Barbary Falcon of the deserts can superficially resemble Lanner (in most plumages), and can be really difficult to separate from adult

Peregrine of race *brookei* and from any race of Peregrine when dealing with non-adults. Nowadays, likelihood of escapes is very high anywhere in region, and extreme caution is required with any large falcon outside its normal range (equally important is to try to determine whether such birds are escapes or true vagrants). Further, recent artificial hybridisation of falcons only exacerbates the problem, and makes some individuals almost certainly unidentifiable.

Structure, Ageing and Sexing Gyr, Saker and Lanner all have more rounded wings (outermost primary shorter than 3rd) and proportionately longer tail than Peregrine and Barbary (outermost primary longer than 3rd) and most forms are generally larger/heavier, but in all species male tends to be distinctly smaller than female (note that large females of smaller species can overlap in size with smallish males of larger ones) and more finely patterned (and normally becomes paler with age). Juveniles generally told by bluish-grey (not clear yellow) feet, cere and orbital ring at least through 1st winter, and tend to have more patterned underwing (first three species) and head and more boldly streaked body (in species where adult barred below, juvenile is mainly streaked); tend also to be darker and less marked above than adults, and usually (most species) to have stronger rusty fringes to upperside and white tip to tail (if not too worn). Adult plumage usually gained by partial moult (often some flight/tail feathers) in 1st winter and complete moult in 1st spring/summer, though sometimes a few juvenile feathers (especially coverts) retained.

Gyr Falcon

Structure and Flight The largest and heaviest falcon, appearing very big, solid and powerful: robustness when perched and wingspan in flight may match those of Common Buzzard *Buteo buteo*, and head proportionately full and broad. In flight, appears heavy, very broad-bodied and full-chested with bulky undertail-coverts, with relatively long but broad-based and rather blunt-tipped

wings and longish tail; often gives impression, particularly when flying away, of a female Goshawk *Accipiter gentilis*, this also due to its rather stiff, shallow wingbeats that appear almost as if executed by hands alone. Larger and heavier than Peregrine, with longer, fuller tail and larger (but proportionately shorter-looking) wings, typically with broader/longer arm, relatively broader hand and distinctly rounded tip, and slower wing action. With experience, told from Saker by broader-armed and blunter-tipped wings, and almost equally longish tail is much fuller and thicker-based, giving impression that body continues into tail (Saker's tail distinctly narrow, especially around vent); body more or less evenly broad from breast to vent (Saker's slim, tapering body recalls a harrier). Clumsy on take-off, rather long flight before really airborne; often glides, but mainly soars (as Saker) on upward-bent wingtips; hunts low down in rather horizontal pursuit (prey often taken on ground), only rarely stooping from height.

Perched Has typical upright posture but robust and deep-chested, with very prominent shoulders; dense belly feathering and bushy trousers almost conceal tarsi (legs more exposed on other species), and wingtips always fall well short of tail tip (tail projection similar to Saker, but much longer than Lanner and especially Peregrine). Note that Greenland Gyr average slightly larger than Icelandic birds and more so than Scandinavian ones.

Plumage Geographical variation complex, with major differences involving frequency of colour morphs. *White morph* of high Arctic (chiefly Greenland, less so Siberia) often vagrant in NW Europe and highly distinctive: white, with dark wingtips and varying amount of dark spotting; juveniles and adults very similar, but former have browner (not blackish) markings and usually not arranged in row-like pattern of most adults. *Grey morph* of lower Arctic predominantly greyish: 'light grey' in S Greenland, Iceland and part of Siberia (paler grey and whiter, with more distinct and finer whitish and grey markings

Adult Gyr Falcon. Typical mid-grey bird. Streaky cheeks, barred upperparts, cross-barring on flanks. Deep chested, bushy trousers.

Large pale-headed juvenile Peregrine.

Juvenile Gyr Falcon. Peregrine-like bird. Compare position of wing and tail tips, tail and upperpart patterns.

Pale juvenile Gyr Falcon. Occasional individuals resemble Saker Falcon. Note pale speckling to upperparts and pale markings within the dark flank patches.

Juvenile Saker Falcon. Small head sparsely marked. Upperparts rufous-toned with complete pale margins. Tail feathers poorly marked with oval spots.

above), with 'darkish grey' birds typical of Nordic countries (rather medium-grey with pale grey barring, but often with brownish cast, and more marked broad 'falcon hood'). Note that 'light grey' birds sometimes occur as genuine vagrants in NW Europe, while 'darkish grey' move very little from their European breeding grounds. Also occurs in a dark morph (N America, unknown in W Palearctic) and intermediate (particoloured) white-and-grey morphs (usually in Greenland); since plumages of these and of white morph are straightforward, following concentrates on identification of Scandinavian grey morphs, which may be confused with Peregrine or Saker. **Adult** Most tend to have pale ashy-grey upperparts with finer slate-grey barring (usually lack obvious brownish cast), and only moderate difference between rather plain translucent flight feathers and slightly darker underwing-coverts, which are typically barred, and underparts rather finely spotted/streaked dark, usually with some

barring on flanks/trousers and undertail-coverts. Differs from adult (and most non-adult) Peregrine in well-defined upperpart barring (indiscernible/diffuse on Peregrine), two-toned underwing-coverts (mostly uniform on Peregrine), typically looser/coarser spotting below with few bars confined to flanks and trousers (Peregrine normally more densely and regularly barred as adult or streaked as non-adult), and more diffuse 'falcon-hood', including moustache, which merges with streaky cheeks (well-demarcated hood and moustache with cleaner cheeks on most adult Peregrine, but less so on non-adults, particularly of race *calidus*: see below). Confusion with Saker normally confined to non-adults of both, but locally adult Saker of aberrant '*saceroides*' variant (which see) may approach Gyr in plumage: such Saker variants can have pale buffish-grey plumage with darker barring above and some bars on flanks, and sometimes even more barred tail, recalling adult Gyr, but usually ruled out by typical Saker shape, head pattern, body streaking and underwing pattern and usually show some typical Saker-like buffy-rufous margins above and slightly more irregular tail barring. *Juvenile* Differs from adult in having little or no pale barring on mostly brown-grey upperparts, more distinct contrast between pale remiges and more solidly darkish underwing-coverts (typically streaked), and densely streaked underparts. Confusion more likely with juvenile Peregrine (chiefly larger and paler *calidus*), since lacks prominent upperpart barring and has streaked underparts and since latter's 'falcon-hood' is more broken and with less clearcut moustache. In most cases best identified by differences in shape and underwing pattern (see above), and most Gyr still have less contrasty head with more streaked ear-coverts than Peregrine (on which moustache usually contrasts clearly with paler cheeks); in addition, Gyr's rump and tail uniform and normally slightly paler than rest of upperparts (tail and upperparts almost concolorous on Peregrine, tail gradually darkening towards tip), and dark central nape patch more clear-cut. Following characters of young Gyr should eliminate superficially similar young Saker (most features also valid for eliminating Lanner, though in practice the two unlikely to be confused). 1 STRUCTURE With practice, wings seen to be broader and rounded (narrower on Saker) and body uniformly broad and bulky (slimmer and tapering on Saker) with broader and thicker-based tail (narrow with slimmer base on Saker), see also above; perched Gyr generally more robust. 2 HEAD PATTERN Pale Gyr and darkish Saker often very similar, but Gyr tends to have larger/broader moustache bordering smaller and variably streaked cheek patch, as well as darker crown with ill-defined eye-stripe, together producing darker head with duskier ear-coverts, but beware that this feature variable. 3 UPPERPARTS/WINGS Always appear more uniform with some grey tinting (and sometimes hint of pale barring), and with variable amount of feathers with incomplete pale tips, and most tend

to have speckled outer webs to primaries; most Sakers show two-toned upperparts, with darkish remiges and variable amount of pale and brownish pigments in upperwing-coverts (effect of paler arm and darker hand), coverts also having narrow and more complete rusty fringes, and plainer outer webs to primaries. 4 UNDERPARTS Juvenile Gyr has more or less evenly streaked breast to undertail-coverts, lacking Saker's considerably paler upper breast contrasting with lower breast and flanks (boldly streaked trousers) and poorly marked undertail-coverts. 5 UNDERWING-COVERTS Compared with all equivalent-aged Saker, but especially juveniles, Gyr has less contrasting and less uniformly brown underwing-coverts, but much variation in both species. 6 TAIL Gyr tends to have more dense and distinct barring, but variation considerable and some more Saker-like, including virtually unmarked central feather pair.

Saker

Structure and Flight Large, rather heavy and powerful falcon, in size similar to or a little smaller than Gyr, but mainly slimmer and lighter in build; wingspan often (females) matches that of Buzzard or Marsh Harrier *Circus aeruginosus*. Larger than Lanner only on average, but stronger/heavier. Varies in size/proportions, but most typically show long wings (arm rather broad but long, hand moderately broad but long and relatively pointed), long slender tail (typically narrow-based) and rather elongated body (though still deep-chested). In flight, differs markedly from Peregrine and Barbary Falcons in usually distinctly larger size, longer wings (longer/broader arm and longer but rounded hand) and slimmer and considerably longer tail, lacking those species' triangular-shaped wings and more rounded body, and less quick and less emphatic wingbeats (though beats often appear fast for its size); from Gyr in somewhat smaller size, with longer and more pointed wings and elongated body (see also above), and perhaps slightly lighter action; and from very similar Lanner in being generally heavier, with broader-based and blunter-tipped wings, deeper chest and somewhat larger head (more agile Lanner's silhouette may recall short-tailed kestrel), and slightly slower and flatter beats (seem more to be executed by hands alone), flight appearing more stable/lazy than Lanner's, but differences subtle and normally require much practice. Hunts at rather low level and stoops in typical large-falcon manner; takes most prey on ground; as Gyr and Lanner, often glides and soars with upcurved wingtips.

Perched Upright posture, but still rather big-bodied with relatively small head; tail distinctly long, producing comparatively long wing/tail projection which is useful in separating from Lanner and Peregrine.

Plumage Varies both geographically and individually; tends to become paler eastwards and also with age, but both paler and darker birds occur anywhere in range and in any age-class. W Palearctic race *cyanopus*, treated here, is unbarred above; Asian races (i.e. *milvipes*), apparently never recorded in region, very different (barred rufous and blackish above, tail and body sides more barred). The aberrant plumages of so-called *saceroides* (not fully understood and nowa-

Adult Gyr Falcon. Pale, blunt-winged. Huge body tapers into tail. Boldly barred body sides and undertail-coverts.

Two juvenile Gyr Falcons. Coverts typically darker than remiges, which are pale with dark tip to wing. Body boldly streaked.

Slight contrast between plainer translucent remiges and typically barred underwing-coverts.

Juvenile Peregrine. Dark beneath, with little underwing contrast. Pointed wings and shorter tail.

Adult Peregrine. Compact outline, dark above, little contrast.

Juvenile Peregrine. Dark above.

Juvenile Gyr Falcon. Appears uniform above, with broken pale-tipped feathers and even, dense barring to tail.

Adult Gyr Falcon Barred above, plainer primary bases.

Juvenile Saker Falcon.

Juvenile Gyr Falcon. Compare keel outlines.

Adult Peregrine.

days even produced among hybrids) apparently represent western end of a cline of the eastern barred races; such birds found locally W Asia and reported in E/C Europe (pending further study). Differences between adult and juvenile often only marginal, and obscured by individual variation, so following summaries serve only as a guide to ageing. *Adult* Usually distinguished from juvenile/1st-winter by bare-part coloration (see above) and by paler head, with reduced and ill-defined eye-stripe, moustache and crown streaking; more complete tail barring (variable, may have tail as juvenile), and more tawny on upperparts (including wing-coverts) owing to wider but more diffuse rufous feather margins, which often form greater contrast against darker remiges. Underpart markings typically of sparser and more rounded streaks or spots, with stronger tendency to be denser/darker on lower breast and flanks; underwing-coverts often less contrasting owing to reduced dark markings, and with larger/whiter remex barring the underwing is generally whiter than on 1st-years (on extreme pale adults, prominent markings almost restricted to greater coverts). For separation from *any* Gyr, see juvenile of latter; usually rather easily distinguished from any Peregrine, including very pale and large juvenile *calidus*, by size/shape, head pattern, underwing pattern and upperwing contrast. Adult and juvenile Saker usually separated from young Lanner by same features (see below, under juvenile Saker). Normally readily distinguished from all adult Lanner by presence of some yellowish rufous-brown unbarred upperparts and upperwing-coverts (barred and greyish on Lanner); by usually paler head with better-developed fine crown streaking bordered by variable but generally prominent whitish supercilium, and quite thick and more diffuse eye-stripe (Lanner has darker and conspicuous head markings, including dark forecrown and clear-cut moustache and eye-stripe, and variable traces of rufous on crown to nape); by minimally barred tail with merely pale spots or with unmarked central feather pair (distinctly and more uniformly barred on

adult Lanner); and by bold dark streaking of flanks and (more solidly) trousers usually contrasting with pale upper breast, vent/undertail-coverts and central belly (adult Lanner tends to be more evenly barred below, with markings less streaked and more spot-like and with variable bars on flanks and trousers). Generally, underwing is more patterned (heavier/denser streaking) and with darker rear coverts than Lanner's more evenly marked coverts (latter with more spot-like streaking and even some bar-like marks, altogether giving Lanner a paler, less patterned underwing). Beware, however, *'saceroides'*-type Saker, which may recall adult Lanner: dusky greyish-brown to buffish-grey or even greyish (as well as partly barred) upperparts and upperwing-coverts, but particularly lower back, rump and uppertail-coverts, more complete tail barring and often variable bars on flanks and on whiter underwing-coverts, while rarely some rufous on crown; at distance, some appear very greyish and uniform and are rather difficult to identify, but in most instances told from Lanner by typical Saker head pattern, some rufous margins on upperparts, and (probably) size and shape. *Juvenile* Differs from adult in bare-part coloration (see above) and in more densely streaked crown with more contrasting/broader pale supercilium and more prominent and usually more solid/broad dark eye-stripe and moustache; upperparts, including wing-coverts, dark earthbrown and less tawny, with only narrow rufous feather margins. Tail bars less complete, oval-shaped, and central feather pair barely or indistinctly spotted; whitish trailing edge distinct and overall tone slightly paler than rest of upperparts at distance. Usually darker and more heavily patterned below, with more longitudinal streak-like markings (instead of more drop-like streaks) spread more evenly over much of underparts and underwing-coverts, but still bolder or widening towards flanks/trousers and rear wing-coverts. For separation from *any* Gyr, see under juvenile of latter. Could be confused with pale large juvenile or immature Peregrine of race *calidus*, though latter lacks Saker's (and Lanner's) longer wings and tail and elongated body and the two-toned underwing with two densities of streaking on coverts and also usually has some barring on lower flanks/trousers and undertail-coverts (never found on juvenile Saker or Lanner); *calidus* also more uniform brownish-grey above (lacking Saker's contrast) and usually has more Peregrine-like head pattern with darker and more complete hood and thicker moustache, reduced pale supercilium and dark crown streaking, and has distinctly paler rump and tail base, while tail/wing projection much shorter than on perched Saker. Separation of juveniles of Saker and Lanner extremely difficult, often further complicated by individual and to some extent geographical variation; in most cases, best achieved by combination of following differences. **1** SHAPE AND FLIGHT ACTION See above. **2** HEAD PATTERN Generally similar, but Saker's crown usually whiter overall and less dark-patterned, and typically has more evenly spaced dark streaks (lacking Lanner's intense streaking on forecrown and crown sides, which may appear horseshoe-shaped on darker individuals, while crown itself is buffish with more irregular and diffuse streaking). Supercilia whiter, broader and typically longer, extending back to meet on nape and forwards partly to join with larger white forehead; Lanner has more buffish, narrower and clearly shorter supercilia not or only just connecting with pale forehead (dark of forecrown meets black eye-stripe) and short dark lateral crown-stripe behind eye (causing supercilium to fade at mid-crown). Rather broad but fainter eye-stripe typically fades in front of and slightly behind eye (forming diffuse loral area, but also much darker upper rear stripe and rear patch), whereas on Lanner eye-stripe slightly narrower but usually darker and solid for most of its length, including in front of eye. Moustache less distinct and generally ill-defined, usually broken below eye and typically more downward-tapering, whereas on most Lanner moustache is darker and more

solid, fully connected with eye-stripe below eye and generally less tapering. (Differences in darkness of eye-stripe and moustache give general effect of pronounced dark eye but indistinct pale orbital ring in the paler surrounds of Saker, and vice versa on Lanner.) **3** UPPERPARTS/WINGS Most juvenile and 1st-winter Saker have variable soft greyish-tawny suffusion on mantle, scapulars and much of coverts (which at close range, if not too worn, show rather striking yellowish rufous-brown margins to feathers) which contrast with darker flight feathers and primary coverts and give paler-arm/darker-hand contrast, though rather obscure on heavily worn or bleached birds; at short to moderate distance, shows slightly darker primary tips and rather marked darker feather bases to greater coverts and as a row on outer scapulars. On Lanner, upperparts darker slate-brown with only narrow pale rufous feather edges (may produce rufous cast when fresh, but as early as autumn bleached and general tone slightly more grey-brown); thus, usually lacks Saker's contrastingly patterned upperparts, though often outer half of hand appears darkest. Some early-moulted Lanner may show new, barred, adult-like upperpart feathers, never found on normal Saker. **4** UNDERWING PATTERN Saker more strongly patterned owing to paler/whiter primaries (paler ground colour and narrower and less complete dark bars than general tendency on Lanner), especially the translucent or silvery-whitish basal and inner section, which contrasts strongly with secondaries and with more sharply defined dark primary tips (small or indistinct contrasts on Lanner); individual underwing-coverts tend to be uniformly patterned with whitish area confined to feather margins (instead of more spot-like pattern of Lanner), which produces prominent streaking, but overlap occurs and rather obscure in extreme pale or dark birds. **5** UNDERPARTS Both Saker and Lanner vary greatly in amount, distribution and shape of underpart streaking, but juvenile (as adult) Saker tends to be darker on mid-breast, flanks and thighs/trousers, where dark streaking broadens and becomes more solid in pattern and even creates all-dark trousers, whereas normal Lanner shows more even and often more dense streaking (with buffish thighs and faintly streaked trousers); some (early-moulted) Lanner may show trace of barring on flanks, never seen on normal Saker. **6 TAIL PATTERN** Rather similar on both, with uniform grey-brown central feather pair, though Saker can show a few small buffish spots (rare on same-age Lanner); otherwise, Saker tends to have more oval/rounded bars which more numerous and prominent on inner webs, whereas Lanner's rectrices have a more bar-like pattern which is more evenly spread on both webs and entire tail. **7 LEG COLOUR** Most Saker retain bluish-grey legs for about a year (often longer); Lanner's legs often become gradually more yellowish (but still largely greyish/bluish-green) during 1st winter and even more so in 1st summer.

Lanner

Structure and Flight Moderate to large, though general proportions and build as Gyr and Saker. Closer to Saker in having long wings (but arm relatively shorter and hand more tapering) and elongated body (but more slender, lacking Saker's broad-chested appearance, and with smaller head); wings usually appear larger (but still narrower and longer) in relation to body, thus kestrel-like head-on, and tail always noticeably narrow and rather long; flight more elegant and graceful, having Saker's effortless manoeuvrability (including impression of only hands working), but lighter and faster in action. Lacks Peregrine's and Barbary's typical bulky body with bull-necked and big-headed proportions and their broader but only slightly shorter tail and typically broader/shorter and pointed wings, and flight by comparison slower and heavier, with less powerful and stiff wingbeats. Ordinary flight therefore rather slow, with flattish and not too deep beats, but accelerates much faster with deeper beats when taking prey in air, though still at low level (as well as stooping); often soars with slightly upturned wingtips.

Perched Shows indistinct tail/wingtip projection (slightly longer on juveniles) as wingtips fall at or marginally (1-2 cm) short of tail tip (about 5 cm on Saker).

Plumage Three races in W Palearctic: *feldeggii* (SE Europe, Turkey), intermediate in size and with much deeper rufous crown, darkest (darker grey-brown), and well-barred above and on leg feathering; *tanypterus* (NE Africa, Middle East), paler brownish-grey and less obviously barred above, crown duller rufous and less heavily and more narrowly streaked, and bars on leg feathering and flanks reduced; and *erlangeri* (NW Africa), the smallest, with palest crown and paler upperparts, and the least patterned below. Juveniles in N Africa and particularly in Middle East average paler on crown but more heavily streaked below and with darker upperparts than *feldeggii*, and tail pattern tends somewhat towards Saker (reduced and more broken bars). Racial differences, however, often merge, especially between N African and Middle Eastern races, and not all (even adults) are identifiable. Given decent views, ageing not too difficult (compared with Saker), though individual variation great. *Adult* Specifically identified and aged by buffish to rufous crown with reduced and narrow streaking, and clear-cut black eye-stripe, forecrown band and moustache; upperparts suffused greyish and variably barred. Basically whiter below and with irregular finer spotting on chest becoming variably shaped transverse spots and bars on flanks and to some extent on underwing-coverts (chiefly greaters, where form a slightly darker central band); rather distinct dark wingtips and trailing edge. Tail generally pale grey with fine, regular dark bars. Although barred above and on body sides, should easily be distinguished from any plumage of Gyr by differences in size/structure, head pattern and other plumage features given under juvenile of latter species. Readily separated from similar Saker (including aberrant '*saceroides*') by detailed differences in shape and in patterns of head, underparts and underwing (see under adult

Adult Lanner Falcon of the race 'feldeggii'. Dark grey and barred above, rufous crown. Note barred flanks and completely barred tail.

Adult Lanner Falcon of the race 'tanypterus'. Browner-grey than 'feldeggii', with paler rufous crown.

Note black forecrown, crown sides, eye-stripe and moustache.

Juvenile Lanner Falcon. Typically plain dark brown above, evenly streaked below. Note head pattern.

Adult Lanner Falcon of race 'erlangeri'. Very pale below and on head. Tail sandy with dark bars.

Juvenile Lanner Falcon. Pale headed birds may closely resemble Saker Falcon.

Juvenile Peregrine of race 'calidus'. Note strong head pattern, pale fringes to upperparts and even spotting beneath, barred to flanks.

1st-winter Barbary Falcon. Compare with Peregrine. Sparse, thin breast streaking, tail barred. Some adult-type feathers moulted in.

Adult Saker Falcon. Pale head, pale around eye. Diffuse pale fringes to upperparts. Dark streaking increases to flanks. Tail markings are enclosed pale spots. Adult has yellow cere and feet.

Two juvenile Saker Falcons. Rufous-fringed upperparts, heavy belly streaking.

Tail obviously longer than primary tips.

77

Saker). Usually not difficult to separate from any Peregrine plumage when combining shape in flight with pattern of head, tail and underparts/underwing (though upperparts may appear rather similarly patterned). Surprisingly, adult Lanner often confused with adult Barbary Falcon in Middle East and N Africa, since latter's smaller size can be difficult to judge and both appear rather greyish-blue above. Adult and most 1st-summer Barbary should, however, be eliminated by their comparatively bulky body and rather short and more pointed wings, proportionately shorter but noticeably broader tail (lacking Lanner's slight expansion rearwards) and bull-necked/big-headed appearance, and rather fitful Peregrine-like flight action (Lanner's shallow/flexible wingbeats more kestrel-like). Lanner also lacks Barbary's two-toned tail and its more hooded appearance with ill-defined or non-existent eye-stripe and rather uniform crown, and has diagnostic dark forecrown band (never on Barbary) and narrower moustache (generally crown dark and nape rufous on Barbary, vice versa on Lanner). Barbary is also buff/rufous-tinged below with finer and coarser spotting and barring, and with more uniform underwing, lacking Lanner's prominent darker central coverts and wider dark wingtip and trailing edge. *Juvenile* Readily aged by bare-part colours; heavy, almost solid blackish streaking on underparts and central underwing-coverts contrasting with pale translucent remiges; darker, unbarred and more uniform upperparts/wings and wide white tail tip; adult-like head pattern, but crown yellowish-to-whitish-buff with extensive dark streaking; and less regularly barred tail, with central rectrices largely unmarked. Note that birds quite often moult as early as 1st autumn/winter and gain somewhat more adult-like head pattern, some barred feathers above and below, and legs turn yellowish. Although has uniformly dark upperparts and fairly evenly streaked underparts rather like juvenile Peregrine and Barbary, should be told from these by same structural and plumage features (chiefly underwing, head and tail patterns)

as given for separating Saker and Peregrine. Separation of juvenile Lanner from any plumage of Gyr and Saker already detailed under latter two.

Peregrine

Structure and Flight Medium-sized but noticeably powerful and stocky, with temperamental action (see below). Often appears rather large, bulky-bodied with heavy chest and bull-neck; wings typically broad-based with long hand tapering to distinctly pointed wingtip, commonly flexed at carpal to form triangular shape. Tail proportionately short, broad-based and square-cut. Flight exceptionally strong, swift and agile; stiff but shallow wingbeats relieved by short glides, but generally rather slow, suddenly accelerating when hunting to fast and deeper beats, usually fairly high up, to perform dashing stoop with closed wings on mostly aerial prey. Wings level or slightly upturned at tips when soaring.

Perched Compact with stout body, head sunk into shoulders; wingtips fall slightly short of tail tip. Females considerably larger (15% longer-winged) than males.

Plumage Three rather distinct races in W Palearctic. Adult *calidus* (east of Lapland) similar to adult nominate (N and C Europe and NW Russia), but on average larger, paler greyish-blue above, with larger white area on cheeks but narrower moustache, and less heavily barred below; juvenile sometimes distinguished from nominate by larger size, less heavily and more narrowly streaked underparts, generally paler upperparts with better-developed whiter forehead, supercilium and nape spot, and narrower moustache. Adult *brookei* in south of region much smaller than preceding races, more rufous (pinker) and densely barred below, darker above, and has varying amount of rufous in nape patch, but cheek patch smaller; juvenile often recognised by its more densely streaked underparts and more rufous/paler area on head. *Adult* Has complete slate-blackish 'falcon-hood' (on some *brookei*, slightly broken on nape) with thick solid moustache, and dark slate-grey upperparts with bluish or often (*brookei*) brownish tinge and often diffuse bars; white to light rufous-tinged below, with fine and dense barring except on upper breast, throat and cheeks, which are plain whitish (most extensive on males). Tail as upperparts but more conspicuously barred, bars becoming darker and broader on rear half. Bare parts mainly yellow. Readily separated from any Saker or Lanner (which see), but confusion possible between *calidus* and dark grey Gyr (compare latter), while *brookei* easily confused with Barbary Falcon (distinctions given under latter). *Juvenile* Shows prominent dark streaks on buffy underparts (though some wedge-shaped bars/blotches in flank-to-undertail-covert region); thin fringes to browner upperparts; head pattern as adult but paler, and some *calidus* have more 'open' 'falcon-hood' with longer/narrower moustache, larger pale cheek patch, forehead and nape patch, even some trace of slightly darker eye-stripe and diffuse pale supercilium, and variable crown streaking. Tail as adult, but browner and more clearly barred. Bare parts dull blue-green or grey. Confusable with all four other species (which see), and best identified by differences in structure and in head and underwing patterns; separation from juvenile Barbary extraordinarily difficult. Both adult and young Peregrine (and Barbary) have similar head pattern to some small falcons (Hobby, pale and/or juvenile Eleonora's and Sooty), but size and proportions, and some plumage aspects, usually markedly different.

Barbary Falcon

Structure and Flight Marginally smaller version of Peregrine; usually rather obviously smaller than nominate and noticeably smaller than *calidus*, but closely approaches *brookei* (which see), with which it shares many plumage characteristics. Powerful, with basic structure of Peregrine, but lighter in build, fractionally less deep-chested and with narrower arm and proportionally slightly longer tail; these relative proportions usually difficult to judge but, once learned, can be

useful, though identification on plumage features more reliable. Females markedly larger than males. Flight behaviour similar to Peregrine's, very strong and direct with rapid but shallow (largely from carpal outwards) beats interspersed with very short glides. Wingbeats distinctly quicker than Peregrine's when hunting, but foraging methods similar; small males even appear very like Merlins *F. columbarius* when hunting, with rapid wingbeats and sudden direction changes. Glides and soars as Peregrine.

Plumage Since southern race *brookei* of Peregrine is closest to Barbary in size and plumage, following text concentrates on these two (reported to overlap in range, they seem to be separated mainly by habitat, with Barbary totally adapted to desert environments); in some areas, and especially in Morocco, there is evidence of 'switching of characters' between the two, with Barbary showing more fully barred underparts and a 'falcon-hood' and the converse in *brookei*. *Adult* Age distinction as for Peregrine (which see). Despite considerable individual variation in plumage, most adults share following characters which separate them from adult *brookei* and these should be given priority. 1 HEAD PATTERN Always has some buffish on forehead (never found on *brookei*, but beware bleached or moulting near-adult which occasionally shows trace of paleness; or conversely it can be rather indistinct on more fully hooded Barbary), buff being especially conspicuous on paler-headed and variegated individuals, which usually show varying amount of rufous supercilium and better-developed rufous on nape (supercilium never found on adult *brookei*, but also missing on some dark Barbary; rufous nape, if present on *brookei*, is duller and restricted in extent, but occasionally extends onto lower crown as on many Barbary). Barbary's moustache distinctly narrower, but most important is resulting much larger and more square-cut cheek patch, sometimes reaching 0.5-1 cm below eye (*brookei* has very broad moustache, often leaving almost no pale cheek patch). Cheek patch is usually also larger than on adult nominate Peregrine but quite similar to that of *calidus*, but both these are predominantly black-headed, white and fully barred below, and usually distinctly larger. **2 UNDERPARTS** Very variable, but most Barbary show strong to duller orangey rufous-buff wash with short dark bars (chiefly flanks) and short streaks and spots (chiefly lower breast and belly) usually restricted to body sides, but sometimes obscure; rarely, more completely (but still more finely) barred below, as *brookei* (on which ground colour more pinkish). **3 UNDERWING** In distant view, Barbary shows diagnostic isolated dark crescent on greater primary coverts and darker and more extensive wingtip on paler underwing, which at close quarters shows paler/greyer, finer and reduced barring on variably buff-washed coverts and generally larger whitish (often buffish) bars on inner webs of primaries which tend to reach feather edges (whitish barring averages smaller and does not reach

edges of inner webs on most Peregrine). On all adult Peregrine, greater primary coverts match general tone and pattern of rest of coverts and remiges, coverts are whiter and dark wingtip smaller and more diffuse. **4 UPPERPARTS** Paler bluish-grey upperparts and upperwing-coverts show more contrast against darker hands and rear half of tail (adult Peregrine distinctly darker slaty-grey or blackish grey-blue with less demarcated darker remex and rectrix tips). **5 TAIL PATTERN** From above (and less so from below), Barbary, unlike most Peregrine, tends to show blacker and more distinct rear two or three bands which become progressively wider/blacker and often produce a wide terminal band, very conspicuous against distinctly pale lower back to basal half of tail or against buffish distal region below; this feature, however, varies individually on both species and can occasionally be similar on Peregrine. Superficially similar upperpart coloration

Adult Peregrine.

Juvenile Peregrine of race 'brookei'. Small. Note dark hood, large moustache and heavily blotched underparts.

Juvenile Barbary Falcon. Note head pattern and thin breast streaking.

Pale-headed juvenile Peregrine. Similar to juvenile Barbary Falcon but larger. Thicker breast streaking (barred to flanks), broad moustache.

Two adult Barbary Falcons, showing range of head and breast markings.

Small adult Peregrine of race 'brookei'. Dark above, heavily barred on pinkish underparts.

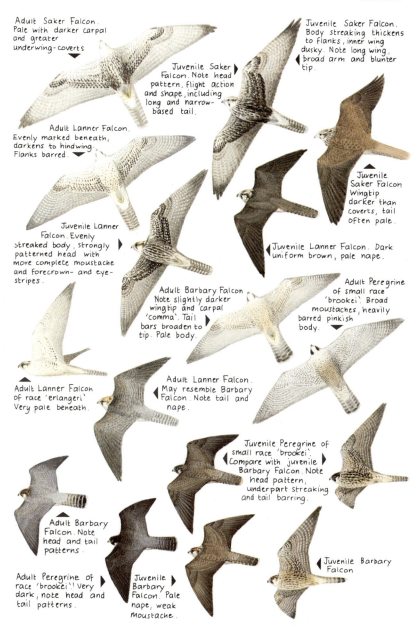

Adult Saker Falcon. Pale with darker carpal and greater underwing-coverts ▶

Juvenile Saker Falcon. Body streaking thickens to flanks, inner wing dusky. Note long wing, broad arm and blunter tip. ◀

Juvenile Saker Falcon. Note head pattern, flight action and shape, including long and narrow-based tail. ▶

Adult Lanner Falcon. Evenly marked beneath, darkens to hindwing. Flanks barred. ▶

▼ Juvenile Saker Falcon. Wingtip darker than coverts, tail often pale.

Juvenile Lanner Falcon. Evenly streaked body, strongly patterned head with more complete moustache and forecrown- and eye-stripes. ▶

◀ Juvenile Lanner Falcon. Dark uniform brown, pale nape.

Adult Barbary Falcon. Note slightly darker wingtip and carpal 'comma'. Tail bars broaden to tip. Pale body. ▶

Adult Peregrine of small race 'brookei'. Broad moustaches, heavily barred pinkish body. ◀

▲ Adult Lanner Falcon of race 'erlangeri'. Very pale beneath.

Adult Lanner Falcon. May resemble Barbary Falcon. Note tail and nape. ◀

Juvenile Peregrine of small race 'brookei'. Compare with juvenile Barbary Falcon. Note head pattern, underpart streaking and tail barring. ◀ ▶

Adult Barbary Falcon. Note head and tail patterns. ◀

Juvenile Barbary Falcon ◀

Adult Peregrine of race 'brookei'. Very dark, note head and tail patterns. ▶

Juvenile Barbary Falcon. Pale nape, weak moustache. ▶

81

may cause confusion with adult Lanner (which see). *Juvenile* Barbary and Peregrine in juvenile plumage show only fine differences; with high degree of overlap, and even intermediate individuals, only those showing extreme typical features suggesting one of the two species should be identified, while a few must be left undetermined. 1 HEAD PATTERN Most Barbary tend to have more variegated and less complete hood with better-developed rufous/buff forehead and supercilia, latter generally meeting at nape patch, and have distinctly narrower blackish moustache but conspicuously larger and unstreaked cheek patch covering entire ear-coverts (and even meeting with rufous of nape and almost reaching eye level) and quite pronounced blacker eye-stripe. Peregrine, especially *brookei*, shows clear tendency towards more complete hood with much smaller pale forehead, no or indistinct supercilium (so eye-stripe not pronounced or clearly separated from crown), smaller/darker nape patch, and much thicker moustache and correspondingly smaller and usually streaked cheek patch. Beware, however, that Peregrine of race *calidus* can approach the 'open-hooded' appearance of Barbary, with rather marked supercilium and large cheek patch, and some small males with such appearance cannot be separated on head pattern from Barbary. 2 UNDERPARTS Barbary's markings, compared with nominate, *brookei* and (less so) *calidus* Peregrine, are distinctly finer and less dense, with slender streaks forming clear and well-spaced long lines (Peregrine's denser, more rounded and broad streaks do not appear as lines); flank barring also reduced (usually concealed beneath wing when perched, but obvious on perched Peregrine), and trousers are finely streaked, usually lacking Peregrine's prominent subterminal spots/streaks/bars. 3 UNDERWING Very similar on both, but Barbary tends to be a little paler as pale bars average slightly larger on both remiges and coverts, and the small lesser coverts are more loosely barred but also streaked and

spotted (unlike most Peregrine); also lacks contrast shown by most Peregrine between paler primaries and slightly darker secondaries (latter also having darkish, incompletely pale-barred distal half, instead of Barbary's more even secondary barring). Barbary's dark wingtip more pronounced. 4 UPPERPARTS Barbary tends to be slightly paler and browner, as ground colour averages browner and rufous margins on coverts, mantle and back slightly broader, and its darker uppermantle patch ('saddle') generally stands out more from surroundings. Individual variation in both species, however (especially when paler *calidus* involved), renders these features of little use. 5 TAIL PATTERN Generally variable and overlapping, but on average Barbary's tail shows more obviously darker central pair (owing to slightly diffuse or incomplete pale bars) and terminal band (rear dark bands average darker/broader and separated by narrower and often less clear-cut pale band) than average Peregrine. 6 SUBSIDIARY FEATURES Juvenile Barbary tends to acquire stronger yellow pigment in bare parts earlier (a few have as much yellow as adults in September), but in both species this varies individually and geographically (in terms of timing of breeding) and can be similar for both. With strong sexual size dimorphism of both, and since juvenile *brookei* is closest in size to though still the most separable by plumage (head/underparts) from juvenile Barbary, while juvenile *calidus* is much larger but somewhat closer in plumage to juvenile Barbary, it appears that the trickiest Peregrine are small male *calidus*, which could be taken for large female Barbary (or vice versa). Although Barbary has rather open 'falcon-hood', it is still readily separated from similar juvenile Lanner by same characters as distinguish juvenile Peregrine from Saker/Lanner (see under Saker).

References Clark & Shirihai (1995), Forsman (1993a, in press), Gantlett & Millington (1992), Shirihai & Forsman (in press).

Partridges

Where and When Red-legged Partridge *Alectoris rufa* is common on farmland, heaths and open lowland country in western Europe east to N Italy and south throughout Spain and Corsica; introduced Britain. Chukar *A. chukar* breeds from NE Greece/S Bulgaria, Aegean islands, Turkey and Crimea eastwards through Middle East (to S Sinai) and east to Manchuria, also introduced in parts of France and Britain and in Sicily (and probably elsewhere); inhabits dry rocky slopes and hillsides (to 4500 m in Caucasus), scrub and semi-desert, locally at lower levels, where also in cultivation. Rock Partridge *A. graeca* occurs in similar habitat to Chukar, though generally remains at high altitudes (mostly on dry, grassy sunlit slopes above treeline), but from the Alps, Italy (including Sicily) and the Balkans east to C Bulgaria, overlapping marginally with Chukar in east of range.

Separating Chukar and Rock

The two are very similar in size and appearance, but their voices differ and their ranges barely overlap. Chukar differs in following plumage characters, but very close views required. **1** THROAT PATCH More buff-tinged or creamy, less clean white (or grey-tinged) than on Rock. **2** BLACK NECKLACE Usually more V-shaped across lower throat and often less well demarcated (sharply defined and evenly rounded on Rock). **3** SUPERCILIUM Generally broader and more diffuse than on Rock. **4** LORES Pale, whitish, with contrasting black lower forehead (on Rock, black of forehead extends to base of upper mandible, giving dark lores). **5** REAR EYE-STRIPE Chukar has fairly obvious broad rufous-brown area in rear eye-stripe (generally much less obvious on Rock). **6** UPPERPARTS AND BREAST Browner, less pure grey, than on Rock (note that Chukar becomes paler eastwards, and very pale sandy/greyish in parts of Middle East, where Rock, however, absent). **7** FLANK BARS Chukar tends to have broader, more widely spaced and fewer bars,

often broken/irregular on lower flanks (bars neater and more regular on Rock), but appearance depends greatly on posture and degree of dishevelment of plumage and often impossible to assess in field.

Voice Chukar has variable advertising call, often a fast rhythmic series of hoarse full notes introduced by short shriller notes, e.g. 'guk-guk-guk- . . . chukARR-chukARR- . . .'; when flushed, 'witu-witu-witu- . . .'. Rock has higher, more grating song, often stuttering and less rhythmic, with harder notes interspersed with choking sounds; alarm a rapid grating 'chituk-chituk-chituk- . . .'.

Red-legged Partridge

Readily separated from both above species by much browner appearance, bold necklace of black streaks over breast and neck sides, smaller white throat patch, and stronger supercilium contrasting with browner crown.

Hybrids

All three hybridise at least occasionally, chiefly following introductions or deliberate releases for shooting purposes.

Red-legged x Chukar Frequent in England (hybrids outnumber pure Red-legged locally), also in France. Can resemble either species but with breast markings and size of throat patch intermediate; flank barring variable, usually with clear black bars on pale ground (produced by twin bars on each feather, more as Chukar and unlike Red-legged's single-barred feathers on darker ground).

Red-legged x Rock Occasional SE France. Much as Red-legged x Chukar hybrids.

Chukar x Rock Limited interbreeding, with hybrids very closely resembling either species. In Sicily (Chukar introduced), local 'Rock' with browner appearance and narrow/broken and more pointed lower border to bib (thus closer to Chukar) may be hybrids. *Reference* Wilkinson (1991).

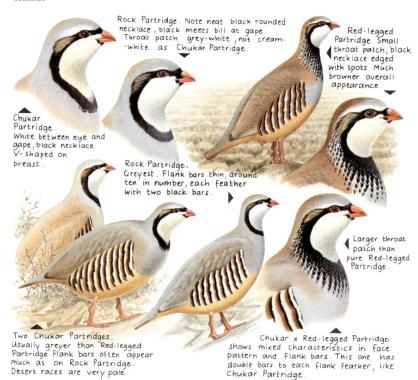

Rock Partridge. Note neat black rounded necklace, black meets bill at gape. Throat patch grey-white, not cream-white as Chukar Partridge.

Red-legged Partridge. Small throat patch, black necklace edged with spots. Much browner overall appearance.

Chukar Partridge. White between eye and gape, black necklace V-shaped on breast.

Rock Partridge. Greyest. Flank bars thin, around ten in number, each feather with two black bars.

Larger throat patch than pure Red-legged Partridge.

Two Chukar Partridges. Usually greyer than Red-legged Partridge. Flank bars often appear much as on Rock Partridge. Desert races are very pale.

Chukar x Red-legged Partridge shows mixed characteristics in face pattern and flank bars. This one has double bars to each flank feather, like Chukar Partridge.

Little and Baillon's Crakes

Where and When Both Little *Porzana parva* and Baillon's Crakes *P. pusilla* frequent marshes, shallow swamps, riparian thicket and stream/pond margins with abundant cover, breeding widely but patchily in much of C and S Europe, with restricted or casual nesting in Middle East and N Africa. Little (also breeds east to Kazakhstan) winters from S Mediterranean and Africa east to India. Palearctic populations of Baillon's winter largely in southern subtropical and tropical areas. Typically, both are very secretive and largely nocturnal, usually observed during very early or late hours of daylight.

General Features The two most closely similar of the W Palearctic crakes. Typically smaller and more slender-looking than much bulkier Spotted *P. porzana* and vagrant Sora *P. carolina* (which always look distinctly larger and heavy-bellied) and with well-defined black-and-white barring on undertail-coverts; Spotted and Sora have plain buffish or whitish undertail-coverts (but beware rare individuals with markings ranging from dark tips to almost perfect barring). Otherwise, Little and Baillon's differ in most aspects of plumage. Interestingly, Little shows clear sexual dimorphism (adult male with rich olive-buff-brown upperparts and slate-blue face and underparts, adult female

♂ Little Crake. Note muddy-brown upperparts. Underpart barring restricted to rear of legs.

Adult ♀ Little Crake has red-based bill, long primary projection, muddy-brown upperparts. Underparts largely plain, barring restricted to rear of legs. ♀ Baillon's Crake closely resembles the ♂.

Juvenile Little Crake resembles the ♀, but eye dark, more buffish fringes above. Less barred than juvenile Baillon's Crake with browner, less rufous upperparts, fewer white blotches above and a prominent supercilium.

Adult Baillon's Crake. Sexes alike. Rich chestnut above, short primary projection; dark grey below with extensive barring. All-green bill.

Juvenile Baillon's Crake. All-green bill, rich chestnut upperparts, extensive barring beneath. Numerous white marks above are ring-like. Primary projection short, but beware drooping wings giving false impression.

mostly buff and brown above and below), whereas adult Baillon's of both sexes resemble adult male Little; juvenile/1st-winter Baillon's recall female Little of same age.

Identification

Basic distinguishing criterion in all plumages is wing structure. Little's primary projection is distinctly longer (almost comparable to tertial length, with at least 5 well-spaced primary tips visible) than Baillon's, which varies from a quarter of tertial length to almost completely concealed (though often shows 3–4 closely spaced and bunched primary tips beyond longest tertial); but beware Baillon's with missing tertials, or, more commonly, with wings not fully folded, which may, seen from above, produce apparent long projection as on Little. Less obvious structural differences include Little's relatively longer wedge-shaped tail (but only slightly longer than greater extension of folded wing) and its more slender and long-necked appearance.

Adult Males Apart from longer wing extension, the most constant and practical features distinguishing Little from Baillon's are its red bill base (green on Baillon's), and its black-and-white flank barring normally being restricted to rear body and not or only just reaching leg line (on Baillon's, barring always extends well in front of leg line). Otherwise, Little is muddy olive-brown above (never chestnut-brown as Baillon's), scapulars and tertials show narrower blackish centres with wide paler olive-buff-brown fringes (Baillon's has broader blackish centres with narrow and warmer brown fringes), and slate-blue of face extends higher above eye than on Baillon's. Male Little from 1st summer onwards have reduced white flecks above, largely blotch-like in shape (Baillon's heavily marked with white streaks and ring-shaped spots).

Adult Female Little Crake In plumage adult female Little resembles buff-brown juvenile/1st-winter of both species, but uniform deep red iris indicates adult; in Baillon's, adult female nearer adult male. Adult female Little has green-yellow bill with quite large red base, long primary projection, paler and broader sandy-buff tertial and scapular fringes with narrower dark centres, and reduced body-side barring (to just in front of leg line), all unlike juvenile/1st-winter Baillon's.

Juveniles/1st-winters This plumage exists at least until late autumn and winter, when adult plumage gradually gained. Good ageing criteria are: iris colour, olive-brown (female) or olive-brown with some orange and red (male), as against deep red on adult; white tips to at least inner primaries (though normally concealed by tertials on Baillon's), lacking on adult; and heavier barring below. Little differs from Baillon's in longer 'primary extension', bill with dark green upper mandible and tip and with extensive yellow and

often also small amount of reddish-orange at base on lower mandible (Baillon's has fairly uniform deep olive-green bill), and much paler fringes to scapulars and tertials with slightly narrower dark centres (Baillon's has broader centres and narrower and warmer-coloured fringes). Ground colour of Little's upperparts and upperwing-coverts is paler olive-brown (warmer rufous-brown on Baillon's), and with far fewer white flecks: on Little, flecks are more like small blotches and normally restricted to inner mantle and back and to greater coverts; on Baillon's, often tend to be more streak-shaped and ring-shaped and extend over most of upperparts, including rump and tail-coverts and both median and greater coverts, where often arranged in rows to form double wingbar (though normally heavily and irregularly scattered on wing-coverts). Both species at this age are heavily barred below, but Little's barring is confined chiefly to rear body and upper flanks, with less on belly or breast (Baillon's much heavier barring often reaches flanks and belly). Little's supercilium is much bolder and contrastingly bordered by much darker crown; Baillon's crown is much less dark and less sharply demarcated, often fading into (or intermixed with) narrower, indistinct, buff or grey-brown supercilium.

Leg Colour The two species have quite similar olive-green legs, but on adult Little sometimes slightly tinged yellow and on Baillon's often appearing deeper and darker green; same on juveniles, but Baillon's legs then often have slight fleshy-brown element (though still predominantly olive-green).

Voice Both sexes of Little have sharp alarm call, 'kweck'; male's song a loud, accelerating 'kuak . . . kuak kuak-kuak-kwa-wa-a-a-a', while unpaired females have shorter song, a rapid 'keck-kuek-kuekwrrr'. Baillon's generally a faster and more jarring trill than Little's, and often gives a 'kek' or 'tek', but male's call and song usually 'chrrrr-wirr-wirr' or 'trrrr-trrrr-trrr' (recalling several frog species); alarm 'tyiuk' or 'check'.

References Becker & Schmidt (1990), Bradshaw (1993), Wallace (1976).

Crested Coot

Where and When Common Coot *Fulica atra* is a familiar bird throughout most of Europe, much of Middle East and locally in N Africa, whereas Crested Coot *F. cristata* occurs very locally in SW Spain (very rare) and N Morocco (scarce). Both live mostly on fresh water, Common also on larger rivers and sheltered coastal waters in winter. Frequently in mixed flocks where both present.

General Shape On water, Common appears more compact than Crested, which generally looks more elongated. Crested frequently floats with rear end higher than fore (often raises rump feathers), appearing much more rectangular and 'straighter-backed' compared with Common's more regularly rounded, rotund body shape (with highest point around centre). Crested's neck often looks longer and also somewhat slimmer, with slight tapering effect from base upwards, whereas Common shows evenly thick neck. Because of its longer body Crested's head (bill base to nape) is proportionately smaller, one-fifth or less of body length compared with about a quarter on Common (not always easy to judge: depends on posture etc).

Head Shape Even in long-range views, head shape can be a good clue to species' identity. Seen side-on, Crested shows a steep forehead with crown peaking level with or slightly in front of eye (at site of knobs when these present) and sloping down immediately into long, rounded nape, producing triangular shape. Common also has a steep forehead, but crown rather flat with peak well behind eye and angling downwards at nape, giving much more rounded shape. Differences usually obvious when the two seen together.

Bill and Bill Shield In good viewing conditions, the species reveal diagnostic differences in bill and in shape of bill shield, visible at reasonable ranges (up to 100 m or more). From the side, Crested's bill shield looks very narrow and confined to forehead; on Common, it generally appears thicker and more obvious and often extends onto crown (but

Three Crested Coots. Bill-shape differences conspicuous at long range. Note head shape, high point of back further back than on Common Coot.

Crested Coot

Common Coot has a sharp indentation of feathers which cut in between the pate and base of bill. Colour of bill tends (if at all) towards pinkish in Common Coot, bluish on Crested Coot.

Two Common Coots. Note head and shield shapes.

In flight, Crested Coot (right) lacks the white on wing of Common Coot (left).

less extensive outside breeding season). More obvious at close range is shape of loral feathering: on Crested, feathering is rounded, squared off or only slightly pointed and does not extend far into bill shield, whereas on Common it forms a strongly pointed wedge, cutting into the shield and almost separating it from the bill. In head-on views, difference even more striking (and detectable at fairly long range): on Crested, shield and bill together form narrow heart shape or elongated inverted isosceles triangle with slight indentation where the two join; on Common, shield is more of an oval shape with rounded upper edge, and is almost detached from the bill (which often appears arrowhead-shaped) by extension of loral feathering. In close views, Crested's bill has a bluish tint (more dusky outside breeding season), is slightly thinner and can appear more drooping than Common's buff/pink-tinged and slightly heavier bill, though differences subtle and by no means always obvious.

Bill-shield Knobs Totally lacking on Common. Diagnostic of Crested, but highly variable in size and often absent/invisible (especially in strong sunlight).

Plumage The only real difference is that, in flight, Crested lacks Common's narrow white trailing edge to secondaries.

Juvenile/1st-winter Young, once independent, separable by same bill/shield features as distinguish adults of the two species. 1st-winters also show above differences in head shape and general body proportions.

Voice and Behaviour Crested has a peculiar moaning or 'mooing' call, 'euugh', apparently not given by Common, and also seems less inclined to graze on waterside lawns, but otherwise little difference.

Reference Forsman (1991a).

Pratincoles

Where and When Collared *Glareola pratincola* and Black-winged Pratincoles G. *nordmanni* are chiefly summer visitors and passage migrants, largely confined to suitable wetlands in south and east; Oriental Pratincole G. *maldivarum* is an exceedingly rare vagrant from Asia. Collared breeds S Europe (and locally N Africa) east to C Asia; a widespread migrant, in southern W Palearctic mainly April-May and July-September (peak early August), often in flocks, and rare/scarce elsewhere. Black-winged breeds on steppes north of Black Sea and east to C Asia; high-altitude and continuous passage chiefly over Middle East in April-May and end August to mid November (peak second half September), with irregular and short stopovers; rare vagrant elsewhere. When not breeding, all three species frequent open ground, usually near damp habitats.

General and Ageing All three closely similar. Diagnostic is combination of tail/wingtip ratio (mainly adults), bill-base colour, and colour/pattern of trailing edge to inner wing and of underwing-coverts. Even close up or overhead a red underwing can look dark/black, so good light (strong sun from side) essential to judge underwing (often as wings held aloft on landing), and trailing edge often hard to judge and can be narrow and invisible on worn bird. Other important characters are structure and small differences in upperpart and head plumages (when comparing same-age individuals): both require good views and previous experience. Sexes (almost) alike and three major plumages distinguishable. *Adult breeding (March-August)*: upperside rather uniform grey-brown, tinged buff and olive; neat black semicircle surrounding creamy-buff throat; deep red at bill base; strong white eye-ring. *Adult non-breeding (August-February)*: as breeding, but breast mottled grey-brown and black throat band replaced by streaks, forming variably ill-defined and broken/reduced border; upperside (mainly crown) shows pale fringes; white eye-ring and red on bill greatly reduced. *Juvenile (June-August/September)*: neat whitish tips to primaries; upperparts tipped grey to buff and with dark subterminal bands; red on bill largely absent; throat line and tail fork/length also reduced. 1st-winter (July-November) much as adult non-breeding (complete post-juvenile moult starts on breeding grounds, suspended in autumn, ends chiefly early winter), but variable amount of retained juvenile feathers; red of bill reduced.

Collared and Black-winged Pratincoles

Note following features. **1** STRUCTURE Tail tip of Collared as a rule about equal to wingtip (on fresh adult, streamers slightly longer); on Black-winged wings clearly project beyond tail tip. Most juvenile Collared (and some adults with heavily worn unmoulted streamers) in early autumn can, however, have tail tip variably shorter than wingtip, so this feature of little value for juveniles and requires careful assessment of abrasion for autumn adults. Black-winged somewhat larger and slightly longer-legged; in flight looks proportionately broader-winged than Collared, and feet normally reach to about central tail feathers (fall short on Collared). **2** UNDERWING-COVERTS AND AXILLARIES Reddish-chestnut/brown on Collared; black and/or blackish-brown on Black-winged. Note that assessment of this feature rather tricky (see above), and intermediates have occurred (see Hybrids below). **3** TRAILING EDGE TO INNER UPPERWING White and rather clear on most Collared; seldom evident on Black-winged. Beware juvenile Black-winged (or 1st-winters with retained remiges) with narrow pale tips, rarely visible in field, while heavily worn Collared may have very narrow secondary tips resulting in virtual absence of white trailing edge. **4** RED OF BILL BASE On adult breeding Collared reaches nostril, on Black-winged restricted to gape area and hardly extends beyond lateral feathering of mandibles; at other ages/seasons, both have reduced red, strongly so on 1st-winters and often absent on juveniles; at comparable ages Black-winged always tends to have less red. **5** ADULT BREEDING Collared generally shows paler (but variable) mantle, scapulars and wing-coverts contrasting a little

with flight feathers; Black-winged averages darker and shows even less/no contrast. In spring, Collared tends to show greyish-brown and buff ear-coverts and nape (greyish-brown with more chestnut suffusion on Black-winged), and on most, even males, black between eye and bill base does not extend to forehead and crown (on Black-winged inter-mixed into crown and forehead, in extreme cases creating rather dark-looking head). Most Collared show fuller, pale eye-ring, with lower half complete and thick, upper half variable but narrower (can be lacking); on Black-winged white restricted to rear two-thirds of lower half. Black-winged also tends to show stronger cinnamon-buff on chest than Collared. **6** ADULT WINTER AND 1ST-WIN-TER Collared tends to have more contrast between remiges and surrounding paler upperparts (upperparts darker and less con-trasting on Black-winged) and to have less clean throat, often (mainly adult) better out-lined by ill-defined band of fine streaks, and plainer crown, nape and ear-coverts with less pale fringing; Black-winged tends to have more and broader pale fringes on head sides and less streaked throat, and shows very little sign of semicircle of pectoral streaks. **7** JUVENILE The two are very similar. Most Black-winged have darker ground colour above, and dark sepia subterminal bars narrower with thinner dark centres to tips, but variable, and much overlap between the species.

Hybrids Have been recorded where breed-ing grounds overlap, and on passage (Israel). Such birds can show mixed characters (or intermediate) between the two species.

Oriental Pratincole

At all ages has some characters of both Collared and Black-winged. Underwing-cov-erts chestnut as Collared, but with broader blackish frame, while rather darkish upper-parts and lack of white trailing edge nearer Black-winged. Juvenile (as that of Black-winged) has very narrow whitish tips to secondaries, normally not visible in field. Red of bill base intermediate between the

Summer Collared Pratincole. Tail tip equal to wingtip. Red bill base reaches nostril. Usually shows reduced black on face and fuller eye-ring.

Juvenile Collared Pratincole. Tail tip feature not reliable on young birds. Usually pale upperparts with large dark subterminal bars.

Juvenile Collared Pratincole. Note wing pattern.

Winter Collared Pratincole. Structural differences useful, often stronger throat markings, plainer head.

Adult Collared Pratincole. Rufous underwing, white trailing edge.

Note contrast in upperwing.

Adult Black-winged Pratincole. Uniform upperwing, underwing blackish. Underwing colours need to be carefully judged.

Juvenile Black-winged Pratincoles. Uniform upperwing, dark underwing, no white trailing edge.

Darker upperparts, more uniform.

Summer Black-winged Pratincole. Note position of tail tip, less red in bill, more black in face than Collared Pratincole. Long legs.

Winter Black-winged Pratincole. Note structure.

Juvenile Black-winged Pratincole. Dark ground colour, thin dark subterminal bars above.

Summer Oriental Pratincole. Mixed characters of other two species, breast warm, tail short.

In Flight, Oriental Pratincole shows rufous underwing but no white trailing edge, upperparts closer to Black-winged Pratincole. Tail short.

Winter Oriental Pratincole. Warm below to flanks. Note short tail reaching halfway along exposed primaries.

other two on adult breeding, and reduced in strength and extent on adult winter/1st-winter and strongly so on juvenile. Otherwise very similar at all times to corresponding plumages of Collared and Black-winged, except that tail as a rule much shorter than on either (falls roughly halfway between tips of primaries and tertials; valid also for juveniles); on Collared and Black-winged tail tip never (even on juveniles) shorter than two-thirds distance along exposed primaries. Due account should still be taken of abrasion and tail moult in judging this. Oriental also differs in its cinnamon-buff suffusion (mainly on chest) which, compared with the other two, is rather extensive in all plumages. Note that some Collared x Black-winged hybrids can approach Oriental in plumage.

Calls Usual call of Collared, in flight and on ground, is rather harsh and high, recalls a tern in pitch, e.g. 'kik', 'kit-ik', often a more rolling combination, e.g. 'keerr-ik-ik'. Black-winged's is lower-pitched and slower/softer, 'pwik-pwik-ik', 'chree-it' or single 'kirip'. Oriental has rather hard 'chik', 'chik-cheik' or rather soft 'chwheet'. Distinguishing between them all requires practice.

Greater and Lesser Sand Plovers

Where and When Both Greater *Charadrius leschenaultii* and Lesser Sand Plovers *C. mongolus* are of very limited occurrence in W Palearctic. Greater breeds sporadically and locally in some Middle East countries (e.g. Turkey, Jordan), and is frequent on passage/ in winter in Levant (e.g. Israel, where may be seen throughout year) but vagrant farther west. Lesser is accidental in Levant and west of there, though variably common on passage and less so in winter in some coastal areas of Arabia/Iran and E Africa.

Identification One of the most difficult species-pairs in the region, especially when dealing with solitary individuals, and normally requires some field experience and awareness of extent of geographical and individual variation. Identification even of breeding-plumaged males of some races not always straightforward. Geographical differences can lead to overlap in some plumage features, or even a degree of reversal of structural characters, and viewing conditions often influence the appearance of birds. Following fairly constant features (though with a degree of overlap), used in combination, should enable separation, but must be used with extreme care. **1** JIZZ When relaxed, Lesser shows more upright and pear-shaped posture, with much of body in front of legs, giving impression that legs are more 'united' with rear body than on Greater (on which legs more in mid-body, producing more horizontal carriage with longer rear end). On Lesser, this, together with its small size (about 10% smaller than Greater), can often produce body shape more like Ringed Plover *C. hiaticula,* as opposed to Greater's rather disproportionately heavy body. **2** HEAD SHAPE Lesser usually has rounded head with steeper forehead, lacking Greater's flattish crown with more sloping and in general broader forehead. **3** BILL Variable on both. On Lesser, normally less robust and with indistinct gonydeal angle, and length approximately equal to distance between bill base and rear of eye, with tip (nail) shorter than rest of bill, and mandibles tapering more steeply, giving blunter, stubbier impression. Greater usually has heavier bill with better-developed gonydeal angle, perceptibly longer than distance between bill base and rear of eye, with nail longer than rest of bill, and usually more smoothly tapering. **4** LEG COLOUR AND LENGTH Lesser has shorter legs (including tarsus and exposed tibia) than the very 'leggy' Greater, on which tibia clearly longer and feet always project beyond tail tip in flight (on Lesser, little or no foot projection). On Greater, legs usually grey with green or fleshy-yellow tinge, sometimes darker on toe joints; Lesser has somewhat darker, mostly grey or dark grey-green legs with toe joints same colour. **5** WINGBAR In flight, Lesser's inner wingbar generally broader on outer secondaries and with fairly straight rear edge on primaries; inner bar on Greater usually narrower and less prominent, but rear edge of outer bar bulges on inner primaries. **6 TAIL PATTERN** Lesser shows less white in tip/sides of tail than Greater and lacks latter's darker (than upperparts) subterminal bar contrasting with paler basal area. **7 FLIGHT CALL** Lesser gives hard 'chitik', 'chi-chi-chi' and 'kruit-kruit', rather short and sharp. Greater has softer, longer trilling 'prrrirt' or 'kyrrrr . . . trrr', somewhat recalling Turnstone *Arenaria interpres*, but Lesser often gives identical trill, especially on ground.

Subspecific Variation Western race *columbinus* of Greater (occurs chiefly Near East) averages smaller, with shortest/thinnest bill lacking strongly arched nail and with almost straight gonys (approaches bill shape of *atrifrons* group of Lesser), and requires great caution in identification. A further complication comes from fact that Lesser has five races, and these may be separated into two groups: *atrifrons* group (breeds C Asia; three races), in which bill and tarsus relatively longer and breeding-plumaged male tends to show more complete black forehead and lacks black line bordering upper breast; and *mongolus* group (NE Asia/Siberia; two races), with comparatively shorter bill and tarsus, and with forehead variegated or largely white and with prominent black band on upper border of breast on breeding male. Variation in Lesser mainly clinal, but bill and leg lengths tend to increase from northeast to southwest over breeding (and in part winter) range. In western winter ranges (e.g. Middle East, NE Africa) some overlap may occur between relatively shorter-billed *columbinus* Greater and relatively longer-billed *atrifrons* group of Lesser, at times rendering bill length/shape of little use (chiefly with lone individuals in the field), though experience shows that for most such birds bill simply requires greater care in examination. Same applies to leg length. Large overlap exists between the species in male breeding plumage, influenced in part also by geographical variation: race *columbi-*

nus of Greater tends (unlike other races) to have wider rufous breast band, almost as on many Lesser; black line bordering upper breast, though often regarded as a good feature of Lesser (mainly of eastern races), also occurs rarely among all populations of Greater; cinnamon tinge to upperparts of Greater (mainly *columbinus*) is often a good feature as against cleaner brown of Lesser's upperparts, but some Lesser may show a little of this and many Greater (mainly of eastern races) lack this altogether; large overlap occurs in head pattern, but full black forehead/mask present in *atrifrons* group of Lesser apparently does not exist on Greater.

General Ageing and Sexing Both species undergo complete post-breeding moult (Greater shortly after breeding, Lesser usually later in autumn), followed by partial pre-breeding moult from midwinter to early spring. Breeding-plumaged male usually strongly coloured/patterned, but Greater more sexually dimorphic, with female usually lacking distinctive breeding plumage and closely resembling winter birds (as many 1st-summers of both species), but very old females of both approach male in plumage. Juveniles differ from non-breeding adults in having pale fringes and variable/indistinct dark subterminal bands to wing-coverts and upperpart feathers; 1st-winter plumage acquired by moult of these parts, but often not fully, and this (retained worn juvenile feathers) distinguishes them from adult winter. 1st-summers usually show very worn remiges and less conspicuous plumage coloration/pattern than adults.

Likelihood of Confusion with Other Species Both species (especially Greater) distinctly larger than Kentish Plover *C. alexandrinus* and in all plumages lack latter's whitish hindneck and have better-developed breast-side patches or complete breast band. Similar-sized Caspian Plover *C. asiaticus* easily distinguished from both in juvenile and non-breeding plumages by its slimmer body with distinctly tapering rear, slimmer bill, narrower wingbar, and bold supercilium with dark-capped appearance and dark ear-

Two summer Greater Sand Plovers of eastern race 'crassirostris'. Some show black on breast. Bill large with 'blob' on tip. Bill equal or greater than length from bill base to rear of eye.

Summer Greater Sand Plover of western race 'columbinus'. Breast band continues down flanks as on Lesser Sand Plover. Upperparts often washed with orange. Bill small on this race.

Non-breeding Greater Sand Plover. Note long legs usually greyish or greenish with darker joints and toes, sloping forehead and bill shape.

Greater Sand Plover

Lesser Sand Plover.

Juvenile Greater Sand Plover.

Legs of Greater Sand Plover extend beyond tail, primary wingbar bulges. Lesser Sand Plover has even-width wingbar, extending further towards body.

Summer Lesser Sand Plover of eastern race 'mongolicus'. No orange in back, small bill.

Lesser Sand Plover in non-breeding plumage.

Juvenile Lesser Sand Plover.

Summer Lesser Sand Plover of southern race 'atrifrons'. Black forehead, broad breast band, no orange to upperparts. Legs dark, shorter in the tibia.

♀ Caspian Plover. Full breast band, tapering body. Note bill shape.

Juvenile Caspian Plover.

Caspian Plover. Note narrower wingbar than Sand Plovers.

93

Lesser Sand Plover. Bill length equal to distance from bill base to rear of eye. Bill less obviously blob-ended; shorter or equal to half of bill, tip blunter.

Greater Sand Plovers. Bill length equal or longer than distance from bill base to rear of eye. Note more obvious blob end to bill, which tapers to the tip.

♀ Caspian Plover. Note long thin bill without thickening at tip.

covert band usually joining clearer buffish/whitish loral region and forehead, all giving distinctive elegant appearance; reasonably fresh adult Caspian also tends to show more obvious narrow pale fringes to upperparts and coverts, and breeding-plumaged male has unmistakable dark lower border to well-developed and complete-looking rufous breast band; in flight (and at rest) wings appear longer and more pointed, with uppersides less patterned and underwings slightly duskier, and often gives sharp 'giut' call.

References Hayman *et al.* (1986), Hirschfeld (1991), Hollom *et al.* (1988), Rogers (1982), Taylor (1982/83, 1987).

Vagrant Stints

Where and When Semipalmated *Calidris pusilla*, Western *C. mauri* and Least Sandpipers *C. minutilla* are Nearctic vagrants, the vast majority to coastal parts of Britain and Ireland, mostly in late summer/autumn (but increasingly in spring, and Least and Semipalmated have overwintered); Semipalmated more or less annual, Least far less frequent, and Western exceedingly rare. Red-necked *C. ruficollis* and Long-toed Stints *C. subminuta* breed in E Siberia: the former has been recorded in the region a mere handful of times (most in Sweden) and the latter on a dozen or so occasions, with no particular pattern but predominantly in early autumn. All need to be distinguished from Little Stint *C. minuta*, which breeds on northern tundra and is common on passage throughout the region, wintering in region mainly in Mediterranean, where locally abundant.

Ageing An essential first step in stint identification is correct ageing. The following summarises briefly the sequence of plumages and their characteristics. Fresh *juvenile* (from about July/August, i.e. when adults in moult) typically has very neat pale fringes to upperparts and wings and is normally the brightest of all plumages (wear reduces crispness and brightness as autumn progresses); scapulars (especially lower ones) smaller than on adults. *1st-winter* plumage (gained by moult of head, body and scapular feathers and usually some wing-coverts, typically during September-November) very like adult winter (see below), but with some retained, worn juvenile remiges and some coverts. Partial moult about December-May (variable number of flight and tail feathers, followed by all head, body and wing-covert feathers) produces *1st-summer* plumage, usually much as adult summer (see below) but variable, and can contain some winter-type feathers; many individuals, however, depending on species, spend 1st summer around wintering area and have plumage much as winter. Complete moult from late June to end September (but flight and tail feathers often not fully renewed until February) produces *adult winter* plumage, comparatively plain greyish/brownish with few distinguishing features, and generally apparent from October onwards. Moult of head, body and some inner wing-coverts in about January-April leads to much brighter *adult summer* plumage: when very fresh, pale upperpart and wing-feather fringes conceal underlying rufous tones, but fringes soon wear off; further wear during summer frequently produces dark-looking, untidy plumage by July/August. In transitional stages (i.e. during moult), birds show contrasting pattern of old, worn (pointed) feathers and fresh (usually much paler and brighter, rounded) ones, and correct ageing and identification requires careful examination of all feather tracts. All these factors, and the fact that some individuals may moult earlier/later than times given, should be borne in mind when interpreting descriptions which follow. **Identification** Additional important features are shape and structure (bill, toes, primary projection, etc) and voice; behaviour can also be a pointer (but no more). Remember that all *Calidris* waders have five rows of scapulars, 3 upper and 2 lower; scapular V is formed by pale outer edges of 3rd row from top, and mantle V by pale edges of outer feathers. It is stressed that all stints are extremely hard to separate in winter plumages, while correct identification of a vagrant requires thorough familiarity with all plumages of Little, hence its inclusion here (Temminck's Stint *C. temminckii*, sufficiently distinct, should cause no problems and is not discussed further; see Harris *et al.* 1989). The stints can be grouped into three pairs of closely related and very similar species, each group having particular characteristics. Descriptions apply mostly to typical individuals. Note that it is essential to use a combination of all features; even so, and with prolonged close views (always necessary) and good photos, odd individuals may still not be identifiable with total certainty.

Little and Red-necked Stints

Shape and Structure Both are rather small-headed, Red-necked having more rounded forehead. Comparatively long primary projection (3-4 well-spaced tips normally visible), but this not always reliable. Importantly, Red-necked has longest wings of any stint, looking elongated and attenuated at rear (can be striking in mixed flocks) and with lower, flatter head-to-tail profile.

Bare Parts Both have stout-based, short black bill: Little's averages marginally longer and fine-tipped, lower mandible showing very slight decurvature; Red-necked's fairly blunt-tipped (sometimes slight 'blob' effect) and straight or slightly decurved. Legs black on both, in some lights can appear tinged greenish, greyish or brownish (beware: mud-covered legs often look pale); toes unwebbed.

Plumage Juvenile Typical individuals reasonably separable. 1 HEAD Red-necked shows somewhat plainer head than Little, with greyer (uniformly streaked) crown, often duller supercilium (no split effect), with white sides to forehead and black lores often rather prominent; more evenly marked ear-coverts (tending to lack Little's paler patch behind eye) also contribute to more uniform head pattern. On Little, dark central crown contrasts with (usually) prominent white supercilium and narrow lateral crown-stripe (split supercilium) and with pale grey nape/hindneck. 2 UPPERPARTS On Red-necked, inner wing-coverts and lower scapulars fairly plain grey with darker shaft streaks (lower scapulars with dark 'lozenge' shape at tip), contrasting with blackish-centred and rufous-fringed upper scapulars and mantle (Little has black centres and sharp pale/rufous fringes to inner greater coverts and to both upper and lower scapulars, not contrasting with mantle); mantle and scapular Vs either lacking or indistinct on Red-necked (mantle V and usually also scapular V very obvious on Little), and tertials greyish-centred with dark shaft streaks and whitish fringes or occasionally some rufous near tip (tertials black-centred with pale to strong rufous fringes on

Juvenile Little Stint. Note dark central crown, split supercilium and cream mantle 'V', also lower scapula pattern and black centred tertials. Buffy or orangey breast patch. A few individuals are much greyer and less strongly patterned.

Summer adult Red-necked Stint. Plain brick-red face and throat, wing-coverts largely grey.

Juvenile Red-necked Stint. Note exact pattern of lower scapulars and grey-centred tertials. Breast streaking greyish, faint but extensive. Head pattern relatively plain.

Summer adult Sanderling can resemble summer Red-necked Stint. Note pale area beneath eye, streaked ear-coverts, distinct pale centres to scapulars, greater coverts and patterned tertials. Sanderling lacks a hind toe.

Summer adult Little Stint. Note white throat speckled face and cream mantle 'V', warm non-contrasting wing coverts and tertials (greyer and contrasting on Red-necked Stint).

Winter Red-necked Stint. Often appears more elongated than shown here.

Winter Red-necked Stint. Dark of lores often runs through eye and across ear-coverts.

1st-winter Little Stint. Dark of lores separated from eye, usually more prominent breast patch and darker feather centres to upperparts, but often impossible to separate from Red-necked Stint on plumage.

Little). Note that occasional Little are much greyer above, with little/no rufous and indistinct V marks, and may, rarely, have rear lower scapulars very like Red-necked. **3 BREAST PATTERN** Red-necked often shows pinky-grey wash on breast sides or sometimes across entire breast, with extensive faint (diffuse) streaking on breast sides. Little has an initially strong orangey/rufous wash on breast sides (sometimes extending faintly across breast), with usually only a few dark, but sharp, streaks. *Adult winter/1st-winter* The two are very similar, rather uniform brownish-grey above with darker shaft streaks, and extremely difficult/impossible to separate on plumage alone. Red-necked averages slightly paler (more greyish) and more uniform above, with less extensive dark feather centres, and often shows dark area on head (blackish lores extending through eye to ear-coverts). Little sometimes has faintly streaked complete pale greyish breast band (apparently never shown by Red-necked). Considerable individual variation, however, and structure (more elongated appearance of Red-necked) more useful in field. 1st-winters of both retain some worn, browner, juvenile wing-coverts. *Adult summer* Typical individuals more easily separable with good views. Best features of Red-necked are: unstreaked bright brick-red coloration of head (crown dark-streaked), throat and breast (breast with extensive white fringes when fresh), but red variable in extent (can include most of head, throat and upper breast or be confined to ear-coverts and a thin band across upper breast); blackish chevrons forming generally complete necklace (beneath the red) on lower breast and distinctly white breast sides, with streaks extending to upper flanks; chin and forehead often white, with pale supercilium (often more prominent behind eye); mantle, scapulars and sometimes some tertials have black centres and broad bright rusty fringes, but inner wing-coverts and most/all tertials (and often some/many lower scapulars) very contrastingly plainer, greyish or brownish (as winter); mantle V variably distinct, can be faint/lacking. Little has orangey or chestnut

head and breast (including sides) extensively streaked/spotted dark (can appear uniform from distance), but throat always white; usually has pale split supercilium (variable); inner wing-coverts, lower scapulars and tertials do not contrast with rest of upperparts; mantle V usually prominent (but less than on juvenile). Note that summer-plumaged Sanderling *C. alba* can resemble Red-necked, but is larger, bulkier, has fine streaking on ear-coverts and throat, lacks hind toe and, when worn, lacks dark necklace (see also Grant 1986).

Voice Little gives a short, sharp, fairly high-pitched 'tit', 'stit' or 'chit' flight call, often in short series; Red-necked's is less sharp, slightly lower and more squeaky, 'week', but often with an 'l' or 'r' sound, 'kreep', 'klüt', 'klürp'. Much practice needed, however, to interpret calls, which also vary depending on bird's 'mood' or degree of alarm.

Behaviour Little is usually very active and lively, making fast runs, but will also pick more slowly and methodically. Red-necked often similar, though frequently more lethargic, more deliberate in feeding actions.

Semipalmated and Western Sandpipers

These two very similar species need also (especially Semipalmated) to be distinguished from Little Stint (see above).

Shape and Structure Semipalmated rather as Little in shape, marginally stouter, and has shortish primary projection (2-3 closely spaced tips). Western similar but with comparatively larger and squarer head and longer body (looks rather flat-backed and often front-heavy), with very short primary projection (1-2 closely spaced tips).

Bare Parts Classic Semipalmated have short (1-2 times loral length), straight, deep-based and blunt-tipped bill, often with lateral expansion at tip ('blob-tipped' effect), but some have longer, slightly decurved or down-kinked bill close to Western (overlap with shorter-billed birds of latter). Western typically has longer/much longer (up to 3 times loral length), slightly decurved, more

Juvenile Little Stint (greyer variant). Note primary projection, longest tertial ends over tip of second visible primary tip. Prominent split supercilium, cream mantle 'V'; lower scapulars and greater coverts black-centred, sharply fringed.

Juvenile Semipalmated Sandpiper. Deep-based blunt-tipped bill. Upperparts greyer than Little or Western, evenly patterned (scaly); lacks mantle 'V'. Broad dark shaft streak and anchor mark on lower scapulars. Breast-side streaking rather extensive. Toes partially webbed.

Juvenile Western Sandpiper. Long bill, slightly curved. Upper scapulars prominently edged rufous, lower scapulars greyish with narrow dark shaft streak and arrowhead; rear lower scapulars more pointed than on Semipalmated Sandpiper. Partially webbed toes.

Summer adult Western Sandpiper. Strikingly rufous-chestnut on ear-coverts, crown and scapulars, wing coverts grey. Arrowhead marks on breast and flanks.

Dull above, no mantle 'V'.

Summer adult Semipalmated Sandpiper with extreme bill length. Heavy breast streaking extends to flanks.

Winter Western Sandpiper. Slightly more uniform and paler than Little Stint. Very like Semipalmated but somewhat greyer, and fine breast streaking usually stronger, more extensive.

Winter Little Stint. Grey, often with darker centres to rear scapulars.

Winter Semipalmated Sandpiper. Slightly more uniform than Little Stint, lacks split supercilium. Feet partially webbed on Semipalmated and Western Sandpipers, not on Little Stint.

tapering and fine-tipped bill (can recall Dunlin *C. alpina*). Both have legs as Little Stint, but toes partially webbed; Western often looks slightly longer-legged than Semipalmated.

Plumage Juvenile Main distinguishing features are: **1** HEAD Typical Semipalmated have prominent whitish supercilium, contrasting with fairly uniformly streaked dark crown (lacks clear split-supercilium effect and dark crown 'ridge'), dark lores and dark ear-coverts; narrow white eye-ring often accentuated by greyish/streaked area above eye. Western can look comparatively 'pale-faced', with prominent white supercilium usually broadest on forehead sides, contrasting with dark loral line, and ear-coverts paler (as nape) than on Semipalmated; streaked crown greyish, usually darker in centre (usually with rufous tones, which also frequently present on ear-coverts); upper half of thin white eye-ring sometimes merges with supercilium. **2** UPPERPARTS On Semipalmated, generally much less rufous and more scaly in appearance than on Little Stint or Western Sandpiper: dark-centred feathers (inner coverts slightly paler) have prominent buff/whitish fringes; rear lower scapulars show broad dark shaft streak with very broad anchor-shaped 'blob' inside whitish tip; V marks lacking or very faint. Western is greyish or rufous above, but always with some rich rufous fringes on at least mantle and prominently on upper scapulars, with lower scapulars and inner coverts normally contrastingly greyer (rear lower scapulars more pointed in shape than on Semipalmated, with narrower shaft streak and dark arrowhead shape inside white tip); mantle and scapular Vs faint or lacking (sometimes more distinct). Note that some Semipalmated can show some stronger rusty tones to upperparts and crown, and the brightest of these can be very like Red-necked, Western or Little. **3** BREAST PATTERN Typical fresh Semipalmated has buffish wash often extending across whole breast, with fairly extensive (but diffuse) dark streaking at sides, while fresh Western has pale to fairly strong orangey-buff wash to

breast, with sometimes better-defined dark streaks at sides (breast markings, however, variable). *Adult winter/1st-winter* Upperparts of both average slightly more uniform than on Little Stint (lone individuals difficult to judge). Semipalmated tends to be a shade browner, less grey, than Western (which is also paler than Little/Red-necked), and below has diffuse streaking restricted to greyish breast sides (centre of breast white), whereas Western has fine but sharply defined streaks on pale grey breast sides (at very close range seen to extend as complete narrow band of very fine streaks across whole breast). 1st-winters of both show worn retained juvenile wing-coverts (browner and more broadly paler-fringed than more uniform, greyer adult winter feathers). Of interest is that most juvenile Western appear to moult earlier (from late August) than Semipalmated, but this may not be relevant to vagrants (which often delay moult). *Adult summer* Relatively easy to separate. Fresh-plumaged Semipalmated dull above, with dark feathers fringed greyish/buff (V marks absent or very faint), lacking obvious rufous (with wear, can show some brighter tinges above and on crown and ear-coverts), but with inner wing-coverts brownish-grey and contrasting with black-centred scapulars; heavy streaking across breast extends to upper flanks. Western normally highly distinctive, with chestnut colour, especially around head, very striking: extensive rufous-chestnut bases to lower scapulars and usually also on sides of crown, ear-coverts and upper scapulars, with fairly contrasting plain greyish inner wing-coverts and tertials; below, arrowhead markings cover entire breast and extend well down flanks, often continuing as streaks onto undertail-coverts (in worn plumage, marks may form almost solid blackish areas on breast). In late summer, when moult to winter almost complete, presence of just one or two arrowheads is diagnostic of Western.

Voice Semipalmated has a coarse, distinctly low-pitched, short 'turp', 'chrrup' or 'krrüt'. Western gives thin, high-pitched 'jeet' or 'krreep', rather drawn-out, but will often utter fairly harsh Dunlin-like 'kree'.

Behaviour Semipalmated much as Little Stint, but also occasionally more hesitant (almost plover-like) in feeding action. Western more akin to Dunlin, tends to be more methodical in surface-picking movements, frequently probes in mud; often wades, in deeper water than other stints.

Least and Long-toed Sandpipers

Shape and Structure Least is the smallest of all stints, tiny, with steeper and more rounded forehead than almost equally small Long-toed's longer, flatter forehead; appears short-legged, short-necked and often hunched (more compact), whereas Long-toed is longer-legged and longer-necked, with smallish head (can recall miniature Wood Sandpiper *Tringa glareola*). Both (especially Long-toed) can look long-bodied, and have very short/invisible primary projection (1 or 2 closely spaced tips). In flight, toes project distinctly beyond tail on Long-toed but not on Least (but latter shows somewhat clearer wingbar).

Bare Parts Both have medium-length, fairly narrow-based and fine-tipped black bill, often slightly decurved (note lower edge of lower mandible); Long-toed has clear pale (yellowish) base to lower and sometimes also upper mandible (whole base always dark on Least). Both have pale (yellowish, yellow-green, yellow-brown, even dull orangey) legs (but beware dark-legged stints with mud-covered legs) and unwebbed, rather long toes; on Long-toed, however, middle toe abnormally long, clearly longer than bill length (about same as bill on Least).

Plumage In most plumages, Least generally appears browner, with fewer bright colours than Long-toed, which can recall Sharp-tailed Sandpiper *C. acuminata* in general pattern (particularly of head). Both can resemble Pectoral Sandpiper *C. melanotos* (exceptionally small individuals of latter not unknown). *Juvenile* Easily distinguished by following characters. 1 HEAD Least is generally plainer and less contrasting, with duller supercilia

meeting across forehead (can occasionally have very narrow darker central forehead) and dark lores, cheeks and ear-coverts with slightly paler area below/behind eye (so dark ear-covert patch may appear more obliquely positioned than on Long-toed). On Long-toed, supercilia normally whiter, stop short of dark forehead (but often drop down to break loral stripe) and continue strongly behind eye to meet paler, grey-brown nape (creating capped effect), often with whitish or pale rufous outer crown-stripe giving split supercilium (can be striking); whole pattern is emphasised by generally more solidly dark rear ear-coverts. 2 UPPERPARTS Overall, Least looks more scalloped above compared with 'stripy' appearance of Long-toed; usually has rufous fringes but colour subdued (and rapidly becomes rather dull, in August/September), and wing-covert fringes complete and more buffish (not white), giving comparatively more uniform pattern (mantle V inconspicuous). Long-toed much brighter rufous, with tertial edges prominently rufous/rusty, and with clear, contrasting whitish tips/fringes to inner median coverts (but pale tips usually broken by thin dark central line), and frequently shows distinctive mantle V; lower scapulars normally longer and with larger black area near tip than on Least. Both become much plainer when worn, but Long-toed should still average somewhat less uniform than Least. 3 BREAST On Least, buffy-brown with rather uniform coarse dark streaks often forming breast band; on Long-toed, streaks finer and often extend to flanks (unmarked on Least), but breast centre often paler/unstreaked. *Adult winter/1st-winter* Both are much browner (less grey) than other stints treated here. Best separated by pattern of scapulars and (mainly inner) wing-coverts: on Long-toed these have well-marked black-ish centres and contrasting broad greyish-brown fringes (on Least, diffuse dark centres/shaft streaks and narrow pale fringes, creating less contrasty pattern). Note that differences become less marked in worn plumage, but Long-toed's larger dark centres still more obvious. Head pattern much as for juveniles

Juvenile Little Stint.
Note primary projection,
leg colour and lower
scapular pattern compared
with Long-toed Stint.

Juvenile Long-toed Stint. Note yellowish
legs, long middle toe, pale base to bill, pale
loral area and split supercilium. Strongly
patterned above, scapulars long with black
centres reaching tip of feather. Breast
centre often unmarked. Distinct pale spot
before eye, loral stripe almost broken.

Summer adult Long-toed Stint
typically shows a split
supercilium. Note pale base
to bill. Brightly patterned
above including broad rusty
edges to tertials.

Juvenile Least Sandpiper. Short pale legs separate
from Little Stint. Note stronger loral
stripe than Long-toed Stint, supercilia
meeting above bill, breast streaking
usually coarser.

Summer adult Least
Sandpiper. Much duller
and browner than
Long-toed Stint. Note
differences in head
pattern.

Winter Least Sandpiper. Less
contrast within upperparts than
Long-toed Stint. Dark
lores, heavily spotted
breast, all black bill.

Winter Long-toed Stint. Browner than
Little Stint, similar to Least Sandpiper.
Note head pattern, more distinct dark
centres to upperpart feathers.

101

(but more subdued). 1st-winter Long-toed normally retains juvenile wing-coverts (well worn), whereas Least can lose some/all coverts in post-juvenile moult. *Adult summer* Least often shows less extensive rufous on mantle, scapulars, wing-coverts and tertials and looks browner and duller than Long-toed, though some can appear equally rufous (but Long-toed generally has broader and brighter rusty edges to tertials); Least not uncommonly has somewhat scalloped shape to pale edges of inner coverts (and occasionally innermost tertials), rarely, if ever, shown by Long-toed; both show fairly obvious pale mantle V. Differences in head and breast patterns and bill colour much as for juveniles.

Voice Least's typical call a very high, rising 'kreee' or 'kreet' (sometimes a lower 'prrrt'), Long-toed's a lower, softer 'chree', 'chuilp' or similar.

Behaviour Both species feed by picking, when Least normally more crouched or hunched. Both frequently adopt upright stance, long-necked and long-legged, recalling Wood Sandpiper, and/or stretch neck well forward (even running in this posture), when remarkably like small crake *Porzana*. Both, and especially Long-toed, also skulk in vegetation at edge of mud.

References Alström & Olsson (1989), Chandler (1989), Doherty (1991), Grant (1986b), Jonsson & Grant (1984).

White-rumped and Baird's Sandpipers

Where and When White-rumped *Calidris fuscicollis* and Baird's Sandpipers *C. bairdii* are Nearctic vagrants (Baird's extending into NE Siberia), most frequently to NW Europe (majority in Britain and Ireland) and mainly in autumn (July-November), most July-August records being of adults (especially in E Britain), later ones mostly juveniles; adults increasingly recorded in spring, in May-June. White-rumped generally favours coastal marshes, salt or fresh (occasional inland), while Baird's tends to prefer freshwater areas (especially inland) but also drier habitats (e.g. airfields, grassland etc); both may occur in any wetland, including open shores.

Identification

Ageing much as for other calidrids (see notes under Vagrant Stints).

Size, Structure and Bare Parts Both are smaller than Dunlin *C. alpina* (though White-rumped can equal small Dunlin) but larger than Little Stint, and markedly long-winged (wings project well past tail tip at rest), appearing elongated. Relatively short-legged. White-rumped has medium-length bill (slightly shorter than head length) which is slightly decurved (note lower edge of lower mandible) and can appear slightly swollen at tip; black, usually with paler (orangey or

pinkish) area at base of lower mandible. Baird's has bill about same length as head (or slightly shorter), somewhat thinner-looking than White-rumped's, virtually straight and with fine pointed tip, and invariably all black. Both have black legs, occasionally with greenish tinge in some lights.

Plumage *Juvenile* Both have streaky head pattern with variably distinct supercilium, neatly pale-fringed upperparts including scapulars and wing-coverts, and white underparts with distinct darker breast well demarcated from white belly. Following should enable separation. 1 HEAD White-rumped usually shows shortish, fairly contrasting whitish supercilium against dark-streaked rusty crown and rear ear-coverts, well-marked dark lores, and greyish hindneck (finely dark-streaked) contrasting with mantle. Baird's has sandy-buff tone to whole head, which is finely streaked all over and lacks any truly contrasting features: usually has slightly paler, indistinct supercilium, and diffuse (but broader) loral bar with prominent white spot above at side of forehead. 2 MANTLE, SCAPULARS AND WING-COVERTS On White-rumped, feathers of mantle and upper scapulars blackish with rusty edges, but outer mantle feathers (often also lower row of upper scapulars) have contrastingly

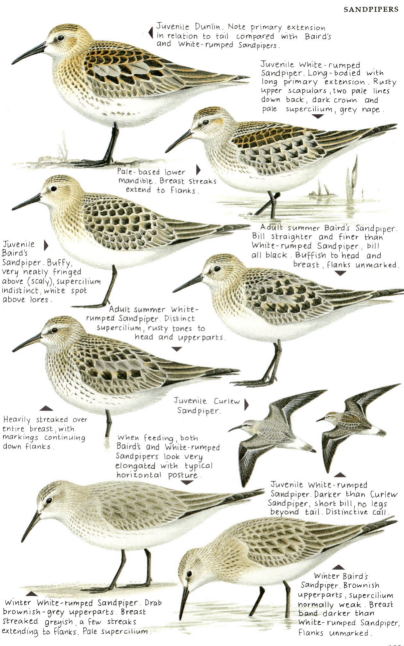

Juvenile Dunlin. Note primary extension in relation to tail compared with Baird's and White-rumped Sandpipers.

Juvenile White-rumped Sandpiper. Long-bodied with long primary extension. Rusty upper scapulars, two pale lines down back, dark crown and pale supercilium, grey nape.

Pale-based lower mandible. Breast streaks extend to flanks.

Adult summer Baird's Sandpiper. Bill straighter and finer than White-rumped Sandpiper, bill all black. Buffish to head and breast, flanks unmarked.

Juvenile Baird's Sandpiper. Buffy, very neatly fringed above (scaly), supercilium indistinct, white spot above lores.

Adult summer White-rumped Sandpiper. Distinct supercilium, rusty tones to head and upperparts.

Juvenile Curlew Sandpiper.

Heavily streaked over entire breast, with markings continuing down flanks.

When feeding, both Baird's and White-rumped Sandpipers look very elongated with typical horizontal posture.

Juvenile White-rumped Sandpiper. Darker than Curlew Sandpiper, short bill, no legs beyond tail. Distinctive call.

Winter Baird's Sandpiper. Brownish upperparts, supercilium normally weak. Breast band darker than White-rumped Sandpiper, flanks unmarked.

Winter White-rumped Sandpiper. Drab brownish-grey upperparts. Breast streaked greyish, a few streaks extending to flanks. Pale supercilium.

white outer edges forming prominent V; lower scapulars largely buff at bases and tipped white; wing-coverts dark-centred with buffish edges and white tips. (Often moult begins early; from late August can show some contrasting grey 1st-winter feathers in mantle and upper scapulars.) Baird's has very different appearance: entire mantle, scapulars and wing-coverts dark-centred (scapulars and coverts often buff at bases, but this rarely obvious) with very neat whitish or pale buff fringes, producing very obvious, regular scaly or scalloped pattern. (Baird's normally delays moult entirely until reaching winter quarters.) 3 TERTIALS Both have dark-centred tertials, but on White-rumped edged rusty or buffish and tipped white and on Baird's edged pale buff/whitish and often tipped white. 4 BREAST PATTERN White-rumped has broad, very pale grey (occasionally faintly buff-tinged) breast band with obvious fine dark streaks, latter generally extending indistinctly down upper flanks (which usually have pale greyish ground colour) and, rarely, being repeated on sides of undertail-coverts. Baird's almost invariably shows distinct buff breast band with very fine short streaks ending abruptly on lower breast to form clear pectoral band (can recall Pectoral Sandpiper *C. melanotos* in sharpness); streaks become more diffuse on breast sides and never extend onto white flanks. *Adult winter/1st-winter* White-rumped is drab-looking, predominantly greyish (tinged brown) above, with darker feather centres/shafts visible mostly on scapulars and mantle; whitish supercilium usually fairly conspicuous against brown-grey crown; white below, with finely streaked, greyish breast and normally a few streaks extending to flanks. (Can acquire largely adult winter plumage as early as August.) Baird's less dull, more warm sandy-brown above (though occasional individuals distinctly grey), often with at least a hint of scaly patterning, and normally with very weak supercilium; buffish breast band (normally somewhat darker than on White-rumped) marked with very fine and indistinct streaks, latter not extending onto flanks (unlike White-rumped). 1st-winters of

both species retain some worn juvenile scapulars and wing-coverts. *Summer* White-rumped differs clearly from Baird's in having light rusty edges to feathers of crown, ear-coverts and mantle (extending to upper scapulars), a usually obvious whitish supercilium, and bold black streaking over whole breast and extending as bold chevrons well down flanks; in very fresh plumage, rusty tones may be concealed by grey feather tips, becoming more prominent as tips wear off. Baird's much less brightly marked, with buff replacing White-rumped's rusty colours (occasionally has a few somewhat brighter, chestnut tinges), supercilium lacking or very indistinct (occasionally more marked), and buff breast band with very fine (but normally quite extensive) dark brown streaks which become more diffuse at breast sides and only exceptionally extend indistinctly onto upper flanks. In worn plumage Baird's becomes very dull (blackish) or patchy above, often with indication of scaly patterning. 1st-summers of both species essentially as adult summer, but some White-rumped may retain some very worn juvenile feathers on upperparts.

In Flight In all plumages, White-rumped shows diagnostic narrow white band across uppertail-coverts, prominent, though smaller than that of Curlew Sandpiper *C. ferruginea.* Baird's looks particularly 'dark-ended' in flight, lacking contrast between dark rump to tail and very narrow white rump sides (white much less extensive than on most other small waders). Both have a thin pale wingbar (on worn Baird's often very indistinct or even absent), and are noticeably long-winged (striking in mixed flocks of small waders).

Voice In flight, White-rumped gives a high-pitched, very thin, squeaky (mouse- or bat-like), rather drawn-out 'tzeeet', often rapidly repeated a few times; occasionally a short 'tit'. Baird's has much lower-pitched short trill, slightly grating or harsh, 'trrrp', 'keerrp' or 'krrt', and occasionally a sharp 'tsik'.

Behaviour Both normally feed in characteristic horizontal posture (long body obvious) by surface-picking. White-rumped, however, sometimes probes and often wades in water;

wading rare for Baird's (which prefers drier margins and often feeds well within vegetation).

References Alström *et al.* (1989), Chandler (1989), Marchant (1985).

Great, Common and Pintail Snipes

Where and When Great Snipe *Gallinago media* is a scarce/rare, local and declining summer visitor to Scandinavian uplands, Poland and east to W Siberia, breeding on marshy slopes and tussocky bogs/marshes in forested areas (locally in dry woodland); migrates through eastern Europe, stopping off in damp fields but often also in dry habitats; vagrant W Europe (but possibly overlooked). Common Snipe *G. gallinago* is common throughout northern half of W Palearctic, breeding in variety of wet habitats; northern and eastern populations migratory, wintering W Europe and throughout Mediterranean region. Pintail Snipe *G. stenura* breeds N Urals to E Siberia and is an extremely rare vagrant (one confirmed record, in Israel).

Identification

On the ground, essential features to look for are structure, bill size and shape, head pattern (especially relative widths of loral stripe and fore supercilium), wing-covert pattern, and (if possible) extent of barring below. In flight, identification generally less problematic (but still far from simple): check shape/structure (including wingtip shape, relative size of head), bill length, strength of central wing panel, presence or not of white tips to secondaries and to primary coverts, tail pattern, any contrast between mantle and upperwing, call, and flight action. Many of these features by no means easy to assess and great care always called for. Juveniles differ slightly from adults, but by 1st winter virtually identical to latter. Note that overlap occurs in most features, and some birds may not be safely identifiable.

Great Snipe

At Rest 1 SIZE, SHAPE AND STRUCTURE Larger and bulkier than other snipes. Plump, with medium-length bill (usually clearly shorter than Common's). Tail projects well beyond tail. **2** WING PATTERN Prominent white tips to median, greater and primary coverts form narrow but usually distinct wingbars (less developed on juvenile). **3** UNDERPARTS Usually heavily barred on breast, rear flanks and thighs (barring stronger, bolder than on Common and Pintail). **4** TAIL Extensive white on outer tail (obvious in flight) may be visible on ground (and highly distinctive in lek display).

In Flight Bulky, with rounded wings. **1** TAIL All tail feathers tipped white, outer 4 largely all white with a few black spots (juvenile with somewhat more dark spots/bars); when tail spread (e.g. on landing or take-off), adults can appear almost white-tailed. **2** UPPERWING Prominent broad white tips to median, greater and primary coverts form two or three narrow but distinct bars across entire wing (less obvious on juvenile), accentuating dark central panel; only when fresh do secondaries show thin, inconspicuous white trailing edge (lacking on juvenile), but this much less obvious than on any Common. **3** UNDERPARTS Breast and flanks very heavily barred, especially on juvenile (can look quite dark below, with belly sometimes also barred); other snipes generally less strongly barred. **4** UNDERWING-COVERTS Uniformly dark-barred, similar to Pintail, but lacking Common's plain white area(s); note, however, that N American race *delicata* of Common (could possibly occur as vagrant) lacks white on underwing.

Call and Flight Behaviour Rises heavily and with noisy wingbeats (can recall Eurasian Woodcock *Scolopax rusticola*), often giving weak croak (this often drowned by wing noise); flight relatively slow and heavy, tends to keep low, often circling around before dropping back into cover. Noisy on breeding

Great Snipe. Bulky. Note white spots to wing-coverts forming bars, heavily barred underparts.

Great Snipe tails, adult (left) and juvenile (right). Note extent of white.

Tails of Common Snipe (left) and Pintail Snipe (right). Only exceptional views would reveal the unique tail feathers of Pintail Snipe.

Great Snipe in flight. Bulky, rounded wings. Note prominent wingbars.

Common Snipe. Long bill, slight toe projection. Pale trailing edge to inner wing. Rakish and erratic in flight. Inconspicuous pale median-covert panel. Usually calls when flushed.

Common Snipe. Long bill, thick loral stripe, long white ear-covert line. Tail projects beyond folded wing. Median coverts appear spotted rather than barred.

Pintail Snipe in flight. Plump and small-headed. Plainer above with obvious median-covert panel. Pale trailing edge barely visible. Toes project marginally further than on Common Snipe, wingtip is rounder.

Pintail Snipe. Short-billed, short-tailed. Lower scapulars evenly edged cream on both sides. Wide pale supercilium, especially before eye, narrow loral stripe, median coverts barred rather than spotted.

Pintail Snipe

Lower-scapular patterns variable, but Pintail Snipe has cream edges of equal width on both sides of the feather, whereas the outer margin is wider on Common Snipe.

Common Snipe.

Pintail Snipe

Great Snipe

Note underwing patterns.

Common Snipe.

grounds, with bill-clattering, gurgles, twitters etc in lek display (solitary at other times).

Common and Pintail Snipes

The two are very similar and correct identification requires prolonged close views. Following tendencies of Pintail, in combination, will help distinguish most from Common.

At Rest 1 SIZE AND STRUCTURE Pintail may look plumper than Common, though not larger (can often appear smaller); bill averages shorter, sometimes markedly so (Common noticeably long-billed), and blunter. Short tail barely projects beyond wingtips, giving 'docked' appearance to rear (on Common, protrudes well beyond wings). **2** HEAD PATTERN Pintail tends to have somewhat narrower loral stripe than Common, and supercilium usually much broader (bulging) in front of eye (on Common tends to taper sharply over lores), giving Pintail a more bare-faced expression; supercilium often concolorous with pale cheek bar (on Common, cheek bar often whiter than buff supercilium). **3** SCAPULARS Lower scapulars with narrow light brown to creamy/whitish edges, often uniform in width on both webs (variable) and giving scalloped appearance; on Common, outer webs broadly edged buff or whitish, inner webs with much narrower (or invisible) and more rufous edges, creating stripy appearance. **4** WING-COVERTS Median-covert panel rather distinct, appears coarsely vermiculated (on Common poorly defined, looks spotted).

In Flight 1 SIZE AND STRUCTURE Pintail generally looks plump and small-headed, with shorter bill and blunter wings than more rakish Common; most of toes project beyond shorter tail (on Common, only tips of toes). **2** UPPERPARTS Pintail averages somewhat duller, browner, above, with pale areas buff or light brown, whereas Common shows richer mix of brown, buff, rufous and white. **3**

UPPERWING Pintail shows contrasting paler panel across median coverts (feathers barred sandy/rufous and tipped whitish), but white trailing edge to secondaries lacking or barely visible (but can show diffuse paler edge to rear wing); on Common, covert panel inconspicuous (medians fringed rufous-brown and unbarred), but broad white tips to secondaries form well-demarcated trailing edge (narrower when very worn, but still more obvious than on Pintail). White tips to primary coverts usually more distinct on Pintail, creating small wingbar (often inconspicuous on Common, not forming bar). **4** UNDERWING Median and lesser coverts uniformly dark-barred, lacking Common's unmarked pale bars/patches (latter normally including much broader tips to median and greater coverts). Beware that American race *delicata* of Common has uniformly barred underwing as Pintail (but still has narrow white trailing edge, different shape/structure, and is also darker and richly coloured above). **5** TAIL Pintail generally has restricted white tips to rectrices, sometimes hardly visible in field, whereas white normally visible on tail of Common; only exceptional views (or in-hand examination) would reveal unique pin-like shape of Pintail's outer 7–9 pairs.

Call and Flight Behaviour When flushed, Pintail may utter a short, throaty, slightly nasal 'scaap' (sometimes repeated), much weaker, less rasping, less disyllabic and less urgent than Common's frequently repeated harsh note. Both occasionally give a much higher, short call, Pintail's being somewhat 'purer'. Latter can appear slightly slower on take-off and to fly a little less erratically than Common, which often towers high and flies far before resettling; the two can, however, show identical flight behaviour.

References Carey & Olsson (1995), Shirihai (1988), Taylor (1984).

Slender-billed Curlew

Where and When A highly endangered species, Slender-billed Curlew *Numenius tenuirostris* breeds in unknown area(s) in C Siberia. Extremely rare (former?) winter visitor to Merja Zerga, Morocco, where prefers muddy, close-cropped freshwater meadows,

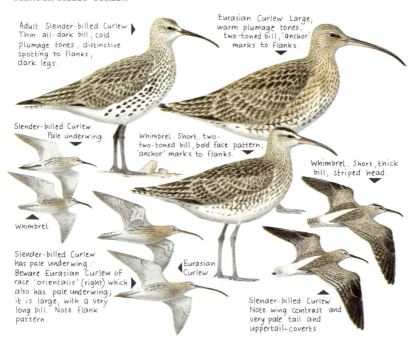

Adult Slender-billed Curlew.
Thin all-dark bill, cold
plumage tones, distinctive
spotting to flanks,
dark legs.

Eurasian Curlew. Large,
warm plumage tones,
two-toned bill, 'anchor'
marks to flanks.

Slender-billed Curlew.
Pale underwing

Whimbrel. Short, two-
two-toned bill, bold face pattern,
'anchor' marks to flanks.

Whimbrel. Short, thick
bill, striped head.

Whimbrel

Slender-billed Curlew
has pale underwing.
Beware Eurasian Curlew of
race 'orientalis' (right) which
also has pale underwing;
it is large, with a very
long bill. Note flank
pattern.

Eurasian
Curlew.

Slender-billed Curlew
Note wing contrast and
very pale tail and
uppertail-coverts.

108

also fields. Recently recorded on passage/in winter also in Italy, Greece, Hungary and Tunisia. Exceptional vagrant elsewhere.

Confusion Species Eurasian Curlew *N. arquata* and Whimbrel *N. phaeopus* the only two possible confusion species in W Palearctic (smaller vagrant Little Curlew *N. minutus* easily eliminated by dark rump, Whimbrel-like head pattern, shorter bill, and much plainer underparts). Slender-billed is closest to Whimbrel in size (wingspans overlap totally); much smaller than Eurasian Curlew (slight overlap in wingspans), and body size distinctly smaller in direct comparison.

Plumage *Head* Crown dark, with well-defined paler streaking (lacks Whimbrel's lateral crown-stripes); can appear to have dark forecrown cap. Pale supercilium contrasts strongly with dark crown, and dark loral bar from eye to bill base prominent

though rather narrow, but pattern can be much subdued (on Eurasian Curlew, supercilium indistinct and dark of lores more in form of diffuse round blob). *Underparts* Obviously paler and more sharply patterned than other *Numenius* species. White/whitish on breast (occasionally with pale brown suffusion), becoming pure white on flanks and undertail, breast overlain with heavy, sharply defined spots and streaks (other two species more diffusely marked on darker background). Flanks show diagnostic, very bold, large, blackish spots (sometimes in fairly regular lines): spots variable in shape and often (not always) round, heart-shaped or triangular, but always quite unlike anchor-shaped flank markings of Eurasian Curlew and Whimbrel. Importantly, note that juvenile Slender-billed has brown streaks on flanks, acquiring spots during 1st winter (though the two other species always show at least some anchor or arrowhead marks at all ages). **Upperparts** Generally somewhat colder in tone than Eurasian Curlew, but this not particularly obvious (especially on lone individuals). **Bare Parts** *Bill* Much shorter than on Eurasian, though juveniles (especially males) of latter may have bill almost as short. Shape, however, distinctive: fairly evenly decurved, and tapering to narrow tip with no lateral expansion (obvious expansion at tip on Eurasian Curlew), and without prominent kink towards tip shown by most Whimbrels. Bill all dark, with no (or only very small) area of pale colour at base (Eurasian Curlew shows extensive pale pinkish area at base of lower mandible). *Legs* Very dark grey (less dark, more bluish-grey, on other two species).

In Flight More extensive white on rump reaches further onto uppertail-coverts and tail (tail can appear very pale) than on Eurasian Curlew or Whimbrel, though this not always conspicuous. Underwing more or less plain white, much as on eastern race *orientalis* of Eurasian (strongly barred on Whimbrel). Upperwing often shows stronger contrast (dark primary coverts and outer primaries, paler inner wing) than on latter two species. **Behaviour and Voice** On ground, tends to move rather more quickly than Eurasian Curlew, with less ponderous steps; often appears more alert, with more upright stance. Voice very like Eurasian's, but slightly higher, less coarse, with faster delivery; often a high-pitched 'kwee' on take-off.
References Marchant (1984), Porter (1984), Serra *et al.* (1995), van den Berg (1990).

Sooty and White-eyed Gulls

Where and When Both Sooty *Larus hemprichii* and White-eyed Gulls *L. leucophthalmus* are gulls of the Red Sea, Sooty extending also along coastal waters of NE Africa, Arabia, Persian Gulf and to about Baluchistan. Breed mostly April-October on islands; resident/partially migratory, with winter numbers much smaller (at least in N Red Sea). Scavenge on beaches and in harbours, but often (at times large flocks) catch fish at sea.

General Features Both medium-sized gulls, rather comparable in structure and plumage pattern, but unlike all other W Palearctic gulls. Dark coloration, blackish underwing, exceptionally long bill, and long wings (in distant flight may recall skua *Stercorarius*; distinctly elongated rear end when perched).

Distinguishing Features Main differences between the two are: **1** BILL On Sooty, thicker and straighter (but gonydeal angle fairly pronounced), pale yellowish with clear-cut black band and small red tip (adult), or pale greyish-yellow or grey with blackish tip (juvenile/immature); on White-eyed, distinctly slender, slightly drooping and with reduced (almost absent) gonydeal angle, dark red with variable blackish tip (adult), or

glossy blackish-brown to brownish-grey and becoming darker/blacker towards tip (juvenile/immature), though never clearly bicoloured as young Sooty. **2** EYE-RING At all ages Sooty has rather prominent white (buff on juvenile) crescent above eye and sometimes also faintly below eye, whereas White-eyed always shows broader and more conspicuous crescent both above and below. **3** SIZE AND STRUCTURE Sooty is slightly larger and more robust, heavy-chested (often gives impression of Lesser Black-backed *L. fuscus*), but with broad, short neck (almost 'neckless') and rounded head with steeper forehead; White-eyed slimmer-bodied, more elongated, and smaller (roughly size of Common Gull *L. canus*), with much less deep chest, narrower neck, and more 'pointed' face with flatter forehead and moderately angled head top. **4** FLIGHT IMPRESSION Apart from heavier bill and more robust body, Sooty's relatively broader and rounded wings produce impression (to experienced observers) of slower and elastic flight, whereas White-eyed always shows more pointed wing and stiffer beats. In all plumages, but most obvious on adults, White-eyed has thin white leading edge to

Juvenile Sooty Gull. Note structure, bill with black tip. Upperparts fringed pale cream.

Breeding adult Sooty Gull. Note thick bill, yellow at base. Eye-ring prominent above eye only. Larger and fuller-bodied than White-eyed Gull. Browner plumage tones.

1st-winter Sooty Gull. Mantle pale brown. Broad pale fringing to wing.

Adult Sooty Gull. Broad and more rounded wings.

1st-winter Sooty Gull. Mantle does not contrast with wing-coverts. Black tail band thinner than on 1st-winter White-eyed Gull.

2nd-winter Sooty Gull.

1st-winter White-eyed Gull. Thin dark bill.

Adult breeding White-eyed Gull. Slender and drooping bill. Prominent eye-ring. Greyer plumage tones.

1st-winter White-eyed Gull. Mantle grey-brown, darker than Sooty Gull, dark mask through eye. Bill all dark.

Adult White-eyed Gull. Slimmer, more pointed wing than Sooty Gull.

2nd-winter White-eyed Gull. Greyer than same-age Sooty Gull. Note bill structure and pattern, eye-crescents prominent.

Juvenile White-eyed Gull. Thin dark bill; upperparts fringed paler, less distinct than on Sooty Gull.

inner wing (lacking/indistinct on Sooty). 5 GENERAL COLORATION Sooty is generally paler brown (1st-year) to grey-brown (adult), and adult's hood dark brown; at all ages White-eyed is greyer, less brown, and adult's hood at most times of year jet-black.

Plumage *Juvenile* Both species show pale fringes to mantle, scapulars, tertials and upperwing-coverts forming scaly pattern (normally less conspicuous on White-eyed owing to narrower, buff-tinted fringes); Sooty's ground colour of rest of upperparts is greyer buff-brown (notably paler forehead/ crown), including neck to chest, while latter less clearly demarcated from body (on White-eyed, more contrast between pale body and typically uniform warmer/darker rufous-brown chest to head). In flight, Sooty paler above, with broader and more conspicuous whitish bars across tips of median and greater coverts and secondaries (narrow and more diffuse on White-eyed) and more contrasting/blacker secondary bar; also much broader white area from tail base to rump (on White-eyed, dark grey-brown extension on rump centre usually reduces white to more of a V shape, instead of wider/squarer patch). Bills differ greatly (see above). *1st-winter* Generally as juvenile, but differs mainly in rather uniform mantle and scapulars, greyish-brown on White-eyed but much browner and often paler on Sooty. Latter's bleached/ abraded tertials and wing-coverts show broader fringes than on White-eyed during same stage of wear. Sooty's head paler brown with some mottling, very different from White-eyed (which has better-defined blackish mask through eye to nape and finer dark crown streaking). For bill and eye-ring differences, see above. *1st-summer* On both, head darker, with more complete hood (mainly on White-eyed); wings and tail become much worn and faded, and tertials and wing-coverts usually lose much of pale fringing. *2nd-winter* Both species approach winter adult, though with browner coverts (retained) and duller upperparts (new/fresh). Fresh remiges have white tips much narrower than on fresh adults but broader than on juveniles;

primary tips from 7th inwards less prominent/narrower on White-eyed than on Sooty (fresh or at same stage of wear). Tail white with variable extent of black subterminal marks. Bill base becomes browner on White-eyed, and may be slightly duller yellowish (though still mostly pale greenish-grey) on Sooty. *2nd-summer* As 2nd-winter, except head and bare parts approaching adult. Bill of Sooty sometimes paler yellow-green with distinct black tip; White-eyed's bill brownish-red at base. *3rd-winter* Sooty still much as 2nd-winter, but with nearly all-white tail, clear black-and-red bill tip and broader white remex tips, while hood paler or with some whitish flecking; white half-collar poorly defined. By contrast, 3rd-winter White-eyed closer to adult winter, though with some vestiges of immaturity (e.g. bare parts). *3rd-summer/adult summer* Sooty's hood dark brown (glossy black on White-eyed). Plumage brightest and features well defined, e.g. half-collar (which somewhat smaller and more diffuse on Sooty). Colour and pattern of bare parts most developed (see Distinguishing Features). *Adult winter* Generally rather similar to adult summer: Sooty has slightly paler brown head (often pale-flecked) and upperparts, with more diffuse half-collar; White-eyed has more distinct winter plumage (e.g. blackish-grey head with paler-flecked forehead/crown, more grey-brown hue to upperparts and ill-defined/greyer half-collar), but very soon wears to very clear pattern as adult summer. Bare parts duller: on Sooty, bill base and legs greyer; on White-eyed, bill more evenly brown-red (lacking distinct blackish tip/bright red base often very clear on breeding adult) and legs much duller yellow. Note also that Sooty's white tips to fresh remiges are broader and clearer, starting from 3rd/4th primaries, while on White-eyed relatively narrow and usually only from 4th/ 5th (none on 3rd or very obscure and quickly worn off). Sooty's plumage, being browner, shows less obvious differences between fresh autumn/winter and worn spring/summer than is often found in White-eyed.

Great Black-headed Gull

Where and When An Asiatic and Middle
East speciality, Great Black-headed Gull *Larus
ichthyaetus* breeds locally from easternmost W
Palearctic (Crimea) east to NW Mongolia.
Winters, mainly December-March, south to E
Mediterranean (chiefly coasts and northern
valleys of Israel, where 1,000+ annually), Red
Sea area, Ethiopian Rift Valley, Persian Gulf,
and coasts of India and Burma. Frequents
shores of large lakes, fishponds and coasts.
Rare vagrant N and W Europe.

General Features In size and proportions
may recall Great Black-backed Gull *L. marinus*, and obviously bigger than Herring Gull
group. Compared with first species is less
heavily built, with longer legs, and distinctly
longer wings (markedly so when perched).
Head shape usually characteristic: longish
and sloping forehead, peak well behind eye.
In flight, long neck/head with heavy bill and
deep chest give front-heavy appearance,
added to by distinctly lazy flight with slower
wingbeats. 3rd-winter and older unmistakable: black hood (unique among large gulls)
frequent from January onwards, and in other
months outside breeding (and at all other
ages) shows dusky or blackish area around
eye and on ear-coverts and from hindcrown
to lower hindneck, concentrated behind eye
and at base of neck. Adult in flight very
distinctive: primaries striking, largely white,
outer 6 having bold black patches forming
subterminal crescent (extreme individuals of
nominate Yellow-legged can show very
restricted black on primaries, though pattern
still very different and back also darker);
white of primaries almost concolorous with
pale greyish/white wing-coverts, giving very
white-looking wing. Bill yellow to orange-
yellow, with neat black subterminal band and
orange-red tip; legs basically yellow.

Non-adult Plumages *Juvenile* Differs from
other large gulls compared here in having
fleshy-grey bill with extensive diffuse black
tip (largely dark on others), rather paler head
(with dusky patches on sides), and prominent

uniform dark centres and clean pale fringes to
feathers of mantle, scapulars and tertials
(other large gulls of same age show obvious
pale internal markings and barred fringes);
distinct breast patches (sometimes form
breast band) created by extension of dark
transverse yoke-like patch at neck base.
Underparts much whiter, and at close range
thin white crescents above and (more distinct)
below eye may be visible. Distinctive also in
flight, with prominent pale upper mid-wing
panel surrounded by darkish remiges and
leading upperwing-coverts, whitish uppertail-coverts and tail with more clear-cut blackish subterminal band, and whitish-looking
underwing with dark tips to some of coverts
and only partly darkish remiges (none of
these features shown by any of above-mentioned large gulls). *1st-winter* Usually
reaches winter quarters having completed
post-juvenile body moult, and differs markedly from all other large gulls in acquiring
mainly grey mantle and scapulars (more as
smaller gulls of similar age). Otherwise as
juvenile, but whiter below, hindneck more
heavily mottled, and breast much whiter
apart from prominent lateral patches; head
whiter, but diagnostic markings better
defined, as are eye-crescents. In flight, upper
mid-wing (median-covert) panel larger and
paler. Bill often becomes yellowish, with
clear-cut black subterminal bar; legs as juvenile or paler, fleshy-brown with greyish-olive
tinge. *1st-summer* As 1st-winter, except: black
head markings more extensive (some even
acquire partial hood); remiges and rectrices
much more worn and faded; upper mid-wing
panel even paler and larger (through moult),
often extending over most of coverts except
lessers, and concolorous with greyish upperside. Often gives impression of older (2nd-
summer) bird when perched, as dark forewing markings largely concealed. *2nd-winter*
Much closer to adult winter in body plumage
and wing-coverts, except brownish feathers
in lesser coverts, blackish in primary coverts

1st-winter Great Black-headed Gull. Large. Mantle grey (like a 2nd-winter large gull), dark collar. Note bill and head shapes.

Juvenile Great Black-headed Gull. Bill fleshy-grey at base. Upperparts scalloped, dark breast sides.

2nd-winter Yellow-legged Gull. Darker mantle, barred inner greater coverts.

2nd-winter Yellow-legged Gull. Dark mantle, no pale mid-wing panel.

1st-winter Great Black-headed Gull. Pale mid-wing panel, clear cut dark tail band.

2nd-winter Great Black-headed Gull. Mainly grey above, dark mask. Bill base yellowish.

2nd-winter Great Black-headed Gull. Extensive pale patches on outer wing, thin tail band.

Adult winter Great Black-headed Gull. Black band over bill, dark mask. Outer wing white with reduced black, obvious in flight (left).

and some dark markings in tertials; amount of black in outer primaries (already intermixed with much white) appears intermediate between adult and 1st-year, but unlike latter shows mainly small subterminal marks on 7th-9th primaries and thinner subterminal black tail band. Legs mainly dusky yellowish-green, pale areas of bill more yellow (less orange-yellow than adult). **2nd-summer** As

2nd-winter, but shows partial or nearly full blackish hood, and primary tips noticeably reduced through wear; more clean grey feathers above (new). Bare parts progressively closer to adult. **3rd-winter/3rd-summer** As adult, but with narrow and broken tail band (at least) and less white on primary tips. *References* Barthel (1994), Grant (1986).

Slender-billed Gull

Where and When   Slender-billed Gull *Larus genei* breeds in scattered colonies at shallow fresh or saline lakes, very locally from steppes of NE Kazakhstan west to Mediterranean and to Senegal coast. Mostly coastal outside breeding season, in similar habitats but also in sheltered bays. Numbers increasing.

General   Unlikely to be confused with other gulls apart from non-breeding Black-headed *L. ridibundus*. Following text concentrates on differences between these two, shape and structure being by far the most reliable.

Shape and Structure   At all times and all ages, best identified by appearance of head and bill and by very long neck. Bill averages longer than Black-headed's (overlap marginal) but not thinner (can in fact be slightly

thicker), with tip somewhat more drooping; feathering extends well onto bill, especially on upper mandible (where front edge of lores appear strongly pointed) and less so on lower mandible (on Black-headed, shorter extension of feathering more equal on both mandibles). Upper-mandible feathering also accentuates the much flatter forehead compared with Black-headed's more rounded profile, and smaller-looking eye seems to be located slightly more to rear (seen side-on, ratio of distances from front of lores to centre of eye and from centre of eye vertically to crown more than 2:1, on Black-headed about 1.5:1). Slender-billed averages somewhat bigger than Black-headed, though this not always noticeable, and has longer neck, wing, tail

Adult winter Slender-billed Gull. Slightly larger than Black-headed Gull. Long necked, pale eyed. Note exact way bill joins head. Flushed pink in summer.

Adult winter Black-headed Gull. Note head markings and bill shape.

Adult Slender-billed Gull. Long neck, rounded tail. Wing similar to Black-headed Gull, less contrast between pale and dark areas on both wing surfaces.

1st-winter Black-headed Gull

1st-winter Black-headed Gull.

1st-winter Slender-billed Gull. Wing markings paler.

1st-winter Slender-billed Gull. Note structural differences of bill, head and neck. Head markings pale or lacking, bill pale with small or no dark tip.

and legs, together with longer bill producing more elongated, elegant appearance. Long neck frequently extended, creating striking 'giraffe-like' appearance; when retracted, in S-shape, produces fuller breast. Although some of these features may be indicated on Black-headed, latter never gives the characteristic total impression of Slender-billed.

Posture When foraging on water, has very characteristic symmetrical appearance, highly distinctive and virtually diagnostic once learnt: long neck stretched obliquely forwards and stern pointing up at similar angle, while head and bill directed down (at right angles to neck); legs often partly visible above water line (rarely so on Black-headed).

In Flight Typical head-and-bill shape and long neck again distinctive, projecting farther in front of wing than on Black-headed, and with tail also longer than latter's and rather rounded (but not wedge-shaped), the whole producing elongated spool- or cigar-shaped appearance. Wingspan greater, mainly owing to longer arm, so wingbeats a trifle slower.

Plumage and Bare Parts *Adult* Mantle and upperwing-coverts a shade paler than on Black-headed; white primary wedge usually slightly broader and often contrasts a little less with dark areas on wing. Otherwise very white, including entire head, but often shows light to intense salmon-pink flush on underparts (though this not uncommon on Black-headed). Deep red bill (often looks blackish or with red confined to base) conspicuous on white head; legs deep red to blackish-red. Eye pale with red eye-ring (eye can appear oddly dark). Little seasonal difference; outside breeding season pink below often fainter or lacking, may sometimes show weak grey ear spot (but much less obvious than on non-breeding Black-headed), and bill and legs more clearly red (not blackish). *Juvenile* This plumage held for very short period: recalls juvenile Black-headed, but paler and greyer, lacking gingery tones. *1st-winter* Differs from

1st-winter Black-headed as follows. Head much plainer, with smaller, paler ear spot which may even be lacking (on Black-headed always distinct, big and blackish) and no or only minute greyish shadow in front of eye (Black-headed usually has obvious dark patch above and in front of eye); never shows Black-headed's diagnostic diffuse bands across crown. Wing-covert bands and trailing edge paler, less blackish, than on Black-headed, and terminal tail band also somewhat paler (and often narrower). May show faint pink tinge below. Iris pale, yellowish/whitish (always dark on Black-headed). Legs yellowish/orange, brighter than on Black-headed. Bill also brighter, yelloworange, with or often without diffuse dusky tip (dark tip more marked on Black-headed). *1st-summer* Head often even whiter than on 1st-winter (Black-headed normally gains variable dark hood); wing and tail markings generally much paler (faded/worn), showing little contrast with rest of plumage (normally darker and more contrasting on Black-headed). Bare parts as 1st-winter, though bill generally uniform orange (on Black-headed, tip normally black and well defined); rarely Slender-billed may show all-black bill. *2nd-winter/2nd-summer* As adult, but bill and legs can average paler or even yellower, and may still retain a few traces of immature plumage (e.g. around carpal region).

Voice and Behaviour Calls as those of Black-headed, but a little deeper and more nasal. Foraging methods include spinning (like phalarope) and tern-like plunge-diving with full submersion (less common in Black-headed).

Leucistic Black-headed Gull Leucistic Black-headed may or may not have dark ear spot, but separated by white upperparts (pale grey on Slender-billed), dark eye and very different structure and silhouette.

Reference Barthel & Königstedt (1993).

Audouin's Gull

Where and When One of the world's rarer gulls, Audouin's *Larus audouinii* is endemic to Mediterranean islands and coasts, chiefly in Spain, Algeria, eastern Morocco and Turkey. Dispersive, winters mainly SW Mediterranean and NW African coast. Accidental SE Mediterranean and north Red Sea, Switzerland , Atlantic coasts of Portugal and France.

General Features Structure and behaviour characteristic, at all ages distinctive from rather similar Herring *L. argentatus* and Lesser Black-backed Gulls *L. fuscus*. Compared with last two, smaller (by 10–15%), slimmer and more elegant, with markedly elongated rear end, less bulging breast, appearing relatively short-tailed and long-legged. Differs particularly in comparatively smaller, rather slimmer head with long sloping forehead (almost concave, peaking well behind eye), and in comparatively shorter and deeper-looking (stout) bill, rather uniform in width, but often held slightly downwards. Legs and feet at all ages darker than on Herring or Lesser Black-backed, dark olive-grey (often appear blackish at distance); eye small and dark, distinctive on white-headed adult. Flight action graceful, with longish wings (broader inner wing and shorter, compact but still relatively pointed outer wing); feeds largely by taking small fish near surface or plunging from low glide (unlike other large gulls).

Plumage and Bare Parts *Adult and 3rd-winter/3rd-summer* Apart from diagnostic dark legs and red bill (with ill-defined black subterminal band and yellowish tip), which both appear blackish at distance, resembles 'Herring Gull group'. Differs in having very little seasonal variation, in fresh winter plumage showing white head lacking dark streaking, (beware: Yellow-legged Gull *L. cachinnans* also lacks or has indistinct head streaking when fresh); and in being very pale grey above, with almost no contrast with whitish head and underparts (at distance appears quite uniform and very pale, apart from black wingtips). At close range, pale greyish coloration extends to hindneck, flanks, belly, rump and underwing, contributing to rather pale, contrastless appearance (this extensive greyish suffusion diagnostic). Otherwise, has inconspicuous whitish crescents on scapulars/tertials and whitish leading and trailing edges, and shows noticeably large black area on outer wings, which lack obvious mirrors (one small one on outermost primary, largely invisible and often absent on 3rd-years). 3rd-years differ from adults in having blackish on outer primary coverts.

Juvenile Resembles juvenile Herring or Lesser Black-backed and shows features of both, particularly former. Normally picked out among other large gulls by dark/blackish legs, but plumage differences also exist. Appears rather uniform grey-brown from head/neck (no obvious ear-covert contrast) to breast sides and underparts, often with contrasting dark patch on rear flanks, and paler/whiter forehead and crown; scapulars and tertials with broad well-defined dark centres and complete broad fringes (fringes sharply notched on other large gulls, creating arc or anchor shapes), centres lacking obvious dark subterminal bar; tail largely uniform black and contrasting with whitish uppertail-coverts, which form distinct U-shaped patch, and with grey-brown upper rump, while from below whitish tail base rather prominent (juvenile Lesser Black-backed often has noticeably broad black subterminal tail band, but from above always shows wide whitish and barred tail base). Upperwing pattern rather like that of Lesser Black-backed, as both show dark secondary bar, dark bar across greater coverts, and inner primaries barely paler than blackish outers, producing almost evenly dark flight feathers and primary and greater coverts combined (thus differing from Herring, Yellow-legged and Armenian Gulls *L. armenicus*, which show pale window to variable degree on inner primaries); underwing pattern clearly differs from that of all above-mentioned species,

Adult Audouin's Gull. Smaller than Yellow-legged Gull, sloping forehead, dark bill and long dark legs. Grey suffusion to body in summer.

Adult Audouin's Gull (left), paler than Yellow-legged Gull (right), slimmer-winged and longer-necked. White mirror in wingtip reduced on Audouin's Gull.

1st-winter Lesser Black-backed Gull. Note scapular and inner greater-covert patterns.

1st-winter Yellow-legged Gull. Barring to wing-coverts and patterned mantle and scapulars.

1st-winter Yellow-legged Gull. Larger than Audouin's Gull, with only partial dark greater-covert bar, and reduced dark in tail.

Juvenile Audouin's Gull. Dark grey legs, dark flank patch, dark centred scapulars, tertials and wing-coverts without bars or notches.

1st-winter Audouin's Gull. Head paler than juvenile, dark hind collar, fresh lower scapulars often with much grey.

2nd-winter Audouin's Gull. Pale grey upperparts, clear-cut tail band. Bill becomes blood-red with black tip.

1st-winter Audouin's Gull. Underwing variegated.

1st-winter Audouin's Gull. Distinctive white 'horseshoe' shape to uppertail-coverts, rump grey, tail wholly dark.

1st-winter Lesser Black-backed Gull. Dark, whitish rump.

having large pale central area (intermixed with dark markings) from greater primary coverts to greater and median coverts and over axillaries (this area more uniform or darker-looking on Herring and Lesser Black-backed). *1st-winter/1st-summer* Head and body whiter and wings and tail much worn and faded (chiefly in 1st spring and early summer); otherwise rather as juvenile, but after partial moults in autumn and spring new scapular fringes greyer, though still with diagnostic pattern mentioned above. Bill, as

117

on juvenile, generally palish with dark tip (much darker on other large ' gulls). *2nd-winter/2nd-summer* Closer towards adult than in case of Herring Gull; differs from latter, Yellow-legged and Armenian in much paler grey upperparts and wing-coverts con-trasting greatly with blackish secondaries and primaries (apart from paler inner primaries), white primary tips broader and better defined; underwing paler than on Herring; bill base usually becoming reddish.

Reference Grant (1986).

Armenian, Yellow-legged and Siberian Gulls in Middle East

Where and When The taxonomy of Arme-nian *Larus armenicus*, Yellow-legged *L. cachin-nans* and Siberian Gulls *L. heuglini* is contro-versial, and their relationships, including with other forms of the Herring/Lesser Black-backed *L. argentatus/fuscus* complex, are still not fully understood. On the basis chiefly of morphological differences, beha-viour and geographical zonation, various authorities have recently accorded specific status to Armenian and Yellow-legged, while some Russian authors have done the same for Siberian Gull: an arrangement that seems to be the most appropriate in the Middle East/Levant, where these three (plus Lesser Black-backed) are identifiable in the field and also differ in status/distribution. Armenian breeds mainly at mountain lakes in Armenia, Caucasus and NW Iran/E Turkey, wintering mainly coastal and inland waters of Turkey, Lebanon and Israel, with variable numbers in other parts of Middle East (e.g. Persian Gulf and Egypt). Yellow-legged breeds rather widely across C Palearctic, the most widely distributed and most recognisable races being *michahellis* (SW Europe, Mediterranean basin), *cachinnans* (Black Sea to Kazakhstan) and *mongolicus* (eastern C Asia); distinctly more coastal, especially in winter, and migra-tory, wintering S Eurasian and NE and NW African coasts. Siberian Gull is a typical low-/subarctic species and occurs in three races, nominate *heuglini* (Kola Peninsula to Yenisei), *taimyrensis* (east of nominate, to Taymyr Peninsula) and *vegae* (east of latter, to NW Alaska); long-distance migrant, winters coasts of S Eurasia and NE Africa, including Middle East (nominate).

Identification Many of the problems invol-ving large gulls are regional. In western half of W Palearctic, they centre mostly around Yellow-legged and Herring Gulls and are well covered in the existing literature (e.g. Grant 1986, Harris *et al.* 1989, Gruber 1995). The text here is restricted to main forms occurring in Middle East, where major problem is the variety of Armenian, Yellow-legged and Siberian Gulls which winters there (presum-ably breeding populations from wide areas of C Asia and Siberia); identifying these, some-times even as adults, is a real challenge, and often somewhat speculative! Further compli-cations arise from clinal populations/inter-mediates (or even hybrids): e.g. the northern and eastern end of nominate *cachinnans* cline produces birds ('*barabensis*', but synonymised with *cachinnans* by Stepanyan 1990) with darker upperparts and larger black wingtip which may be confused with Armenian. As considerable variation exists in non-adult (and sometimes adult) plumages, with many individuals difficult to allocate to species, the effect of feather wear and especially of bleaching, as well as individual size variation, should be borne in mind; only birds showing all features (including structural) suggesting one of the species should be identified. Following summaries are based on 'obvious' birds, but serve as a useful key to identifica-tion and ageing.

Separating Armenian and Yellow-legged

Size and Structure Armenian averages smaller and has distinctly shorter and rela-tively stouter and blunter-tipped bill (with shorter distance between feathering and nos-tril) than Yellow-legged (on which longer, narrower bill also widens more obviously at gonys). Armenian's short, stout bill the single most useful feature at any stage; in addition, crown is relatively high but distinctly flat, with steep slope to forehead and an angular look to rear head (Yellow-legged has more evenly rounded crown shape, with moderately shallow forehead slope and with slight mid-crown peak). Although a 'large gull', Armenian's short (but stubbier) bill, combined with high crown (but appears rather round-headed) and on average smaller size and more 'chubby' appearance (stocky neck and chest, but with flat belly and well-attenuated rear end), can give a rather gentle-looking impression somewhat recalling Common Gull *L. canus*, unlike the more powerful-looking Yellow-legged (which has more angular structure, with deep chest and broad sturdy body); these differences subtle, however, noticeable only on extreme birds and only to observers with some practice. Interestingly, studies in Israel revealed that nominate Yellow-legged and Armenian are the least variable in nostril shape: on former, nostril very narrow with almost parallel edges and with indistinct broader front end; on Armenian, much broader (i.e. easy to see through) and almost triangular, with distinct narrow rear and broad front end.

Adults Armenian's structure combined with its highly distinctive full adult plumage (see below) should readily distinguish it from W European Herring (*L. a. argenteus/argentatus*), as also should its yellow legs, bill coloration, dark eye, darker grey upperparts and wing pattern, but confusion can often arise with Yellow-legged, major differences between the two being given below. Both Armenian and Yellow-legged acquire winter plumage by complete moult from early/late May to November/December. **1** UPPERPART COLOUR Armenian has slightly darker grey upperparts than Yellow-legged of race *michahellis* (or marginally more so than nominate *cachinnans*). Unlike Armenian, however, Yellow-legged, especially nominate, is quite variable in this respect: although with palest *cachinnans* differences from Armenian are obvious, some darker birds (often associated with '*barabensis*') are inseparable. Further, it

must be stressed that extreme caution is demanded when assessing grey tone of gulls' upperparts, as different viewing angle and lighting can easily lead to misjudgements! **2** UPPERWING PATTERN Armenian has wider blackish wingtip, black extending to primary coverts on outermost 3 or 4 primaries (giving impression of triangular blackish wingtip), smaller white primary tips, and well-separated smallish white mirror on outermost primary (obvious also on underside of folded wing); Yellow-legged has smaller blackish wingtip on which black extends to primary coverts only on outermost primary (and with progressively more basal grey from penultimate primary inwards, making demarcation between black and grey concave rather than straight), and distinctly larger white primary tips and mirrors, which sometimes may even meet or partly meet to form extreme large white (but broken) wingtip and black subterminal band. Beware, however, 4th-winter/summer Yellow-legged having larger black wingtip and smaller mirrors. **3** BARE PARTS Considerable variation and overlap in both species. Armenian, however, unique in developing a broad blackish subterminal band across bill, obscuring red gonys. Although Yellow-legged can show dusky on bill, this is mainly a remnant of immaturity (and is never as Armenian's band, which is broad and so close to tip that it runs through the much-compressed curved section of upper mandible, producing effect of an extremely small pale tip). Armenian's diagnostic bill band, however, seems to disappear on a few adults for a short period during spring and mostly towards early autumn, leaving extensive red spot at gonydeal angle with only small or no subterminal band. Armenian has dark brownish or grey-brown irides (in some become paler from early spring and through summer, in a few dull yellow throughout year), so typical birds look distinctly black-eyed in field, whereas most Yellow-legged have pale or yellowish irides (sometimes greyish-olive, when may look dark-eyed, as Armenian). Both typically have yellow legs (brightest in late winter, as spring advances), but Yellow-legged's are often not quite so bright as most Armenian's and tend to have some greyish-flesh pigment. 4 SUBSIDIARY DIFFERENCES Upper wingtip pattern is also shown on underwing, the black area being larger on Armenian; remainder of remiges below are predominantly grey on Armenian (but not so much as on Lesser Black-backed Gull), whereas on Yellow-legged almost white on both primaries and secondaries (as on Herring Gull *sensu stricto*). On standing Armenian, white scapular and tertial crescents usually much smaller and often not visible, but some may develop rather large crescents, almost matching the typically large ones of Yellow-legged. *Greatest confusion risk* Trickiest Yellow-legged is near-adult having extensive dark at wingtip (with smaller mirrors) and on bill and darker eye (see in plate).

1st-winters In many ways, Armenian is somewhat intermediate between Yellow-legged and Herring Gulls, sharing former's whitish head and underparts and all-dark bill but differing in structure, notably bill and head shape (see above), and in following plumage characters. 1 UPPERWING PATTERN Armenian's inner primaries are distinctly paler brown than Yellow-legged's and show marked contrast with outer primaries and secondaries, as Herring Gull (but window not so conspicuously pale as latter's); Yellow-legged has darker and more uniform primaries approaching pattern of Lesser Black-back. Both in flight and perched, Armenian shows pale, well-barred greater coverts (again approaching Herring, but not so heavily barred) and quite wide pale tips and very narrow, reduced pale fringes to fresh tertials, as opposed to Yellow-legged's darker and more uniform greater coverts (form dark inner wingbar, approaching that of Lesser Black-back) and wider pale, but barred, fresh tertial tips and fringes. Beware some variation in Armenian, some of which exhibit slightly darker inner-primary and greater-covert pattern. 2 TAIL Uppertail-coverts of Armenian very white, as on Yellow-legged, but dark tail band distinctly narrower and more

cleanly demarcated (extremes approach pattern of Common Gull, and thus also differ from Herring). 3 SUBSIDIARY DIFFERENCES The relatively white-headed Armenian as late as February has fine but dense streaking from forecrown to neck and on side of head (generally darkest around and behind eye, producing dark eye-crescent), so that (especially darkest individuals) it is much like Herring Gull, though paler individuals rather white-headed but never as Yellow-legged. Generally, Armenian's fresh mantle and scapulars tend to have narrower and more anchor-shaped centres (less even in width), but assessment of this hampered by bleaching and wear. Unlike many Yellow-legged (the cleanest below), many Armenian have brownish-grey spotting on upper breast sides and extending to upper flanks and across lower breast, and flanks may be washed greyish (in last feature somewhat approaching Herring). Most Armenian show dark-flecked paler brown underwing than Yellow-legged, and with wear (or bleaching) ground colour of underwing-coverts becomes almost whitish and dark flecks more obvious, latter forming lines of marks following contours of coverts and axillaries. *Note* By midwinter, or even from October/November, many Armenian, as Yellow-legged, begin to exhibit high degree of abrasion on coverts, creating bleached white patches (starting on outer parts of median and lesser coverts).

Subsequent Immature Plumages *1st-summer* Many features discussed under 1st-winters are useful for separating Armenian and Yellow-legged in 1st-summer plumages, too. Owing to feather wear, however (e.g. dark area of wing becomes faded and lighter, reducing contrast on primaries in Armenian, or conversely enhancing contrast in case of Yellow-legged), a higher percentage of individuals will remain inseparable, and often 'speculative identification' relies much on structure. Bill frequently becomes paler at base on Armenian, and even more so on Yellow-legged. Both may gain a few new grey scapulars (as for adult, showing tone of the particular species). *2nd-winter/2nd-summer*

Adult winter Armenian Gull. Short, stubby bill with black band just before tip. Dark eye. Upperparts dark grey with little white. Note underwing-tip pattern.

Adult summer Armenian Gull may lose bill band.

Adult Yellow-legged Gull of race 'michahellis'.

Adult winter Yellow-legged Gull of race 'cachinnans'. Some show dark eye. 4th-winter bird (right), note bill pattern.

Adult Yellow-legged Gull of race 'cachinnans'.

Adult Yellow-legged Gull of race 'cachinnans' (left) and 'michahellis' (below).

Adult Armenian Gull.

Note subtle differences in wingtip patterns.

4th-year Yellow-legged Gull of race 'cachinnans'.

Adult Lesser Black-backed Gull of race 'graellsii'. Black primary area sharply defined from grey upperparts.

Adult winter Siberian Gull of race 'taimyrensis'. Leg colour yellow or pink. Note underwing-tip pattern.

Adult winter Siberian Gull. Dark as or darker than Lesser Black-backed Gull of race 'graellsii'. Huge, bold head streaking.

Adult Siberian Gull. Black primary area merges with grey upperparts, only outermost primary uniform black.

Adult winter Lesser Black-backed Gull of race 'graellsii'.

Small mirrors, often on outermost primary only.

1st-winter Armenian Gull. Inner primaries paler, pale rump, neat tail band.

2nd-winter Armenian Gull. Dark grey mantle, blunt bill. Generally somewhat more advanced than 2nd-winter Yellow-legged Gull.

2nd-winter Yellow-legged Gull of race 'cachinnans'.

1st-winter Armenian Gull. Fine streaking to head and body, barred greater coverts. Underwing paler than on Yellow-legged Gull.

1st-winter Yellow-legged Gull.

1st-winter Yellow-legged Gull. Pale head and underparts, dark outer greater coverts.

1st-winter Yellow-legged Gull. Slightly paler inner primaries. Dark secondaries and outer greater coverts create two bars across wing.

1st-year Siberian Gull. 2nd-year similar but worn owing to slow progression of moult.

Note diamond shapes on lower scapulars, all dark bill and dark tertials.

1st-winter Siberian Gull. Plainer wing, pale 'saddle' and extensive dark in tail.

1st-winter Lesser Black-backed Gull. Small and dark. Tertials and outer greater coverts dark. Bill black, pale forehead often gives 'hooded' effect.

3rd-winter Siberian Gull. Moult progresses slowly, dark grey mantle develops, eye turns pale.

1st-winter Lesser Black-backed Gull. Plain dark wings and back contrast with pale rump and dark tail band.

Plumage is advanced more or less as in Herring Gull, e.g. mantle and scapulars variably become clearer grey and adult-like, giving saddle-like appearance, inner primaries more obviously pale, secondary bar bolder and more blackish-brown, and tertials more strongly patterned (with reduced dark centres). Bill and legs very variable: bill from almost wholly dark to having paler basal two-thirds, and legs from fleshy-coloured to distinctly yellow. At this stage, Yellow-legged is usually less adult-like. Structure of head and bill (which see) and wing pattern are useful for separating Armenian from Yellow-legged: some of latter show a small mirror spot, and sometimes a white primary tip, unlike Armenian (which rarely has a small, generally invisible, mirror spot). Tone of upperparts also a useful guide, being usually darker on Armenian. *3rd-winter/3rd-summer* Much more like adult, but predominantly grey wing shows vestiges of dark markings, especially on primary coverts, and both taxa also have larger black area on outer wing than adult, with reduced white primary tips and mirrors (often absent on Armenian, but typically some obvious on Yellow-legged). Both also have strongly yellow legs, and typically rather yellow bill with broad clearcut black tip (chiefly Yellow-legged) or very wide subterminal band (chiefly Armenian). Besides structural features, the bill and iris colours (approaching respective adult) and to some extent wing pattern and ground colour of upperparts are useful distinctions. *4th-winter/4th-summer* Basically as adult, including primary markings. Birds with vestiges of dark markings on primary coverts and less advanced in bare-part coloration are presumed to be this age, at which there is risk of confusion between Armenian and Yellow-legged. Some adult-looking Yellow-legged can have slightly more blackish markings on outer primaries than full adult, much-reduced white primary markings, and dusky subterminal markings on bill, all suggesting adult Armenian. Extreme care is essential with such birds.

Siberian Gull

Size and Structure Averages larger and bulkier than Yellow-legged and much more so than Armenian, often almost recalling Great Black-back *L. marinus* (but, as with all large gulls, considerable size variation exists and smaller females may be as small as former two species). On immatures in particular, the large and powerful bill with prominent gonydeal angle and the proportionately long legs are often more helpful than any plumage characters in identifying this gull. Moreover, Siberian's upper mandible, unlike Armenian's, is not parallel with lower but runs slightly below horizontal from base towards tip, emphasising gonydeal angle. Always appears big-headed (bulky behind eye); rear crown typically rather flat but runs slightly downwards from crown peak, while forehead slopes less than on Yellow-legged but more than on Armenian.

Moult Adult has complete post-breeding moult from (August-)October/November to February/March(April), which often useful in identification (chiefly after December): adult Siberian is frequently fresher than Armenian and Yellow-legged and may even be still moulting outermost primaries in second half of winter and spring. Unlike standard cycle of most other large gulls, primary moult of immature Siberian seems to be completed later than that of adults; such extremely retarded moult means that full 2nd-winter plumage hardly occurs in winter, and it is probably better to combine 2nd-winter and 2nd-summer plumages as '2nd-year' and so on.

Plumage *Adult* Distinctive. Dark slate-grey upperparts, as *graellsii* Lesser Black-back or somewhat darker, but considerably darker than Armenian and Yellow-legged, and strikingly heavy coarse head streaking is most prominent on lower nape and hindneck and retained much later into winter/early spring. Obvious characters also shown in flight, when major differences in upperwing: wing-tip pattern generally closer to *graellsii*, but black primary area contrasts less (merges) with dark slate-grey of rest of wing than on *graellsii* and Armenian; and mirror on outer-most primary typically small and well iso-lated, and shows very small/no mirror on second-outermost (visible also on folded wing). Apart from very different upperpart colour and primary pattern, Siberian differs from Yellow-legged in its rather dark greyish underside of remiges. Besides distinctly larger size and above-mentioned upperwing con-trast (grey and black), differs from adult *graellsii* in having only outermost primary mostly uniform black (on *graellsii*, two outer-most almost uniform black), the rest having diffuse dark grey tongue on inner webs; mirror on second-outermost primary is usually smaller than that of *graellsii*. Although full adults (chiefly in spring) typically have red spot on gonys, many also show distinct dusky area in this region (even as subterminal band), but this mainly remnant of immaturity. As well as nominate, a further race of Siberian occurs less frequently (in Middle East): *tai-myrensis*, which has duller grey upperparts and often pink legs (see plate). *1st-year (1st-winter/summer)* May recall Great Black-back in general appearance, including structure and (sometimes) size, bold pattern of mantle and scapular feathers, very whitish head and underparts, and heavy all-black bill. Owing to whitish areas, the barely noticeable pale window on inner primaries and rather plai-ner, less barred greater coverts, resembles Yellow-legged more than Armenian, but dif-fers in somewhat larger and heavier build, solidly dark-centred tertials with very narrow whitish fringes all around (instead of obvious indentations near tips), and very broad, almost solidly dark tail band with only very small white spots near bases of outer feathers (instead of well-barred base and much dirtier rump). On typical Siberian, scapulars (but as soon as winter/early spring usually restricted to rear inners, some of which newly acquired in late-autumn/winter moult, but often miss-ing during active moult) are strongly pat-terned with diamond-shaped blackish-brown centres and are also usually surrounded by variable arrow- or anchor-shaped central marks on middle and upper scapulars. These bold diamond-shaped marks on inner rear scapulars never occur on *cachinnans*, and although Armenian may show a rather simi-lar pattern it is never prominent. Beware that bleaching and wear make assessment of scapular and also tertial characters very difficult and often impossible. Observing 1st-winter Siberian and Lesser Black-back together (a common occurrence in Middle East) is a real eye-opener: striking structural, size and plumage differences should easily separate them. *2nd-year* Some features dis-cussed under 1st-year are often useful also for separating 2nd-year Siberian from the other two. 2nd-year plumages even more striking, as most have combination of heavily abraded wings (faded, brownish primaries) and tail and bleached head, wing-coverts and body, but with (in autumn) many fresh scapulars with blackish diamond-shaped centres, creat-ing broad chessboard pattern. Also differ from 1st-years in distinct (but variable) pale bill base and sometimes pale eye; sometimes show single slate-grey (adult-like) scapular/ mantle feathers, acquired in winter/early spring, at which time diamond marks con-fined (through wear) to inner rear scapulars. *Subsequent immature plumages* In *3rd-year* plumage (gained by prolonged moult during previous winter/spring as well as into sum-mer/autumn), autumn Siberian show many adult-like grey feathers on mantle, back, scapulars, tertials and upperwing-coverts, though with clearly more variable vestiges of immaturity than in congeners of correspond-ing age, while tail feathers still show wider black subterminal marks than on other forms treated here; distinct but variable bold head streaking, chiefly in late autumn/winter; bill (usually with obvious subterminal band) and legs remain predominantly pink and eye is distinctly pale. Many are still moulting outer primaries in January/February, at which time often show new slate-grey upperpart feathers. Owing to extremely retarded moult, *4th-year* Siberian looks very different from adult: distinct features are slate-grey upperparts, whitish iris and dark subterminal bill band (legs and bill still mostly pinkish-yellow or dull yellow). Extensive grey feathering approaching adult, but all parts are in various active moult during autumn, winter and even early spring; new secondaries and tail usually indistinctly dark-centred, while black area on primaries obviously wider than on adult (some birds stop moulting before early-spring migration and migrate north with old, worn outer primaries), and new/fresh primaries in winter have smaller white tips and mirrors. When still fresh, shows extensive dark bold head streaking. *5th-year* generally as adult, but (unlike congeners) still shows vestiges of immaturity in plumage and mainly in bare parts. Apart from very distinctive (late and retarded) primary moult, Siberian's size and structure, particularly of head and bill, are always important for identification in these transitional plumages.

Juveniles

Juveniles of the three species are darker than their respective 1st-winters, with large, dark brown, pale-edged scapulars typical of juve-nile large gulls. Armenian differs, however, from Yellow-legged in its slightly smaller size, stouter bill, paler inner primaries, and greater-covert, tertial and tail patterns (see 1st-winters of those species); juvenile Armenian also has narrower scaly-fringed scapulars, giving overall darker, more *fuscus*-like rather than (as juvenile Yellow-legged) *argentatus*-like appearance. Juvenile Siberian is also distinguishable from Armenian and Yellow-legged: head to belly predominantly dark (not unlike *fuscus* and also similar to *argentatus*, but distinctly browner, less greyish in tone); generally dark brown above and below, approaching *armenicus* and *fuscus*, but characteristically patterned with more solidly (less notched) blackish central marks on scapulars; head rather dark, if not too worn shows diagnostic demarcated dark ear-coverts; otherwise rather distinct, with shape and other plumage features (e.g. remex/tail pattern) just as 1st-year (which see).

References Grant (1986, 1987), Gruber (1995), Shirihai *et al.* (in prep.).

Orange-billed Terns

Where and When Caspian Tern *Sterna caspia* is a cosmopolitan species, in W Palearctic being a local summer visitor to coastal and inland waters in Baltic, Spain, N Africa, Middle East and Romania eastwards, some wintering at coasts/estuaries in south of region; vagrant elsewhere. Royal Tern *S. maxima* breeds in America, and in W Palearctic only on offshore islands in Mauretania (Banc d'Arguin), dispersing north to S Spain; vagrant elsewhere. Lesser Crested Tern *S. bengalensis* is a summer visitor in W Palearctic to Libyan coast and Red Sea and Persian Gulf (sporadically elsewhere around Mediterranean, often in colonies of Sandwich Tern *S. sandvicensis*, with which has interbred), also regular (dispersal/passage) NW African and Atlantic coasts and sometimes winters in extreme south of region; vagrant north to Britain. Crested Tern *S. bergii* possibly breeds on islands of Red Sea and Persian Gulf (status unclear), but virtually unknown elsewhere in region. Elegant Tern *S. elegans* is a rare vagrant from W America, usually associating with Sandwich Terns.

Identification Main points to look for are bill shape and colour, tone of upperparts and any contrasts with rump and tail, underwing pattern, and leg length. Note, however, that evaluating tones of grey is often very difficult, especially in strong sunlight (even when direct comparison possible). Juveniles (usually accompany parents on autumn migration) have shorter bill, shorter/less pointed wings and shorter tail until 1st autumn.

Moult Adults have complete post-breeding moult, with remiges usually not fully replaced until late winter, when a partial moult (head, some body feathers, inner primaries and some rectrices) produces summer plumage (primary moult suspended in spring). Upper surfaces of primaries become darker with wear and gradual moult leads to dark outer wing or dark wedges on upperwing. From autumn, juveniles have partial moult to 1st-winter; contrast between retained juvenile outer primaries and their coverts and new inners most obvious in 1st summer.

Caspian Tern

Structure and General Appearance Should be identifiable by size alone: the largest of all terns. Huge and heavily built, approaching size of a large gull. Massive, blunt, scarlet bill characteristic; head large and angular, with flat crown and often almost perpendicular nape/hindneck; legs relatively long. Has distinctive shape in flight, with long pointed wings and relatively short, barely forked tail but powerful head/neck (appears front-heavy). Closest to Royal Tern, but latter smaller, less heavy in build, somewhat narrower-winged, longer-tailed and with smaller and more pointed bill. At all times Caspian shows diagnostic large dark area on under primaries.

Plumage and Bare Parts *Adult* Pale grey above with white rump and tail (outer tail often with some grey feathers); outer 3–6 primaries have blackish-grey tips and inner webs. Underwing with blackish primaries (only innermost being paler), forming diagnostic large dark patch (reported rarely to have black restricted to broad tips on outer 5–6 primaries). Cap black with insignificant nuchal crest. Bill bright red with small yellowish tip and variable dusky subterminal ring; legs black. Outside breeding season, forehead, lores and central crown mottled black and white (look uniform grey at distance), with more solid broad black band from rear lores to nape sides (most have winter cap from late autumn to about February, whereas Royal moults out summer cap from start of nesting); outer primaries become darker in winter with wear; bill often duller, with broader dark ring (rarely, whole tip dark). *Non-adults* Juvenile less heavily patterned than other juvenile terns, occasionally almost unmarked: cap dark brown, spotted white/sandy (appearing uniform from distance), but

forehead/crown sometimes paler; resembles non-breeding adult, but with variable dark V-shaped marks above (especially on scapulars), faint dark lesser-covert and secondary bars and thin dark terminal tail bar; bill duller, more orange-red. Legs yellow-brown at fledging, quickly turning blackish. Wing markings become more obvious with wear during 1st winter (retained juvenile primaries then very dark) and normally retains some juvenile markings (e.g. on tail) until 1st summer. Subsequent immature plumages much as adult.

Flight Behaviour and Call Flight slow, ponderous, with deep beats; makes spectacular gannet-like plunge-dives from various heights. Typical call loud, deep and croaking, recalling a heron, 'krraah'. Juveniles with adults give high-pitched sharp 'weee'.

Royal and Lesser Crested Terns

Structure and General Appearance The two are similar in general shape and build, but Royal is larger (much larger and bulkier than Sandwich Tern, with heavier head/breast area and with stronger bill, approaching Caspian). Bill of Royal varies in shape, that of vagrant American race being clearly deeper with more prominent gonydeal angle. Perched Royal not unlike a small, slim, short-legged Caspian with narrower bill (often held slighly upwards); wingtips level with or projecting a little beyond tail tip (on Caspian wing projection longer). Lesser Crested close to Sandwich in size, but has longer, narrower wings and more elongated body; compared with Royal, has straighter, narrower and less deep-based bill and shorter legs, and looks more delicate, less full-chested, with longer wing projection.

Plumage and Bare Parts *Adult breeding* Following are the most important distinguishing features. 1 BILL On Royal deep orange (not red) with darker orange base, becoming yellower at tip (lacks dark subterminal ring of many Caspian); may occasionally have red bill (especially nominate American race). Lesser Crested has bright orange-yellow bill, becoming yellower at tip.

Lesser Crested Tern. Close in size to Sandwich Tern, but upperparts darker.

Sandwich Tern.

Caspian Tern. Huge. Blunt scarlet bill, pale upperparts, long legs.

Royal Terns, showing variation in bill and amount of black in crown of non-breeders.

The larger Crested Tern has bill cold green-yellow without orange tint. Dark upperparts. White forehead at all times.

Caspian Tern. Dark under primaries diagnostic. Non-breeding birds have pale forehead.

Royal Tern. Underwing pattern similar to Lesser Crested and Elegant Terns.

Lesser Crested Tern.

Elegant Tern.

Note bill shapes and prominence of gonydeal angle.

Elegant Tern. Note bill shape, shaggy crest, white rump.

Royal Tern. Much larger than Sandwich Tern, heavy bodied. Very pale above, shortish crest.

Elegant Tern in breeding plumage. Size and upperparts as Lesser Crested Tern.

Lesser Crested Tern. Smaller and darker than Royal Tern, looking shorter-legged.

Royal Tern

Juvenile

Lesser Crested Terns. Both Royal and Elegant Terns share this plumage sequence. Note grey rump of Lesser Crested.

Lesser Crested Tern. Royal Tern is paler, larger, with white rump.

1st-winter

1st-Summer.

1st-winter Lesser Crested Tern. In immatures the bill is not fully formed and the colour washed out.

127

2 HEAD Both have all-black crown with prominent shaggy crest, but note, importantly, that Royal's forehead quickly becomes white once breeding started, most having white forehead by June. 3 UNDERWING Both lack Caspian's extensive dark hand below. Instead have dark trailing edge to underside of primaries, distinct on Royal and rather less so on Lesser Crested. 4 UPPERPARTS Upperparts of Royal very pale grey (average slightly darker on American race) with white rump and tail; Lesser Crested a shade darker grey (especially in Mediterranean population), with (when fresh) paler grey remiges and pale grey rump and tail; contrasts, however, often not obvious. *Adult non-breeding* Both tend to have duller, less orange bill (that of Royal sometimes tinged greenish/brown) and have forehead and crown white. Royal has relatively narrow blackish U-shaped band from rear eye across nape (can also show some dark spots/streaks on rear crown) and black loral spot, separated by fairly distinct broad white eye-ring (thus forehead, crown and lores whiter than on Caspian, lacking mottled appearance, and with more complete white eye-ring). Lesser Crested generally has broader, more solid dark band behind eye and across nape and more obvious and more extensive dark streaking on rear crown; eye-ring less distinct, often obscure in front of eye. Note, however, that Royal starts to gain black on crown early, from February or before, when differences less clear (most Royal have complete cap from March/April). *Juveniles* Juveniles of the two are very similar. Head as respective adult winter, but with broader black band and more heavily spotted/streaked rear crown (eye-ring less clear-cut); back, scapulars and tertials with variable brownish/grey centres and pale fringes; outer wing largely dark (feathers edged pale); inner wing grey (somewhat darker on Lesser Crested) with dark grey bars on lesser coverts, greater coverts and secondaries and with contrasting pale medians (bars, especially that on lesser coverts, often less marked on Lesser Crested than on Royal); tail pale grey with dark terminal band and sides,

rump a shade paler; white underwing shows dark trailing edge (more complete than on adult and most obvious on secondaries) and sometimes pale grey lesser coverts. Bill duller, paler, more yellowish, than on adults; legs also paler (often yellowish or orangey, especially on Royal), but quickly darken (though some Royal may apparently still have pale legs in 2nd winter). *Subsequent immature plumages* Both species share similar plumage sequence and are very difficult to separate by plumage. During 1st winter upperparts become more uniform grey (Lesser Crested with grey rump, whiter on Royal), bars on wing somewhat faded (occasionally broken), and central area of wing very pale (whitish), and dark tail band obvious; new pale grey inner primaries contrast strongly with retained juvenile outers. Bill of Royal generally becomes orange, that of Lesser Crested similar or more yellow-orange. In 1st summer closer to winter adult (with rather more extensive dark head markings), but usually still show at least traces of dark secondary and lesser-covert bars and some dark-tipped feathers in tail; unmoulted juvenile outer primaries and their coverts dark and contrast with fresh pale inners (can have three generations of primaries, with central ones most worn), whereas adults have more uniform primaries in spring/early summer. By 2nd winter/2nd summer much as adult (but with darker outermost primaries); some show traces of secondary bar and (more rarely) lesser-covert bar.

Flight Behaviour and Call Both recall Sandwich Tern, but the larger Royal has somewhat slower, heavier flight. Typical calls grating, very like that of Sandwich but slightly deeper and less clearly disyllabic.

Hybrids Vagrant Lesser Crested in Europe have formed mixed pairs with Sandwich Tern and sometimes produced hybrid young. See especially Gillon & Stringer (1994).

Aberrant Sandwich Sandwich Terns with yellow/orange bill may possibly occur very rarely in W Palearctic. Lesser Crested best separated from such very similar-looking individuals by its slightly deeper-based bill, broader white wedge between gape and black of forehead, and slightly darker grey upperparts and grey rump and tail.

Crested Tern

Structure and General Appearance Large, with slightly decurved bill and short legs. Crest shaggy and very long (longer than on all but Elegant). Resembles Royal in size and build, but slimmer and less full-chested; bill has more obvious gonys and more decurved tip (distal part of lower mandible can even appear concave) compared with most Royal. Appears front-heavy in flight, with narrow wings angled (primaries pressed back) and bill drooped. Has darkest grey upperparts of all crested terns, forehead white at all times. and bill always yellowish. Lesser Crested is much smaller and paler, with straighter, narrower bill.

Plumage and Bare Parts *Adult breeding* Head pattern similar to Royal, but lower forehead white even in breeding plumage. Upperparts and upperwing-coverts very dark grey (rump slightly paler, tail sides white), contrasting with paler mid-grey primaries and outer secondaries; underwing pattern as Royal. Bill cold yellow (very rarely tinged orange in breeding season), shading paler at tip and often green-tinged at base. Legs black. *Adult non-breeding* Head pattern more diffuse than on Royal, with more extensive dark on nape (heavily mottled white) merging with white central crown and often some dark marks running down rear ear-coverts; eye-ring obscure. Upperparts somewhat paler than on breeding adult (but still much darker than other terns); worn primaries darker, contrast less with rest of wing. Bill usually strongly tinged dull greenish rather than pure yellow (can be pale yellow) and often darker at base. *Juvenile/immature* The most heavily patterned and darkest of all species. Similar to juvenile Royal/Lesser Crested, but darker above with more contrasting (blackish) markings and crown more spotted/streaked; inner primaries paler than wing-coverts. Bill much as adult winter; legs often dull greenish-yellow, soon becoming blackish. By 1st winter

upperparts and upperwing-coverts greyer and more uniform, and median coverts fade with wear and contrast more with secondary and covert bars; by 2nd winter much as adult, but with retained juvenile outer primaries and their coverts and some secondaries and variable dark tail band.

Flight Behaviour and Call Has strong, buoyant and rather bounding flight, foraging over wide distances. Typical harsh, grating call is slightly deeper than that of Sandwich, recalling Royal's.

Racial Variation Red Sea race *velox* described above. Slightly smaller southern race *thalassina* (could possibly occur as vagrant) much paler grey above, with whitish rump and tail; similar to Lesser Crested, and best distinguished by bill features.

Elegant Tern

Identification of vagrant Lesser Crested and Elegant Terns in Europe is still disputed: individuals of both (but mostly former) have occurred in colonies of Sandwich (and interbred). Possible (but unconfirmed) existence in W Palearctic of Sandwich with 'yellow' bill poses further problems, and such birds, if they do exist, would be most difficult to separate from Elegant (except longest-billed).

Structure and General Appearance Very close to Lesser Crested in size and build, recalling a slender Sandwich Tern with very slim, long orange bill. Bill distinctly longer, thinner (though rather deep-based) and obviously curved, especially on upper mandible, and gonydeal angle inconspicuous; longest-billed birds striking, but females (average shorter-billed) and juveniles (bill still growing) have more orange and less curved bill and could cause problems. Adult's crest longer and shaggier than on all other *Sterna* terns, drooping well down nape even when sleeked.

Plumage and Bare Parts Differs from Lesser Crested as follows. *Adult breeding* 1 BILL Typically reddish-orange, at least at base (where often red), becoming yellower along culmen and at tip; more orange-yellow on

Lesser Crested. 2 HEAD Crest much longer and more ragged than Lesser Crested's, and often shows narrower area of white between eye and bill than latter (more as on Sandwich). 3 UPPERPARTS Pale grey (close to Sandwich in tone) with contrasting whitish rump and tail; on Lesser Crested slightly darker (difficult to judge on lone individuals), with rump and tail somewhat paler (but grey, not white). Note that on Lesser Crested fresh primaries appear paler than inner wing, but no obvious contrast on Elegant. 4 UNDER-PARTS Breeding-plumaged Elegant may have faint pink tinge, never shown by Lesser Crested. *Adult non-breeding* Head band averages broader than on Lesser Crested, and usually shows no white eye-ring (thin ring visible only at very close quarters); Lesser Crested has at least partial (obscure)

eye-ring. Bill paler, more sandy-red, than on adult breeding, but still usually somewhat more orange-looking than on non-breeding Lesser Crested. *Juvenile/immature* Compared with Lesser Crested, juvenile Elegant (most unlikely in region) more strongly patterned, with dark brownish bases and subterminal marks to feathers of mantle, scapulars and wing-coverts, and bill more orange-tinged, often with diagnostic darker upper mandible. Plumage sequence as Lesser Crested (and Royal), but may lose lesser-covert bar earlier (by 1st summer) than Lesser Crested. Older immatures best told by same differences as for adult.

Call Typical call much as that of Sandwich.
References Alström *et al.* (1991a), Gillon & Stringer (1994), Malling Olsen & Larsson (1995).

White-cheeked Tern

Where and When White-cheeked Tern *Sterna repressa* breeds locally on coast and islands of N Indian Ocean, including from Kenya northwards along Red Sea to Tiran Island. In N Red Sea summer visitor (March to end November), and throughout range more pelagic in winter over northern Indian Ocean (some southern populations also winter along coast near breeding grounds). Flocks of tens to hundreds regular in spring-autumn southern Sinai; variable numbers, mainly 1st-summers, oversummer at Eilat.

General Features and Structure A medium-sized tern, closest to Common *S. hirundo* but slightly smaller, with shorter tail streamers, and bill generally looks proportionately longer, thinner and slightly drooping. In flight appears rather stout, with comparatively shorter but considerably narrower wing and shorter tail. Hovers low and splashes on to surface with wings raised, catching prey at or near surface (cf. plunge-diving and partial/complete immersion typical of Common and Arctic). In some plumages superficially resembles marsh terns *Chlidonias*, but tail always longer and deeply forked, wing and bill longer and pointed, and always shows

some differences in plumage and wing pattern; also, habitat exclusively marine. General impression is of a graceful sea tern, at all times darkest and most uniform of its medium-sized congeners and with rump and tail concolorous with grey back and wings.

Plumage *Adult breeding* Mostly uniform dark ash-grey to sooty-grey, with obvious white facial streak separating black cap from grey underparts (but beware dark race *longipennis* of Common, which passes through/winters in Middle East and E Africa; conversely, occasional White-cheeked with paler underparts can resemble Common). In flight, upperparts uniform, lacking contrast between rump and tail (cf. white/very pale grey rump and whitish tail of Common and Arctic, and uniformly pale upperparts of Roseate Tern *S. dougallii*); upperwing generally uniform with upper body, but when fresh also shows white secondary tips (can be difficult to detect, dependent on wear) and contrast between whiter inner primaries (well visible when fresh, after moult in December-April) and darker outers (mainly tips). Dark trailing edge broad and long, extending well towards secondaries (looks shorter on Common, nar-

Adult summer White-cheeked Tern. Mid-grey, white cheek, thin dark bill (with dark red base at close range).

Adult summer White-cheeked Tern. Note underwing pattern, dark rump.

Adult summer Common Tern.

Adult summer Common Tern. Slightly larger, paler beneath, may show dark bill in some races.

Adult summer Whiskered Tern. Note small size, blunt bill, white undertail-coverts, short tail and longer-looking legs.

1st-summer White-cheeked Terns. Rump and tail grey as back, dark carpal and secondary bars, blackish outer primaries.

1st-summer White-cheeked Tern. Rump and tail grey.

Juvenile White-cheeked Tern. Greyish rump and tail, broad dark subterminal crescents to lower scapulars and tertials.

1st-summer White-cheeked Tern near end of moult to 2nd-winter.

Juvenile Common Tern. Upperparts scalloping brownish, legs pale.

rower on Arctic). Underwing diagnostic: coverts whitish-grey, contrasting with dark grey secondaries, primaries (mainly tips) and sooty-grey (even blackish-grey in strong sun) belly, but often shows whiter central area, from carpal to body (contrast marked in some lights). Whiter rump sides than rump centre and belly, on some creating light patch, often a good feature even at long range. In such plumage bears striking resemblance to Whiskered Tern *C. hybridus*, but separated by structural features and lack of white undertail-coverts and lower belly. Legs orange-red and often dark brownish-red (normally not so red as Arctic or Common). Darker red bill

with extensive black tip looks all dark at distance. *Adult non-breeding* Forehead mottled and underparts wholly white, but retains ash-grey upperparts (including rump), tail and secondaries, as well as grey/white underwing-coverts and axillaries (thus differs from Common, Arctic and Roseate). Upperwing pattern (see above) also retained, but shows more contrast (unlike Common and Arctic). Lacks streamers, and bill becomes black or blackish-red. Structural features help separate it from marsh terns in non-breeding plumage; latter also differ in being varyingly less uniform and comparatively paler above and in having restricted black (in different pattern) on head. *1st-winter and 1st-summer* Bill and legs blackish. Plumage somewhat more similar to same-stage Common Tern, with forehead and forecrown, hindneck and underparts basically white and crown and nape blackish, but differs in obvious grey rump and tail always concolorous with rest of upperparts. In this plumage often most like marsh terns, but latter have rump and tail (especially tail base) variably paler than back. Again, structure differs considerably from that of marsh terns and Common/Arctic Terns. More striking are upperwing and underwing patterns, which diagnostic. On upperwing, carpal bar (dark greyish-brown lesser coverts) most conspicuous; outer primaries (retained from juvenile plumage, for more than six months) blackish, with inner webs whitish-grey; remaining primaries and secondaries dusky-grey with distinct brown tips, creating secondary bar. 1st-summers show even stronger upperwing contrast of darkish (old) outer primaries and whiter (new) inner ones; secondary bar also broken by new whiter feathers. Underwing mostly white, primaries and secondaries darker grey (on extremely 'contrasty' birds, particularly in strong sunlight, can recall underwing of Bridled Tern at long range). Surprisingly, White-cheeked may also be confused with 1st-summer Little *S. albifrons* and Saunders's Terns *S. saundersi* in strong sunlight (which makes these very small terns appear bigger): apart from smaller size, both can be separated by shorter tail, more pointed and straighter (not slightly decurved) bill, and quicker flight with faster, more flickering wingbeats; they also show narrower and less distinct carpal bar and are much (Little) or moderately (Saunders's) paler above, with less blackish on primaries. Little (but not Saunders's) also shows contrast between white tail/rump and more greyish back. *Juvenile* Generally as juvenile Common, but scapulars and tertials have fringes varyingly notched sandy to cinnamon and broader darkish subterminal areas creating clear scalloped pattern, unlike Common (which tends to show brownish 'saddle' area on scapulars, and on latter as well as tertials subterminal markings are more diffuse/narrower and closer to feather tips). In fresh plumage, forehead tinged greyish-brown, similar in colour to juvenile Arctic and greyer than buff-tinged forehead of juvenile Common. Legs and bill base greyish-tinged (with some indistinct flesh-pink areas), lacking the rather obvious orange-reddish of Common and Arctic. Dark appearance of juvenile White-cheeked bears some resemblance to juvenile Black Tern *C. niger*, but plumage paler and less scalloped and head pattern differs. Jizz and structure again important.

Sooty and Bridled Terns

Where and When Two terns from tropical/subtropical waters, generally dispersing offshore or pelagic outside breeding season. Bridled Tern *Sterna anaethetus* is a local and uncommon summer visitor to S Red Sea and Persian Gulf, and accidental north to Britain. Sooty Tern *S. fuscata* is a rare vagrant.

General Features Bridled is slightly smaller, slimmer and relatively shorter-winged and longer-tailed than Sooty (latter about size of Sandwich Tern *S. sandvicensis*). Bridled has elegant and buoyant flight with slow, elastic beats (body moving with each stroke), feeding by hovering and dipping to surface or by short plunge-dives. Sooty has stronger, more purposeful flight with deep beats, and often wheels and soars, feeding in similar manner. Adults of both are entirely blackish above and have white underparts.

Adults Most useful distinguishing features are as follows. *Breeding* 1 FOREHEAD On Bridled, white extends back to rear of or up to 1 cm past eye as a pointed supercilium, and uniformly broad black loral stripe extends to base of upper mandible (Sooty has broader, more rounded white forehead patch reaching to front of eye but not extending beyond, and loral stripe tapers from eye, where broadest,

Head on, Sooty Tern shows much more white on forehead than Bridled Tern. The black mantle ends abruptly at the base of the neck, a thin stripe connects mantle to crown.

Sooty Tern. Note exact extent of white over forehead and eye, and where loral stripe meets the bill, and compare with Bridled Tern below.

Bridled Tern. Reduced white forehead, diffuse pale collar.

Sooty Tern. Heavier than Bridled Tern. Note darkened primary tips without white 'fingers'.

Sooty Tern. Contrastingly black and white, no pale collar, browner when worn.

Bridled Tern. Slighter and more buoyant than Sooty Tern. Note thin 'finger' of white down outer primaries.

Bridled Tern. Note diffuse collar. Upperparts brownish slate-grey (but in a distant view may appear blackish), rump and tail slightly greyer.

to meet bill narrowly at gape). **2 UPPERPARTS CONTRAST** In favourable lights, Bridled shows fairly clear contrast between black crown, greyish to mid brown mantle and secondary coverts and blackish-brown remiges (Sooty uniformly blackish above, browner when worn, showing virtually no contrasts). Bridled can in some lights appear to show pale-collared effect (greyish nape/uppermost mantle), but this normally difficult to see and generally lacking on western Indian Ocean race *antarctica* (and never shown by Sooty, though on worn individuals white feather bases often revealed on nape/

upper mantle). **3 UNDERWING** Both have white underwing-coverts and axillaries. Bridled has tips of primaries and secondaries broadly dark grey and outer web of outermost primary dark grey, showing only diffuse contrast with pale grey/whitish primary bases, but with white inner webs to outer three primaries creating a very pale fan-like patch towards leading edge. Sooty has more contrasting pattern, with underside of flight feathers wholly blackish-grey. **4 TAIL** Bridled has tail dark grey-brown (more dark grey on Atlantic race *melanoptera*), whereas tail blackish on Sooty. Atlantic Bridled has white on outer three feathers (amount of white decreasing inwards); *antarctica* and Sooty have only outermost rectrix white. **Non-breeding** Both are somewhat paler above than in breeding plumage, with pale-spotted crown and lores (i.e. less contrast with white forehead, and loral stripe sometimes absent) and with pale edges to mantle feathers (on Bridled sometimes also scapulars; on Sooty sometimes also back, rump and tertials). Bridled, however, still shows effect of pale supercilium (often broader behind eye than in breeding plumage). Sooty's upperwing-coverts often appear variegated black and brown and outer tail can show even less white. Note, however, that many adult Sooty show no plumage change between seasons.

Immatures 1st-winter/1st-summer Bridled much as non-breeding adult, but with very worn retained juvenile outer primaries and secondaries (more pointed than on adult) and sometimes some coverts (can show contrast between dark lesser coverts and paler med-

ians/greaters), and with shorter outer tail feathers (with no or less prominent white); as adult from 2nd winter. Immature Sooty rather different: resembles juvenile (latter sooty-brown apart from dirty pale lower underparts and distinctly pale-spotted upperparts), but with paler forehead, nape and entire underparts (forehead and lores and to lesser degree crown spotted brown/grey; throat pale with dark streaks/spots, can form diffuse dark throat bar); in 1st summer throat and lower underparts become paler (may be greyish-white), and by 2nd-winter/2nd-summer as adult but with diffusely dark-mottled underparts (mottling may be seen on a few even up to 6th calendar-year).

Voice At breeding colonies, Bridled has a barking or yelping 'wep-wep' and Sooty a very loud and characteristic 'ker-wak-awak'. Both rather silent at other times, but feeding flocks of Bridled utter short harsh calls.

References Alström *et al.* (1991a), Harris (1988), Malling Olsen & Larsson (1995).

Sandgrouse

Where and When Pin-tailed Sandgrouse *Pterocles alchata* occurs in steppe, semi-desert and desert edge, chiefly on flat or slightly rolling plains, and strongly attracted to partly dry cultivated areas, breeding SE France and parts of Iberia (accidental elsewhere S Europe), NW Africa, parts of Levant and S Asia; resident and nomadic, with some true migration. Black-bellied Sandgrouse *P. orientalis* is found in similar habitat, also ascending to higher and broken areas, and has similar distribution, but more sedentary (accidental north to Belgium and Germany). Lichtenstein's Sandgrouse *P. lichtensteinii* is apparently the most desertic and resident sandgrouse (in region), quite widespread in parts of N Africa, Arabia, SE Iran to NW India but very restricted in W Palearctic; best observed in S Israel and Sinai, where inhabits stony mountain wadi beds with some scattered scrub and acacias, always in very dry, hot areas. Crowned Sandgrouse *P. coronatus* breeds N Africa, S Levant, Arabia and east to

NW India, where largely resident in extreme desert (high-lying stony deserts, fewer in absolute desert); best observed in Morocco and Israel. Spotted Sandgrouse *P. senegallus*, widespread in N Africa and S Middle East east to NW India (accidental Italy), is the most numerous desert sandgrouse and highly nomadic; favours sandy and stony deserts, chiefly open lowland with little/no plant cover but often sparse shrubs and grasses, in winter often shifting to dry cultivated fields. Chestnut-bellied Sandgrouse *P. exustus* breeds Africa (mainly south of Sahara), parts of Arabia, Iran and east to Indian subcontinent, in semi-desert and steppe to very dry areas (prefers open rolling sandy/stony tracts), where resident and nomadic; status in Near East unclear, apparently some extensive invasions between mid 19th and early 20th centuries (and one record Hungary), but none since (except in Egypt). Pallas's Sandgrouse *Syrrhaptes paradoxus* breeds in steppe/semi-desert from about Caspian Sea east to Mongolia; partially migratory, and also periodic eruptions, some reaching Near East/Europe west to Britain and Spain.

General Most sandgrouse are medium-sized with robust body but comparatively small wings, normally producing fast flight with whirring wingbeats. Terrestrial, they walk or waddle on short legs, and head-and-bill always looks small. All are attractive, in soft shades of brown, red-brown, buff or yellowish and grey, often with black and white markings, so look pale and 'dense-plumaged'; strong sexual plumage dimorphism. All have characteristic plumage features and diagnostic calls. Most distinctive are their long flights to drink at favourite freshwater sources, either at dusk (Lichtenstein's) or in the morning (all others). Although all are easily separated, particularly at close quarters, a general lack of familiarity with them combined with the complexity of their plumage patterns (too many identification features) can lead to unexpected confusion, chiefly in areas where several species occur and especially when seen at long range.

Pin-tailed Sandgrouse

In Flight, and Voice The only one to show pure white underbody, below breast; joins with white underwing framed in black. From above, less contrast between blackish-grey remiges and golden-green/grey upperbody and chestnut and buff-yellow coverts, but coloration visible only at short range. Distinct in its long and pointed rear body with long tail-streamers (missing during moult, or lacking on juveniles and 1st-winters, or just not visible even from rather close proximity) and its long narrow wing, which gives unique appearance with rather deep and regular wingbeats, producing apparently very fast flight; often likened to Golden Plover *Pluvialis apricaria*. Call a loud 'catar catar' suggesting Jackdaw *Corvus monedula*. Highly gregarious, collects in large dense flocks (chiefly in winter, locally can number thousands), like pre-roost starling gatherings.

On Ground Most intricately patterned and colourful. Distinguished by having crown to tail greenish-buff, slightly mottled with yellow, but generally looks rather plain/darkish (male) or yellowish-brown/buff closely barred black/grey (female), and by deep rufous-buff (male) or ochre (female) chest bordered above and below by narrow black bands; male has black throat, unlike female, which instead has additional narrow black band on uppermost breast, and both have pronounced black line through eye. Juveniles and 1st-winters show 'ghost pattern' of respective adult.

Black-bellied Sandgrouse

In Flight, and Voice Bulkier, with the most robust body, broad and rounded wings and relatively short tail lacking streamers, giving slower take-off and slower flight action on straight course. Combination of broad black belly and contrast on underwing (white coverts and black remiges) diagnostic; only Chestnut-bellied and Pallas's show rather extensive black on underbody, but both are slimmer-bodied with narrower wing and normally (adults) elongated central tail feathers, and have wholly black (former) or largely white (latter) underwing. Call distinct, rather gruff yet soft, gurgling or bubbling, often rolling 'churr-urr-urr', suggesting Black Grouse *Tetrao tetrix*.

On Ground Noticeably larger and heavy-bodied, also looking rounded, but thick neck comparatively longer and legs slightly taller, which often contributes to a more grouse-like appearance and often makes black belly visible. Male told from other sandgrouse by combination of black and chestnut throat, black band dividing grey breast and buff-white upper belly, and basically yellow-ochre upperbody and wing-coverts (with/without olive-brown centres); female has similar pattern, but breast and head area mainly buff-sandy and spotted, throat pale buff with narrow black lower band, and upperparts barred/scalloped/spotted. 1st-winters show 'shadow appearance' of respective adult, but reduced in coloration. Juveniles of both sexes much nearer female, but develop adult-type feathers soon after flying.

Lichtenstein's Sandgrouse

In Flight, and Voice Seen mainly at dusk during arrival/departure at drinking sites. The smallest, shortest-tailed and most round-winged; generally looks rather pale grey and buff (but extremely densely marked), with strong upperwing contrast of dark (brownish-black) remiges. Underwing wholly dark greyish-brown, with little or no contrast. As normally observed in daylight only at close quarters (when flushed), detailed plumage pattern can be checked even in flight (see below). Flight call 'wheet-wheet-wheet' and 'qwee-oo'; also guttural 'krerwerwerwer'.

On Ground Small, with more compact appearance, and generally closely barred blackish on yellow-buff (mainly male) or grey (mainly female). Adult male distinct: has buff-yellowish breast traversed by narrow bands, one across centre and one dividing breast from belly; also black and white forehead and face and orange bill, unlike other sandgrouse of region, as well as pale gold-buff bars across wing-coverts. Female much paler, duller, with bars (and vermiculations) finer and closer and rather even, thus not interrupted by bold black markings on head and breast, but shows wide whitish area around eye and has blackish bill; similar only to female Crowned Sandgrouse, but smaller and lacks that species' strong yellow throat and its isabelline-brown upperwing-coverts with large buff/white spots (in fact, at close range, almost all corresponding feathers different in pattern), and underwing patterns also differ. Juvenile largely resembles female. 1st-winters much as adults, but male shows (until first pre-breeding moult) only partial or even no black-and-white facial marks and reduced and paler wingbars and chest bands.

Crowned Sandgrouse

In Flight, and Voice Smallish, with broad wing base but long and pointed primaries; short-tailed, but rear body looks rather long. General appearance of pale sandy-brown upperbody and upperwing-coverts, contrasting with solid blackish remiges (on second-

aries only tips visible, forming narrow black line along rear edge), and pale sandy/buff or whitish underbody and underwing-coverts, also contrasting with black flight feathers. In flight confusable with closely similar Spotted Sandgrouse (both often share same areas, sometimes seen together), but latter normally shows elongated tail and narrow black patch on central belly (detectable only from close range) and has different upper- and underwing pattern with much less contrast. Flight call a repeated guttural chatter but loud, 'ch-ga ch-ga-ra' or 'gatut-gadidada'.

On Ground Short-tailed, but still has horizontal stance and slender body (chiefly rear); legs very short. Male distinguished by combination of black facial marks (see plate) and pale rufous crown, surrounded by pale blue-grey, and by having small well-defined spots (unlike those of Spotted, compare on plate) from mantle to wing-coverts; female almost wholly and evenly close-barred, vermiculated and flecked with dark brown or black, except for deep ochre-yellow throat, differing strongly from female Spotted, which has unmarked belly (except narrow black central patch) and dark-spotted (not barred) chest and upperparts. Juvenile nearer female, but throat whitish; both differ from juvenile/female Lichtenstein's in lacking streaked throat and in having large pale tips (speckles) over all wing-coverts and scapulars, as well as in pattern of barring and size. 1st-winters resemble respective adult, but male lacks or has reduced black facial marks and general head coloration indistinct, more or less intermediate between adult male and female; may be confused with male Spotted, but latter lacks well-defined pale spots on mantle, scapulars and lesser coverts and shows black belly streak and different wing pattern (when wing-stretching or in flight).

Spotted Sandgrouse

In Flight, and Voice Close to Crowned Sandgrouse in size, but looks slimmer-bodied with pointed tail (often long streamers) and more narrow-based and pointed wings. Unlike Crowned, has plain and pale belly (including female) except for narrow longitudinal black central patch which should easily be seen from close range. At long range, it should be distinguished from Crowned (apart from by diagnostic call) by different, relatively indistinct and rather pale wing pattern: lacks prominent contrast of pale coverts and solid black flight feathers shown by Crowned on both sides of wing, and instead shows pale upperwing except for dark trailing edge along entire wing and brown patch on central median and greater coverts, while underwing has whitish lesser and median coverts and paler grey primaries but distinct solidly blackish patch over rear inner wing (greater coverts and secondaries) and also blackish primary tips. Flight call a bubbling, guttural 'quitoo quitoo'.

On Ground Stands rather low and short-legged, and black belly patch only just visible (normally only behind legs). Male distinct, with deep yellow-orange throat, pale grey-blue supercilium which merges with greyish sandy-isabelline neck and chest, and indistinct pink-brown crown; otherwise rather pale sandy olive-brown above, with only pronounced dark area on large wing-coverts (with contrasting sandy tips). Female has spotted and slightly mottled upperparts, wing and chest. As in flight, the long tail-streamers are difficult to see, unless at close range. Juvenile nearer female, but also barred, with whitish throat, and lacks streamers; best separated from juvenile Crowned by its plain belly except for blackish central streak. 1st-winter nearer adult, but overall pattern and coloration generally indistinct and paler and often shows some old juvenile feathers.

Chestnut-bellied Sandgrouse

In Flight, and Voice Small, but with comparatively long, pointed tail with streamers (indistinct on female) and very long and narrow wing; uniform dark underwing diagnostic, especially combined with blackish-chestnut belly. Above, shows contrastingly dark flight feathers with visible white trailing edge to primaries and yellowish-buff band along rear coverts, the rest predominantly sandy-brown. Flight call a guttural chuckle, 'whit-kt-arr', 'vitt-kerr-kerr' etc.

On Ground Rather small-looking but somewhat long-legged, making dark underparts quite visible. This, combined with following features, diagnostic. Male predominantly olive-greyish-brown above, buffy face merging into dusky isabelline chest, with horizontal black line dividing lower breast and upper belly, where colour becomes increasingly warm towards blackish-brown belly; pale yellowish-sandy spots edged olive/black (quite diffuse) on mantle, back, scapulars and tertials and (well marked, bold) on wing-coverts. Female's basic pattern approaches that of male, but all upperparts and head to chest are well spotted/barred/vermiculated, with yellowish throat pronounced, bold black-edged yellow spots on wing-coverts are more distinct (produce 4–5 broad bands), and tail-streamers shorter. 1st-winters as adults, but paler. Juveniles differ from adult female in having neck and breast with brownish scallops and pale fringes (instead of spotted/streaked) and upperparts and wing-coverts are warmer-coloured, with finer vermiculation. Could be confused with Black-bellied, but differs in size, structure and wing-covert pattern.

Pallas's Sandgrouse

In Flight, and Voice Smaller than Black-bellied, less bulky than Pin-tailed, with most elongated tail with longest streamers, and longest, narrowest, most curved wings with elongated tips. These features combined with wholly pale underwing (indistinct dark narrow trailing edge and small spots on axillaries) and small but conspicuous black belly patch diagnostic; upperwing generally looks weakly patterned and pale, showing yellowish coverts but with indistinct chestnut band on rear coverts, narrow dark trailing edge to secondaries, with pale greyish primaries. Both sexes have boldly mottled/spotted and coarsely barred upperparts. Commonest flight call a low-pitched 'cu-ruu curuu cu-ou-ruu'; also 'quut' or rolling 'por-r-r-r'.

On Ground Relatively large-looking, about

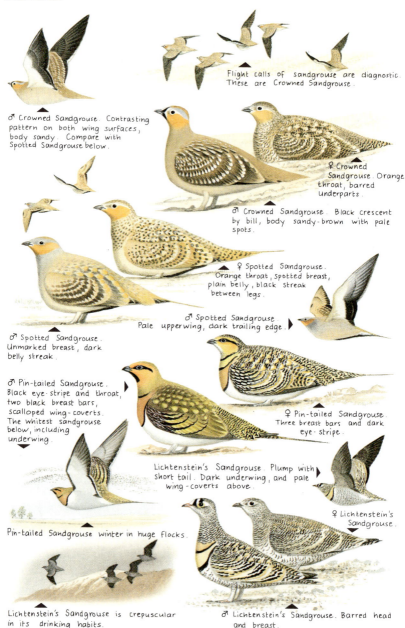

Flight calls of sandgrouse are diagnostic. These are Crowned Sandgrouse.

♂ Crowned Sandgrouse. Contrasting pattern on both wing surfaces, body sandy. Compare with Spotted Sandgrouse below.

♀ Crowned Sandgrouse. Orange throat, barred underparts.

♂ Crowned Sandgrouse. Black crescent by bill, body sandy-brown with pale spots.

♀ Spotted Sandgrouse. Orange throat, spotted breast, plain belly, black streak between legs.

♂ Spotted Sandgrouse. Pale upperwing, dark trailing edge.

♂ Spotted Sandgrouse. Unmarked breast, dark belly streak.

♂ Pin-tailed Sandgrouse. Black eye-stripe and throat, two black breast bars, scalloped wing-coverts. The whitest sandgrouse below, including underwing.

♀ Pin-tailed Sandgrouse. Three breast bars and dark eye-stripe.

Lichtenstein's Sandgrouse. Plump with short tail. Dark underwing, and pale wing-coverts above.

Pin-tailed Sandgrouse winter in huge flocks.

♀ Lichtenstein's Sandgrouse.

Lichtenstein's Sandgrouse is crepuscular in its drinking habits.

♂ Lichtenstein's Sandgrouse. Barred head and breast.

Black-bellied Sandgrouse. Heavier and slower flight action than other sandgrouse.

♀ Black-bellied Sandgrouse. Large, short-tailed. Note black belly, speckled head and breast with dark throat collar. Wings ochre as ♂, with speckling.

♂ Black-bellied Sandgrouse. Black remiges and white coverts beneath. Both sexes show black belly. Tail short.

♂ Chestnut-bellied Sandgrouse. Dark underwing and body diagnostic in both sexes.

♂ Black-bellied Sandgrouse. Orange throat, grey breast, black belly.

♀ Chestnut-bellied Sandgrouse. Smaller than Black-bellied Sandgrouse, no throat collar, long tail.

♂ Chestnut-bellied Sandgrouse. Note head and wing patterns, long tail.

Pallas's Sandgrouse. Note elongated wingtips and long tail in both sexes.

♂ Pallas's Sandgrouse. Both sexes show almost wholly pale underwing and small dark belly patch.

♀ Pallas's Sandgrouse. Note spotted sides (but not centre) to breast, black throat collar. Belly patch similar to ♂.

♂ Pallas's Sandgrouse. Similar to Spotted Sandgrouse. Note exact pattern of orange face, barred mantle and spotted wings.

139

comparable with Pin-tailed, also having quite elongated rear body and long tail-streamers, but extremely short legs make underbody almost invisible. Unmistakable. Male has mantle to wing (except remiges) sandy-buff, with bold blackish-brown spots and coarse barring chiefly on upperparts down to scapulars and tertials and large spots (restricted) on rear central wing-coverts; head to chest greyish-sandy, outlined by narrow pectoral band of fine flecks on lower breast, and face and nape/hindneck indistinctly orange. Female generally resembles male, but paler, with coarse bars/spots extending also over neck and breast sides and crown and over

much of wing-coverts, and fine flecks penetrate onto rear ear-coverts and throat; narrow band borders the yellowish-buff throat, but lacks male's bar across lower breast. 1st-winters mostly as adults, but juveniles (both sexes closer to female) distinguished by following features: tail not elongated; breast brownish-tinged, with fine markings, no ochre on head; paler and browner upperpart barring more crescent-shaped; throat pale buff, and dark belly patch restricted; most upperwing-coverts show more irregular brown subterminal crescents, less spots/mottling; and lacking the black necklace on lower breast.

Oriental Turtle Dove

Where and When Oriental Turtle Dove *Streptopelia orientalis* is an Asiatic species, breeding west to about Urals (race *meena*). Northern populations of *meena* and of nominate *orientalis* are migratory, wintering south to S India and Indochina; almost all vagrants in western Europe have been in Fennoscandia and Britain, mostly October-February, several having overwintered (often with suburban Collared Doves *S. decaocto*).

Identification and Ageing The only problem is in separating this species from very similar Turtle Dove *S. turtur*, a widespread summer visitor to most of region (though scarce Fennoscandia). With good views, adults should not be too difficult to identify, but younger (chiefly juvenile) birds and all individuals of smaller race *meena* of Oriental require great care. Important features to note are size, general plumage coloration, tail pattern and, particularly, pattern of wing-coverts (with younger birds, entire wing pattern important). Ageing an essential first step: juveniles (in which plumage late-hatched individuals migrate) are characterised by browner plumage, lack of neck barring, and less contrasting wing and scapular patterns (fringes narrower, browner, less bright). Timing of moult varies in both species, depending largely on hatching date; most gain adult plumage during 1st winter,

when can show a mixture of fresh, bright adult feathers and faded, worn juvenile ones. **Size and Structure** Oriental Turtle Dove is larger, much bulkier (nominate up to 75% heavier), fuller-breasted, broader-winged and slightly longer than Turtle Dove, but with proportionately somewhat shorter tail. In general shape recalls Stock Dove *Columba oenas* more than the more delicate, slender-looking Turtle Dove.

Adults General plumage of Oriental Turtle Dove is perceptibly darker than that of Turtle Dove, though this often not so apparent in race *meena*, which can be very close to latter in plumage tones. Lone adults should, however, be fairly readily separable in good views by combination of following features. **1 HEAD AND NECK** Nape and hindneck deep brown or pinky-brown, contrasting with grey crown and forehead, though hindcrown sometimes with some brown feathers (on Turtle, nape is grey, as crown). Neck bars vary in number, 4–6 narrow black bars being usual (3–4 broader ones on Turtle), but in both species apparent thickness depends on posture, looking thicker when neck extended. A useful indicator can be colour of intervening pale bars: usually with bluish tint on Oriental Turtle (white on Turtle), but southern populations of Turtle (and especially race *arenicola*) can show some blue while rarely race *meena* of Oriental Turtle

Adult Turtle Dove. Small. Note wide rufous fringes to scapulars and wing-coverts (pattern of scapulars same as inner coverts). Mainly olive rump, clean grey wing panel, whitish belly, neck marks black and white, nape grey.

Adult Turtle Dove. Note tail pattern, particularly outer web of outer feather.

Juvenile Turtle Dove. Coverts and scapulars dark-centred, fading gently to feather edges (centres more extensively dark on Oriental Turtle Dove). Pale grey nape, buffy lower rump.

Juvenile Oriental Turtle Dove moulting into adult plumage. Dark breast extending onto chest, wing-coverts more solidly dark centred. Dark nape and mantle, deep slate rump.

Adult Oriental Turtle Dove of race 'meena'. Usually lacks grey wing crescent of Turtle Dove.

Oriental Turtle Dove of race 'orientalis'. Note grey tail tips, and extension of black onto outer web of outer tail feather.

Adult Oriental Turtle Dove of race 'meena'. Only slightly darker than Turtle Dove. Nape pinky-brown, neck bars usually grey and black. Mantle dark, tertials and scapulars dark centred.

Adult Oriental Turtle Dove of race 'orientalis'. Thin rufous fringing; wing-covert tips cream, forming wingbars.

141

DOVES

may lack blue tint and then show black and white neck barring. **2** MANTLE TO RUMP Pinky-brownish mantle (more or less concolorous with nape/hindneck) contrasts with blue-grey back and rump (on Turtle, back and rump much browner, showing varying degree of contrast with grey nape). Note, however, that a few Oriental have fairly prominent brown tips to uppertail-coverts, while *meena* has brown rump and is blue-grey only on back, and that Turtle of race *arenicola* from WC Asia (migrate through Middle East but could also turn up in western Europe) generally show extensive grey on rump. **3** SCAPULARS AND UPPERWING Scapulars and tertials extensively blackish with well-defined deep orange-rufous fringes (Turtle has broader, paler, orangey fringes and smaller, dark centres, latter also often browner, less black). Wing-coverts with large, rounded black centres and narrow, contrasting, pale buff to whitish fringes, latter contrasting also with scapular fringes (on Turtle, centres more clear-cut black and pointed or triangular, with fringes relatively broader and more or less same colour as scapular fringes). Tips of greater and median coverts often produce effect of double wingbar, and sometimes lesser-covert tips also create barred effect (Turtle rarely gives this impression). Outer greater and median (and often lesser) coverts often fringed greyish but have blackish centres, and so do not create such an obvious grey panel as on Turtle Dove (which has outer coverts rather uniform pale bluish-grey, forming contrasting panel), but note that *meena* can have more Turtle-like pattern on median and lesser coverts and very occasionally has outer coverts blue-grey (reaching to carpal). Primaries more distinctly tipped pale when fresh (but beware individuals with worn primaries, very similar to Turtle Dove). **4** UNDERPARTS Breast dark pinkish-brown, sometimes tinged bluish at sides, paling gradually towards vent and becoming diagnostically grey on undertail-coverts (Turtle's breast paler violet-pink, lacking brown elements, and fading rapidly towards belly/vent, becoming pure white on undertail-coverts). Race *meena* of Oriental

rarely may have paler breast colour similar to Turtle and usually also has white undertail-coverts, though is still normally darker (and more extensively so) below than latter. **5** TAIL Nominate Oriental Turtle always has grey tips to tail feathers (always white on Turtle Dove) and black extends onto outer web of outermost feather (outer web all white on Turtle), this often producing impression of grey terminal tail band (though central feathers can virtually lack paler tip). Race *meena*, however, often has white rather than grey tips, and black area on outer web of outermost rectrix often much restricted (can be almost invisible in field), producing effect of paler surround to entire tail very like that of Turtle Dove. Moreover, both races of Oriental (particularly adults) have more black at base of undertail, commonly extending beyond and surrounding undertail-coverts (on Turtle, black largely concealed by coverts), this often creating U-shaped frame to coverts and detectable on distant perched birds. **6** EYE AND BARE FACIAL SKIN Oriental usually looks 'small-eyed', with eye more at midhead, and has more circular and very narrow, at times almost imperceptible ring of bare skin around eye (normally broad, more elliptical and well visible on Turtle), which can make Oriental's loral area appear more extensive and with greater distance between eye and gape than on Turtle. Skin colour varies on both, usually red/pinkish (or not uncommonly grey on Oriental).

Juveniles/1st-winters Crown and upperpart differences much as for adults (note that young birds of both species are browner overall), but juveniles of both lack neck bars and have far less contrasting wing and scapular patterns. At this age, separating the two by plumage alone can be extremely tricky and requires great care (and often experience), since differences frequently slight. Oriental Turtle has darker breast than Turtle, and dark colour reaches further down belly; breast can have diffuse orange-pink feather fringes (Turtle occasionally shows pale ochre fringes). Oriental's scapulars, tertials and wing-coverts are generally more solidly dark-centred with contrasting paler/rufous fringes (Turtle shows pale brownish centres with diffuse blackish shaft streaks, and less contrasting paler fringes). In fresh juvenile plumage, Oriental's primaries very dark with very well-defined rufous fringes (browner and with more diffuse and paler fringes on fresh Turtle), and greater primary coverts generally show no (or only very narrow) pale tips, looking all dark (Turtle usually has broad tips). It is important to check age of feathers: both species moult into adult plu-

mage in 1st winter (some fully adult by December/January), so a variable number of fresh adult feathers often present among faded juvenile ones; these new feathers, usually first in scapulars, coverts, tertials and primaries, aid the identification process.

Voice Oriental's four-note repeated cooing (more like a *Columba* dove, quite unlike Turtle's continuous purr), if given by spring vagrants, should clinch identification.

References Hirschfeld (1992), Hirschfeld & Svensson (1985).

Striated Scops and Scops Owls

Where and When Striated Scops Owl *Otus brucei* is a fairly widespread but local breeder in Iraq and adjacent countries west to SC Turkey and N Syria and from S Iran east to about Pakistan, and to limited (but largely unknown) extent also in easternmost Arabian Peninsula (populations in S and SW Arabia seem to match the form *pamelae*, nowadays considered conspecific with African Scops Owl *O. senegalensis*). Striated frequents dry to arid open country, semi-desert, open cultivated areas and dry stony hillsides with some scattered trees, groves, large gardens or riverine forest; southern populations largely residents or partial migrants, while northern ones are mainly summer visitors (e.g. in Turkey and Iraq) and apparently the main winter visitors to Levant and Arabia. Most reliable W Palearctic site for Striated is the 'tea park' in Birecik, Turkey, where a few pairs regular late March to early October; recently quite regular in winter and on early-spring passage in acacia wadis in Israel (Eilat and Ein Gedi). Scops Owl *O. scops* breeds widely across C Eurasia and winters Africa (resident and partial migrant Mediterranean region), with passage mainly mid August to mid October and mid February to late April: generally inhabits lightly forested regions, in open or broken forest, riverine forest, parkland or areas with scattered trees, i.e. better-vegetated and less dry areas than Striated, but on passage in arid areas both species favour acacia wadis and date palms.

Identification Before any plumage features observed, song (territorial/contact calls) is the best way to identify these two species: Scops has characteristic loud, rather musical whistle, 'tyuu', repeated every 2–4 seconds; Striated's calls are all extraordinarily soft, recalling Stock Dove *Columba oenas*, 'OO-ooo', with 4–8 notes rapidly repeated every 2–5 seconds (can be almost inaudible to human ear at 10 m). Owls are often discovered by chance, roosting in a tree by day, which usually gives best light conditions to discern fine plumage details; at night, artificial light tends to change appearance of colours and feather patterns (deep brown can appear grey-washed and vermiculated feathers can appear plain greyish or even white), so observer needs good experience to determine colours and feather patterns correctly in such circumstances, which can even influence apparent size and structural features. Remember also that shape and structure vary according to bird's activity and state of agitation: at day roost, especially when disturbed, the owl often stands bolt-upright with plumage sleeked and head feathers, notably ear-tufts, raised, appearing very slim with triangular, flat-topped head; during most night-time activities, usually appears dumpier, with 'relaxed' body plumage and more rounded head, or with only slightly sleeked upright posture and ear-tufts only slightly raised. In our region Scops is more variable than Striated, much variation being geographical but also strongly evident within a population (affecting general grey-ness and the pattern/depth/intensity of streaking and barring, and strength of rufous, creamy or sandy colours or amount of white speckling on upperparts): in European races, some populations contain both 'rufous' and 'grey' individuals, and latter (or pale greyish eastern races of Scops) may approach Striated in coloration. Separation of Striated from most European and Levant races of Scops (nominate, *mallorcae* and *cycladum*) should be fairly straightforward, but complicated by existence of pale greyish eastern races of Scops, mainly *turanicus*.

European/Levant races of Scops

Striated of races *obsoletus* and *exiguus* are best separated from European/Levant races of Scops by voice (see above) and by combina-tion of following features (but requires the best of views and reasonable light conditions). 1 SIZE AND STRUCTURE Striated averages larger and marginally bulkier-look-ing than Scops. Comparing birds in same plumage stage and same posture, Striated may appear dumpier and rounded-looking, with slightly lower forehead, even when plumage sleeked and ear-tufts fully raised (i.e. less strongly triangular shape to head and tufts than in Scops, and tufts appear slightly shorter and rounded, but can be identical). Tips of fully folded wing never project beyond tail tip (slight projection on most Scops), and normally tail appears marginally longer; primary projection slightly shorter (half to two-thirds of exposed tertials; three-quarters or equal on Scops) and only 5–6 primary tips visible (usually 6–7 on Scops), but this often impossible to discern in field. 2 FACIAL PATTERN Striated's facial disc is paler, greyer and much plainer-looking (lacks Scops's darkness around eye), and often shows obvious whitish wash (mainly between central face and eye) so that face may appear paler than crown (darker and almost concolorous with crown on most Scops); feathers of ruff bordering facial disc dull black, narrower/neater and more shar-ply demarcated from surrounding area

(rather broader, sometimes more diffuse or browner on Scops). 3 UNDERPARTS Striated has generally paler (greyer or sandier) ground colour, and at close quarters shows notice-able, precise longitudinal black 'feather-centre streaks' and variable indistinct broken dark horizontal bars, but background rather uni-form and faintly vermiculated; Scops's under-parts often show rather similar (often slightly broader or more diffuse) dark streaks and often heavy dark bars, with pale horizontal panels and darker broad warm brown cross-bars (narrower, indistinct or absent on all Striated), and general tone is darker and often browner. Both species have varying degree of bold blackish feather centres, chiefly on chest sides, but at very close quarters these may appear to become narrower and sharper towards tips on Striated, whereas on Scops they normally become slightly broader and more diffuse (best to examine several feather centres, to avoid being misled by any single abnormally patterned feather). 4 UPPER-PARTS In general, Striated is paler greyish, often with slight sandy wash (never any of the obvious rufous that predominates on most Scops, though often shows indistinct rufous-buff hindneck-collar but largely hid-den when head sunk between shoulders) and with streaking on average much neater, and always lacks prominent cross markings shown by most Scops chiefly on mantle and scapulars. Striated as a rule lacks Scops's large and conspicuous white spots on scapu-lars and the smaller ones on hindneck, mantle and wing-coverts (but beware that great deal of variation exists in amount and size of spots, which on some Scops very few and inconspicuous); primary coverts of Striated have richer pattern, with distinct and very broad horizontal whitish-sandy bars promi-nent on both webs of each feather, unlike Scops's ill-defined and narrower (also war-mer buff) bars that are largely restricted to outer webs. 5 'SHOULDER-STRAPS' On Striated, the large pale spots on outer scapu-lars are sandy to warm buff, often pale cream or sandy, but never whitish as on most Scops, but beware that light conditions greatly affect

Striated Scops Owl. Note shorter primary projection, longer tail, wide cream bars to primary coverts, warm rufous-buff or creamy 'shoulder straps'. Overall plainer above, with less spotting on nape than Scops Owl. Lacks white bars to breast.

Brown-phase Scops Owl. Striated Scops Owl does not show a rufous plumage phase.

Grey-phase Scops Owl. Primary projection long, equal to tail tip. Note pale nape spotting, pale cream-buff 'shoulder straps' and whitish bars to breast.

Striated Scops Owl. Paler face, dark streaks below without pale bars, but with uniform horizontal vermiculations.

Striated Scops Owl tends to have more rounded 'ears'. Compare with Scops Owl (left).

Grey-phase Scops Owl. Darker around eyes, lower belly shows pale cross-panels or squares.

Grey-phase Scops Owl. Both species are very approachable when roosting.

In close view, Striated Scops Owl (far right) shows feathering extending onto the toes, unlike Scops Owl (near right).

Central tail feather of Scops Owl (near right) is evenly barred to tip. Striated Scops Owl (far right) has wider bars, indistinct at tip.

reliability of this feature. **6** SUDSIDIARY FEATURES Striated's foot feathering usually extends onto bases of toes (on Scops always limited to tarsus, leaving toes bare) and, often on third toe, feathers reach along top of second phalanx; this feature, however, hard to see, and Striated in active moult tends to show partly or fully bare toe bases. All tail feathers of Striated have fewer light bars beyond uppertail-coverts (4–6 bars; 5–8 on Scops), and the bars are much wider and less speckled at borders; on central rectrices only 2–4 bars (5–7 on Scops) visible beyond tail-coverts and about 1 cm of feather tip freckled grey and pale buff, without traces of bars out to tips (on Scops, continuously marked with 5 or more virtually unspeckled buff or cream bars right out to feather tip, each bar rather narrower and with irregular and diffuse black upper edge). *Juveniles* Separation of juveniles relatively simple: Striated's underparts completely barred (very different from adult), whereas juvenile Scops similar to adult. *In flight* The two are similar in shape and flight action, though Striated appears somewhat slower, more like Little Owl *Athene noctua*, with slightly more rounded wing; in exceptionally good view, it may show wider and clearer pale barring on flight and tail feathers and primary coverts, and (unlike Scops) almost unmarked underwing-coverts.

Greyish eastern Scops

Race *turanicus* of Scops is even closer to Striated, showing generally paler and colder, more silvery-grey (less warm grey-brown) plumage with narrower and more contrasting streaks. Striated is best separated (apart from by calls) by patient and careful checking of following characters. Above-mentioned structural differences still apply, but some *turanicus* (as well as *cycladum*) have very short ear-tufts, even shorter than Striated's. Striated's lack of white spots and rufous-brown tone on hindcrown, mantle, scapulars and upper-wing-coverts is also useful (but beware that *turanicus* also often has these features reduced), while the buff or warm sandy rather than cream or white 'shoulder-straps' are still a constant difference between the two. Striated's more uniform underparts with narrower black 'feather-centre streaks' than on Scops (without latter's conspicuous fine dark bars and white subterminal bands) usually help distinguish it from *turanicus*, but existence of very pale individuals of *turanicus* limits use of this feature, especially in poor light conditions; in such cases, Striated's lack of white subterminal bands and the shape of its bold black feather centres (narrowing and becoming sharper towards tip; converse on Scops) are apparently the most important underpart features. Both Striated and *turanicus* show pale and uniform facial disc, but ruff framing this is less developed, generally narrower, on most Striated. Other features (tail pattern, primary coverts, foot feathering) that separate Striated from western races of Scops also eliminate eastern *turanicus*.

In the hand

As some silent, atypical or intermediate-looking individuals need to be trapped for identification, in-the-hand features are summarised. In Striated, outermost (10th, counting outwards) primary falls between 4th and 5th or may equal either, wing length 139–169, tail 66–78, and tarsus 26–35 mm; respective measurements for Scops are 5th–7th, 143–167, 60–76, and 23–29.

References Byers (1992), Cramp (1985), Hollom *et al.* (1988), Shirihai (1993), van den Berg *et al.* (1988).

Nightjars

Where and When Nightjar *Caprimulgus europaeus* is a numerous summer visitor and widespread on passage over much of Palearctic, wintering Africa and parts of Middle East.

Red-necked Nightjar *C. ruficollis* is confined to SW Europe and NW Africa, wintering slightly south of breeding range; vagrant elsewhere in western and southern Europe. Egyptian

Nightjar *C. aegyptius* breeds in deserts and semi-deserts of N Africa and Middle East to WC Asia, winters chiefly N and C Africa, and is regular on passage in Middle East and accidental north to Sweden. Nubian Nightjar *C. nubicus* is mainly E African, with local populations in deserts and semi-deserts north to eastern Israel.

General Confusion arises frequently owing to poor observation conditions (often at distance and in weak light), but, with care, flight behaviour, shape and plumage features should prevent mistakes. Separation complicated by sexual dimorphism and age and racial differences in plumage tone and patterning. Main problems are in distinguishing Nightjar and Red-necked Nightjar (mainly in W Europe); eastern races e.g. *unwini* of Nightjar from Egyptian (most of region) or from Nubian (Middle East); and separating the last two species (Middle East).

Red-necked Nightjar and Nightjar

On Ground Red-necked is larger (30-32 cm), against Nightjar's 26-28cm) and more robust, with relatively larger head and longer tail; wingtip always falls roughly half to two-thirds way along tail, reaching to about third/fourth tail bar counted from tip (on Nightjar, extends about three-quarters along tail, to about third tail bar, giving shorter tail projection). Red-necked is a greyer brown, has distinct rufous half-collar on nape (inconspicuous and largely greyish on Nightjar), and both sexes show pronounced, larger white throat patches and cheek bars (much weaker/smaller on Nightjar); rufous tone often extends to adjacent head area, particularly around throat patches and reaching to lower throat/upper breast, forming rather reddish 'face' compared with more grey-brown of Nightjar. Wing-coverts not so variegated in pattern, as relatively broader buffish tips to outer webs of longer lesser and median coverts contrast less with surrounding plumage and each is more separated from the next, together creating ill-defined and broken wingbars; Nightjar as a rule shows dark panel across upper lesser coverts contrasting with rest of wing, bordered below by pronounced buff-white wingbar and broad paler panel on central inner wing. Red-necked's second row of upper scapulars is usually sharper-patterned, with clear black inner-web centres and contrasting wide buffish/rusty outer-web fringes. Otherwise, most Red-necked have more cinnamon/buffy overall suffusion, although some rusty-brown extremes of Nightjar (of Mediterranean race *meridionalis*) can in certain lights approach general tone of brownish nominate Red-necked (SW Europe). Moreover, full-grown juvenile Red-necked has above features less evident/lacking, often superficially resembling Nightjar, but latter always shows the above 'negative features' and indeed juvenile lacks white primary spots of juvenile Red-necked.

In Flight All Red-necked have large white to buffy spots on distal halves of outermost three primaries and on tips of two outer pairs of rectrices; on Nightjar, spots smaller (males) or absent (juveniles/1st-winters and most females). Algerian race *desertorum* of Red-necked distinctly paler, with more sandy or pink/rufous-cinnamon suffusion, finely vermiculated, and often approaches Egyptian Nightjar in general tone, but primary pattern very different (and other Red-necked features present, can be checked on close-range perched birds). Flight action of Red-necked more powerful and swooping (looser action) with deep beats, often noticeably buoyant and graceful, but speed never reaches Nightjar's and wheels and twists less easily (fewer erratic dips and sideslips), while larger head and longer tail often noticeable.

Egyptian Nightjar and Nightjar

On Ground Egyptian is slightly smaller (24-26 cm) than Nightjar, with relatively short tail (wingtip falls not far short of tail tip, reaching roughly to second tail bar from tip). Egyptian has pale sandy-grey to pinkish grey-buff general plumage; Nightjar generally darker and browner, predominantly greyish-brown (but greyish or sandy eastern forms such as

Red-necked Nightjar. Note long tail at rest, rufous nape collar, prominent white throat and cheek bar.

Red-necked Nightjar. Both sexes show white wing patches, smaller or absent on Nightjar.

Nightjar. Smaller than Red-necked Nightjar, with proportionately shorter tail. Greyish nape, less obvious white throat patch, dark lesser-covert patch.

Egyptian Nightjar. No white wing patches, outer wing darker than inner wing.

Nubian Nightjar.

Red-necked Nightjar.

♂ Nightjar. Pale wing-coverts, dark leading edge to inner wing.

Nightjar of the race 'unwini'. Pale, but note streak over crown, long white streak under eye, dark ear-coverts, darker lesser-coverts.

♀ or 1st-year Nightjar. Uniform barred underwing.

Nubian Nightjar. White wing and tail patches, blackish primaries, underwing orangy.

Egyptian Nightjar. Large head which is inconspicuously patterned. Short tail. Underwing pale.

Nubian Nightjar. Small, pale with streaked crown, cinnamon hind-collar. Short wing projection and tail. Rusty secondaries.

Wingtips rounded.

148

unwini or *plumipes* can easily approach paleness of Egyptian). Though some Nightjars can appear very pale, both species have many features which rule out the other. Egyptian differs from Nightjar in following respects. **1 HEAD** Larger and inconspicuously patterned, generally unmarked or finely flecked, and lacks distinctive appearance of Nightjar (which always shows bold black streaks in centre of head top and dark ear-coverts). Also has very small throat patches, and indistinct cheek bars hardly extend beyond eye (always do so on Nightjar). **2 UPPERPARTS AND UPPERWING-COVERTS** At close range Egyptian's upperparts are complex, but less than Nightjar's, lacking latter's distinct bold dark streaks on mantle and scapulars and dark and pale wing panels; instead has black freckles (formed by black centres and wavy black subterminal 'bat shape' on each buffy feather), big on scapulars and tertials and small on wing-coverts.

In Flight Egyptian has Kestrel-like contrast above, with paler coverts, body and tail and darker remiges (Nightjar tends to appear darker with less/no contrast, but shows pale bar/panel on longer lesser and median coverts respectively); underside generally paler, with darkish remiges (owing to conspicuously widely spaced dark brown bars) and all-dark outer primary tips, but much paler and finely vermiculated underwing-coverts and chest, and has white flash at primary bases as well as cleaner buff belly to undertail-coverts (Nightjar rather uniformly barred below and more tinged with rufous-brown). These features apply to both sexes and all ages and races, even when distinguishing Egyptian from pale young female Nightjars of race *unwini*; to inexperienced observers, latter's palish appearance often recalls sandyish Egyptian. Egyptian's lack of white patches above in outer primaries and outer rectrices of limited value, as most female and all young Nightjars also lack these; on the other hand, well-spread wing of Egyptian can expose white serration along inner webs of outer primaries, often giving impression of pale patch (distal scallop quite large on some,

showing as white spot on outer primaries). Egyptian has rather broader arm than Nightjar and flies with looser, slower beats, giving heavier look (despite slightly smaller size). When feeding, Egyptian tends to make long-range approaches and to keep to low and medium levels, with less erratic flight than Nightjar; nearly always rests on ground, not on trees or posts/stumps (Nightjar will perch anywhere).

Nubian and Egyptian Nightjars

On Ground Nubian is smallest of all (21-22 cm), large-headed, moderately short-tailed but with very short wing. Tail projection beyond wing nearer that of Egyptian, short; primary projection, however, the shortest, with only 3-4 exposed tips visible beyond tertials (4-6 on other three species), and with distinct gap between 3rd and 4th (counted from wingtip). Owing to less complex markings, with minimal bold black, and predominantly sandy-grey or buffy-grey ground colour, has been confused with Egyptian. Main W Palearctic race of Nubian (*tamaricis*) differs from Egyptian in following plumage feaures. **1 HEAD AND NAPE** Crown prominently streaked, ear-coverts darkish, indication of diffuse pale grey supercilium/crown (no hint of this on Egyptian, which appears almost uniform), and distinct tawny-buff hindneck-collar (on Egyptian pale buff-grey, little different from rest of upperparts). **2 SCAPULARS** Feathers of middle row show pointed black centres, with most of outer webs prominently buff (cf. Egyptian).

In Flight Nubian has conspicuous white patches on outer wing and outer tail feathers (lacking on Egyptian), and both above and below shows distinct pale chestnut/buff area on inner wing (bases of innermost primaries and secondaries and part of coverts) which strongly contrast with solid blackish primaries (Egyptian's wing looks paler, less variegated, lacks chestnut inner wing). Nubian's wings appear shorter, broader, more square-shaped; flight erratic, with fast mechanical beats and zigzagging. As Egyptian, keeps low and perches mainly on ground, but when feeding flies shorter distances from resting spots.

Separating Nubian from Nightjar In Middle East, Nightjar has been misidentified as Nubian: both have white patches in primaries and rectrices, and some eastern races of Nightjar often have overall buff-brown to cinnamon-brown (rather than greyish-brown) suffusion. Nubian's small size, short primary and tail projections, rufous half-collar on nape and distinctive variegated wing pattern (including more prominent primary patches) should, however, separate it from any rusty and pale Nightjars. Nubian also has less distinct black streaks on central crown and upper scapulars, and upperwing lacks dark lesser-covert panel always shown by Nightjar.

Calls

Nightjar: territorial call a shrill 'coo-ic'; song a continuous loud churring, rising and falling in pitch. Red-necked: low-pitched 'tuuk', or rather harsh 'kuituk' or 'churuk'; song a long monotonous series of double 'knocking' sounds, 'cut-ock cut-ock cut-ock...' or 'kutuk kotok kotok...', altogether different from Nightjar. Egyptian: main territorial call a single or repeated 'tok' or 'klak'; song a rapidly repeated 'kworr' or 'kre-kre-kre', or sounds like rapid hammering on wood, 'toc, toc, toc', or sewing-machine-like 'kroo-kroo...'. Nubian: territorial call as Nightjar's but harsher, e.g. 'kwua'; song like muffled yelp of small dog but rather soft, 'kwua kwua' or 'poww poww', normally a double bark, rarely longish series (even accelerating). All species also wing-clap, Egyptian less loudly.

References Cramp (1985), Swash & Cleere (1989).

Bar-tailed Desert, Desert and Dunn's Larks

Where and When Three Saharo-Sindian arid-belt breeders, quite widespread in Middle East and N Africa. Desert Lark *Ammomanes deserti* occurs in all types of arid desert in Sahara, Sinai, and east through Arabia, S and E Israel to about Pakistan and Kashmir. Bar-tailed Desert Lark *A. cincturus* breeds locally in N Africa east to Egypt and N Sudan, into Arabia, S Israel and east to about Afghanistan and Pakistan; accidental Italy and Malta. Dunn's Lark *Eremalauda dunni* has a disjunct distribution across northern/central Africa and deserts of Arabia and Jordan; casual breeder Sinai and S Israel and accidental north to Lebanon. All three are mostly resident, but partly nomadic outside breeding season. A degree of overlap in range, but normally segregated by habitat: Desert inhabits desert badlands and highlands, on barren rocky and stony hillsides or mountain slopes, narrow wadis in mountain areas etc (places never frequented by the other two), also often in flat or rolling desert including mouths/sides of wadis; the other two almost exclusively in arid flattish or rolling desert, always much more open, Dunn's preferring plateaux or open mouths of wide wadis with much sand and low annual grass and a very few low desert bushes, while Bar-tailed Desert prefers more open and more sandy areas and can also be found on edges of sand dunes and coastal alluvial areas with less vegetation. In winter, Dunn's and Bar-tailed Desert form mixed flocks of tens to hundreds (may also breed alongside each other); Desert tends to flock less, but can occur in single-figure groups.

Identification

All three differ from all other W Palearctic larks in having 'desert-type' upperpart coloration: sandy or sandy-rufous and usually fairly uniform (unlike the well-marked upperparts of all larks of genera *Alauda*, *Galerida*, *Calandrella* and *Melanocorypha*), in fact lacking any particularly contrasting plumage patterns and usually with no distinctive head pattern. They also differ in structure, having longer legs, more 'dwarfish' body, short tail and larger, more rounded head. Separating these three is fairly straightforward for the careful observer provided all features are checked (note that strong desert light can alter apparent proportions, e.g. Bar-tailed Desert's bill can appear larger than it actually is). Combination of behaviour, size, structure and colour of bill, primary projection, tail pattern, pattern of back feathers, facial pattern (profile) and call will permit certain identification even for the inexperienced; but fairly close views required before confirming bill shape and head pattern. Note that distinctive tail patterns are best seen when tail spread immediately before landing or in flight overhead. Intensity of coloration varies individually and also depends on light and on viewing angle (e.g. tertial colour is more obvious when viewed from behind, and intense sun tends

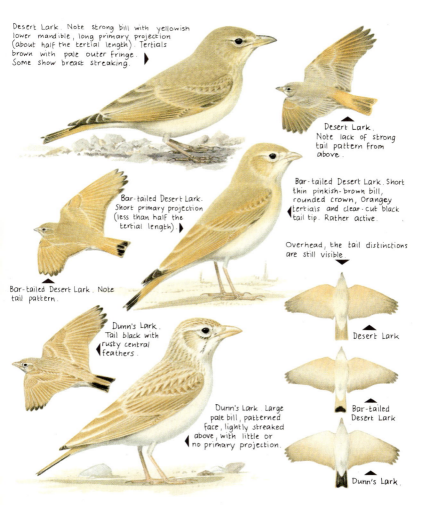

Desert Lark. Note strong bill with yellowish lower mandible, long primary projection (about half the tertial length). Tertials brown with pale outer fringe. Some show breast streaking.

Desert Lark. Note lack of strong tail pattern from above.

Bar-tailed Desert Lark. Short primary projection (less than half the tertial length).

Bar-tailed Desert Lark. Short thin pinkish-brown bill, rounded crown, orangey tertials and clear-cut black tail tip. Rather active.

Overhead, the tail distinctions are still visible

Bar-tailed Desert Lark. Note tail pattern.

Dunn's Lark. Tail black with rusty central feathers.

Desert Lark

Bar-tailed Desert Lark

Dunn's Lark. Large pale bill, patterned face, lightly streaked above, with little or no primary projection.

Dunn's Lark.

to 'burn out' subtle buff and orange tones). Following descriptions and plate relate to fresh-plumaged birds after complete late-summer/autumn moult, when all ages look similar. By spring/summer some individuals become highly worn and faded (e.g. a few Dunn's have faded markings and much weaker head pattern). Desert Lark varies more than the other two, chiefly geographically but also individually, this affecting upperpart coloration, strength of rufous on primaries and flanks, and bill size.

Separation of Bar-tailed Desert and Desert Bar-tailed Desert has a short, relatively thin, mainly pinkish-horn bill with dark grey culmen and tip (Desert has longer and thicker bill tapering evenly to a point, with most of upper mandible and the tip dark and lower mandible always pale yellow), which together with rounded crown gives shape recalling other small larks (Desert is larger, heavily built, flatter-crowned and longer-tailed, with shape like other medium-sized larks). Bar-tailed Desert has comparatively short primary projection, only about a quarter to a third tertial length, with only 2-3 primary tips visible and contrasting greatly with paler, buff-orange tertials and to lesser extent remiges and inner wing-coverts (Desert's projection about half tertial length, usually with 4 tips visible and not contrasting greatly with rest of wing, which is less rusty, with inner webs of tertials always dark brown and outer webs sandy); tail rusty or sandy-rufous with clear-cut blackish (sub)terminal band (Desert's tail almost uniform, with diffuse and much broader blackish terminal band showing little contrast with rusty tail base). Less obvious differences are Bar-tailed Desert's whitish/greyish lores (Desert normally has dark grey loral stripe); its whitish belly centre contrasting with buff-sandy flanks (Desert has almost entire underparts including belly centre uniform grey or grey-buff); on most a pale crescent below ear-coverts (much less prominent on Desert); its rather plain warm buff upperparts and breast (greyish on Desert, though upperparts quite heavily suffused rufous in some popu-

lations, and often quite heavy breast streaking). Bar-tailed Desert almost always active, with clockwork-like runs with sudden brief stops to peck for food, seldom still for long; Desert less energetic, stops and pecks at ground for long periods or perches prominently for some time. Flight call (and some contact calls) of Bar-tailed Desert usually 'twer'; song very distinctive, like creaking of iron gate (or pub sign!) in wind, 'zoo-ee' or 'te-eh, te, eh'. Desert has weak, monosyllabic flight call, a whistled 'chwee'; song often recalls Long-billed Pipit, e.g. 'chup-chup choo-oo-ee'.

Separation of Dunn's from Desert and Bar-tailed Desert Dunn's bill is normally strikingly large, thick-based and swollen, often decurved near culmen tip to give blunt-ended shape, and almost wholly pale pink or horn (Bar-tailed Desert's bill is short/delicate, Desert's usually long and pointed with dark culmen and tip). Dunn's also looks big-headed and stocky. Its streaked crown, thick pale eye-ring and obvious blackish moustachial stripe are distinctive, and its very short or non-existent primary projection, streaked scapulars and mantle, and black tail with pale central and outer feathers are diagnostic; other prominent features include varying amount of breast-side streaking, strong buff-orange tone to upperparts and wing (chiefly fresh birds), and cleaner whitish belly and flanks. Dunn's recalls Bar-tailed Desert in general behaviour, but not so constantly active. Its typical flight call is a monosyllabic 'bshz' or 'wazz', urgent but soft and quiet, and often repeated in series; song from ground a rising and falling trill, somewhat recalling Bimaculated Lark, but often flutters in one spot at height of up to 20 m emitting deep whistles and rattling notes.

Likelihood of Confusion There should be no real problem in separating these three from any other W Palearctic larks. Only Dunn's, having light streaking above, may perhaps be confused with Short-toed and Lesser Short-toed, but it differs clearly from latter in its big, heavy bill and short primary projection (Lesser Short-toed has small, dainty bill and long primary projection) and in head-profile pattern and pattern of feather centres of mantle, scapulars and tertials (see Lesser Short-toed plate). Although Short-toed has similar primary projection, the two differ particularly in bill colour and shape (Short-toed's is narrower, pointed and less heavy,

with dark culmen and tip) and in wing pattern (Dunn's generally lacks Short-toed's relatively obvious wingbars and well-defined dark tertial and covert centres), as well as in several other aspects (see Short-toed plate). *References* Shirihai (1994b), Shirihai *et al.* (1990).

Bimaculated and Calandra Larks

Where and When Bimaculated Lark *Melanocorypha bimaculata* is a typical steppe breeder of the northern Middle East (from much of N and C Turkey) and in areas east of Caspian Sea to C Russia: some winter on southern edge of breeding range, but most well south of it from NE Africa and southern Middle East to Pakistan and NW India; Middle Eastern breeders present mainly mid April to late September, nesting in montane and rocky areas with dry heath and submaquis-type vegetation/low shrubs at 1200–2000 m, occurring on passage (March-April, September-October) also in other open areas, including desert and semi-desert. Calandra Lark *M. calandra* breeds more widely across southern Europe and in N Africa, Middle East and S Russia; partially migratory, it occurs mostly on open lowland plains and upland plateaux, primarily on grasslands. Much of Spain provides good sites for Calandra, best areas for Bimaculated being Eilat and Nizzana desert in Israel (migration) and Golan Heights in N Israel and highlands of N and C Turkey (breeding); last two areas unique in holding both species. Both are vagrants west to Britain and north to Sweden.

General and Diagnostic Features in Flight

Both are typically large, robust larks with large head and heavy bill; wings broad, tail comparatively short. In song flight (when wingbeats much less deep) wing shape more obvious, on Bimaculated generally more pointed (starling-like impression) but on Calandra broader and rounder-tipped; former also quite often shows widely fanned tail. Bimaculated is easily separated in flight by

combination of lack of white trailing edge to secondaries and white edges to outer tail, but with white terminal tail band, Calandra having distinct white trailing edge to secondaries and white tail edges but lacking obvious white at tail tip. Otherwise, Bimaculated lacks Calandra's contrast between dark remiges and paler upperwing-coverts, appearing rather uniform and paler; in most lights also lacks Calandra's striking solid blackish underwing, instead showing plain darkish grey-brown underwing or slight contrast of paler underwing-coverts (can be difficult to discern in poor lighting, while at other times underwing may appear darker than it really is). These differences apply to all plumages.

Identification on Ground

The two species when perched are closely similar in general appearance, especially in juvenile plumage, when best distinguished by flight features (juveniles moult soon after fledging, and then more adult-like). From 1st winter onwards there are a number of fairly constant differences (though with degree of overlap), of which following are most important. **1** SIZE AND STRUCTURE Bimaculated is marginally smaller, the robust, chunky-bodied and powerful-headed appearance slightly less marked than in Calandra, and tends to show (when in good feather condition: close view and extra care needed) shorter tail projecting less beyond wingtip and marginally shorter primary extension; such differences, however, difficult to judge on lone individuals, and some experience required. **2** BILL When comparing local races in Near East, bill shape a good feature: although may at first appear very similar,

Bimaculated Larks. Posture greatly alters black throat markings. Note white supercilium, strong facial pattern, longer bill which is darker on the upper mandible.

Bimaculated Larks. Note pale tipped tail and absence of white trailing edge to wing.

Bimaculated Lark tail pattern.

Spring Calandra Lark. Weak face pattern, breast streaked.

Fresh-plumaged Bimaculated Lark. Strong streaking on back, very little to breast.

Calandra Larks in Flight. Dark underwing, white trailing edge to wing.

Fresh-plumaged Calandra Lark. Upperpart streaking and face pattern subdued. Note bill colour and shape, although with some variation. In both species, general colour often matches habitat.

with practice Bimaculated seen to have proportionately (relative to body/head size) larger, longer and deeper-looking bill (and with straighter culmen but more acutely pointed), producing almost flat-headed appearance, whereas Calandra shows medium-sized (relative to its total size) bill and usually a slight decurve along whole culmen length. Some variation, however, and difference may not always be apparent, or impressions may even be reversed (if extreme large-billed race of Calandra compared with extreme small-billed race of Bimaculated), so relative differences in bill size and shape may be of limited value with lone vagrants of either species. Both have bicoloured bill, but that of Bimaculated shows mostly darker culmen and tip with rather contrasting pale or deep yellow lower-mandible base, while most (not all) Calandra show less contrast in bill and lower mandible tends to have a more horn or pinkish-yellow colour; some overlap occurs, however, as do intermediate-looking individuals. 3 HEAD PATTERN With experience, head pattern normally allows ready separation, even from distance. Bimaculated has more contrasting and complex facial markings: more prominent and purer white supercilium and eye-ring (often looks more 'bespectacled') and more rusty tone to ear-coverts, which are contrastingly bordered by bold blackish-brown eye-stripe (including line below eye-ring), rear ear-coverts and moustachial stripe, and white patch at lower front corner of ear-coverts also usually more distinct. Wide variation within each species, however, and a few Bimaculated (often 1st-winters or heavily worn adults) may approach Calandra, or vice versa in the case of well-marked Calandra (chiefly fresh nominate or some local Middle East populations). **4 UPPERPARTS AND FOLDED WING** To experienced observer, Bimaculated tends to show more contrasting mantle and scapular streaks (feather centres more accentuated by paler sandy-cinnamon inner fringes, while almost whole of outer webs dark and concolorous with the broad 'shaft streaks'), paler nape, and darker and broader centres with narrower and better-defined fringes to tertials and median coverts (may create rather pronounced median-covert bar); most (not all) Calandra show less contrasting mantle and scapular streaks (but in form of more pronounced shaft streaks, more diffuse centres and wider fringes on both webs), less obvious pale nape, and paler centres and diffuse fringes to tertials and median coverts. **5 UNDERPART MARKINGS** Blackish crescents on upper chest sides slightly narrower on Bimaculated, and on most extending further towards centre (and more often narrowly

meeting at front) than on Calandra; its chest and breast sides are paler (pale buff to off-white) and generally with rather indistinct dark brown spotting, while chest virtually unmarked and usually appearing uniform, unlike the normally (not always) much more heavily streaked Calandra. Wide variation within both species, however (also influenced by age differences, bleaching and abrasion), renders chest/breast markings of little or no value with lone vagrants, though rather useful in distinguishing spring/early-summer adults of local Turkish and Israeli populations on breeding grounds. **6 TAIL** Fresh Bimaculated quite often reveals diagnostic whitish-tipped tail (on Calandra, pale tip much narrower and warmer-coloured or lacking), though pale tip soon worn off. **7 VOICE** Songs sometimes indistinguishable, but Bimaculated's is perhaps a shade harsher, harder and with shorter phrases, less varied and less Skylark-like, with less mimicry. Flight calls also similar, but Bimaculated's slightly more reminiscent of *Calandrella* larks but deeper, harsher, 'tcheRRup-tcheRRup', often preceded by short 'tchup-tchup'; Calandra has a dry, rolling, often coarse and raucous 'kchürrük' or 'prrruuup', with jingling tone of Skylark and slightly quarrelsome tone of Starling.

References Cramp (1985), Mild (1990), Ullman (1990), van den Berg (1987).

Lesser Short-toed and Short-toed Larks

Where and When Lesser Short-toed Lark *Calandrella rufescens* breeds quite widely (but locally) across S Palearctic, from Spain and N Africa east to C Asia, generally in quite barren and dry habitats, from shrubby steppe to semi-desert and plain desert, but usually prefers grassy areas, often cultivation and grazing land; W Palearctic populations resident or partially migratory, though largely nomadic. Short-toed Lark *C. brachydactyla* generally breeds more widely in much of C and S Palearctic, adapted to less dry areas than Lesser Short-toed though sometimes sharing breeding areas; all populations

migratory apart from some in N Africa and Middle East (which partially migratory), wintering well south of breeding area. During migration period often in large flocks, mainly Short-toed, but sometimes the two mix together. Lesser Short-toed is a very rare, irregular vagrant north to N Europe, while Short-toed more widely recorded in much of Europe and quite regularly north to Britain and Sweden.

Identification

Both species show considerable variation, much of it geographical, but also individually within one population, and abrasion and bleaching often have marked influence on appearance. Variation affects mainly colouring (e.g. some individuals pale sandy-brown or greyish-sandy-brown, others distinctly darker and very dingy with reddish-yellow or browner tone to upperparts), but to lesser extent pattern (e.g. breast markings, head pattern). Identification should be based on following **structural features** and more constant plumage characters, as well as **voice. 1 WING** Lesser Short-toed shows prominent primary projection (3 primary tips visible), whereas Short-toed's very long tertials more or less completely cloak primary tips (beware birds in moult or in abraded plumage having worn/broken, missing or incompletely grown tertials, thus showing slightly exposed primary tips). Less conspicuous differences include Lesser Short-toed's less distinct dark bar across median coverts owing to the wider pale tips and/or less clearly defined dark centres, whereas medians of Short-toed (albeit with degree of overlap with Lesser) clearly show the feather contours, median-covert centres appearing very dark and well defined but tips narrow, which may produce (chiefly when worn) a dark bar across wing; and outer web of central alula feather of Lesser Short-toed narrowly and diffusely fringed, as opposed to Short-toed's much broader and clearly defined pale-fringed central alula feather (pale often extending over much of outer web). **2 BREAST MARKINGS** Neck side, breast sides and chest are closely/uniformly and finely streaked on Lesser Short-toed; Short-toed is either unstreaked (but with diffuse flecks) or has some streaks on sides, but often (mainly in spring) rather obvious (variable) blackish patches on neck/upper-breast sides accompanied by some indistinct streaks. On Lesser Short-toed, however, streaks rarely (perhaps more often in eastern races) merge to form vague dark spot on breast sides, while pale races (chiefly in N Africa and Middle East) sometimes show much narrower/paler streaking, appearing almost obsolete from distance; Short-toed, on the other hand, frequently shows continuous

narrow streaks across upper breast (though still concentrated at sides) and/or has dark breast-side patches so reduced that they cannot be detected even from close range. Otherwise, chest streaking of some Lesser Short-toed tends to diffuse into fine buff-brown streaks on flanks, unlike on Short-toed. **3 HEAD PATTERN AND BILL** Lesser Short-toed generally shows combination of less striking head pattern (less prominent pale supercilium and vague darkish eye-stripe, ear-coverts often heavily flecked, and with fine crown streaks usually reveals more evenly and finely streaked head, recalling Linnet *Carduelis cannabina*) and much smaller, stubby bill (generally shorter, deep at base and appearing more curved on both mandibles); Short-toed combines well-defined and richer head pattern (nearly always whiter and often broader supercilium and varying degree of dark eye-stripe, rather uniform ear-coverts) with usually rather longer and somewhat heavier bill (generally appearing relatively slender and acutely pointed). Lesser Short-toed tends to have quite distinct malar stripe (lacking or very narrow on Short-toed), while some Short-toed have contrastingly rufous crown and/or unstreaked or faintly streaked forehead (unlike Lesser Short-toed's more uniformly and finely streaked crown). Moreover, on most (not all) Lesser Short-toed the feathering covering nostrils is fully white, normally showing as unbroken continuation of supercilium along forehead, whereas on Short-toed the inner part of nostril feathering is usually dark, separating supercilia at culmen base. Variation frequent, however, and all head-pattern features can be confusingly similar on the two species, while bill differences may not be apparent, especially when comparing some eastern races of Lesser Short-toed (bill slightly larger, stronger and more conical) with a relatively small-billed Short-toed. **4 SUBSIDIARY FEATURES** Lesser Short-toed looks slightly more compact, with marginally shorter legs and shorter tail (even against the relatively short wings), and head usually more rounded with comparatively high-crowned appearance (instead of more

Lesser Short-toed Lark. Note short stubby bill, lightly streaked breast, and primaries extending beyond tertials.

Lesser Short-toed Larks. Note variation in breast pattern. Eastern birds typically more heavily streaked.

Short-toed Lark. Note larger bill, clean supercilium, dark collar mark (sometimes concealed), strong back pattern and median covert bar. Primaries do not extend beyond tertials.

Note variation in breast pattern of Short-toed Lark.

Some Short-toed Larks lack neck mark.

Beware worn Short-toed Larks with primaries exposed by worn, broken or moulted tertials.

Some Short-toed Larks show warm plumage tones and 'capped' appearance.

flattish crown of Short-toed), but latter character not species-specific since Short-toed, particularly males in display, frequently raise crown feathers. Generally, both species show quite similar upperpart pattern, but dark feather centres (particularly of scapulars) of Lesser Short-toed are sharply demarcated and narrower, tending to produce impression of shaft streaks; on Short-toed, however, mantle feathers show bolder/broader and often slightly more diffuse dark centres, while scapular centres well defined and narrow but usually tending to merge into warm buff-brown over much of outer webs (this pattern never or only indistinctly shown by Lesser Short-toed). 5 VOICE Commonest calls rather dissimilar. Lesser Short-toed has characteristic rippling, drawn-out but loud and dry 'prrrit-prrrir' or 'prrirrick' and 'chirrr-de'. Short-toed gives much harder and more trilling or clipped, sparrow-like or Skylark-like notes (but less rippling than latter's), 'tchirrup' or 'chichirrp', 't-trip-trip-chip-chip' or 'trriep-diu'. Song of Lesser Short-toed continuous and varied, often recalling Crested Lark or changing over to trill like Calandra's, but superficially similar to that of Skylark (and with excellent mimicry), thin and high-pitched, with musical quality; given either from ground or in randomly circling song flight (without undulations) with unbroken slow wingbeats. Short-toed sings with more regular, accelerating and higher-pitched notes, still variable and melodic but almost without mimicry, often a descending musical trill, 'tee-tee-ti-ti-te-too-too-too'; rather simple phrases and delivered in synchrony with wingbeats in undulating flight.

Juveniles Both species show rather similar pale and white speckles above (feathers black subterminally and buff-white terminally), but full-grown birds differ in primary projection: distinct on Lesser Short-toed, almost absent on Short-toed (see above).

Likelihood of Confusion Both, and in particular Lesser Short-toed, sometimes confusable with small, medium-sized and even large larks (e.g. Dunn's, Oriental Skylark and *Melanocorypha* species, which see), but confusion less likely with these than with each other. In fact, they really resemble only the much larger Skylark, but both Lesser Short-toed and Short-toed have proportionately shorter, stubbier bill, much shorter crest, tail and hindclaw, and very different jizz; also differ from Skylark in less heavily streaked upperparts and less prominent head pattern. Skylark normally shows more fully streaked chest, and reveals obvious white trailing edge to wing (lacking on both Lesser Short-toed and Short-toed) in its characteristic flight, which often accompanied by different call and can include hovering before landing.

References Alström *et al.* (1991b), Cramp (1988), Dennis & Wallace (1980), Svensson (1992).

Thekla and Crested Larks

Where and When Thekla Lark *Galerida theklae* has rather restricted distribution, but locally quite common in SW France, much of Iberia, Balearic Islands, and west and central N Africa (also locally central E Africa). Crested Lark *G. cristata* is much more widely distributed across middle and southern Eurasia and down through middle of Africa. Both are mainly resident and dispersive, and occur in rather poorly vegetated areas in sandy steppe, semi-desert or desert, in coastal dunes with sparse tufted vegetation, on dry hillsides and lowlands with scattered shrubs, and also in open cultivation around human habitation. Thekla is less of a lowland bird than Crested, in certain areas occurring more frequently on rocky mountainsides which may have more bushes or even small trees. Overlap and

competition limited to restricted parts of their ranges, where problems of identification may aggravate difficulties of ascertaining their habitat differences.

Identification

The considerable amount of variation among the many races of these two species can lead to overlap in some plumage features, or even to a complete reversal of structural characters, and their morphology is extremely 'flexible' and reflects habitat colours. Most observers meet the two in Iberia, where patient stalking should allow most distinguishing characters (bill shape, streaking/spotting on hindneck, upperparts and chest, contrast of uppertail-coverts and rump, facial pattern etc) to be checked; these distinctions also valid in part

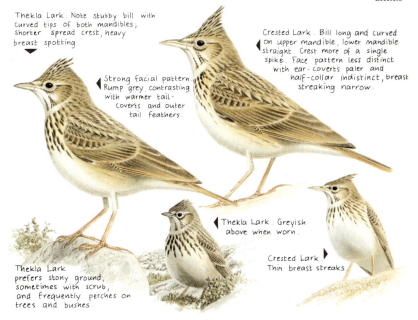

Thekla Lark. Note stubby bill with curved tips of both mandibles; shorter spread crest, heavy breast spotting.

Crested Lark. Bill long and curved on upper mandible, lower mandible straight. Crest more of a single spike. Face pattern less distinct with ear-coverts paler and half-collar indistinct, breast streaking narrow.

Strong facial pattern. Rump grey, contrasting with warmer tail-coverts and outer tail feathers.

Thekla Lark. Greyish above when worn.

Crested Lark. Thin breast streaks.

Thekla Lark prefers stony ground, sometimes with scrub, and frequently perches on trees and bushes.

for populations of coastal NW Africa, but not for inland races (Thekla in latter region approaches Crested in having less heavily marked plumage and longer bill), and sometimes identification must rely on habitat and voice. Differences between these two larks are neither striking nor easy to assess and much care is required, while some individuals may be impossible to identify in the field (some may even be hybrids!). Nevertheless, with experience, the following features (relating to Iberian and coastal NW African races) are significant, but it must be stressed that identification should be based on a combination of characters, especially when dealing with a lone bird. **1 BILL** Thekla has shorter, deeper and stubbier bill, with almost straight culmen tapering slightly (more steeply curved towards tip) and somewhat spiky, and also with convex lower mandible; Crested's is obviously long and tapering, with gradual curve along whole length of culmen

(often looks slightly decurved), and lower mandible appearing much straighter. **2 CREST** Fully erected crest of Thekla is slightly shorter (often appearing as such even when crest depressed), less spiky, and rises from forecrown; Crested's is longer (but beware worn/moulting crest) and more strongly rising, and when fully erected usually rises from around mid-crown or above eye, so forecrown remains depressed. This, however, can be difficult to judge (and experience required on part of observer), as Crested with half-raised crest can give appearance of Thekla, while converse applies to Thekla with unusually strongly raised crest (e.g. in strong tail wind). **3 FACIAL PATTERN** Generally, supercilium of Thekla is shorter behind eye, but cleaner, whiter and better defined, and this, together with whitish feathers below eye and wider pale area on lores, creates more open facial expression (often even appearing 'bespectacled'); most Crested have longer, slightly diffuse supercilium and lack obvious white feathering below eye, but much variation in both species. Otherwise, Thekla's ear-coverts usually appear darker (and more heavily and evenly marked) than Crested's, accentuated by fairly clear and broad whitish half-collar (obscure on Crested), and Thekla tends to have more distinct black-brown centres to feathers of nape, hindneck and neck sides, as well as crown. 4 UNDERPART MARKINGS Thekla's whitish half-collar extending below ear-coverts and throat is emphasised by longish black-brown nape/breast-side markings that terminate sharply across upper chest – usually a fairly good feature (and may recall Skylark) against the rather poorly marked Crested. Thekla usually shows rather bold blob-like markings on cleaner, whitish chest (sometimes as obvious as breast spotting of Song Thrush *Turdus philomelos*), which tend to be more distinct and dense towards chest sides and to extend onto flanks, whereas Crested tends to have finer and less well-defined chest streaking less often (or less obviously) extending to flanks, though this character varies racially (but not affecting identification of most Iberian birds, as the most heavily streaked races of Crested occur in Middle East, well outside Thekla's range; unfortunately, however, least-streaked forms of Thekla occur within range of Crested inland in NW Africa). 5 UPPER-PARTS AND WING Mantle and scapulars of Thekla show more distinct/wider (chiefly on outer webs) but diffuse black-brown feather centres (on Crested generally more sharply defined, showing mainly as dark shafts), and uppertail-coverts and lower rump usually rusty-toned, contrasting with greyer upper rump, back and tail feathers (Crested with only slight rusty tinge and contrast, or almost uniform). Fresh tertials almost cloak primaries on Thekla, whereas Crested shows slight extension of (at least 2) primary tips beyond tertials, and Thekla has more conspicuous, well-demarcated pale tertial margins (diffuse fringes on most Crested); but beware that appearance of tertials varies somewhat with angle of light and viewing angle, and greatly so with wear, *so tertials of either species can sometimes appear much as those of the other*. Median coverts of most Thekla usually broadly and boldly (but always diffusely) dark-centred and with less obvious or no dark shafts, whereas on Crested centres are generally paler, showing clear dark shafts and demarcated margins, but some variation in both species and rarely some Thekla show same or nearly same pattern as Crested. 6 SUBSIDIARY DIFFER-ENCES Other differences subtle, but Thekla usually shows greyish to sandy-buff underwing-coverts (light rusty to brownish-pink on Crested) and outer pair of rectrices tends to show more rufous-buff colour (mainly buffish-brown on Crested), and to experienced eye Thekla may appear marginally smaller and more squat. Again, however, these features difficult to discern in the field, and some variation and overlap render them of little use. 7 VOICE Song of Thekla resembles that of Crested, but with softer, lower-pitched and more fluted notes, 'doo-dee-doo-deeee' (with many variations) and with long final syllable rising and then falling; commonest call 'wee-te-tee' or 'hwee-hwee-hwee'. Song of Crested distinctive: both short and long whistled or twittering phrases (e.g. 'wee-too-wee too-chee-too twee-too-chee twee chee'), and more so than Thekla's contains imitations of other birds' calls and even of human whistles; commonest call 'diui' or softer 'du-i' or 'tui-tui-tioo'. *References* Delin & Svensson (1988), Robertson (1989), Ullman (1994), Wallace (1984).

Oriental Skylark

Where and When Oriental Skylark *Alauda gulgula* is found across a wide area of C and SE Asia. It largely replaces Skylark *A. arvensis* of C and W Palearctic, but the two meet in C Asia, mainly in autumn and winter. Much of Oriental's habitat is desert and semi-desert areas, but it does occur in wet and green areas more typical of Skylark. Mostly resident, but race *inconspicua* breeding west to C Asia and Iran migratory (winter quarters largely unknown). First recorded W Palearctic at Eilat, Israel, early 1980s, since when regular (flocks of up to about ten) at Eilat and elsewhere in (mainly E) Israel as migrant and winter visitor late September to mid April; subsequently recorded in areas east of Israel. Form involved in Israel differs somewhat from *inconspicua*, suggesting one of the more eastern races (or an undescribed race).

Identification

Main confusion species is Skylark, especially of smaller and greyer races (which winter in Levant). Given good views, however, the careful observer should not find separating them a serious problem. Oriental's call commands attention, and differs from that of any other lark. Resembles Skylark in coloration but Woodlark *Lullula arborea* in shape and flight; from distance may even be confused with Short-toed or Lesser Short-toed Larks.

Separation from Skylark Oriental Skylark is about 15% smaller than Skylark, with squat appearance, clearly shorter tail (extends less beyond wingtip), and short wing and primary projection, latter projecting little, if at all, beyond tertials (obviously longer on Skylark, exposed primaries always showing 2–3 widely spaced tips). On ground, Oriental shows obviously rusty tone to ear-coverts, and distinctive rusty fringes to secondaries and primaries form warm-coloured panel when tightly folded; broader supercilium and strikingly wide loral area are sandy-coloured (narrower and whiter on Skylark, which also more often shows blackish line or spot between eye and bill), and as a rule has rather plain pale sandy underparts (belly to undertail-coverts white on Skylark) with brownish streaking which often extends to whole of chest and upper fore flanks (Skylark has bolder, short streaks forming pectoral band on buffish ground colour), as well as lacking spotted throat of most Skylarks; scapulars normally appear as a wide brownish area with broad and well-defined sandy fringes to outer webs (Skylark shows predominantly blackish centres). In flight, Orien-

Oriental Skylark. Thin bill, 'open-faced' expression, very short primary projection beyond tertials, orangey wing feathers and pale sandy underparts.

Skylark is larger with longer primary projection, brown wings, white belly.

In flight, Oriental Skylark (above) shows shorter tail and warm brown wings without white trailing edge of Skylark (below).

tal's short tail and short, rounded wings are apparent, as is sandy trailing edge to wings (broadly and contrastingly white on Skylark) and sandy outer tail feathers; flight action much slower, and tends to hover and flutter its wings when low over a field (less than 1 m above ground) or before landing. Commonest flight call a diagnostic harsh, buzzing 'baz, baz' or 'baz-terr', often ending with 'pyup' (quite unlike Skylark's usual liquid, rippling, disyllabic 'chirrup' or 'prrrp').

Separation from Woodlark Woodlark, though approaching Oriental Skylark in size and structure, shows several different and diagnostic features, e.g. characteristic buffy-white tips to black primary coverts (form black-white-black-white 'wrist' patches) and to tail, noticeable chiefly at rest but often in flight, and well-exposed primary projection (intermediate between Oriental and Skylark). Less obvious differences include Woodlark's better-developed crest, whiter supercilium which is conspicuous above and behind eye, even reaching rear crown (on Oriental predominantly sandy, well marked above and often concolorous with lores, but shorter behind eye), and rather diffuse fringes to tertials and greater coverts (well defined on Oriental). The two also differ in facial, scapular and breast-streaking patterns, and Woodlark has characteristic jerky, strongly undulating flight and melodic 'toolooeet' call.

Separation from Short-toed and Lesser Short-toed Larks Oriental differs from both in its thicker and more prominent breast streaking and noticeably longer and narrower bill; also slightly larger and more squat in comparison. Also lacks long primary projection of Lesser Short-toed and blackish breast-side patches of many Short-toed, and has very different facial and scapular patterns, flight action and call (see pp. 155–158).

Reference Shirihai (1986).

Lesser-known Martins

Where and When Crag Martin *Ptyonoprogne rupestris* is mainly resident in Mediterranean area from NW Africa and Iberia, in central and southern France, the Alps and Italy to Balkans, Turkey and east to China, breeding mostly in mountain areas, most northern populations moving short distances south in winter; signs of northward spread (and vagrant to NW Europe). Rock Martin *P. fuligula* is mainly an African species, but race *obsoleta* breeds from Dead Sea area south to Egypt and parts of Saudi Arabia and SW Iran, and *presaharica* from Atlas mountains south to Mauritania; prefers more arid areas than Crag. Brown-throated Sand Martin *Riparia paludicola*, with nearest breeding area in W Morocco, has been recorded as vagrant in Saudi Arabia and elsewhere in Middle East.

General Features All three are rather plain, lacking any striking features, with grey or brown upperparts and paler underparts. Brown-throated Sand may sometimes be picked out by its tiny size and weak and fluttering flight (lacking power and fast dives of other two), but it often moves very quickly. Look for underwing pattern, colour/pattern of underparts and tone of upperparts.

Crag and Rock Martins

Crag is more robust with broader wing base (recalls 'fat' House Martin *Delichon urbica*) than Rock, which is closer in shape to Sand Martin *Riparia riparia*.

Upperparts Crag is uniform cold grey or brownish-grey above (often tinged sandy when fresh), with darker flight and tail feathers. Rock is normally slightly paler above, much less brown (difficult to judge in strong sun), with better-developed pale fringes/tips, notably on tertials and inner greater coverts, also paler inner wing and darker primaries and their coverts and notably alula; often slightly paler area around rump/uppertail-coverts (which rather clearly pale-tipped). Note that some races of Rock in N Africa and SW Arabia are darker above, close in tone to Crag.

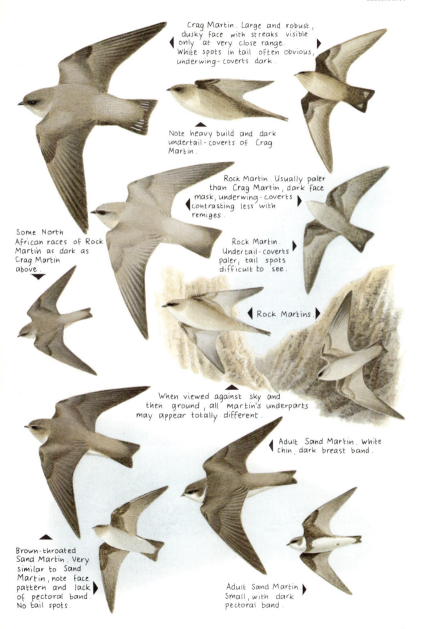

Crag Martin. Large and robust, dusky face with streaks visible only at very close range. White spots in tail often obvious, underwing-coverts dark.

Note heavy build and dark undertail-coverts of Crag Martin.

Rock Martin. Usually paler than Crag Martin, dark face mask, underwing-coverts contrasting less with remiges.

Some North African races of Rock Martin as dark as Crag Martin above.

Rock Martin. Undertail-coverts paler, tail spots difficult to see.

◄ Rock Martins. ►

When viewed against sky and then ground, all martin's underparts may appear totally different.

◄ Adult Sand Martin. White chin, dark breast band.

Brown-throated Sand Martin. Very similar to Sand Martin, note face pattern and lack of pectoral band. No tail spots.

Adult Sand Martin. Small, with dark pectoral band. ►

Tail Spots Whitish spots on inner webs of rectrices (except central and outermost pairs) tend to be somewhat larger on Crag than on Rock, but this of no use in field. Note that spots visible only on well-spread tail (even then can be difficult to see, especially on Rock), and most obvious from below.

Underparts Crag has dirty white or greyish-white chin and throat sides, with (at very close range) grey-brown streaks and spots which extend to sides of face (often form bar or stripe on cheeks); ground colour becomes pale buff (wearing to whitish) on breast, pale brown-grey on flanks and belly and dark brown-grey (blackish-looking) on vent/undertail-coverts (latter with pale tips forming diffuse bars, visible close to). Rock is much paler below, generally whitish-grey with pinky-buff tinge (strong when fresh), including on throat (no contrast with breast, unlike Crag), but becoming darker mouse-grey on upper flanks and especially undertail-coverts. Note that on Crag Martin dark rear end contrasts with less dark belly (Rock shows little contrast).

Underwing Crag Martin has grey-brown underwing with contrasting dull black or blackish coverts (greaters slightly less dark). Rock also has underwing-coverts darker (dark brownish) than flight feathers, but contrast less than on Crag, and underwing often appears all pale with dark confined to axillaries and leading edge of inner wing (notably marginal/lesser primary coverts). Beware that in strong desert light, chiefly against sky, Rock's underwing-coverts (including greaters) can appear solidly darker than translucent remiges, so close views vital for correct assessment of this feature.

Juveniles Can be harder to separate. On both, upperpart feathers edged/fringed paler (rufous-sandy on Crag, more buffish on Rock). Juvenile Crag can virtually lack dark spotting on cheeks/chin, but other features distinguishing adults of the two still apply.

Brown-throated Sand Martin

Very small, drab, and with relatively weak, fluttering flight on rather stiff wings (but can fly fast); closely tied to water (unlike above two species). Told from both Crag and Rock Martins also by its olive-brown upperparts (rump slightly paler) and lack of tail spots. Sides of face and neck, breast and flanks uniform grey-brown (slightly paler and greyer than upperparts), becoming dull brownish-grey (greyer when worn) on chin and throat (on some, breast appears darker than throat), gradually merging into whitish lower underparts, with contrastingly dark tail. Underwing dusky brown (darker than on Crag and Rock), with coverts somewhat darker but showing little contrast with rest of underwing. Has darker face and throat than Sand Martin and lacks dark breast band, but can be very difficult to separate from Sand, especially of southern races (chiefly Middle East and eastwards); some fresh Sand Martins (in spring) have paler, more diffuse breast band (broad pale tips to feathers) and also rather obvious brownish-flecked chin/throat, and are clearly smaller, as small as Brown-throated Sand. The biggest problem is that these birds move too fast for features to be confirmed easily, so very good and prolonged views essential, especially when dealing with possible vagrants in Middle East.

Long-billed Pipit

Where and When In our region, Long-billed Pipit *Anthus similis* is a very local resident in Middle East (endemic race *captus*) in rocky mountainous parts of Israel and surrounding areas, usually not above 700 m (above which Tawny Pipit *A. campestris* starts to breed in overlap zone). Tawny also breeds widely across C and S Europe and Asia and south to N Africa; frequent on passage, but scarce/vagrant in N and NW Europe.

General Adult Long-billed is a uniformly patterned large pipit, lacking prominent markings on predominantly dull, dun ground colour. Combination of general build and coloration, facial pattern, bill shape, tail pattern and voice will permit correct identification even by first-time observers. Both Long-billed and Tawny undergo complete post-breeding moult, juveniles moulting on breeding grounds into adult-like 1st-winter plumage, and correct ageing is often crucial to identification. 1st-winters often retain variable number of juvenile upperwing-coverts and tertials which are almost identical on the two species, whereas freshly moulted or adult ones frequently differ between the two species. These plumage areas on juvenile are as a

rule contrastingly patterned, with distinctly narrower, whiter and better-defined fringes than on adults; juveniles also show heavier streaking/spotting below, with more marked head pattern including moustachial, submoustachial and malar stripes. Some of the features separating birds in adult-like plumage are also valid for juveniles.

Identification Compared with Tawny, Long-billed is slightly heavier/larger and has deeper breast and belly (less sleek and *Motacilla*-like than Tawny), but proportionately small head, long tail (distinctly fuller,

Adult Long-billed Pipit. Uniform large pipit. Stout bill curved on upper mandible; open-faced expression with tapering supercilium. Moustachial stripe indistinct. Note pattern of median coverts, diffuse streaking on breast. Tail dark.

Juvenile Long-billed Pipit. Dark tail, poorly marked head (no spots on ear-coverts).

Poorly defined breast streaking, pale cinnamon underparts. Note median coverts

Adult Tawny Pipit of greyish eastern races most resemble Long-billed Pipit. Note strong square ended supercilium, thin but obvious malar and moustachial stripes, buff breast, white belly.

Juvenile Tawny Pipit. All markings more clearly defined, particularly on throat, breast and mantle. Median coverts sharply edged palest cream, belly white.

1st-winter Tawny Pipit. Note tail feathers pale-edged and not darker than rest of bird. Warm plumage tones, obvious median-covert bar.

mainly when flushed) and typically longer and stouter bill with drooped appearance created by distinct curved culmen (Tawny has slim bill tapering to more pointed tip). Further structural differences are Long-billed's relatively short legs and wing, latter also appearing broader in flight. In fairly close views, Long-billed's head pattern can be checked: generally poorly marked and rather bland, with more open-faced or gentle expression in which dark eye prominent, but with weaker curving supercilium generally narrow but quite long and often diffusing onto nape (Tawny has obvious thick, squared supercilium emphasised by dark crown sides and eye-stripe) and with inconspicuous narrower loral line than Tawny. Moustachial stripe indistinct (on Tawny, thin but conspicuous and usually extending below eye and/or along lower edge of ear-coverts) and malar stripe reduced, paler and diffuse (usually well marked on Tawny); submoustachial region therefore inconspicuous and lacks contrast shown by Tawny. General impression is of rather flat grey-brown upperparts (lacking Tawny's sandy or buffy tone), but beware Tawny with grey upperside usually belonging to eastern race *griseus*, which migrates through breeding area of Long-billed. Closed tail of latter always darker, contrasting more with rest of plumage, but less striking pattern when spread as outer edges/tips of two outermost rectrices average less pure white (more buff). Exceptionally close views may also enable examination of adult-type median coverts (of use chiefly when fresh): on Long-billed, dark centres protracted into a long 'tooth' usually reaching feather tip, though centres more diffuse, mainly on inner webs, than on Tawny (on which blackish centre of each covert contrastingly cut off and rarely central part may be slightly drawn towards tip, but more crisply defined). Greater-covert pattern/coloration duller, with more diffuse centres than on Tawny. Underparts usually show minimal contrast with upperparts, as former, including undertail-coverts, are saturated buff-grey (lacks Tawny's contrastingly whiter underparts with two-toned appearance to flanks and belly); also with diffuse breast streaking, lacking on adult Tawny (but variably rather heavy on juvenile and subsequent immature Tawny). *Juveniles* Where breeding ranges overlap (chiefly Israel), juveniles of both species may mingle, even before acquiring 1st-winter feathers. Juvenile Long-billed separable by its weaker-patterned upperparts (diffuse centres, colder/greyer edges), lacking Tawny's distinct scaly pattern; also (unlike Tawny) has poorly marked head which lacks any distinct spots on ear-coverts and moustachial stripe and has much weaker malar stripe and some poorly developed small triangular brown spots sparsely scattered on chest and breast sides, producing pattern less different from adult than is the case with juvenile Tawny; underparts rather uniform pale cinnamon (on most Tawny generally whitish, especially belly). Note also Long-billed's usually contrastingly dark tail and pale cinnamon (instead of whitish-cream) edges to median coverts, which (unlike on Tawny) have short and less tapered centres.

Habits and Voice Long-billed inhabits rocky, grassy hill and mountain slopes with exposed boulders, on which it perches in rather typical upright posture; generally less energetic than Tawny, occasionally flicks and partially opens tail (rather than Tawny's typical wagging action). Voice diagnostic. Song of two far-carrying phrases separated by a pause, first phrase rising and second falling, 'tir-ee . . . tiu', or in full song 3–4 phrases (lacks Tawny's monotonous repetition of rising 'chee-ree'); commonest flight call 'djeep' or 'tchup' (unlike Tawny's disyllabic 'tsilip' or 'tchriip'). Note that Desert Lark can give call similar to Long-billed Pipit's.

References Cramp (1988), Laird & Gencz (1993).

Buff-bellied Pipit

Where and When *Anthus spinoletta*, formerly regarded as one polytypic species of Holarctic distribution, was in 1986 split into three species (based on habitat choice, morphology, plumage, voice, and from studies of relationships of adjoining populations): Rock Pipit *A. petrosus*, a partial migrant of coastal NW Europe from Iceland through Britain and N France to Scandinavia and NW Russia; Water Pipit *A. spinoletta*, breeding in alpine meadows from Pyrenees via Alps, N Turkey, Iran and central-southern Russia to Lake Baikal, wintering in or south of breeding range but also north/west to Britain; and Buff-bellied Pipit *A. rubescens* of tundra and mountains, extending northeast across Siberia, Alaska and Canada and down each side of Rockies, a migratory species wintering mostly well below breeding areas. Siberian race *japonicus* of latter (sympatric with Water Pipit of race *blakistoni* near Lake Baikal) winters mainly China, with a few regularly October-March as far west as Middle East (in similar habitats to Water Pipit). In W Europe, Buff-bellied most likely as autumn vagrants of nominate N American race.

Identification

Superficially, Buff-bellied recalls corresponding plumages of Water Pipit, but in typical plumage and with ideal views is rather easily identified (in non-breeding plumage confusion more likely with Meadow Pipit *A. pratensis*). A useful feature is Buff-bellied's call, a high, short 'zzeep' or 'tsiit', lacking usual shrill quality of Water's or Rock's calls, generally more like calls of Meadow though higher-pitched, thinner/sharper and more squeaking or drawn-out; on take-off gives rapid series of 'tsi-tsip' or 'tsiip-iip-iip', higher/sharper and more nervous than Meadow's. All species can, in very broad terms, be aged as follows. Adult in spring/summer has rather uniform orangey/pink-buff underparts with reduced streaking, and usually varying degree of tonal or colour contrast between head and mantle; autumn/winter adult is markedly streaked below, more uniform above, with wing-coverts of uniform age with fresh, rather broad and warm-coloured edges (at least until midwinter); 1st-winter similar, but tends to show variable number of new coverts and tertials among more worn/ bleached and whitish-tipped retained juvenile ones. Most 1st-summers inseparable from spring adults. Note that most Rock Pipits are heavily streaked below in all plumages, and thus easily separable from the others in summer.

Separation from Water Pipit Buff-bellied is marginally smaller and shorter-tailed than Water, with proportionately finer and shorter Meadow-like bill; ground action somewhat daintier (sleek-plumaged), with erratic bursting movements more reminiscent of Meadow than Water Pipit. In all plumages differs from Water in having complete and conspicuous white eye-ring and plain (but often very faintly/diffusely flecked) loral area, whereas Water's obvious dark loral stripe breaks white eye-ring. Other head characters compared with most Water include: more prominent deep yellow base to lower mandible; dark olive-brown forehead and crown (slightly paler and greyer in spring/summer) with very faint dark streaks; whitish supercilium usually quite distinct from surroundings but sometimes rather ill-defined; dark olive-brown ear-coverts bordered below by rather distinct dark moustachial stripe (almost obsolescent on Water); more distinct malar stripe (begins rather faintly but broadens into obvious blackish patch or wedge on side of lower throat) bordering pronounced creamy and unstreaked submoustachial stripe, chin and throat. Upperparts uniform dark olive-brown (non-breeding) or greyish olive-brown (breeding), unstreaked or with very indistinct dark feather centres (recalling Olive-backed Pipit *A. hodgsoni*, but darker and less greenish), lacking Water's pale, grey or buff-brown, ground colour and clearly defined darkish

Winter Water Pipit. Strong supercilium, broken eye-ring, dark lores, underparts whitish with streaks to upper breast. Dark legs.

Winter Buff-bellied Pipit of race 'japonicus'. Dark plumage, pale lores complete white eye-ring.

Strongly streaked below, obvious wingbars and often pale legs.

Winter Buff-bellied Pipit of race 'rubescens' Pale lores and complete pale eye-ring. Plain above, entire underparts buff with thin streaking, dark legs.

Summer Buff-bellied Pipit of race 'japonicus'. Note pale lores, poor supercilium, thick streaks to orange-tinged breast.

Summer Water Pipit. Greyish head, pale supercilium, dark lores, thin streaks to sides of breast.

Meadow Pipit. Note pale lores, heavy streaking above and below, pale legs.

Rock Pipit. Very dark; heavy but diffuse streaking to underparts, weak face pattern. Outer tail feathers creamy (white on Water and Buff-bellied Pipits).

centres. Compared with all races of Water, underparts in non-breeding plumage show much heavier, bolder, clearer-cut and darker spots or streaking (chiefly race *japonicus*; nominate *rubescens* has less extensive and narrower/sharper streaking), and with longer blackish-brown streaks down flanks, resembling Meadow or Red-throated Pipit *A. cervinus*; remainder of underside whitish to pale buff (chiefly *japonicus*) or much richer buff (most nominate). In breeding plumage, however, underparts mostly pale/warm pinkish-buff or cinnamon-sandy with more orange tone and usually still strongly streaked/spotted, hence not so predominantly pinkish or pale vinous nor with markings much reduced (or even absent) as on all races of Water. Ground colour of remiges and greater and median coverts very dark greyish olive-brown, coverts and tertials tipped and fringed whitish/creamy, creating two obvious wing-bars and framed tertials on 1st-years and less obviously so on adults (see ageing), unlike most Water in equivalent plumage. Legs of race *japonicus* yellowish- to reddish-brown, darker than Meadow's but paler than Water's (beware that latter, mainly juveniles in summer, may have pale legs); nominate *rubescens*, however, usually has dark/blackish legs. Otherwise, Buff-bellied shows more white on outer tail feathers than Water.

Separation from Rock Pipit The relatively darkish, plain-backed Rock Pipit, distinctly greyish-olive and slightly brown-tinged (*petrosus*) or slightly olive-tinged grey-brown (*littoralis*) and with rather heavily marked underparts, may present a pitfall to inexperienced observers. Buff-bellied, however, is clearly smaller and daintier-looking than bulkier Rock, with less horizontal stance, longer legs and noticeably finer bill as well as a fuller tail (same structural differences as between Meadow and Rock). At all ages has plainer and more dusky olive-brown upperparts (Rock always shows varying degree of dark feather centres) and more obvious white wingbars and supercilium (Rock's wingbars usually more diffuse dull creamy-buff, supercilium more often indistinct/subdued and creamy), and as a rule has unbroken white eye-ring and distinctly whitish outer tail feathers (on Rock, conspicuous loral stripe breaks eye-ring and outer tail feathers are creamy or pale brown). Racial differences may complicate underpart features. Non-breeding Buff-bellied's underparts, however, are predominantly whitish-buff (*japonicus*) or deeper buff (nominate), with respectively bolder and denser or rather heavy but narrow streaking, lacking Rock's warm yellowish-olive/cream ground colour with heavy broad (but mainly diffuse) streaks. Breeding Buff-bellied uniformly orange-tinged below and always streaked, whereas Rock has restricted pinkish-vinous tinge on chest (*littoralis*, normally lacking on nominate *petrosus*) and more heavy and diffuse streaking. Differences in moustachial stripe and leg colour as between Buff-bellied and Water.

Separation from Meadow Pipit In size, structure and calls (see above), Buff-bellied recalls Meadow and could be dismissed as such. In particular, a warm/dark and less-marked Meadow is very like non-breeding *japonicus* Buff-bellied, which also has pale legs; latter told by (among many other small differences) its obviously darker and more greyish olive-brown upperparts with much fainter dark feather centres, lacking Meadow's purer pale greyish- or greenish-olive tone with well-defined blackish centres (most prominent on crown, mantle and scapulars). *References* Alström *et al.* (1991a), Knox (1988), Shirihai & Colston (1987).

Nightingales

Where and When Nightingale *Luscinia megarhynchos* and Thrush Nightingale *L. luscinia* are both summer visitors, wintering Africa. Former breeds from W Europe and NW Africa east to Mongolia, while latter has more northerly distribution, from S Fennoscandia and Denmark south to Romania and east to WC Asia, with isolated population in Caucasus. The two overlap marginally in Europe and in Caucasus, but can occur together on passage, especially in E Mediterranean area; either could turn up as vagrants almost anywhere (and in any habitat) in region. Thrush Nightingale breeds in damp habitats, often in broken forests or wooded areas by water; Nightingale will use similar habitats, but prefers wooded areas with dense undergrowth, shrubbery, etc in drier areas and also dry sunny hillsides.

General Although typical individuals can, with good views, be separated fairly easily, others, and especially silent passage migrants skulking in dense vegetation, can be extremely difficult. General appearance greatly influenced by such factors as lighting conditions, state of moult and age, and great caution and prolonged good views (not easy!) often essential. Differences in coloration often subtle, and structural features can also overlap. Hardly any feature is on its own reliable for field identification, and a combination of as many structural and plumage features as possible is essential.

Structure The two appear identical in size and shape. To experienced observers, Thrush Nightingale may sometimes look somewhat bulkier, with proportionately shorter tail, longer wing and slightly longer primary projection often giving relatively short-tailed appearance; its bill averages shorter but stronger. *Wing* Number of primary tips visible on closed wing differs between the two species: Thrush shows 8 equally spaced tips (9th primary shorter and concealed, 10th greatly reduced); on Nightingale, usually only 7 tips visible (sometimes 8, but distance between outermost two then minute). With patient observation, length of greatly reduced outermost primary (not to be confused with alula) can often be determined: on Nightingale longer than greater primary coverts, and often visible briefly as bird lands or after short hopping movement (before primaries quickly refolded); on Thrush very much shorter, not extending beyond primary coverts (thus rarely discernible). Good photos may also reveal difference in emargination of primaries: on Nightingale 7th and 8th emarginated, on Thrush only 8th. Note, however, that heavy wear or active primary moult (mid June to mid August) can invalidate structural differences while a few individuals (and hybrids!) can exhibit intermediate structures, and may not be identifiable.

Identification

Both have forehead to nape more or less concolorous with brown of mantle; head of Thrush Nightingale appears somewhat more uniform and darker than that of Nightingale, with crown often rather richer brown (can recall female Blackcap *Sylvia atricapilla*). Typical of most Nightingales is slight grey tone on neck sides, reminiscent of Garden Warbler *S. borin* (though sometimes shown by Thrush),

with chin and upper throat forming relatively large whitish area (on Thrush less extensive and more often diffusely spotted). Note that in worn plumage both species become on average paler overall, with great variation. Despite great overlap between the two, each shows certain tendencies; structure and the following characters, used in combination, will aid identification. **1** SUPERCILIUM On Thrush somewhat lighter brown and poorly indicated (on Nightingale rather greyer, reaches farther behind eye, and often very broad in front and joining with pale lores, hence more conspicuous). Occasional overlap, but loral region of Thrush usually diffusely dark, whereas on Nightingale often paler. **2** EAR-COVERTS On Thrush mottled grey-brown, appearing somewhat dirty (uniformly brownish on Nightingale). **3** MALAR STRIPE Thrush Nightingale often shows more obvious malar stripe formed by poorly defined row of spots (rarely present on Nightingale), and area between dark spotting along lower ear-coverts and dark malar stripe often pale and unmarked, suggesting a submoustachial stripe. **4** EYE-RING Nightingale's dark eye on pale face accentuated by whitish eye-ring (Thrush's eye-ring on average less conspicuous, more brownish-tinged). **5** UPPERPARTS On Thrush generally duller, dirtier and darker earth-brown, sometimes somewhat greyer, or even olive-brown recalling Song Thrush *Turdus philomelos* (Nightingale tends towards brighter, warmer reddish-brown, looking very reddish in direct sunlight, but can appear much duller in dark surroundings). Note, however, that Thrush Nightingale can very occasionally appear more reddish above and, conversely, some Nightingales are quite dark brown. **6** TAIL/UPPERPARTS CONTRAST Both have reddish-brown tail, but on Thrush darker and duller, more dull chestnut-brown, whereas on Nightingale usually bright rust-brown. Difference usually more obvious when compared with colour of rest of upperparts: on Thrush uppertail-coverts usually dark brown (as mantle and back), so reddish tail frequently shows quite strong contrast (on Nightingale uppertail-coverts about same colour as tail,

Thrush Nightingale. Note dark brown plumage with grey or olive tones. Dark malar stripe with contrasting paler throat and submoustachial stripe, dappled grey breast, dark tips to undertail-coverts often evident.

Nightingale. Warm rufous, especially the rump and tail. Pale lores and vague supercilium, non-contrasting throat, underparts creamy. Primary tips gradually spaced. 1st primary longer than primary coverts.

Evenly spaced primary tips. Note 1st primary very short, not reaching tips of primary coverts.

Some birds ambiguous. This Nightingale is greyer than usual, though the tail and rump are still rufous. In long careful observation the length of the 1st primary can be judged.

often resulting in lack of strong contrast on upperparts). **7** UNDERPARTS Typical Thrush Nightingale averages somewhat darker and dirtier greyish-white below than Nightingale, with breast almost always obviously darker and usually with clear grey-brown spotting (can even show checkered pattern), diffuse spots normally extending to flanks, where often appear as indistinct streaking, and frequently also faintly onto belly; some, however, are confusingly pale and uniform below. Nightingale is typically paler, whiter and cleaner below, generally lacking breast-band effect of Thrush. Unfortunately, some overlap occurs, and viewing conditions can often radically change appearance of birds. Nightingale often shows variable grey-brown wash to breast (sometimes contrasting sufficiently with white belly to form breast band), and at certain angles of light flanks can look spotted/ streaked as on Thrush. Note also that Nightingale's breast may become soiled (looking 'spotted') from ground foraging, while 1st-autumn (and even 1st-spring) Nightingales can retain odd dark juvenile feathers on breast giving spotted appearance very like Thrush. **8** UNDERTAIL-COVERTS Thrush Nightingale's darker, brownish-grey undertail-coverts have brown spots/bars, diagnostic when seen; on Nightingale always unmarked and on average paler, from whitish to light red-brown (if reddish, often contrasting with white belly and extending to lower flanks). Note, however, that dark markings on Thrush occasionally restricted to feather bases, so not visible in field. **9** BILL AND LEGS Both have blackish-brown bill with paler lower mandible: on Thrush Nightingale, however, only inner half of lower mandible paler (light brown to dirty flesh-coloured, sometimes faintly tinged yellow-orange); on Nightingale more often entirely pale (greyish-flesh to clean pink). Legs brownish-flesh, on Nightingale averaging somewhat paler (often dark pinkish or greyish-flesh to pale horn-brown), on Thrush somewhat darker (usually light brown). 10 TAIL-WAGGING Nightingale wags its tail rapidly downwards several times, and only on final wag brings it slowly back to original position. Thrush Nightingale describes an oval shape with its tail tip (recalling a shrike *Lanius*), with no slow final upstroke. 11 SUBSIDIARY DIFFERENCES On closed wing, primary tips appear more blackish on Nightingale and contrast more with brighter rusty-brown of rest of wing; contrast less marked on Thrush Nightingale, owing to less bright chestnut-brown wing-coverts and edges of remiges. Underwing-coverts and axillaries of Thrush darker, more brownish (yellowish-white on Nightingale).

Age-related Variation Juvenile plumage (moulted quickly, seen only close to breeding site), with typical thrush-type spotting, extremely similar in both species, but Thrush somewhat darker and less reddish above, with pale wing spots more whitish; safely distinguished only by wing formula. 1st-winters of both, before first complete moult (in 1st summer), have greater coverts and tertials, and less obviously uppertail-coverts, tipped brownish-yellow (somewhat paler on Thrush), and smaller tips to tail feathers; some tips retained (especially on wing) into 1st spring, when also often have darker and more heavily abraded rectrices and more heavily worn remiges than adults.

Racial Variation of Nightingale Nominate Nightingale shows minor geographical variation in upperpart tone and wing and tail lengths, but of no significance for identifica-

tion. Eastern races, however, are greyer, less rufous, above and paler below and can show variable hint of breast band (structural and biometric details often needed to support field identification). C Asian *hafizi* (migrates through Middle East; has appeared as vagrant W Europe) is bigger, with longer wing and tail, sandy to light grey-brown upperparts, whitish underparts with extensive white throat and with undertail-coverts usually lacking or having only weak brownish tone, and often shows clear pale edges to tertials and greater primary and secondary coverts. Race *africana* (breeds Caucasus and Iran) is closer to nominate European *megarhynchos* in plumage, but tends more towards a grey tinge above (like Thrush) than a red tinge, has grey-brown breast and averages distinctly larger, with clearly longer tail.

Voice Alarm calls differ. Thrush Nightingale utters uninflected 'iiht', recalling Collared Flycatcher *Ficedula albicollis*; Nightingale has disyllabic, slightly rising 'hüit', with final syllable stressed, somewhat recalling Willow Warbler *Phylloscopus trochilus*. Songs basically similar: that of Thrush sounds louder, richer, more powerful, with phrases longer, and without the almost sobbing, 'pew-pew-pew-. . .' phrase typical of most Nightingales; tends also to lack latter's short terminal flourish. 'Mixed' singers occur in and near overlap zone, where differences less clear-cut anyway.

Other Confusion Risks In W Europe, both species could possibly be confused with vagrant American *Catharus* thrushes, especially Veery *C. fuscescens* (which has only weakly spotted breast). Careful observation of size, structure and all plumage features, plus voice, should, however, rule these out.

References Barthel (1993), Cramp (1988), Svensson (1992).

Wheatears
Introduction
Although wheatears are a most difficult group, with practice and experience most

individuals are identifiable. While females and immatures pose greatest problems, plumage morphs and racial differences add to the difficulty in the case of some males. Tail pattern often (not always) useful. It helps to group species by similarity and distribution, as done here, but, since most are at least in part migratory, locality is not always a reliable guide.

Moult and Ageing

Most wheatears have a partial post-juvenile moult (head, body, often some inner wing-coverts) soon after fledging, producing 1st-winter plumage: much as adult female winter (but see male Hooded and male Pied), though all tail and most/all wing feathers (and sometimes some scapulars) retained and look duller and relatively worn. Partial spring moult (some/all head and body feathers) in winter quarters produces 1st-summer plumage: when fresh resembles fresh adult summer, but in early spring often distinguishable by pale-flecked, slightly duller appearance (and by faded, browner, retained juvenile remiges, primary coverts and varying amount of outer greater and median coverts). Complete moult in breeding area in late summer/autumn gives adult winter plumage: as 1st-winter (with pale fringes to body and wings), but males usually brighter. Partial spring moult (some/all head and body feathers, sometimes some inner wing-coverts) in wintering area produces adult summer plumage: when fresh often much as adult winter, but loss of pale fringes to head, body and wings soon gives full, bright plumage in early spring. (Note that partial spring moult does not occur in Black and probably also some other species, and can be fully or partly suppressed in others.)

Isabelline and Northern Wheatears

Where and When Northern Wheatear *Oenanthe oenanthe* is a summer visitor and/or passage migrant throughout W Palearctic (a few winter irregularly N Africa, S Middle East). Isabelline *O. isabellina* is a summer visitor to southeast of region (present all year in parts of Middle East) and very rare vagrant to NW Europe.

Size, Structure and Posture Isabelline is larger, more robust and longer-legged than Northern, with bigger, broader head and deeper- and broader-based, longer bill (length sometimes accentuated by dark lores); primary projection (equal to or shorter than exposed tertials) shorter than Northern's (exceeds tertial length). Tail, though relatively shorter and fuller-looking, projects further beyond folded wings, wings reaching only to level with tip of undertail-coverts or (from above) to much less than halfway down black area of tail (on Northern, wings extend well over halfway along tail, often to within 1 cm of tip). Isabelline often stands very upright, appearing pot-bellied or (head-on) even pear-shaped, when longer legs (long thigh) even more striking, as is the shortish tail (ends well above ground, so tail-wagging 'freer'). Race *leucorhoa* of Northern large, but criteria of primary and tail projections still valid.

Plumage Isabelline varies little, basically fairly uniform sandy-coloured with relatively few contrasting features. Needs to be distinguished from all plumages of Northern except breeding adult male. Main constant features of Isabelline are as follows. 1 UNDERWING Underwing-coverts and axillaries very pale, white to pale buffish (greyish to blackish, on Northern), and remiges, though slightly darker, can be almost as pale, so whole underwing appears paler than on Northern. This diagnostic difference may be impossible to confirm in field, but Isabelline's almost translucent underwing may be detected in flight. 2 UNDERPARTS Tends to show more even sandy/whitish-buff suffusion from breast to vent (on Northern, warmer colour, especially in autumn, forms broad breast band extending to flanks, contrasting more with whiter belly), but overlap occurs and also affected by wear, while spring female Northern may be equally pale. 3 ALULA Largest (and second largest) alula feather very dark brown (can appear blackish), darkest part of entire upperparts, usually contrasts strongly with much paler coverts (on Northern, alula also dark but does not stand out, as rest of wing normally almost as

Tails of Northern Wheatear (left) and Isabelline Wheatear (right).

Spring ♀ Northern Wheatear. Superciliun weak, upperparts greyish-brown, wings dark. Tail reaches ground in upright posture.

Spring Isabelline Wheatear. Dark line of wing broken by pale primary coverts. Thick bill, supercilium whitish before eye, indistinct behind. Long-legged.

1st-winter Northern Wheatear. Supercilium poor before eye, stronger behind. Wings dark to feather centres.

1st-winter Northern Wheatear of large Greenland race 'leucorhoa'. Breast may be dark rusty. Dark centres to wing feathers.

Fresh plumaged Isabelline Wheatear. Very pale, wing pattern evident but does not contrast with upperparts, notably the tertials. Lacks stronger pectoral band of Northern Wheatear. In upright posture tail does not touch ground.

dark and at least some dark-centred coverts always present). Note, however, that alula often hidden by breast-side feathers, and heavy abrasion of wing of Isabelline may obscure this feature. 4 WING AND MANTLE CONTRAST Isabelline shows little contrast between folded wing and rest of upperparts (Northern's wing always looks darker, at least in part, than mantle/back). Again, this strongly influenced by wear/bleaching, as well as by light and viewing angle: e.g. abraded Isabelline in strong light appears more contrastingly patterned than usual, while reverse can apply to Northern. 5 TAIL-AND-RUMP PATTERN Dark inverted T on tail averages deeper (usually extends half to two-thirds up tail) and shorter-stemmed than on Northern (a third to half of tail), but often

hard to assess and overlap occurs (note also that young Northern have broader band than adults). White restricted to upper tail sides and uppertail-coverts, thus smaller than on Northern (where reaches further onto tail and extends onto rump), this obvious on take-off/landing, when inverted-T effect much reduced. On perched Isabelline, border between white area and sandy of rump about level with pale tips of longest tertials (on Northern, white to well above tip of tertials). 6 SUPERCILIUM Whitish, most pronounced (broadest and palest) in front of and above eye, shortish and often buffish and tapering to point behind (on Northern, washed buffish and less distinct in front of eye, whitish and more obvious behind). Care needed with paler/grey winter Isabelline, on which supercilium often less distinct. (Note that lores vary on both species: often dark, but can be pale.)

Pied, Cyprus Pied and Black-eared Wheatears

Where and When Pied *O. pleschanka* breeds from Bulgaria east to China, migrating via Iraq, Iran and Middle and Near East to winter E Africa; rare vagrant NW Europe (mainly late autumn). Cyprus Pied *O. cypriaca* breeds Cyprus (vagrant Turkey, Balkans), migrating mainly September-October to E Africa and returning to Cyprus from mid March; rare on passage Levant and Egypt, but could possibly occur elsewhere in Mediterranean (or beyond?). Black-eared *O. hispanica* is a summer visitor to Mediterranean region and east into Iran; fairly common on passage in south and rare vagrant elsewhere.

SEPARATING PIED FROM BLACK-EARED

General Both are slim, with rounded head, smallish bill and longish tail. Differ little in structure; primary projection on Pied equal to/clearly longer than tertials, on Black-eared shorter to slightly longer than tertials. Tail patterns normally not distinguishable (rarely, Black-eared's outer tail almost all-white). Females and autumn/winter birds require great caution. Here, Black-eared refers mainly to eastern race *melanoleuca* (though many points apply equally to western *hispanica*) and primarily black-throated morph.

Spring Males Usually distinct. Pied has extensive black throat patch meeting black/brownish-black mantle and wings; on Black-eared, mantle pale, and dark throat of black-throated morph usually less extensive and never broadly connected to wings (though on hunched bird dark throat can seem to meet scapulars/wing). Pied may still show grey fringes on crown and nape, and pale fringes on throat (sometimes also mantle, scapulars and wings) often present well into spring; Black-eared can retain dusky/sandy on crown and mantle and/or slight pale fringes on throat/scapulars. 1st-summer males of both normally have varying amount of more obvious pale fringes (can produce ill-defined

pattern above and on throat), and crown usually duskier. *Females* Pied is sooty-brown to greyish olive-brown (but still usually rather dusky) above, normally somewhat darker than Black-eared (which can show rusty tinge), and never with contrasting blackish ear-coverts of some Black-eared, but many are virtually identical above. Pied has extensive but highly variable dark grey-brown/blackish patch across lower throat extending to neck sides, upper scapulars and upper breast, where border may be diffuse (occasionally much of breast darkish, or, with wear, some extremes may appear 'black-throated'), and chin normally pale/pale-fringed. On dark-throated Black-eared, throat patch smaller, not reaching scapulars or upper breast, and can show some/many pale fringes (though need not produce isolated whitish chin); pale-throated morph has white to creamy-buff (rarely, dusky) throat, but very rare white-throated morph '*vittata*' of Pied virtually identical. Rest of Pied's breast normally grey-buff or off-white, usually cold-toned but occasionally with faint warm tint (Black-eared usually shows orange-rufous band, as in autumn). Individuals with greyish-brown upperparts, white throat and warm-tinged but rather indistinct breast band may be unidentifiable (but white-throated Pied extremely rare).

Autumn Adult males Fresh adult male Pied has extensive sooty-grey crown and nape; lores, ear-coverts and throat black with some pale fringes; mantle and back feathers pale-fringed with black centres (when worn, mantle all black, unlike Black-eared); and entire wing feathers, especially lesser coverts, have very broad pale fringes. Adult Black-eared much as in spring, but mantle less white; may show pale fringes to black of scapulars and throat (throat patch less extensive than on Pied, not reaching onto neck sides); wing and tail feathers pale-fringed, but lesser-covert fringes very narrow (broad on Pied). Note that some adult male Pied in autumn resemble 1st-winters (but remiges black, not brown-black); thus, with even more variegated and broader-fringed upperparts and impression of more contrast between blacker scapulars and paler mantle, can be hard to separate from 1st-winter Black-eared (see below). *1st-winter males* Very difficult to separate. On Pied, heavy fringing often obscures black on mantle and scapulars, and, although throat patch reaches upper breast, fringes can conceal lower part of patch and its connection to wing. Black-eared may look 'less tidy' (extensive pale fringing), with dark throat obscured. Wear reveals diagnostic difference in feather centres of mantle, black on Pied but white or buff on Black-eared (in very fresh plumage, detectable only in hand or if feathers lifted by wind). *Females* Separating females (all ages) in autumn extremely difficult and at times impossible; overlap occurs, and some show features of both species. Following features helpful. 1 UPPERPARTS Typical fresh Pied looks rather uniform, with neat pale fringes to cold grey-brown feathers of crown, mantle and scapulars (usually distinct until November) often giving pale appearance (typical Black-eared usually rather plain warm darkish brown above with slight rufous tinge, occasionally with neat but faint fringes to scapulars and mantle). 2 THROAT Pied's throat usually extensively dusky (can show hint of malar stripe), with whitish border below narrow/indistinct or lacking (usually broader and pronounced on Black-eared), and usually with faint whitish submoustachial stripe; pale-throated morph of Black-eared often identical, but some have cleaner, cream-tinged whitish throat (as does rare *'vittata'* Pied). On both species, throat can be dark with pale feather tips (dark may extend to upper breast on Pied, never so on Black-eared). 3 BREAST Pied's breast often has slight creamy/buffish tinge (can be greyish), forming diffuse patchy breast band, darkening near wing; on Black-eared, usually rather broad, better-defined, orange-rufous band (more brown-grey near wing), contrasting more with throat and lower breast. Difference, however, not always marked, and both can show pale orangey breast (generally more extensive and better defined on Black-eared).

Intermediates/hybrids The two hybridise in Caspian area, where (as also with such birds on passage) separation often impossible.

SEPARATING CYPRUS PIED FROM PIED

Structure and Essential Features Cyprus Pied is smaller than Pied, with shorter wing (noticeable in flight) and shorter primary projection; 1st primary clearly longer than primary coverts (only slightly longer on Pied), but this of little use in field. Bill and tarsus average marginally shorter on Cyprus Pied (on extremes of Pied can be distinctly longer). Cyprus Pied differs markedly also in male-like plumage of female, and in all plumages shows two constant diagnostic features. 1 RUMP PATCH Uppertail-coverts to rump/lower back whitish (still buff-tinged in early spring) for 1.5-2.5 cm, ending level with tip of shortest/central tertial and generally not covering lower back, length being about two-thirds that of black on central tail (Pied has 2.5-4 cm of white, reaching to lower back, about level with tip/base of smallest tertial, equal to or slightly shorter than black on central tail); beware that size of patch varies individually but also with sex/age (notably on Cyprus Pied), 1st-winters and females tending to have smaller white area. 2 OUTER TAIL Black on outer feathers averages longer, extending up to two-thirds along outer edge from tip (on Pied about a half).

(Note that, although the following compares corresponding plumages of the two species, there is often more risk of confusion among different ages/sexes: see below and also Moult and Ageing above.)

Spring Adult males Apart from features given above, main distinctions as follows. 1 UNDERPARTS Cyprus Pied shows more extensive black on upper breast, and breast sides may have some black (often hidden by folded wing); breast and flanks rich cinnamon-buff, becoming paler with wear and can be mainly white by April (underparts whiter on Pied, with yellow-buff tinge to breast in early spring; rare *'vittata'* morph has chin and throat white). 2 CROWN Very variable on both. On fresh Cyprus Pied, crown and nape have extensive dark sooty-brown tips (Pied's crown usually greyer-brown, somewhat paler). Crown of both wears to whiter/white, but at corresponding stages Pied appears cleaner-headed. 3 MANTLE On Cyprus Pied, black of back extends to upper mantle (latter white on Pied). *1st-summer males* Cyprus Pied is much like adult female (see below), with black areas brownish and with more dark on crown; Pied can also have darker crown and normally retains some brown mantle fringes, but paler overall than Cyprus Pied. *Females* Fresh Cyprus Pied has brown tinge to black areas and some paler fringes on throat, but with wear becomes much as male. Pied very different: grey-brown above (contrasting with darker wings, unlike Cyprus Pied), with creamy or buff-white supercilium (flares behind eye) and variable amount of reddish-brown on ear-coverts; chin and throat black or greyish-buff, rest of underparts whitish, or sometimes warm pale rufous on breast.

Autumn Adult males Cyprus Pied has whole top of head and hindneck blackish-brown (variable pale flecking on hindneck/nape), isolating buffish-white supercilium; rest of upperparts much as adult summer, but with indistinct brownish-grey fringes to black areas (most obvious on scapulars); wing-coverts fringed buffish, secondaries and tertials edged white; black feathers of chin to upper breast variably tipped buff, rest of underparts warm pale cinnamon. Fresh autumn adult Pied has paler, buffish or brownish, crown with paler tips; black of mantle to upper back can be totally obscured by olive-brown fringes; wing-feather fringes distinctly paler and broader (especially on greater coverts, secondaries and tertials) than on Cyprus Pied, and primaries (notably inners) broadly tipped white; black of throat shows more extensive, broader and paler fringes than Cyprus Pied, with upper breast a paler warm buff and fading downwards (pale cream vent). *1st-winter males* 1st-winter Cyprus Pied differs from adult in greyer forecrown, buffer supercilium and hindneck flecks, bolder fringes to upperparts and throat, duller underparts, and on average

smaller, more buffy rump patch. Pied normally quite different, more like pale version of adult (but with prominent pale edges to primary coverts, sometimes some new inner wing-coverts with buffy-white edges and black centres), though some more like female. Note that, since some 1st-winter male Cyprus Pied are much paler/greyer when very fresh, they progressively approach relatively dark fresh adult male autumn Pied (same occasionally applies to 1st-winter male Pied), but size/structure, rump patch and tail pattern should minimise this problem. *Females* Female Cyprus Pied is virtually identical to male (though 1st-winters slightly duller than adult females and usually markedly duller than any autumn male plumage). Fresh adult winter female Pied much as in spring, but has pale buff or cream edges/tips to wings and upperparts, and pale creamy throat with some intermixed dark feathers (1st-winters variable, often identical to adult, sometimes buffer below and 'frostier' above). Note that 1st-winter female Cyprus Pied, being the dullest autumn examples of that species, are very like 1st-winter male Pied; structure, rump patch and tail pattern again the most useful differences between the two.

Behaviour and Voice Cyprus Pied often uses elevated perches (wires, buildings etc), Pied preferring lower sites. Has rasping 'bizz...-bizz...bizz...' song, quite unlike Pied's musical whistling (though Pied may begin with buzzing notes and includes mimicry).

Some Near Eastern wheatears: Desert, Red-rumped, Red-tailed and female Hooded

Where and When Desert *O. deserti* breeds in desert-like areas in Near and Middle East and N Africa (two further races Asia), wintering from N Africa and Dead Sea area southwards; rare vagrant elsewhere in region. Red-rumped *O. moesta* is resident N Africa and a few scattered localities in Jordan, S Israel (casual), Syria, W Iraq and NW Saudi Arabia. Red-tailed *O. xanthoprymna* breeds in mountains from E Turkey to southern Caspian (and to W Pakistan), most wintering N Africa and

Spring ♂ Black-eared Wheatear of eastern race 'melanoleuca'.

Spring ♂ Pied Wheatear. Very pale below, white rump extends high up back. Crown sharply defined

1st-winter ♂ Pied Wheatear. Summer pattern hidden by buff fringes. Note grey-buff fringes to upperparts.

Pied, Cyprus Pied and Black-eared Wheatears have similar tail patterns.

Spring ♂ Black-eared Wheatear of western race 'hispanica'. Both races can have full or half mask.

Spring ♀ Cyprus Pied Wheatear. Dark crown, peachy breast.

Winter ♂ Black-eared Wheatear of orangey western race 'hispanica'.

Spring ♂ Cyprus Pied Wheatear. Breast peachy, white rump reaches smallest tertial. Shorter primary projection than Pied Wheatear.

1st-winter ♂ Black-eared Wheatear, race 'melanoleuca'.

Mourning Wheatear. Wing pattern diagnostic.

1st-winter Cyprus Pied Wheatear. As ♂ Pied, but smaller, darker back and less extensive white rump.

♂ Finsch's Wheatear. Stocky, heavy bill. Pale back stripe.

1st-spring ♂ Black-eared Wheatear of eastern race 'melanoleuca'.

Mourning Wheatear. Both sexes similar in Near East, very different in North Africa. Note warm flush to undertail-coverts.

♂ Hooded Wheatear. Long-billed and short-legged. Note tail pattern (right).

SW Asia. Hooded *O. monacha* is mainly resident in barren stony/rocky deserts from W Jordan and Israel to N Egypt east of Nile.

DESERT WHEATEAR

General Features Rather small and compact, with relatively long tail and diagnostic tail pattern. Tail frequently pumped.

Plumage Tail-and-rump pattern distinctive in all plumages: tail all black (very small amount of white at very base of outer feathers), so no inverted-T impression; rump white (often with buffish tinge). Note that some Isabelline can approach this pattern (see above). For ageing, both in spring and in autumn, see Moult and Ageing above. *Spring males* Adult male unmistakable (tail pattern; black throat joins black of wings; sandy upperparts, tinged pink in N African race *homochroa*); often fairly obvious pale area along outer scapulars. 1st-summer male has similar pattern but less contrasting, with browner wings, more greyish-buff upperparts and pale tips to throat feathers. *Autumn males* Fresh winter adult has generally darker (greyer) upperparts, pale supercilium contrasting with darker crown, pale buffish wing-feather edges, and whitish fringes breaking up black of throat. 1st-winter male similar, but blackish areas browner and dark of throat sometimes wholly obscured by pale fringes. *Females* Pale sandy-buff or buffish grey-brown above and buffy-white below; indistinct but broad pale supercilium, brownish ear-coverts, brownish-black (not black) remiges with sandy-buff edges; throat usually pale as rest of underparts, but can be blackish or mottled dark. Tail pattern as male's (rump usually more buffy) and also shows same pale area along outer scapulars.

RED-RUMPED WHEATEAR

General Features Large-headed and robust, with long legs, fairly strong bill, and distinctive tail pattern (fans tail widely).

Plumage *Spring males* Black-throated summer adult distinctive: crown and hindneck white (crown centre mottled grey or reddish-brown), merging into dull black mid-mantle (more grey-black on Middle East race *brooksbanki*); rump rufous-buff, or mainly greyish,

or off-white with rufous uppertail-coverts (paler, whitish-buff, on *brooksbanki*); and tail all black with restricted rusty bases to outer feathers. Rather prominent pale tips to median and especially greater coverts produce double wingbar (occasionally panel). Looks pale-winged in flight (remiges silvery below, contrasting with very dark coverts). 1st-summer as adult, but black areas generally browner. *Autumn males* Adults have greyish crown and hindneck (isolating whitish supercilium), not well demarcated from slaty-grey mantle; rump darker, deeper rufous or greyish. 1st-winter (from July) more brown-grey above, crown often tinged rufous. *Females* Buffy- or sandy-grey (or grey-brown) above and somewhat paler below (sometimes slight rusty-buff wash to breast). Head has variable but usually distinctive cinnamon or rufous-buff tone and brown wings show prominent buffy panel (both features lacking on female Red-tailed). Tail as male's but with much more rufous (dark colour confined to central feathers and diffuse terminal band); rump also similar to male's, but usually paler on 1st-winter females.

RED-TAILED WHEATEAR

General Features Smaller, less robust than Red-rumped, with fairly heavy bill but short tail; recalls Rock Thrush *Monticola saxatilis* in shape. Male western *xanthoprymna* much more contrastingly patterned than drab eastern race *chrysopygia* (females of both rather variable).

Plumage *Western males* Fresh male looks dingy grey above, with darker head sides and black throat and prominent narrow whitish supercilium; sooty-brown/blackish wings (meeting black of throat, but less clearly than on Red-rumped) broadly fringed pale on greater coverts and remiges, but do not contrast much with scapulars/mantle; whitish below, with slight rufous or pinky-brown tinge (especially on breast and ventral area). When worn, mantle becomes more sandy and wings darker (almost black in carpal area), thus showing more contrast, and underparts a dirty white. Rump reddish-chestnut or rusty (darker than Red-rumped), with base of outer

1st-winter ♀ Cyprus Pied Wheatear. Smaller and darker than Pied, less extensive rump patch and shorter primary projection.

Winter ♀ Pied Wheatears. Note pale fringing to cold brown upperparts, pinkish-brown breast band diffuse and extending onto upper chest. Dark-throated forms (below) with extensive dark throat not separated from grey breast. Dark sides of breast merge into centre.

Autumn ♀ Black-eared Wheatears of eastern race 'melanoleuca'. Back warmer, less fringed than Pied Wheatear. Breast orange-tinged. Throat coloration variable.

Autumn ♀ Black-eared Wheatear of western race 'hispanica'. Note warm upperparts, more orangey than Pied Wheatear.

Dark throated Black-eared Wheatears have breast patches separated from throat by pale crescent.

Spring ♀ Black-eared Wheatear of western race 'hispanica'. This race also occurs in pale- or dark-throated forms.

Spring ♀ Black-eared Wheatears of eastern race 'melanoleuca'. Cold brown above.

Spring ♀ Pied Wheatears. Dark of throat spreads over breast. Pale-throated birds are exceptional.

♂ Red-tailed Wheatear

♂ Red-rumped Wheatear.

♀ Red-tailed Wheatear. Tail pattern diagnostic. Some females look like males.

♀ Desert Wheatear in fresh plumage. Tail all dark, wing variegated. Rather chat-like, distinctive tail-wagging.

♀ Red-rumped Wheatear. Strong orange tones, especially to head; pale wing panel. Tail pattern diagnostic.

♀ Hooded Wheatear in spring. Tail pattern diagnostic (but variable). Large with long bill and short legs.

♀ Red-tailed Wheatear of eastern race 'chrysopygia'. ♂ similar. Tail pattern diagnostic.

♀ Northern Wheatear in fresh autumn plumage. Note supercilium, mantle colour and tail pattern.

♀ Finsch's Wheatears in spring.

♀ Mourning Wheatears from North Africa. Head pattern variable. Sandy above, undertail-coverts cream. Primary coverts pale-tipped.

♀ Finsch's Wheatear. Variable head pattern, back silvery-grey, underparts whitish. In autumn (right) plain-faced, ear-coverts warm, pale wingbars, undertail-coverts whitish.

rectrices contrastingly white (occasionally orange-buff or pale rufous); tail appears much less black (black only on central feathers and as narrow terminal band) than on male Red-rumped. 1st-winter male resembles adult of eastern race (see below). *Western females* Female *xanthoprymna* can resemble male, but normally paler above, has less rufous (more pale brownish) rump and sometimes also slightly rufous-tinged ear-coverts; rather often lacks black throat, which instead is dirty whitish or greyish (= pale-throated morph). *Eastern males* Very different from western: greyish overall, appearing relatively plain brown-grey above and grey-white below (no black throat); base of outer tail rusty (not white), not contrasting with rump, and tail shows typical inverted T (but tail has less black than on female Red-rumped, which also shows cinnamon/rufous on head and pale wing panel). Spring birds show warm brown tone to ear-coverts, warm buffish flanks and reddish-buff vent/undertail-coverts; in autumn greyer, but with broad cream-buff fringes to wing-coverts and tertials, somewhat brighter rump, and pronounced pale brownish-orange tip to tail (absent on Red-rumped). *Eastern females* Indistinguishable in field from eastern males. *1st-winters* 1st-winters of both races resemble adult of eastern race, but worn retained juvenile feathers (wing, some coverts, often tertials and/or tail) distinctly browner.

Intermediates Some individuals show characters of both races (black throat and rusty tail sides, or pale throat and white tail sides), but other features should enable identification.

FEMALE HOODED WHEATEAR

General Features Big and long-bodied (noticeably long rear end), with very long bill and large-winged appearance but short legs, and relatively uniform plumage. Structure and plumage generally sufficient for separation.

Plumage Basically sandy-grey to sandy-brown above and dirty white below. When fresh, looks slightly darker above (but with clearly fringed wing-coverts and secondaries) and reddish-buff below, with rump pinkish-

buff and tail reddish-brown with brownish central feathers and tips to outers (tail lacks obvious terminal band). When worn, wings darker (with narrower but still pronounced covert fringes) than rest of more grey-sandy upperparts, and rump and base of outer tail a paler creamy-buff (rest of tail rather dark brown), and underparts dirty grey-white with buff wash to breast sides, flanks and undertail-coverts. In reasonable view, confusion with other wheatears unlikely.

Finsch's, Mourning and male Hooded Wheatears

Where and When Finsch's *O. finschii* breeds in narrow band from S Turkey eastwards (a few Lebanon, Syria), northernmost breeders wintering Middle East areas. Mourning *O. lugens* is largely resident in Near East and parts of N Africa, some eastern breeders moving short distances in winter. Hooded *O. monacha* is a desert specialist (see above).

FINSCH'S WHEATEAR

General Features Stocky and large-headed. Male can recall dark-throated morph of Black-eared in plumage, while female and 1st-winter somewhat similar to female/1st-winter Pied and Black-eared. On landing, typically flicks and cocks tail and hugs ground.

Plumage *Adult male* Creamy-white or pale buff nape, mantle and back (pale grey tips when fresh) and black throat connected by broad black area to black of wings distinctive (black also extends further onto upper breast than on similar dark-throated Black-eared, which in addition has pale neck sides). Tail has neat black inverted T of fairly uniform width (unlike Black-eared) and very narrow white terminal band. Creamy-white underparts tinged buffish when fresh. In flight, underwing shows striking contrast between black coverts and silvery flight feathers (far less contrast on Black-eared). *Female and 1st-winter* Forehead and ear-coverts often tinged rufous-brown (and can show diffuse pale supercilium, mainly above and behind eye, where sometimes rather obvious); rest of upperparts grey or sandy-grey. Wings dark brown, with distinct, almost solid dark greater-covert panel bordered by fairly prominent whitish/buff median- and greater-covert bars, with prominent grey lesser coverts; primary coverts distinctly fringed. On fresh female, throat can be pale (especially eastern race *barnesi*) or variably blackish, whole throat (and even upper breast) becoming blackish when worn; if not fully dark-throated (chiefly in spring, or older birds) or if not too fresh and with whiter/cleaner throat (as many 1st-winters), tends to have dark lower-throat crescent which together with dark malar stripe encloses pale chin/upper throat. Rest of underparts much as male. Separated from Black-eared by colder tone above and by paler scapulars (on Black-eared, scapulars often dark, and eastern race brownish above in autumn), by tail pattern (approaches that of Northern) and by wing pattern (see above), as well as by shape and behaviour. Dark-throated females can resemble female Mourning of race *halophila* (the two can occur together in winter in Egypt), but paler and greyer above and lack latter's pale rusty-orange on ventral region.

MOURNING WHEATEAR

General Features Smaller than Hooded, with more 'standard' proportions. Confusable with male Pied (see above), but has less black on upper breast (almost confined to throat) and lacks extensive pale mantle/scapular fringes when fresh; white appears to be restricted to head (extends to upper mantle on Pied).

Plumage *Males* Distinguished by pale wing panel formed by whitish inner webs to primaries and outer secondaries, obvious in flight and most marked on eastern race *lugens* (less distinct, more greyish, on N African *halophila*). Distinctions from Pied also include: larger area of white on rump (extends further onto lower back); smaller area of black on throat, and rest of underparts cleaner white but with pale orangey-buff (wearing to off-white) ventral region, vent averaging paler on *halophila* (Pied's black bib extends a little onto upper breast, rest of underparts buff-tinged and with white ventral region, though latter may be buffy in autumn); pale of nape not reaching onto upper mantle; black tail band

more or less uniform in width. In flight, blackish underwing-coverts contrast strongly with pale remiges. In autumn, normally shows uniform mid-grey crown and hind-neck (autumn Pied's crown usually darker, with white supercilium) and lacks Pied's prominent pale fringes on mantle and throat. *Females* Adult female *lugens* resembles male. Female *halophila* differs: pale buff-grey/buff-brown above (paler and not so cold grey-brown as female Finsch's), ear-coverts sometimes with warm brown tone; wings dark, more uniform (pale panel lacking or indistinct; also lacks Finsch's dark greater-covert panel and pale wingbars), but, when fresh, broad whitish tips/fringes to primary coverts create rather prominent small patch; chin and throat variably blackish (may extend to upper breast), though some lack blackish altogether, and rest of underparts white/buffy-white with orangey-buff or buff ventral region (entire underparts dirty white when worn). Diagnostically, when perched, black of central tail reaches to 2nd-3rd exposed primary tip (on Finsch's, usually shorter than or equal to wingtip, rarely appears to reach 2nd primary tip), and in flight shows extensive pale area on remiges (remiges more uniform on Finsch's). *Immatures* 1st-autumn/winter birds similar to respective adult, but in particular have prominent white tips to retained, brown primary coverts and some pale or buff fringes/tips to lower back and tertials. For 1st-summer, see Moult and Ageing.

MALE HOODED WHEATEAR

General Features A large, slim, black-and-white wheatear, long-tailed and remarkably long-billed (bill may even give hint of bee-eater *Merops* impression).

Plumage Distinctive and in reasonable views unmistakable. Forehead to nape white; rest of head, mantle and wings black; lower back to uppertail-coverts white; tail white, with black central feathers and black corners to outers (no black terminal band); chin to mid-breast black, remaining underparts white. (Large wings can conceal white belly area on distant perched bird, which may thus resemble White-crowned Black Wheatear *O. leucopyga*, which has similar tail pattern, but Hooded has more white on head and much longer bill.) Black underwing-coverts contrast with pale flight feathers. Fresh autumn adult and 1st-winter males have pale fringes to black areas (mantle can at times appear somewhat greyish) and buffish tint to white areas (on 1st-winter, crown yellowish-buff and white areas and all pale fringes have distinct yellow-brown tone).

References Alström *et al.* (1991a), Clement (1987), Cramp (1988), Flint (1995), Hollom *et al.* (1988), Jonsson (1992), Small (1994), Svensson (1992).

Moustached Warbler

Where and When Moustached Warbler *Acrocephalus melanopogon* is restricted to the southern W Palearctic and SW Asia (vagrants recorded north to Britain). Nominate race is a local resident or summer visitor from coastal NW Morocco and E Spain east to Ukraine and western Turkey; resident or dispersive, but most inland and northern populations move to coasts to winter. Eastern race *mimica* breeds Transcaucasus, Caspian, S and E Turkey and Levant; resident and summer visitor, wintering Middle East area and NW India.

Main Problems In most of region, this species has to be distinguished from the common and far more widespread Sedge Warbler *A. schoenobaenus*. For careful observers this should not be too difficult, as the two are fairly distinct. Eastern Moustached of race *mimica*, however, much duller and longer-winged and thus far closer to Sedge in general appearance, is more likely to cause problems, but can with care be safely identified.

Habitat and Behaviour Moustached generally prefers wetter areas with vertically structured vegetation (especially *Typha*), largely avoided by Sedge, though the two overlap little in breeding range; habitat on passage, however, of limited value. Moustached's high tail-cocking (especially when alarmed/flushed) is well known, but Sedge occasionally performs this action and Moustached often holds tail straight out for extended periods (particularly when feeding). Moustached often climbs to top of reed stems (may sing from exposed perches), but tends to feed at/near ground level, often hopping about; can be very inquisitive, and quite easily attracted by imitating its song.

Structure and Shape Moustached's tail is distinctly more graduated than Sedge's and appears longer, owing mainly to its shorter primary projection (about a quarter to a third of exposed tertials, against three-quarters in Sedge) and its relatively shorter undertail-coverts; eastern *mimica*, however, has longer projection (about third to half tertial length) which can even overlap with Sedge's. Reduced outer primary of Moustached is longer than primary coverts and sometimes visible in field (usually shorter and not shown on Sedge). Moustached has a slightly more delicate, finer bill than Sedge.

Adult Plumage Most Moustached have brighter and deeper (rufous) colour than Sedge and stronger head pattern, but eastern *mimica* much drabber and (with its longer wings) more closely resembles Sedge. Apart from structure, the following plumage features should enable all Moustached to be identified. 1 HEAD PATTERN Crown unstreaked blackish, with slightly paler central area (nominate) or noticeably plain centre and forehead (*mimica*), feathers edged brownish when fresh (can appear faintly mottled); Sedge has paler edges to brownish-black crown feathers, usually appearing streaked, but wears to unstreaked dark grey with blacker lateral crown. Moustached's supercilium is contrastingly white to greyish-white, very broad throughout its length (especially behind eye), and normally ends abruptly just beyond ear-coverts (often square-ended); on Sedge, supercilium has pale buffish or creamy tinge (becoming whiter with wear), is clearly narrower and tapers at both ends. Both species show dark eye-stripe, but on Mous-

Worn adult Sedge Warbler. Note long primary projection, crown blotchy or streaked, supercilium cream and fades at nape. Rump contrasts with back, underparts pale, flanks warm buff.

Adult Moustached Warbler. Note short primary projection, crown blackish, not streaked. White supercilium ends abruptly, thick eye-stripe. Very rufous, no rump contrast, flanks dark.

Bill thin, legs dark, back usually strongly streaked.

Adult Moustached Warbler of eastern race 'mimica'. Closer to Sedge Warbler, head pattern still distinctive, rufous flanks and upperparts less contrasting, rusty neck sides. Primary projection longer than on western birds, but still shorter than Sedge Warbler.

tached this is blackish and broadens slightly behind eye (on Sedge, slightly thinner and dark olive-brown rather than black, becoming slightly darker behind eye). A narrow dark moustachial stripe is normally distinct on Moustached (particularly nominate), whereas Sedge lacks this or has only faint suggestion of a very short stripe (often a small arc shape). Moustached has dark, rufous-blackish ear-coverts, often slightly paler below eye (sometimes looking solid in nominate), and well defined by moustache and eye-stripe (often making paler ear-coverts of *mimica* appear 'hollow'); on Sedge, ear-coverts more uniform pale olive-brown, less prominent and show less contrast with throat. **2 UPPERPARTS** Nominate Moustached very distinctive above, being deep rufous-brown with rufous neck shawl extending well onto neck sides and with broad black mantle streaks, quite different from Sedge's dull grey-olive ground colour to mantle and contrasting rufous-

grey/yellow-brown rump and uppertail-coverts (also, many Sedge appear virtually unstreaked when worn, whereas Moustached normally/always shows some streaking); *mimica*, though duller/greyer than nominate, always shows some indication of rusty tones on mantle and lacks rump contrast. Both races of Moustached have tertials black-centred when fresh or moderately so (on Sedge, ground colour usually more dark olive-brown and appears paler than on Moustached at corresponding stages of wear), and often a rusty panel on secondaries (paler, duller on Sedge). **3 UNDERPARTS** Moustached has very white throat (emphasises head pattern) and white or greyish-white central breast and belly, with extensive rufous-buff wash from breast sides, through flanks to thighs and undertail-coverts (wash less extensive and less rufous on *mimica*, but still distinct); faint streaks may be visible on upper breast of some. Sedge never shows any hint of rufous below, being washed a paler buffish-olive, and never any hint of streaking (but see juvenile, below). **Autumn** Significantly, Moustached has complete moult on breeding grounds, so both adults and 1st-winters fresh in autumn, when adult Sedge (moults in winter quarters) heavily worn.

Juvenile/1st-winter Fresh, bright juvenile Moustached distinguished from any age of Sedge by same characters as for adults (note also that adult nominate Moustached moult early, from July, and ageing not feasible much after August). Juvenile Sedge much brighter than adults, having buff feather edges above, spotting across breast and usually a distinct buffish central crown-stripe; confusion with any age/race of Moustached unlikely.

Voice Moustached's song sounds like a mix of Reed and Sedge songs: series of clear mellow notes followed by a chatter, but either element may be omitted. Sedge gives very fast, varied chatter interspersed with whistles and churrs (and much mimicry, including of Moustached). Calls of Moustached include hard 'tak', a softer 'chak', a 'tic' (recalling chat *Saxicola* or *Sylvia* warbler) and occasionally 'trrrp', all fairly distinct from Sedge's harsh 'churr' or repeated scolding 'tuc'.

In Flight Moustached's short, rounded wings and longish graduated tail, bold head pattern and (at least in nominate) rich rufous colours often give clue to its identity when flushed (flies low for short distance, then briefly perches with tail cocked high).

Separation from Paddyfield Warbler In SW Asia and even E Turkey, where Moustached (*mimica*) and Paddyfield Warbler *A. agricola* breed together in same habitat, worn adults can cause problems. In June-July, both are very heavily worn and look so similar (faded sandy-grey with almost no pattern in plumage) that they are best identified by size, shape and voice; Moustached usually also shows remnant of blackish centres to (mainly smallest) tertials and slightly darker crown, and its bill (unlike Paddyfield's) is all dark. *Reference* Madge (1992).

Small Unstreaked Acrocephalus *Warblers*

Where and When Marsh *A. palustris* and Reed Warblers *A. scirpaceus* are common summer visitors to Europe east into Asia, former largely in rank, damp sites with tall herbage (not necessarily near water), Reed in waterside reedbeds and luxuriant vegetation; widespread on passage to/from Africa. Blyth's Reed *A. dumetorum* and Paddyfield Warblers *A. agricola* breed eastern Europe eastwards to Asia, former at edges of marshes, in willow/tall grass interspersed with lightly wooded damp areas, near or far from water (and often overlapping with Marsh), latter in patches of low reed at lakes and marshes in river valleys and steppes (often sharing habitat with Moustached Warbler, less so with Reed or Sedge); both winter S Asia, but only rare vagrants elsewhere in W Palearctic. On passage all occur in any vegetated habitat, but preferably near water. **General** To identify Blyth's Reed Warbler, extensive field knowledge of Marsh and Reed is essential, so these are addressed first but preceded by an equally essential clarification of differences between the genera *Hippolais* and *Acrocephalus*. Paddyfield is distinctive (extremely short wings/long tail, strongly patterned plumage) but rather variable, and poorly patterned or worn birds cause problems with Blyth's Reed and Booted Warblers, so is included here (text only).

Separating *Hippolais* and *Acrocephalus*

Structurally the two genera are very close, and confusion is not rare, particularly between above *Acrocephalus* species (except Paddyfield) and Olivaceous Warbler or between Paddyfield and Booted. Following differences should in combination determine genus. **1 UNDERTAIL-COVERTS** Long on *Acrocephalus*, reaching to three-quarters of tail length, and much farther behind wingtip point (but beware birds with longest undertail-coverts missing); much shorter on *Hippolais*, fall roughly halfway along tail, slightly beyond wing point. 2 TAIL SHAPE Round-ended on *Acrocephalus*, square-ended (or very slightly graduated) on *Hippolais*. 3 OUTER-MOST RECTRICES On *Acrocephalus* rather uniform, sometimes with hint of paler tips and edges; *Hippolais* usually shows paler tips and edges. 4 BILL AND HEAD *Acrocephalus* have slightly rounded/angular head (flatter on Olivaceous) and generally less deep and broad-based bill than Olivaceous, which, with flattish head and deeper and broader bill base, always shows paler, open-faced and gentler expression than *Acrocephalus*. 5 UPPERPARTS *Acrocephalus* have more 'undulating' shape from head to tail, rather than relatively straight back-to-tail line of *Hippolais*; latter also paler, much more greyish (not always obvious when comparing Olivaceous with extremely pale/worn Reed of race *fuscus* or with Blyth's Reed), with no trace of rufous or warm brown/olive. Olivaceous also has distinctly paler (greyer/sandy) fringes to tertials but particularly to secondaries, often forming pale panel (never apparent on any *Acrocephalus*, on which fringes more buff-brown). 6 ACTIONS *Acrocephalus* never nervous and 'clumsy' like *Hippolais*, which constantly (Olivaceous) twitch tail downwards.

Racial variation of Reed and its separation from Marsh

The following summarises the most significant differences, but also emphasises seasonal plumage variations (essential for further comparison with other species). 1 UPPERPARTS Marsh generally has distinct greenish or olive tone, with faint yellowish-brown tinge to rump; autumn young can be warmer with slight brown/rusty tinge, mainly to rump, but still paler (never saturated with rufous as Reed) and always suffused olive with almost no contrast effect; adult wears to paler/greyer, with brownish olive-grey rump by end of summer. Reed generally has warm brown to greyish-brown tone, never olive, and rump always obviously orange-brown to rufous-brown; autumn young rustier; adult

wears to greyish, with little rufous by end of summer. 2 WING Both show long wing and primary projection (70–100% of tertial length), but that of Marsh looks longer and pointed; both also have rather evenly spaced primary tips (on Reed often slightly bunched towards wingtip) with narrow whitish tips when fresh (slightly wider and more pronounced on Marsh). Dark centres and pale fringes to tertials and alula, usually (variable) not concolorous with rest of wing, shown by both species, but on average more pronounced on Marsh. Otherwise, longest tertial always slightly longer than longest inner secondaries on Marsh, but equal or slightly shorter on Reed. All wing features, however, of little or no value on worn individuals. 3 HEAD AND BILL Bill of Marsh fractionally shorter and stouter (also seems thick, with broad pinkish lower mandible), which, together with more rounded crown, gives Marsh a large-headed *Sylvia*-like appearance; average Marsh also shows relatively well-marked whitish eye-ring and whitish-buff supercilium, latter rather broad and bulging in front of eye, fading behind eye, but generally apparent. Reed has long, rather sloping forehead-crown, appearing flattened (gentler-looking), accentuated by long and more pointed bill; vague eye-ring and supercilium (latter indistinct and often absent behind eye). 4 LEGS Marsh has yellowish-flesh to pale brownish or straw-coloured legs, but always with tawny shade; claws pale yellowish-brown and distinctly small and dainty. Reed shows pale brownish-grey/flesh tarsus but nearly always tinged with true grey or dark bluish-grey; claws longer, less rounded and distinctly darker greyish-brown. (Leg colour less reliable for adults than for young birds, but claw colour always valid.) 5 UNDER-PARTS Marsh washed rather uniform yellowish-cinnamon (paler on fresh adult, deeper on 1st-winter), always with only little or no contrast between throat and breast. Nominate Reed tends to have more cinnamon yellowish-buff wash (warmer and darker than Marsh at all corresponding ages) and always strongly on flanks and breast sides; throat

Spring Reed Warbler. Warm plumage tones, especially rump, dusky flanks. Shorter primary projection than Marsh Warbler, with primaries slightly bunched at tip.

1st-autumn Reed Warbler. Warm rufous wash to plumage, especially rump. White throat conspicuous.

Spring Reed Warbler of race 'fuscus'. Greyer above, flanks paler.

1st-autumn Reed Warbler of the race 'fuscus'. Buff-brown above, very pale below.

Spring Marsh Warbler. Note olive plumage, no warm rump, long, evenly spaced primary projection. Straw-coloured legs, and short pale claws.

1st-autumn Marsh Warbler. Browner than adult, stout bill.

Spring Blyth's Reed Warbler. Short distinct supercilium, often a dark spot at tip of lower mandible. Very pale underparts.

Spring Blyth's Reed Warbler. Uniform tertials, upperparts greyish-brown; no rump contrast.

Short primary projection.

Adult Olivaceous Warbler. Hippolais warblers are best separated from the Acrocephalus by shorter undertail-coverts, square-ended tail, pale-edged outer tail feathers, open-faced expression and pale, broad-based bill (from above).

1st-autumn Blyth's Reed Warbler. Warmer than adult, particularly in the wing. Primary projection short, primaries bunched at tip.

often rather whiter. Both species wear to dirty white below. **6 TAIL** Outer tail feathers of fresh-plumaged Marsh show on average slightly more obvious/wider pale tips and edges than on Reed, though overlap common (with wear, feature reduced or lacking on both). EASTERN REED WARBLER (*fuscus*) Existence of this race adds further complications. Generally, upperparts (chiefly crown and nape) and fringes of upperwing distinctly greyer than nominate *scirpaceus*, less brown and more dusky olive-grey; rump paler, more buff-brown (instead of rufous); supercilium, eye-ring and underparts whiter, with very restricted greyish-cream area on body sides and chest. Juvenile/1st-winter has buff-brown (instead of rusty-brown) upperparts, with underparts extensively pale buff (never cinnamon as nominate) and even paler/whiter than Marsh. The dingiest closely approach both Marsh and Blyth's Reed, but still tend to have some rusty/brown tone to rump and lack any green tinge above. Some extreme pale individuals in spring (in Israel) very grey or dusky grey, approaching Olivaceous in many aspects (but see above).

Blyth's Reed Warbler

Upperparts Head to back and rump area uniform (almost no rump contrast), paler, rather greyish. On fresh spring adult cold, earthy olive grey-brown, wearing to greyish-brown in autumn; 1st-winter has slight rufous wash, but never as rufous nor as bright as Reed or Marsh of same age (latter also show varying degree of rusty on rump area). Spring adult never shows distinct olive tone of Marsh nor warm brown tone of nominate Reed; although eastern Reed can show rather comparable (greyish-brown) upperpart tone, it always has varying amount of rusty-buff on rump which Blyth's Reed lacks. *Wing* Wing and primary projection clearly shorter (55–80% of exposed tertials) than on Marsh and most Reed; primaries bunched towards wing-tip, producing mainly 6 widely spaced tips (on Marsh and most Reed 7, occasionally 8, well-spaced tips). Tertials and alula generally concolorous with rest of wing, with hardly

any contrasting pale fringes and never showing prominent dark centres (but beware tricks of light and angle: diffuse tertial fringes can look well defined in side view); base colour of remiges also rather pale, contributing to rather uniform wing which (when fresh) almost lacks pale tips to primaries normally visible on Marsh and Reed. Latter species show more contrasting wing, with rather prominent dark-centred and pale-fringed alula and tertials. 1st-winter Blyth's Reed frequently has remiges tinged rufous (quite broad on fringes), unlike Marsh and Reed. *Head and bill* Although head shape varies with mood, posture and climate, Blyth's Reed shows lowest (flattish) forehead-crown, often creating rather long-billed impression, but bill in fact is intermediate in length between Marsh and Reed and is broad-based and tapering, making species look more like Olivaceous Warbler (but see above). Tip of lower mandible often shows dark smudge (unlike Marsh and Reed). Supercilium short but distinct (often accentuated by short dusky eye-stripe), whitish-buff, rather broad and bulging in front of eye, often fading behind eye; generally, this and eye-ring are more apparent than on Marsh and Reed. *Underparts* When fresh (1st-winter and spring), paler and the most uniform, with (often restricted) greyish-buff tint, chiefly on flanks and breast sides. *Legs* Pale greyish-flesh with some purple tone; claws same, short and with shape as Marsh's (see above).

General Impression Compared with both Reed and Marsh, tends to appear long-tailed (owing to short wings), and frequently cocks, fans or flicks tail; this, combined with upward-slanted head and neck, forming arc, is often referred to as 'banana posture', but this should be used only as *contributory* evidence in identification. Undertail-coverts somewhat shorter than on Marsh and Reed, but still always over half tail length. Importantly, note that no single one of above features is diagnostic of Blyth's Reed, combination of several (if not all) being essential. Comparison between species must be made with same-age/plumage individuals: beware worn autumn adult Reed and Marsh, which can be very similar in upperpart coloration to some pale 1st-winter Blyth's Reed. Can also be confused with Paddyfield and Olivaceous.

Paddyfield Warbler

Usually distinctive. Smaller, with proportionately shorter bill; also shows shorter (rounded) wing and primary projection (30–40% of exposed tertials), strongly contributing to longer-tailed appearance. Tail strongly rounded (most apparent when slightly raised or cocked on landing). Short primary projection and wing also characteristic of Blyth's Reed, but Paddyfield's wing shorter, bluntly rounded and with primary tips bunched, though wings often held drooped. Although forehead-crown flattish, feathers are often raised. In fresh plumage upperparts greyish-brown, but vary from olive-tinged (mainly spring) to light/deep rufous (mainly 1st-winter), and often with rather contrasting greyer crown/nape and (variably) rustier/warmer rump and uppertail-coverts. Supercilium usually striking (though can be rather obscure on poorly patterned or worn birds), whitish-buff from bill to well behind eye, where most conspicuous; frequently accentuated by darker border above and by obvious thin dark line through eye (can be reduced on 'featureless' birds); ear-coverts paler brown and blotchy. Underparts vary, but normally sandy-buff with warmer colour on body sides and often broadening onto breast, ventral region and undertail-coverts; white on throat and breast reaches to neck sides, creating prominent whitish wedges on strongly coloured individuals. Lower mandible pinkish-horn at base then blackish to tip (very rarely, all pale). Bases of remiges and rectrices are darkest area on most individuals, and tertials and alula show pale fine fringes, all producing relatively contrasting pattern. General first impression is of fairly rufescent small warbler with strong supercilium, sometimes likened to Moustached (and note that heavily worn adults of both can also lead to confusion: see Moustached Warbler). Autumn adult wears to more olive grey-brown above.

Such worn Paddyfield, or even fresh but colourless or 'featureless' individuals, with their small size, often give rise to confusion with Booted Warbler, but latter always shows (even when worn) whitish outer tail feathers, distinctly square-ended and shorter tail and shorter undertail-coverts, and is much less warm in colour; Paddyfield always has rufous rump, unlike Booted. Moreover, fresh 'featureless' Paddyfield (not uncommon among juveniles) is not easily separated from Blyth's Reed, which is sometimes only fractionally larger and longer-winged. With caution, however, some structural features (including longer and more rounded tail) and general jizz (lacks latter's resemblance to Olivaceous) can be used, and although plumage characters obscured it still tends to show, at least, relatively more obvious dark-centred tertials, rather distinct supercilium and warmer-coloured rump and body sides.

Hybrids

Hybridisation has occurred between Reed and Marsh and between Marsh and Blyth's Reed. Offspring may resemble either parent species or appear intermediate, and biometric data often confusing. Discussion of these, however, is beyond the scope of this book.

Voice

Reed: song 'chirruc-chirruc-chirruc-puipui-pui-trer-trer-tjetje-tetje . . .' repeated many times, usually from cover, also mimicry; call a low 'churr' but mainly a slurred 'tchar'. Marsh: song very flowing, rich and mimetic, varied in presentation and speed, but with characteristic harsh 'zi-cheh, zi-cheh' interposed, mainly from exposed perch with fully open bill (Reed's bill partially open, rarely almost fully); call a soft 'churr' or 'twik', often stuttering 'st-t-t-t'. Blyth's Reed: song somewhat like Marsh's as also a brilliant mimic, but *much* slower, and single notes repeated 5–10 times, often with interposed clicking 'chek chek', also from high perch; call distinctive, frequently uttered 'thik'. Paddyfield: song again like Marsh's, but highly variable, often quite imitative, and softer, lacking harsh notes; call a harsh 'chr..chuck' or sharp 'schik' or 'cheer', often hard 'trr'.

References Alström *et al.* (1991a, 1994), Cramp (1992), Dowsett-Lemaire & Dowsett (1979), Grant (1980), Harrap (1989), Harris *et al.* (1989), Harvey & Porter (1984), Jännes (1987), Kennerley & Leader (1992), Parmenter & Byers (1991), Pearson (1981, 1989), Schulze-Hagen & Barthel (1993), Svensson (1992), Williamson (1967a).

Large Acrocephalus *Warblers*

Where and When Great Reed Warbler *A. arundinaceus* is a widespread summer visitor over much of central W Palearctic, being scattered on passage south of breeding areas and vagrant to north. Clamorous Reed Warbler *A. stentoreus* is a resident and partial migrant from Israel and Egypt eastwards, rarely recorded outside normal range. Basra Reed Warbler *A. griseldis* is a local summer visitor to southern Iraq; occasionally on passage Arabia and straggles to Israel. Eastern Great Reed Warbler *A. orientalis* and Thick-billed *A. aedon* are rare vagrants from E Asia.

Taxonomy and General Features In Levant, separating Clamorous Reed from Great Reed (both nominate and *zarudnyi*) is relatively easy, using former's combination of short wing and wing projection, long bill, and long-looking and more deeply graduated tail; but slightly farther east race *brunnescens* of Clamorous Reed is longer-winged with (slightly) longer wing projection, shorter bill and less graduated tail. Eastern Great Reed (sometimes lumped with Great Reed) is closer to Clamorous Reed, having rather short wing and short primary projection and rather rounded tail. Racial variation in plumage tone complicates identification process, this also often compounded by individual variation and by effects of abrasion and bleaching, plus existence of birds intermediate in appearance between Great Reed of race *zarudnyi* and Eastern Great Reed (recorded on passage Israel, apparently originating from areas of intergrading/interbreeding). Nevertheless, each species retains specific combination of structure and plumage, distinguishable in good viewing conditions.

Clamorous Reed and Great Reed Warblers

Nominate Clamorous Reed differs from Great Reed in longer and pointed, slightly decurved (instead of shorter and broader) bill, and shorter wing with only about 6 primary tips visible beyond tertials, creating short primary projection half to two-thirds tertial length, and in longer and deeply rounded tail (Great Reed has longer wing and primary projection, latter more or less equal to tertial length and with 8–9 exposed primary tips, and tail proportionately shorter and less deeply graduated). Clamorous Reed shows smooth, rather flattish head profile (more angular on Great Reed, often with steeper/elongated forehead, though quite rounded), producing, with longish bill and tail, much gentler expression than Great Reed; singing Clamorous Reed shows crown peak just behind eye (above or just in front of eye on Great Reed). Clamorous Reed also shows extensive darker/warmer pigments (but much variation, from light olive buffy-brown to deep brown: see plate), with restricted area of whitish (often absent) on mid belly and throat to chin; Great Reed paler and suffused more rufous-brown (nominate) or greyish-olive (*zarudnyi*) above and distinctly paler and whiter below, with deeper buffy colour restricted to body sides. Clamorous Reed's supercilium is rather weak, and shorter/indistinct behind eye (often absent or nearly so); on Great Reed appears pronounced and longer (but variable) and normally also present behind eye, and emphasised by darker and sharper lores and upper ear-coverts and often also by darkish lateral crown and forecrown. Clamorous Reed has greyish or dull pale bluish-grey legs and feet, with soles often tinged olive; on Great Reed predomi-

Spring Clamorous Reed Warbler. Note short primary projection, long tapering bill, weak supercilium, greyish legs. ▶

Spring Clamorous Reed Warbler. Dark variants occur, they lack face markings. ▶

Spring Great Reed Warbler. Broad, blunt-tipped bill, strong supercilium, warm upperparts, whiter underparts, long primary projection. Legs brownish. ▶

Clamorous Reed Warbler of race 'brunnescens'. Close to Great Reed Warbler (particularly of race 'zarudnyi'). Note bill shape, short but strong supercilium. Intermediate primary projection. ▲

Spring Great Reed Warbler of race 'zarudnyi'. Paler, less warm than nominate. ▶

1st-winter Thick-billed Warbler. Short, thick bill, round head, pale lores giving open-faced appearance, short wings, long rufous tail. ▶

Spring Basra Reed Warbler. Midway in size between Reed and Great Reed Warblers. Whitish below, colder olive-brown above. Thin supercilium whitish, extending behind eye. Dark tail least graduated of this group. Slim bill. ▲

Eastern Great Reed Warbler. Shorter-winged, rounded tail with whitish tips, whiter underparts, often with sharp streaks on breast. ▲

nantly pale brown or mouse-grey. Race *brunnescens* of Clamorous Reed much less distinct and often (chiefly when not fresh) inseparable: pale olive-brown or greyish-olive upperparts and paler, whiter underparts with smaller area of greyish-olive on body sides make it rather like Great Reed (mainly *zarudnyi*), but its shorter (but often strikingly whitish) supercilium, very slightly longer and slimmer (dagger-like) bill, and somewhat shorter primary projection, about two-thirds tertial length (instead of about equal) with 6–7 primary tips visible, as well as slightly longer and more graduated tail, should enable identification by experienced observers in good conditions; overall field impression is always of a paler (less saturated with brown), longer and slimmer bird than the robust and chunky Great Reed. Complete post-nuptial moult of *brunnescens* takes place in September-November (nominate *stentoreus* moults in winter), so many young and adults by then in heavy moult while any passage Great Reed at same time and place (e.g. Arabia) show no active moult; where both occur in spring (as in Arabia, where *brunnescens* breeds and Great Reed on passage), *brunnescens* always more worn, chiefly at primary tips, than Great Reed (which has complete moult in winter quarters).

Eastern Great Reed Warbler

Smaller than Great Reed, with shortish primary projection (about two-thirds of or equal to tertial length, roughly intermediate between nominate Clamorous Reed and Great Reed), and has more olive-grey tinge to upperparts and whiter underparts (but largely comparable with Great Reed of race *zarudnyi*), often with rather distinct sharp streaks on lower throat and chest; also whiter, longer and sharper supercilium. Most, when fresh, have broader and whiter tips to rectrices (buffer and narrower on Great Reed). Moult-strategy differences between *brunnescens* and Great Reed (see above) also apply for separating Eastern Great Reed from Great Reed: former moults before autumn migration, latter in African winter quarters. Eastern

Great Reed is often confused with Clamorous Reed (chiefly paler/greyer and short-billed *brunnescens*), but generally latter still has longer and more pointed bill, unstreaked breast, deeper-coloured underparts, less pronounced (often lacking) whitish supercilium and tail tips, and proportionately longer tail and short primary projection (converse on Eastern Great Reed). Eastern Great Reed also has slightly less graduated tail.

Basra Reed Warbler

Much smaller than preceding species (size between Reed and Great Reed), including tail, with moderate/longish and slender bill and long primary projection (about equal to tertial length and often longer). Upperparts more or less uniform cold olivaceous-brown/-grey, slightly greener and darker than *zarudnyi* and with darker tail, and lacking warm rufous tinge of nominate *arundinaceus* (but suffused creamy-yellow or slightly pale rufous-brown when faded); whiter below than preceding species, with restricted cream-yellow tinge to flanks, and pure white throat without faint streaks on breast. Supercilium whitish (cream or buffish on most of preceding forms) and quite prominent, extending well behind eye, and often with well-marked dark eye-stripe. Also has the least graduated tail. Legs look greyish (not brownish-grey as Great Reed). Moults in E African winter quarters. Otherwise, relatively long wing, short tail and slender bill give impression of slim 'large warbler' (instead of 'small Great Reed'), with distinctive darkish remiges and (particularly) tail contrasting with rest of plumage. Above features should separate Basra Reed from Reed and other smallish *Acrocephalus* warblers.

Thick-billed Warbler

Distinctive. About size of Great Reed, but bill relatively shorter (rather deeper, thick); rounded head lacks supercilium and loral stripe (but lores uniformly paler, giving open-faced appearance). Also, has short wing and primary projection, very long and graduated tail (very different from Great

Reed, but rather comparable to Clamorous Reed), and is distinct in its plain fulvous olive-brown upperparts (but with rufous-brown remex fringes, rump and uppertail-coverts) with whitish-buff underparts, but deeper ochraceous on breast, flanks and undertail-coverts. Lower mandible pale (variably dark tip present on most Great Reed); legs and feet bluish-pink. General impression shrike-like, with long tail, this reinforced by its preference for more bushy areas and often mixed forest.

Voice

Clamorous Reed: call a loud, deep 'tak' or 'chak', or rather soft 'karrk'; song very loud, powerful, rather melodious, but not so varied, 'pthara-pthara-tuckii-tuckii' (always preceded by clicking call note), often in repeated series and always high-pitched and with broken rhythm. Great Reed: call a deep

'chak' or 'tsek' or harsher 'trrak'; song not so loud and harsh as preceding species but somewhat more melodious, with many variations and longer phrases, 'karra-karra-karra-keek' or 'karre-karre-keet-peet dree-dree-dree trr trr'. Eastern Great Reed: call and song as Great Reed's. Basra Reed: call quite different, a rather harsh 'chaarr' (louder than similar note of Reed Warbler); song quieter, lacks guttural, grating quality of Great Reed's, e.g. 'chuc-chuc-churruc-churruc-chuc'. Thick-billed: call a loud, harsh, fast-repeated 'cherr-cherr-tschok' or sharper, metallic 'clik, clik', 'tack-tack' or 'chok-chok'; song highly melodious and varied, mimetic, beginning with several 'tschok' notes.

References Cramp (1992), Laird (1992), Pearson & Backhurst (1988), Shirihai *et al.* (in press), Svensson (1992), van den Berg & Symens (1992).

Hippolais *Warblers*

Where and When Largely W Palearctic. Olive-tree Warbler *H. olivetorum* is confined to open oak woodland or olive/almond groves with much scrub, from southern Balkans to SW Turkey and south to N Israel (late April to late August), wintering E and S Africa; and Upcher's Warbler *H. languida* breeds in mountain scrub and rocky areas with very sparse thorn trees on slopes or in wadis, from Transcaucasia and lower Turkey south to C Israel (migration much as Olive-tree; on passage in desert areas, both favour acacias). Olivaceous Warbler *H. pallida* is a summer visitor to habitats with tamarisks or damp woodland, often near water but also in arid areas or parks and olive groves, breeding Spain, N Africa, Balkans, Turkey, Levant and Arabia east to W China, on passage mainly August-September and April-May; rare vagrant elsewhere in Europe. Booted Warbler *H. caligata* is a summer visitor to shrubby and tall herbaceous thickets in European Russia eastwards and south to Caspian area (winters chiefly India); rare vagrant, mostly autumn, to most of Europe and Near East (has

summered N and E Europe). Icterine *H. icterina* and Melodious Warblers *H. polyglotta* are summer visitors (mainly March-October): former to mature dense broadleaf areas and tall shrubs, also forest edge, in warmer boreal to temperate zone of much of Europe east to C Russia and N Iran, on passage April-May and August-October; latter to similar habitats but with lower, denser shrubs in warm-temperate parts of C and W Europe and NW Africa, passage March-April and August-September.

Identification Genus is typified by relatively short undertail-coverts (beware some *Acrocephalus* with short-looking undertail-coverts), usually square-ended tail, flattish forehead and relatively long, strong, broad-based bill (except Booted and some Olivaceous); frequently show rather straight profile from mantle to tail, and rather front-heavy, often seeming 'clumsy and careless' in movements through cover. Adult Icterine and Melodious generally greenish and yellow, others greyish or grey-brown; bland facial expression, often variable pale wing panel and outer rectrices.

Spring Olive-tree Warbler. Large, long-winged, with white in wing and tail prominent. Dark tail frequently waved from side to side. ▶

Worn Olive-tree Warbler. May lack white wing panel. Large orange bill, legs grey. Head slightly darker than upperparts. Wings often slightly darker than rest of upperparts. ▼

Spring Upcher's Warbler. Slightly smaller and paler brown than Olive-tree Warbler, with weaker bill and high crown. Supercilium often runs behind eye. Note tertial spacing, dark tail, legs pinky-grey. ▶

Worn Upcher's Warbler. Wings and tail slightly darker than upperparts. ▶

Note structure of wing. Tail movement often reminiscent of Olive-tree Warbler. ▲

Fresh autumn Olivaceous Warbler of eastern race 'elaeica'. Greyish-brown. Tertials equally spaced. ▶

Worn Olivaceous Warbler. Flattish crown, short supercilium. No wing contrast. ▶

Fresh autumn Olivaceous Warbler of western race 'opaca'. Cold olive, slight wing panel. Tail of Olivaceous Warbler less 'full' than Upcher's Warbler's. Olivaceous Warblers pump tail downwards rhythmically with 'tak' calls. ▶

Worn Olivaceous Warbler of western race 'opaca'. Bill base very broad (from above) in this race. ▶

195

Within genus, main problems (depending on region) involve separating Olive-tree from Upcher's, Upcher's from Olivaceous, Booted from some Olivaceous, and Icterine from Melodious (grey individuals of last two, mainly 1st-winters, can also be confused with Olivaceous). All have complete moult in winter quarters: in autumn, fresh birds are juvenile/1st-winter and heavily worn birds are adults; spring birds are fresh or very slightly worn. Individual variation, abrasion and bleaching, and existence of intermediates are further complications.

Olive-tree Warbler

The largest (about 15 cm); characterised by long, broad, powerful bill, long(est) and pointed wing and primary projection, and blackish long tail with most prominent white edges (frequent tail-waving). Predominantly grey above, contrasting markedly with tail and extensive whitish wing panel (beware heavily worn summer/autumn adult with reduced/no panel). *Fresh plumage* Differs from Upcher's in heavier bill with orangey-yellow lower mandible (pinkish-grey on latter), larger size with much fuller tail, latter with blacker ground colour (more dark brown on Upcher's) and purer and larger white areas on tip and sides which are noticeable in flight/tail-waving (on Upcher's, white quite prominent but less pure, narrower and less contrasting); darker grey above, often with impression of lead-grey or light bluish suffusion (Upcher's duller/paler grey-brown); longer primary projection more or less equal to exposed tertials, with 7-8 widely spaced tips (on Upcher's, projection about three-quarters tertial length, with 6 slightly closer-spaced tips), and more prominent whitish edging to remiges and tertials forming extensive secondary panel (on Upcher's fringes narrower, greyer, forming indistinct panel, and tertial edging more diffuse). Moderately angled forehead (when excited appears rather steep and shorter than Upcher's) and crown (peak generally slightly behind eye) never look really flattish. *Worn adult* Close to Upcher's in having indistinct

wing panel and browner tail with less obvious white on outer feathers, but size, shape and actions, upperpart colour and size/shape and colour of bill should separate the two. Other differences include: bluish-grey tarsi (grey-brown or dark pinkish-grey on Upcher's); fairly indistinct supercilium, largely in front of eye or even absent (on Upcher's rather indistinct but usually visible, from bill base and extending slightly behind eye); greater contrast between upperparts and underparts, head always darker (indistinct demarcation between these areas on Upcher's, on which tail and wings typically darker than rest of upperparts); call much louder, a deep 'chuk' recalling Great Reed Warbler (Upcher's quite loud but much less deep, approaching Olivaceous). Tail action more waving (like shrikes) and performed throughout year, whereas Upcher's cocks and fans tail up and down or from side to side (tail movement mostly restricted to breeding grounds). In Levant, migrant 1st-winter/summer Barred Warbler occasionally misidentified as Olive-tree: note former's shorter and grey-based bill, variable amount of barring/pale edges on scapulars, flanks and undertail-coverts, whitish wingbars, well-fringed tertials and wing-coverts, and different behaviour.

Upcher's Warbler

Smaller (about 14 cm) than Olive-tree, less stocky and 'pear-shaped', but slightly larger (and remarkably heavier) than Olivaceous: second-largest of genus. Rather close to Olivaceous in general proportions and coloration, identification requiring caution. Tendency towards rounded head, and shows (mainly when excited) steeper, long forehead to crown, peaking just/well behind eye (together with thickset neck, tends to give heavy-headed appearance recalling large *Sylvia*); bill rather long and comparatively thicker than on Olivaceous, but owing to typically rounded large head does not look obviously long; tail long, thick and full. Flight feathers, wing-coverts and tail dark brown, contrast markedly with rest of upperparts, which much paler and greyish or very pale greyish-brown; shows faint suggestion of wing panel, shortish supercilium, and tail usually with conspicuous white tips and outer webs of outer feathers (unless very worn); legs and wings (and primary projection) long. Considerable individual variation, however: proportions and size, and darkness/contrast of tail and wing, depend partly on angle of light and view and partly on background/habitat, as well as on degree of wear and abrasion (producing intermediates between Upcher's and Olivaceous), so much practice and experience essential (and some individuals still not safely separable). Upcher's (mainly adults on breeding grounds) repeatedly wave tail vertically and horizontally (both fanned and, less often, closed) in circular movement quite like that of Olive-tree (as latter, also moves rather slowly through foliage); Olivaceous flicks tail downwards, which Upcher's also does but mainly on passage. Nesting Upcher's habitually perches on rocks, unlike other *Hippolais*. Combination of many/most of following features of Upcher's essential for field separation from Olivaceous: 1 SIZE, PROPORTIONS AND BEHAVIOUR Large (size of Whitethroat *S. communis* or larger), with longer, broad tail, thick bill, rounded heavy head joined to plump body by thick short neck, with much less pot-bellied appearance; moves rather slowly and quite often perches prominently. Relatively smaller Olivaceous (recalls small *Acrocephalus*), often with relatively angular head shape and rather flattish forehead to crown and narrower but broad-based bill, longer and slimmer neck, rather elongated body, but comparatively shorter (and less full) tail than Upcher's, more horizontal posture with low belly and more nervous, clumsy and faster movements. (Much overlap, however; differences in proportions most obvious when birds in action or flying between bushes.) In addition, Upcher's has slightly longer primary projection (three-quarters tertial length; half to two-thirds on Olivaceous) and usually shows outer tertial tips closer together than inner two (spacing equal on most Olivac-

eous), but this extremely difficult to see and variation in both species plus differences in age/wear of feathers render it of limited use. Tail-action differences also important (see above). 2 TAIL AND WING COLOUR Darker tail and wings (including broad dark centres of coverts and tertials) usually more striking (against Olivaceous), particularly on adults from late spring to autumn (when lack of paler fringes creates conspicuous, contrasting dark tail and wings), but some Olivaceous may appear slightly darker and contrasting and a few Upcher's look paler and less contrasting (especially in strong desert light); note that these feathers appear darkest when viewed from behind or slightly from side, and paler in profile view. Most Upcher's in spring and fresh young in autumn show fairly marked and quite sharply defined whitish fringes to wing-coverts and tertials, as well as to remiges, and variable whitish secondary panel (most Olivaceous also show clear pale fringes and may have hint of similar panel, but these often buffish and diffuse). Both species show whitish tips and margins to tail, but on Upcher's these on average broader, more distinct (contrast with darker tail) and usually obvious in flight (but this feature inconstant, and relatively useless for heavily worn birds). 3 OTHER DIFFERENCES Most Upcher's have paler crown and ear-coverts (almost as pale as whitish throat) and are largely whitish below and distinctly grey above, whereas most Olivaceous have slightly darker/warmer ear-coverts (and sometimes crown) often well demarcated from whitish throat and often have very faint yellowish-brown suffusion to breast sides and flanks, and may show more obvious brownish/olive/sandy tinge above (though many just as Upcher's). Supercilium in front of eye can be either thin or rather broad or indistinct on both, but on Upcher's tends to be slightly deeper and whiter and equally strong to rear edge of (or to distance of less than eye diameter behind) eye, while on Olivaceous it usually does not extend behind eye or on a few extends further than eye diameter behind eye (but then only faint/indistinct). Upcher's lower mandible tends to have some pinkish (chiefly fleshy-yellow on Olivaceous), with gape always reaching fore edge of eye-ring (ends slightly before on most Olivaceous), and has 3 or 4 rictal bristles (3 on Olivaceous). Leg colour varies: on Upcher's mainly brownish (mainly fleshy-grey on Olivaceous). Upcher's 1st (shortest) primary reaches about tips of primary coverts or shorter (much longer on Olivaceous). **4** VOICE Upcher's 'chuk' is obviously louder and deeper than Olivaceous's 'tchak' or 'tek'; other rattling 'churr' calls louder from Upcher's. Song very variable, slower in tempo, with rich and open vowel sounds, 'unsteady', melodious, with warbling quality: very different from Olivaceous, which gives repeated (with little variation) song like Reed Warbler's but more monotonous, harsher, more chattering.

Olivaceous Warbler

More variable than other *Hippolais*. Much variation geographical and highly marked, with three races: *opaca* (NW Africa, Iberia), nominate *pallida* (NE Africa, possibly with other N and C African populations) and *elaeica* (SE Europe, Middle East; includes synonymised form '*tamariceti*' in east). Field characters (and variations) as follows. **1** STRUCTURE AND JIZZ Medium-sized (about 13 cm), with long, flattish but broad-based bill, longish tail, shortish primary projection (varies from half to two-thirds tertial length); some, however, appear larger, relatively long-billed and long-tailed, with much broader bill base (race *opaca*), others rather smaller and daintier with slightly shorter tail and bill, and less broad bill base recalling *Acrocephalus* (race *elaeica*), and others even smaller with much smaller bill and tail and very narrow bill base (easternmost *elaeica* and other small African races). Normally gives impression of long, low profile (flattish crown), pot-belly, but quite delicate with elongated body. **2** CALL AND BEHAVIOUR Has 'tak' calls like Lesser Whitethroat's *S. curruca*, and with each call pumps tail downwards; many other *Hippolais* have similar call and may occasion-

ally flick tail downwards, but action never so conspicuous (and not combined with call). Quite nervous and clumsy in movement. **3** GENERAL COLORATION Noticeably pale. Upperparts vary from fawn, through various shades of grey tinged with slightly colder olive (*opaca*) or greyish-brown (*elaeica*), to pallid plain grey or sandy (some N African birds, a few Middle East populations), or largely greyish-brown (some easternmost *elaeica*). Underparts off-white, often with greyish or buffish wash on flanks and breast. Wing usually appears slightly darker, with pale fringes forming variable (generally indistinct) secondary panel. Usually shows clear off-white outer-web fringe, tip and distal inner web of outer tail feathers, narrow but often quite sharply defined; this feature quite variable in contrast and depth (and beware that against light outer tail of all *Hippolais* looks pale). All races wear to paler greyish-brown or greyish-olive (and are much more similar in colour) on breeding grounds. **4** SUPERCILIUM AND FACE Has typical bland facial expression of genus, with rather indistinct pale supercilium to (or just behind) eye, though sometimes more distinct and occasionally extends (but largely faint) well behind eye, or often concolorous with lores; in field, supercilium usually appears restricted to fore area. Most have pale area below eye (actually surrounding eye), which may also contribute to bland expression.

Booted Warbler

Smallest of genus (about 12 cm, little bigger than Willow Warbler *P. trochilus*), but does not appear delicate. Characteristic in comparatively heavy head with rather high crown and short, slender bill, and relatively shortish tail, but pot-belly and short wings (primary projection about half tertial length) make it look rather long-tailed. Also strikingly pale brown above ('pale milky tea': valid for most fresh autumn young or most spring birds, but summer and autumn adult wears to very pale grey-whitish-sandy) and markedly pale off-white below. Unlike other *Hippolais*, has rather strong facial pattern, with prominent (though frequently diffuse) supercilium always extending well behind eye (as far as in front) and square-cut at rear, and often with darker upper border, also often offset by thin dark eye-stripe, which, combined with shortness of bill, can create *Phylloscopus*-like appearance. Wing feathers (including coverts and particularly tertials) typically darkercentred with broad pale fringes, sometimes creating faint wing panel. Tail fairly square, outer feathers with variable whitish outer web, tip and distal part of inner web, though this hard to see (or strongly reduced, even on fresh birds). At close range, often shows quite distinct pale eye-ring and, on some, more

buffish suffusion on rump and uppertailcoverts. Very active, typically moves through undergrowth with slight upward-flicking of tail and wings (but, unlike Olivaceous, no persistent tail-dipping); may also flycatch and rarely even hover (again recalling *Phylloscopus*). At distance, appears plain-headed. Much of Booted's variation is geographical, but some also within same population: e.g. some have dark eye-stripe and lateral crownstripe reduced/lacking and/or supercilium weaker, shorter or only just visible behind eye and closely approach bare-faced expression of other *Hippolais*, also often have stronger and slightly longer bill, paler greyish-brown

1st-winter Booted Warbler of race 'caligata'. Distinct supercilium flares behind eye, bordered darker above. Short slender bill. Short primary projection.

Worn Booted Warbler of race 'rama'. Compared to 'caligata' greyer above, paler below, thicker billed and longer tailed.

Primary projection approaches that of some Olivaceous Warblers.

Booted Warblers often phylloscopus-like; bill and legs sturdier, tail edged pale.

Small 1st-winter Olivaceous Warbler resembling Booted Warbler. Note longer primary projection, less distinct supercilium. All pale lower mandible. Pumps tail rhythmically with 'tak' calls.

Large 1st-winter Olivaceous Warbler. May show pale wing panel like Icterine Warbler; typically has more white in tail. Pumps tail rhythmically with 'tak' calls.

1st-winter Melodious Warbler. Yellow wash at least to face. Shorter primary projection than Icterine Warbler, wing panel poor or lacking, domed head.

1st-winter Icterine Warbler. Pale wing panel, long primary projection (equals tertial length). Legs steely-grey.

upperparts and paler cream underparts (these are normally race *rama*, particularly in spring), all quite different from normal nominate *caligata* described above; many are intermediate in characters.

Confusion species Can be confused with Paddyfield Warbler *A. agricola*, chiefly in spring or when individuals worn: see p. 190. Also with *Phylloscopus* warblers, notably Chiffchaff *P. collybita* and Bonelli's *P. bonelli*: size and bulk, combined with longer/heavier bill and lack of black legs, should separate it from former, and lack of green or yellow from latter; Willow Warbler *P. trochilus* of race *yakutensis* approaches Booted in coloration, but shows long primary projection, much longer and sharper supercilium, *Phylloscopus*-type bill, yellowish (not greyish-brown) legs and notched tail; Dusky Warbler *P. fuscatus* can be greyish, but always has rufous-buff suffusion to ear-coverts, flanks and undertail-coverts. Booted's call differs from that of any *Phylloscopus*. Within *Hippolais* genus, confusable only with Olivaceous (mainly *elaeica* or small N and C African races), but is smaller, more delicate, with rather shorter/finer bill, and general shape and behaviour somewhat approaching *Phylloscopus*; bill pale orangey-flesh or horn with dark culmen and tip (Olivaceous has all-pale lower mandible, but rarely indistinct blackish tip); also has more complex facial pattern, with at least prominent supercilium behind eye (where faint/absent on Olivaceous), often hint of eye-stripe and quite obvious lateral crown-stripe, but very rarely Olivaceous may have slightly stronger supercilium behind eye and slightly darker border above supercilium (conversely, some Booted have weaker facial pattern). Booted's upperparts normally browner, and breast to flanks smudged with cream-buff (unlike most Olivaceous), also more prominent dark centres/pale fringes to wing-coverts and tertials, more flesh-brown or greyish-horn legs and more contrasting darker feet, slightly shorter primary projection and more square-cut tail. More active when feeding, without tail-wagging of Olivaceous (though can give slight upward flicks or rarely slight

downward flick, but never pronounced or repeated). Some larger Booted with slightly bigger bill or weak facial pattern and paler/greyer above, and some smaller Olivaceous with smaller bill or faint supercilium and brownish tinge above, can be impossible to separate in field (some even in hand), but calls differ: Booted has single or repeated hard and rather harsh 'tick' or 'chet' (never Olivaceous's repeated 'tak' with downward tail flicks).

Melodious and Icterine Warblers

Although both typical *Hippolais* (but olive-brown, green-grey and yellow to just whitish and buff), often confused with some other warblers. Garden Warbler *S. borin* has short, comparatively deep, greyish bill (never long and broad-based or with orangey lower mandible), is plain greyish-brown/olive-brown above, dingy below, and has rather plain face with large eye. Willow Warbler smaller, restless, flitting, has typical *Phylloscopus* appearance, very thin bill, stronger facial pattern (always very long supercilium) and different call. In autumn, both, though mainly Melodious, sometimes confused with Marsh or Reed Warbler: see Identification, above, also 'Small Unstreaked *Acrocephalus* Warblers' (p. 186), and compare plates. Icterine and Melodious in spring (fresh) differ from all other *Hippolais* in being rather pale olive greenish-grey (Icterine) or greenish olive-brown (Melodious) above and rather uniform (variable) yellow below; summer/autumn adults wear to pale greyish-green/olive above (though Melodious generally more brownish-tinged), whitish-yellow below, with worn browner remiges, when 1st-winters distinctly paler grey-green (some very pale greyish-buff) above and off-white with variable yellowish wash below (some lack yellow, resemble Olivaceous: see below). Following features separate Melodious from Icterine (any plumage). **1 WINGS** Melodious has short primary projection, roughly half length of exposed tertials, and wing panel usually absent/less solid (Icterine has long primary projection roughly equal to tertials and always has conspicuous wing panel). Note that wing fringes whitish (Icterine) or whitish-buff (Melodious) on autumn immatures, but mainly yellowish on fresh spring birds, while on worn autumn adults of both species panel can appear whitish, or as series of white lines, or (as on many Melodious) be non-existent. Both can, rarely, show primary projection of about two-thirds tertial length, so primary spacing important (on Melodious tends to be even, on Icterine wider-spaced towards wingpoint) or, perhaps better, wing/tail ratio (on Melodious, projection half as long as wingtip to tail tip and never covers tail-coverts; on Icterine, about same as wingtip to tail tip and covers coverts). 2 SUBSIDIARY FEATURES Melodious slightly more rounded-looking (less elongated and slim), with head more rounded, with steeper forehead and peak around/just before eye (rather domed crown); Icterine has flatter forehead, with crown peak well behind eye. Both have short, ill-defined supercilium mostly before eye, but this often extends slightly more behind eye (though more diffuse) on Icterine. Melodious usually has brownish-grey legs (bluish-/lead-grey on Icterine), but hard to see and both species can have greyish legs. Both lack clean white on outer tail, but edges tend to light brown on Melodious (slightly whiter on Icterine), more obvious in flight. Most Melodious show stronger yellow on throat/upper breast (Icterine often more uniform and duller yellow below), this more useful with 1st-winters. 3 BEHAVIOUR Melodious tends to skulk/remain long in same clump, and feeds more slowly and methodically (Icterine often perches in full view, is more lively and impetuous, often shoots off with dashing or flycatcher-like flight). 4 VOICE Song of Melodious a persistent, rapid *Sylvia*-like chatter with less mimicry, starts hesitantly then goes into softer, smoother but faster and more sustained musical rambling lacking Icterine's 'rough bits'; latter has a more varied and pleasing, high-pitched *Acrocephalus*-like refrain, perhaps recalling Marsh or Blyth's Reed, but with discordant whistling, and unstructured, rather hoarse and strained, but with long-drawn notes and includes much mimicry (and usually sings from higher perch). Call of Melodious variable, mainly a short sparrow-like chatter, less often a sharp 'tic'; Icterine (rarely calls in autumn) has a short, hard 'teck' or 'tec-tec-tec', in alarm tongue-clicks, and has (mainly in spring) musical 'tey-te-dwee'.

Problems with Olivaceous Occasional 1st-winter Olivaceous suffused more buff and olive resemble 'colourless' Icterine/Melodious (1st-winter or heavily worn adults), but have primary projection between the two. Latter two occasionally flick tail down, but never so conspicuously as Olivaceous and not combined with call. Olivaceous always has outer tail feathers edged off-white, this normally indistinct/lacking on other two (but reduced/absent on heavily worn individuals of all three). Olivaceous normally has long, low forehead/crown (flattish head), unlike more rounded crown of Icterine/Melodious, which also have more prominent orangey lower mandible and very pale ear-coverts (in extremes almost concolorous with throat or crown, quite unlike warmer, well-defined ear-coverts of Olivaceous). Icterine has much more obvious wing panel (little use with heavily worn birds). Folded wing of Melodious usually shows 5 primary tips; most Olivaceous show 6, but quite often 7 (as most Icterine).

References Alström *et al.* (1991a), Cramp (1992), Fry (1990), Glutz von Blotzheim & Bauer (1991), Harrap (1988), Hollom *et al.* (1988), Jonsson (1992), Shirihai (1987b), Shirihai *et al.* (in press), Svensson (1992), Ullman (1989), Wallace (1964), Williamson (1967a).

Dartford and Marmora's Warblers

Where and When Two typical *Sylvia* warblers of fairly open (mainly Marmora's *S. sarda*) to thick (mainly Dartford *S. undata*) scrub with dense thorny, shrubby areas. Sympatric and with less distinct habitat differences in some parts, but Dartford more widespread, from S England south to Morocco/Tunisia, including Balearics (Minorca only), and east to Italy and Sicily, with Marmora's in Corsica, Sardinia, Pantelleria islands and Balearics (except Minorca). Residents or partial migrants; Marmora's vagrant as far north as Britain, Dartford north to Sweden and east to Greece and the former Czechoslovakia.

General Features The two are very close in structure: smaller *Sylvia* warblers with small body, short wings but very long tail. Sexual dimorphism slight; minor plumage differences between 1st-winter and adult, though juvenile differs markedly. Adults and most 1st-winters of the two are easily distinguished: Dartford is reddish-brown or pinkish-brown below, where Marmora's predominantly lead-grey and suffused with dull brownish-white/buff. Confusion arises with juveniles, which are extremely similar; some 1st-winter female Dartford lack real pinkish-

brown below (or it is very subdued) and some 1st-winter female Marmora's (and all females of race *balearica*) have pinkish-grey and buff shading below, thus having almost identical underparts.

Juveniles Juvenile Marmora's has slate-brown upperparts almost concolorous with or showing little contrast with dark tail (most juvenile Dartford more grey-brown, though still often quite warmer, with prominent tail contrast), and is dark slaty-brown below (thus lacking slightly paler colour with buff or sandy-pink tinge of most Dartford). This, however, subject to individual variation (some appear intermediate) and also to lighting, so time and different viewing angles may be required before true coloration determined. Note also that juvenile Marmora's of race *balearica* tends to be slightly paler or sandier below, and may not be separable on this feature. Both species have pale throat, but this contrasts less with breast on Dartford.

Juvenile Dartford Warbler. Usually pale buff beneath, browner above. Lores paler than ear-coverts.

Juvenile Marmora's Warbler. Usually greyer above, grey-brown beneath. Lores usually concolorous with ear-coverts.

Calls remain the best way to separate these two species in non-adult plumages.

Minute differences in the alula pattern may be useful.

Dartford Warbler.

Marmora's Warbler.

1st-winter Dartford Warbler. Pale individual. Most show pinky underparts, pale belly. Dull birds show pale lores. No contrast within the upperparts.

1st-winter ♀ Marmora's Warbler. Note whitish chin, grey nape, browner back. Darker flanks and vent contrast with pale belly.

Further, juvenile Marmora's has lores almost same colour as ear-coverts and crown, its orbital ring tends to be dark reddish-brown and eye-ring feathers generally grey or buff-brown (Dartford shows whitish lores, with fair contrast with rest of head, clearer orange/red orbital ring and usually pinkish-sandy eye-ring). Much overlap between the two, however, and best separated in field by calls (see below).

1st-winter Females For individuals lacking (or almost so) diagnostic underpart coloration, main distinctions as follows. Marmora's shows sharper contrast between grey crown and brown-washed mantle, has more whitish throat contrasting with grey sides of breast, and flanks and vent are darker and contrast with lower belly; Dartford shows less crown/mantle contrast (in *toni* and nominate *undata* uniform grey-bluish, in *dartfordiensis* darker

slaty-brown), and is generally more uniform below with usually at least suggestion of pinkish-buff suffusion (rarely, absent), but never gives Marmora's white-throated impression. Marmora's tends to have darker loral and often also ear-covert area (Dartford paler), outer web of largest alula feather is broadly and evenly fringed and tipped pale (narrow fringe on Dartford, becoming broader towards tip), and its orbital ring is more dark pink or brown (on Dartford, strong red-orange, thicker and better developed), but this difficult to check. Again, best separated by call.

Call Marmora's commonest contact and alarm is sharp, clear, short rattle, 'trrut' or 'drrut', very unlike Dartford's harsher, longer and softer 'chaihrr-er' or 'tschirr'.
References Gargallo (1991), Shirihai *et al.* (in prep.).

Spectacled Warbler and Closely Similar Species

Where and When Spectacled Warbler *S. conspicillata* is a local resident and partial migrant in Mediterranean region, on rather dry open hillsides and lowland plains with low scrub but no trees, occasionally in dry saltflats of coasts or desert edges and even in denser mountain vegetation at up to 2200 m; relatively common S France, Spain, NW Africa and Israel, vagrant W and C Europe. Subalpine Warbler *S. cantillans* is a summer visitor to thorn scrub and open woodland undergrowth of Mediterranean; on passage or as vagrant in much of Europe and Near East. Whitethroat *S. communis* is a common summer visitor to much of Palearctic, in low shrubbery, scrub, open woodland or farmland edge. Tristram's Warbler *S. deserticola* is local breeder in valleys and open scrub in hilly country, mostly above 1000 m, in NW Africa.

Identification That confusion has occurred with these species may surprise some people, as each has plenty of distinctive features. Yet, difficulties have been experienced in field separation of Spectacled from female Subalpine and from Whitethroat; Spectacled also

closely approaches Tristram's in plumage pattern. The following outlines main features allowing Spectacled to be distinguished from the other three in the field, dealing only with those plumages which cause problems.

Separating Spectacled and Subalpine Warblers

Problem restricted to separating 1st-winter/summer female Spectacled from anomalously rufous Subalpine in equivalent plumage. Following features of Spectacled are the most significant. **1 STRUCTURE AND BEHAVIOUR** Usually slightly smaller, with short, rounded wing (primary projection about one third tertial length, only 4-5 primary tips visible) and comparatively long-tailed in relation to wing and body size, giving impression always of a small and delicate bird with rounded head shape and steep forehead. Subalpine has more solid build (though still rather delicate), with relatively short tail and longer, more pointed wings (primary projection between half and two-thirds tertial length, 5-6 primary tips easily visible), and flatter/less rounded head, but bill sometimes looks marginally shorter and broader-based than Spectacled's. Spectacled prefers low, sparse bushes and frequently hops on ground, as well as raising tail and vigorously wagging it from side to side; Subalpine prefers taller, denser vegetation and also trees (where Spectacled seldom seen), and performs less tail-wagging. 2 WING PATTERN Prominent and extensive rusty fringes to much of wing feathers, broadest on secondaries and tertials, on folded wing forming solid rusty panel extending widely over wing-coverts as well; pattern of middle tertials important, showing sharply demarcated blackish central area, wide at visible base and tapering cleanly to sharp point along feather shaft, showing from rear as clean 'arrowhead'. Subalpine often shows marked pale rusty-brown or sandy edges to most of wing feathers, but fringes clearly 'isolated' and paler, and seldom more than a faint and smaller wing panel, while dark tertial centres are not clear-cut but diffuse, and more rounded at end. 3 TAIL PATTERN Rectrices contrastingly patterned, with black base and centre and a large area of white on both webs of outer feathers, next-to-outermost pair having clear white tips and edges to outer webs: from below, produces fairly white tail when perched and a contrasting pattern in flight; from above, closed tail very dark and contrasts with rest of upperparts. Subalpine's tail is largely brown and concolorous with upperparts, and when spread lacks strong contrast, having relatively small and diffuse sandy tips and edges to outer and second-outer feathers, from below giving indistinct (and rather pale grey-brown) pattern; beware moulted new (adult-like) tail feathers producing slightly more contrasting pattern, though above differences still obvious. 4 SUBSIDIARY FEATURES Eye-ring appears thicker and broader above eye than below, standing out in field, whereas Subalpine's looks uniform in width throughout. Other differences are Spectacled's less conspicuous head pattern (often giving bland facial expression), fairly uniform pale whitish-sandy/buff underparts, fleshy-yellow-

brown tarsus and brown or black hue to orbital ring, against Subalpine's marginally stronger facial pattern (sometimes with variable faint greyish supercilium, often tending to surround ear-coverts, this chiefly on 1st-winter male), clearer contrast between whitish throat and belly centre and buffy breast sides, flanks and vent, occasionally clearer white submoustachial stripe contrasting with dingier throat centre, much darker fleshy-brown legs and at least some reddish in orbital ring. 5 CALL Spectacled has drawn-out, straight 'trrrrrr, trrrrrr'. Subalpine gives hard 'tak tak' or 'trec trec' (but in Corsica a rather hard rattled 'trrrrrt' similar to Spectacled's, though latter is softer and more prolonged (rattlesnake-like)).

Separating Spectacled Warbler and Whitethroat

Despite conspicuous size difference, these two are quite often confused; most frequently Whitethroat is misidentified as Spectacled through misjudgement of size (also influenced by its slight size variation), while both also have similar plumage pattern. Identification problems are not restricted to specific ages or plumages (though involve mainly 1st-winters), and following features are broadly usable for all birds. 1 STRUCTURE AND BEHAVIOUR Whitethroat is larger and more robust, with longer, thicker and heavier bill, and has longer primary projection, just over half length of tertials (6-7 tips visible), whereas on Spectacled it is about one-third (only 4-5 tips visible). Whitethroat moves tail very little, unlike the more excitable Spectacled. 2 WING PATTERN Compared with Spectacled's more complete and solid rusty wing panel, Whitethroat's rusty edges to coverts are less broad and some dark feather centres are usually visible, breaking up wing panel and reducing its impact (rusty tertial edges also thinner and cover smaller area, and dark centres more rounded in shape and not sharply demarcated as on Spectacled). 3 TAIL PATTERN Whitethroat's tail pattern resembles Subalpine's (but even

1st-autumn ♀ Subalpine Warbler. Warm brown individuals may cause confusion. Note primary projection, diffuse brown centre of middle tertial, thick bill, buff flanks, white belly.

1st-autumn Whitethroat. Large, longer primary projection than Spectacled Warbler, tertial centres rounded, less black. Upperparts warm brown, heavy bill.

Calls are very useful in identification, see text.

Spring ♂ Spectacled Warbler. Small. Dark head, darker lores (and often forehead). Centre of throat grey. Note exact pattern of middle tertial. Short primary projection accentuates long dark tail.

1st-autumn ♀ Spectacled Warbler. Short primary projection, thin bill, clean 'arrowhead' mark on middle tertial, uniform buff underparts, throat white.

Adult ♂ Whitethroat. Lacks dark forehead and lores. Throat all white.

Adult ♂ Tristram's Warbler. Similar to Dartford Warbler in structure, plumage and actions. Note rusty-edged wing, pale diffuse submoustachial stripe.

1st-autumn Tristram's Warbler. May recall 1st-winter ♀ Spectacled Warbler. Structure and action close to Dartford Warbler (including long slim tail often cocked). Note warm colour to most of underparts, rufous wing panel smaller, less solid, less rufous on primary and median coverts. Smallest and middle tertials with diffuse centres to inner webs.

205

more poorly defined: edges of outer feathers, of a faded sandy colour, merge into centres and cover relatively small area, just outer web); from below gives same impression of indistinctly grey-brown tail, and from above tail almost concolorous with upperparts, as opposed to Spectacled's well-patterned tail which also contrasts with much paler upperparts (see above). **4 SUBSIDIARY FEATURES** Almost all 1st-winter and adult (but chiefly 1st-summer and older) male Spectacled show an area of blackish on lores and forehead which also emphasises white eye-ring, whereas Whitethroat always appears to have uniform head pattern, but beware that female and some 1st-winter male Spectacled have rather plain head approaching corresponding plumages of Whitethroat. Some male Spectacled, chiefly in spring and mainly 2nd-winter or older, also have a dark grey throat and breast and often a clear submoustachial stripe bordering grey throat. Spectacled's legs usually appear more pinkish-yellow with slight reddish tone (Whitethroat's are slightly darker, more yellowish-brown) and its bill usually shows small area of black at tip and on culmen (Whitethroat has entire upper mandible dark, and larger dark area at tip). **5 CALL** Whitethroat's usual call is a long drawn-out 'chairr', or 'chuck' or 'che', very different from Spectacled's calls (see above).

Separating Spectacled and Tristram's Warblers

Adult Tristram's generally unmistakable, as it shares characters of Dartford Warbler (size, shape, warm vinous-pink underparts), of Subalpine (bluish-grey upperparts, variable submoustachial stripe) and of Spectacled (rusty wings, similar tail pattern); while some are not so long-tailed, combination of tail length and rather big head gives most a characteristic Dartford-like impression. 1st-winter Tristram's, however, is very like Spectacled in plumage pattern and colour; more-

over, its affinities with the 'long-tailed *Sylvia* warblers' are not always obvious, and in shape and proportions it can appear just as Spectacled. Besides vocal differences (Tristram's has throaty 'tchak', weak sparrow-like 'chip' or sharper 'chit'), the following should separate the two in 1st-winter plumage. **1 TAIL LENGTH AND ACTION** Most (but not all) Tristram's show proportionately slightly longer tail, giving somewhat Dartford-like appearance (unlike Spectacled), and tail is more strongly and more frequently cocked. **2 UNDERPARTS** Tristram's is warm buff (even rufous-buff) below except on central belly, while Spectacled almost always whiter (with yellowish-buff restricted mainly to body sides and appearing to merge with rest of underparts). **3 WINGS** Spectacled's rusty wing panel appears wider and more solid, having broader rufous margins and including rufous-fringed median and sometimes primary coverts; Tristram's margins, mainly those on inner remiges, average narrower, with slightly broader dark centres, its medians are darker-centred with relatively narrow sandy/sandy-rufous (female) to grey-brown (male) fringes, and its primary coverts largely indistinctly fringed and more sandy than rufous. Unlike Spectacled, female Tristram's has lesser coverts at least partly greyish (mostly greyish on males), usually showing clear contrast with sandy-rufous fringes of medians and greaters. Marginal difference (but much overlap and usually undetectable in field) in tertial pattern, focusing on small and central tertials: on Spectacled, blackish centres on inner webs often more sharply defined, narrower and restricted to shaft area, whereas Tristram's tends to show ill-defined but broader blackish area on inner webs (on some, even reaching fringes). **4 BILL STRUCTURE** Tristram's bill often looks longer, thinner and slightly drooping.

References Shirihai *et al.* (1991), Svensson (1992), Williamson (1967c).

Some Poorly Known Sylvia *Plumages*

Where and When Subalpine *S. cantillans*, Ménétries's *S. mystacea*, Sardinian *S. melanocephala*, Cyprus *S. melanothorax* and Rüppell's Warblers *S. rueppelli* occur in unique combination in Levant and other parts of Middle East (only some occur together in other areas). Their identification requires great caution, and 'non-adult-male' plumages in particular (unfamiliar to most birders, who have little opportunity to study them) are regularly misidentified. Subalpine is a summer visitor to Mediterranean areas east to W Turkey and winters Africa; regular vagrant to much of Europe and Near East. Ménétries's is a local summer visitor and partial migrant from SE Turkey east to around Afghanistan, wintering Arabia and S Iran (and very rarely elsewhere in Levant and NE Africa). Sardinian is largely resident (partially migratory) throughout Mediterranean region, wintering south to N Africa; recorded widely as vagrant in much of Europe. Cyprus breeds (chiefly summer visitor) in Cyprus; winters mainly S and E Israel, Jordan and Sinai, less so Arabia and Egypt (mid October to late March). Rüppell's is a local summer visitor to Greece, Crete and W and SW Turkey, migrating mainly through Sinai and NE Egypt in autumn (September) and mainly through NE Egypt and Israel in spring (March-April).

Identification The five are normally readily distinguished in typical adult male plumage (acquired by some species in 1st winter, by some highly migratory species only from 1st summer) at all seasons. Some very old females often show trace of, or even close resemblance to, male's coloration and pattern, and are also fairly straightforward. Real problems occur mainly with 1st-winter and 1st-summer females, or with 1st-winter males of Subalpine, Ménétries's and Rüppell's (often closely similar to their immature females); surprisingly, however, separation of males quite often problematic, e.g. males of Sardinian and Ménétries's, or latter and some old females of Subalpine. The following treats only the main identification problems.

Ménétries's Warbler

Characteristic in having rounded head profile, moderate-sized wings, but long and fully blackish tail (constantly raised and vigorously wagged from side to side and up and down) which contrasts highly with distinctly pale bluish-grey (male) or sandy-grey (female) upperparts; bill relatively strong. Diagnostic harsh and low buzzing call. Main problems involve separating male from male Sardinian and from poorly marked male or very old female Subalpine, and to lesser extent from 'dark-hooded' female Rüppell's; also separating 1st-winter/summer females from same-age Sardinian and Subalpine.

Male In size, structure and coloration, most closely resembles male Sardinian of Levant race *momus*, differing in having broad and ill-defined greyish tertial fringes which merge diffusely with indistinct darker centres (Sardinian has blackish centres and narrower and sharply defined whitish fringes); note, however, that appearance of tertials varies slightly with angle of view and light, so Ménétries's tertials can appear rather dark in centre with narrower and even pale edges when bird in profile, and beware also that heavily worn tertials can sometimes produce narrow whitish fringes as well (so tertial pattern should be examined critically from behind and from horizontal position). Less conspicuous and less constant differences shown by Ménétries's include: slightly longer primary projection, varying between a third and half tertial length and tending to show 6 primary tips, with spacing increasing progressively outwards (on Sardinian, quarter to third tertial length, with usually 5 closely and equally spaced tips); middle and longest alula feathers always show broader whitish edges (narrower on Sardinian, and especially narrow and indistinct on longest feather); remex fringes often tinged sandy-grey (bluish- or whitish-grey on Sardinian); crown duller black, often suffused with greyish at rear and

1st-winter Subalpine Warbler. Brownish, greyer rump, buff breast and flanks. darker-centred tertials.

Adult ♀ Subalpine Warbler in spring. Old birds approach ♂ Ménétries's Warblers, note tail does not contrast with rest of upperparts, clear sandy fringes to tertials.

Adult ♀ Ménétries's Warbler. Pale and uniform above including wings; darker tail. Bill thick, pink-based. Regularly cocks tail.

Dark alula broadly edged pale.

Adult ♂ Ménétries's Warbler in spring. Thick bill pinkish-based, plain tertials, dark tail, often cocked. Hood merges into nape.

♀ Sardinian Warbler of Near East race 'momus'. Grey head, dark brown back, warm flanks. Pale tertial edges, less contrasting tail than Ménétries's Warbler. Bill base greyish.

Adult ♂ Sardinian Warbler of Near East race 'momus'.

1st-spring ♀ Rüppell's Warbler. Large droopy bill with grey base. Long primary projection, distinctly fringed tertials and (less distinctly) greater coverts. Tail dark and contrasts with paler upperparts.

1st-year ♀ Cyprus Warbler. Similar to ♀ Rüppell's Warbler, but bill smaller, pink-based, shorter primary projection, tail less contrasting.

Old ♀ Rüppell's Warbler. Head mottled black, throat too. Note grey flanks and rump, pale fringed wings, long primaries and blackish tail.

Note scaly undertail-coverts. Most develop some dark crescents beneath by spring.

on rear ear-coverts, and tending to grade into lead-grey upperparts which are often tinged sandy (Sardinian tends to show deeper black crown, normally sharply divided from cleaner and darker bluish-grey upperparts), but beware that intermediate individuals occur (with overlap in characters) which render this feature of less use. Otherwise, throat and upper breast normally show varying degree of pinkish, and are separated from dark ear-coverts by ill-defined whitish moustachial stripe (Sardinian never shows any distinct pink, but beware birds with dirty throat from fruit-eating or other discoloration), though many Ménétries's of westernmost population have only faint suggestion of pale pink or sandy wash and occasionally this lacking altogether, then appearing just as on Sardinian; moreover, most Ménétries's tend to have whitish-sandy or very pale buff suffusion to breast sides and flanks, less often pale greyish (on Sardinian, always darker grey-brown and sometimes creating contrast with white throat). Most Ménétries's have fleshy or pinkish lower mandible (always lead-grey on Sardinian). Male Ménétries's may also be confused with poorly coloured male or very bright (very old) female Subalpine, which can show similar amount and same tone of pinkish as male Ménétries's, but Subalpine have paler and greyer crown, obvious and sharply defined whitish- or greyish-sandy tertial fringes, longer primary projection (often exceeding tertial length and usually with 7 widely spaced primary tips), and browner/paler (blackish on Ménétries's) ground colour to tail feathers, which show much less contrast with upperparts and also, when spread, show poor contrast (from below, undertail appears indistinctly patterned with whitish/grey and brown). Ménétries's has contrasting, quite different tail pattern (similar to Sardinian's), with black base and centre and with large area of white on outer feathers. Both Ménétries's and Sardinian are typically active and continually fan and cock tail, former more nervously and with sideways swinging and vertical wagging; Subalpine only occasionally wags tail,

and much more shallowly. **Calls** Commonest call of Ménétries's is a harsh and soft buzzing and rather rattling 'tzerrr' or 'trzerr-r-r'; of Sardinian a harder, fast and mechanical 'tjrett-ett-ett-ett' or just a single 'tsche'; and of Subalpine a hard ticking 'tak tak'.

Female Separating 1st-year females of Ménétries's, Sardinian and Subalpine is extremely difficult and requires greatest care. Ménétries's is intermediate between Sardinian and Subalpine, showing characters of both: e.g. plumage coloration very similar to latter's, but tail as Sardinian, giving most Ménétries's an obvious appearance of blackish tail contrasting greatly with pale upperparts. Subalpine's longer primary projection, paler/ browner and indistinctly patterned tail, paler/sandy upperparts and buff body sides should rule out any typical Sardinian; it also appears slightly slimmer and daintier than the other two, with less 'fluffy-plumaged' impression and different behaviour. All three should also be separable by call (see above). Thus, main problem is separating Ménétries's. Following differences, applicable to all ages, are most important. 1 TERTIALS As a rule, Ménétries's tertials indistinctly darker-centred, normally merging into broad and diffuse slightly paler fringes and sometimes concolorous with latter; Subalpine and Sardinian have darker centres and sharply defined fringes of, respectively, pale sandy-buff and pale brown. Differences, however, often obscured by wear and distorted by viewing angle (see above). 2 ALULA See Male. 3 TAIL On Ménétries's, typically blackish and clearly contrasting with pale sandy-grey upperparts; Sardinian also shows blackish tail, but upperparts much darker/warmer brown or grey-brown, never giving same contrast, while Subalpine has pale sandy-grey upperparts (similar to Ménétries's) but tail paler and browner from above and almost concolorous with upperparts. Subalpine's tail pattern, particularly in this plumage, lacks strong contrast: outer feathers have relatively small sandy edges and tips which merge with centres, from below producing almost uniformly brown-grey appearance with no distinct pattern when closed, rather than sharp contrast of black and white of Ménétries's and Sardinian (see above). 4 PRIMARY PROJEC- TION Primary projection and spacing of tips (see above) often helpful in this plumage, but difficult to judge in field; Ménétries's intermediate between the other two. 5 SUBSIDI- ARY FEATURES Other useful features include colour of lower mandible, largely pinkish- flesh on Ménétries's, mainly fleshy on Subalpine and mostly blue-grey or lead-grey on Sardinian; underpart colour, suffused pale sandy-grey on flanks and breast sides on most Ménétries's and Subalpine, but usually much darker and warmer brown on Sardinian (where noticeable on ventral area). Sardinian's crown and ear-coverts often appear darker grey, which, with warmer breast, gives strong impression of white throat, unlike Ménétries's and Subalpine (which usually show indistinct demarcation between ear-coverts and throat, as well as more conspicuous pale loral region).

Rüppell's Warbler

1st-summer and older males unmistakable (diagnostic white submoustachial stripe dividing blackish throat-breast area); 2nd- summer and older females to varying degree approach male in plumage. 1st-winter (both sexes) and 1st-summer female plumages less straightforward. Latter often have prominent blackish-grey head grading into grey mantle, thus often misidentified as male Ménétries's, though Rüppell's relatively larger size and more robust appearance, longer primary projection (about two-thirds tertial length) and obvious tertial and greater-covert fringes should separate it (and should also separate 1st-winter Rüppell's from same-age Méné- tries's). Compared with any female Sardinian, Rüppell's is slightly larger, and has much longer primary projection, with 7 (instead of 5) tips well visible, and more marked whitish tertial and greater-covert fringes. Rüppell's 'problematic plumages' also lack Sardinian's warmer brownish upperparts and body sides, being instead greyish above and slightly pale greyish-buff on body sides, mainly on rear

flanks; unlike any female Sardinian, many tend to have at least trace of submoustachial stripe, and tail pattern approaches that of Subalpine. 1st-winter/summer Rüppell's often resemble corresponding ages of Subalpine in having same proportions (including primary projection), rather similar tail pattern and well-marked tertial and covert fringes; nevertheless, Rüppell's should be separable by its obviously larger size, whiter tertial fringes contrasting with blacker centres (Subalpine has more brownish centres and more sandy-buff or greyish-sandy fringes), and greyish lower mandible and greyish body sides (Subalpine has fleshy lower mandible and buffish-yellow body sides), as well as its often darker head, at least on ear-coverts (mainly in 1st spring), and Whitethroat-like jizz. Note that, in Levant, Rüppell's is frequently confused with Whitethroat, especially of paler race *icterops*, but any rufous (instead of whitish) in wing, pinkish (not grey) lower mandible, greyish-brown (not reddish) orbital ring and different tail pattern should easily separate latter at any age.

Cyprus Warbler

Apart from 1st-winter (and a few 1st-summer) females, identification straightforward: varying amount of black or dark brown/grey spots or blotches on chin and throat and/or breast, and even down to belly and body sides. 1st-year females, however, often lack these markings altogether and can be very hard to separate from all above-mentioned species, except by their species-diagnostic undertail-covert pattern of grey bases with whitish scaly-barred tips/edges. Bold and well-defined whitish tertial and greater-cov- ert fringes and warmer olive-buff body sides (chiefly rear flanks), as well as slightly darker greyish olive-brown (instead of greyish- sandy) upperparts, also usually help separate Cyprus from 1st-year female and 1st-winter male Ménétries's. Besides undertail-covert pattern, 1st-year female Cyprus should also be separated from any female Sardinian by having marked and more sharply defined whitish (instead of largely warmer greyish-brown) edges/tips to tertials and part of wing-coverts, therefore showing paler-patterned wing (darker and more uniform on Sardinian); also by lacking Sardinian's warmer, browner upperparts and body sides, being instead slightly paler and predominantly suffused greyish-olive. Also has pinkish or pinkish-flesh (not grey) lower mandible and usually greyish or whitish dots above lores, unlike Sardinian. Ground colour of tail mainly blackish, as Sardinian's, but tail pattern intermediate between that species and Subalpine or usually somewhat approaching latter. Owing to pale wing edgings, 1st-year female Cyprus is occasionally confused with Subalpine of '1st-year-female type', but latter should always be distinguished by lacking

Cyprus's undertail-covert pattern, by being paler sandy-grey/buff above, with browner tail, and by having pale buff body sides and tertial fringes. In structure and behaviour Cyprus is closer to Sardinian, and similarly performs quite obvious tail-raising and tail-wagging, unlike Subalpine. Cyprus could also be confused with 1st-year female and 1st-winter male Rüppell's, but latter's slightly larger size and robust appearance, more uniform greyish/whitish undertail-coverts, grey lower mandible, longer primary projection, and slightly greyer upperparts and whiter underparts are among many useful field distinctions between the two.

References Cramp (1992), Shirihai *et al.* (in prep.), Svensson (1992).

Large Sylvia *Warblers*

Where and When Three large *Sylvia* warblers occurring in W Palearctic can, in certain plumages and regions, cause identification problems. Barred *S. nisoria* breeds from Sweden south to Italy and east to China, migrating over much of region (in W Europe recorded chiefly in autumn) to winter Arabia and E Africa. Orphean *S. hortensis* breeds around Mediterranean and east to the Pamirs and Baluchistan, wintering tropical Africa, Arabia and India. Both inhabit woodland, open forest edge or orchards, always with undergrowth including bushes and shrubs. On passage/in winter they meet Arabian Warbler *S. leucomelaena*, a sedentary desert breeder of acacia and bush savanna, from SE Israel/Jordan south to Somalia/Ethiopia.

Regional Identification Problems Over much of W Palearctic, main regional problem is separating 1st-winter/summer (unbarred) Barred Warblers and 1st-winter/female Orphean (latter also confusable with Lesser Whitethroat *S. curruca*). Arabian Warbler is also confusable with migrant Orphean. The following focuses on the specific regional problems, rather than embracing all aspects of these species' identification.

Orphean Warbler

Separation from Barred Warbler The two are similar in size and structure, but differ greatly in most plumages. Problems arise only with unmarked (largely 1st-winter, less so 1st-summer female) Orphean and unbarred (largely 1st-winters and 1st-summer female) Barred Warbler. Orphean has darker, more grey-brown upperparts (paler sandy-grey on Barred) and distinctly longer and pointed bill, and as a rule lacks any obvious pattern above, whereas Barred has noticeable white tips/edges to median and greater coverts forming double wingbar, as well as pale well-defined scaly fringes to tertials (beware indistinctly patterned 1st-winters and heavily worn 1st-summer Barred, which can sometimes lack these features). Other helpful features are Barred's more conspicuous pale edges to undertail-coverts and whitish eye-ring, which largely indistinct on Orphean. Most (not all) Orphean at this age tend to have some bluish suffusion to crown and slightly contrasting darkish ear-coverts, unlike Barred's plainer and paler, non-contrasting head pattern.

Separation from Lesser Whitethroat Although Orphean is 15–20% larger than and almost twice as heavy as Lesser Whitethroat,

Adult ♂ Arabian Warbler. Note dark eye and broken white eye-ring. Head blackish-chocolate.

Juvenile Arabian Warbler. Browner than adult.

Adult ♀ Arabian Warbler. Midway between Orphean and Sardinian Warblers in size. Dark head and eye, pale edges to tertials. Tail appears all dark from above, frequently dipped.

1st-autumn Lesser Whitethroat. 1st-year Orphean Warbler exhibits very similar plumage.

Adult ♂ Orphean Warbler. Note heavy bill, dark ear-coverts and forehead, pale eye. Primary projection long compared with Arabian Warbler. White in tail usually obvious, tertials plain. Older males may have a complete blackish hood.

1st-summer ♀ Orphean Warbler. Dark eyed.

1st-winter ♀ Orphean Warbler. Compared with Barred Warbler usually darker above, greyer head with slightly darker ear-coverts. No eye-ring. Similarly plumaged Lesser Whitethroat much smaller, with shorter tail and bill, partial white eye-ring and uniform undertail-coverts.

1st-autumn Barred Warbler. Plainer individuals may resemble Orphean Warbler. Note paler upperparts, shorter, stubbier bill, pale eye-ring and pale feather tips.

the two are surprisingly often confused in field (usually, latter misidentified as 1st-winter/female Orphean, or the reverse). Problem results largely from similar plumage pattern and coloration plus frequent misjudgement of size. Following constant features should obviate this. Orphean is much more robust and heavy-bodied than (and never so nervous and 'clumsy' as) Lesser Whitethroat, with diagnostically longer and thicker bill and 'plenty of tail', and shows indistinct (or lacks) white eye-ring (quite obvious and more complete on most Lesser Whitethroats); rear body appears much darker, undertail-coverts always showing variable amount of dark centres and pale fringes, sometimes producing *Locustella* pattern. Undertail-coverts of Lesser Whitethroat look largely uniform whitish or pale buff; it also shows little contrast between tail and upperside, and undertail pattern is pale/faded, whereas Orphean's tail looks darker with at least some contrast with upperparts and shows more clear white on outer edges of rectrices (some experience needed to judge this correctly). Voice differs greatly between the two. Orphean's main calls are 'tjeck', rather sharp but deeper 'taak' or harder 'tchak' and often an explosive, loud and chattering 'trrrr'; Lesser Whitethroat's 'teck teck' is much shorter, higher and harder (more like Blackcap *S. atricapilla* or Olivaceous Warbler), and migrants in Middle East often give high, loud, very fast trill. Orphean has a vigorous thrush-like warbling song, in quality often resembling Nightingale's, e.g. 'tru tru tru sheevu sheevu, yoo-yoo-yoo-bru-treeh'; Lesser Whitethroat has a soft warbling chatter followed by a quick louder rattle.

Arabian Warbler

Average Arabian is between Sardinian Warbler and Orphean in size, but generally looks larger, approaching latter species (partly result of strong desert sunlight). Slow, heavy movements recall Orphean or Barred (though actually freer, with more deliberate and less frequent jumps from perch to perch), lacking quick, sprightly, tail-cocking habits of smaller

Sylvia warblers. Tail held in line with body or slightly drooping, is diagnostically flopped downwards rather repeatedly (somewhat recalls Olivaceous). Combination of short/rounded wings and proportionately longer tail gives Arabian a much longer-tailed look than Orphean. Also has much shorter primary projection, one-third or less of exposed tertials, than Orphean (about half tertials), and shorter and more slender bill; Orphean's longer, deeper-based and evenly tapering bill appears (mainly on N African and Near/Middle East races) strikingly long, heavy and dagger-shaped. Arabian's head profile distinctly rounded. Other plumage features of adult Arabian helpful in distinguishing it from any Orphean include: **1 HEAD** Rather uniformly dark with less contrastingly dark ear-coverts, giving almost complete hooded pattern; Orphean (apart from 2nd-summer and older males, which have almost complete blackish hood) generally shows paler head with obviously darker ear-coverts, recalling Lesser Whitethroat. **2 EYE-RING** Usually shows obvious, complete or broken white eye-ring (beware worn or actively moulting birds almost lacking this); eye-ring largely absent or very faint greyish on Orphean. **3 TERTIAL PATTERN** Except when heavily worn, shows well-defined and rather broad white fringes; Orphean's tertials appear uniform or with diffuse narrow greyish edges. **4 TAIL** Usually blackish and contrasting greatly with upperparts; adults show white tips to outer/shorter two pairs of rectrices (visible from below) and thin white fringes to outermost pair, but indistinct or lacking on juveniles. Orphean's tail is generally grey-brown and less contrasting, and at all ages has clear and broader white tips and outer webs to outer three pairs (visible from most angles).

Iris Colour Both sexes of Orphean from 3rd calendar-year onwards show at least some whitish or grey in iris (less in 2nd calendar-year). Arabian has dark iris at all ages, but note that most 1st-winter/1st-summer Orphean have dark-looking iris.

Plumage Variation of Arabian Warbler Adult male Arabian of Israeli race *negevensis*

has upperparts pale brownish-grey or clean bluish-grey with very slight brownish tinge, merging gradually on nape with brownish-black crown (nominate of Arabia differs slightly: more brownish than grey above, with browner cap). Adult female rather similar, except slightly browner upperparts and head and slightly more contrasting darkish ear-coverts; eye-ring normally less prominent and always more broken. Juvenile nearer adult female, but crown and nape more grey-brown with stronger darkish ear-covert contrast and with rather prominent whitish spot above lores; no white eye-ring, and upperparts much browner with distinctive rusty fringes to wing-coverts and tertials. Tail almost all black apart from indistinct fine pale fringes on outer pairs of feathers.

Voice Call a quiet, soft 'chuck, chuck', repeated up to three times with pauses (Orphean has deeper 'tchak'). Song very different from Orphean's: loud and far-carrying, with great deal of individual variation.

References Shirihai (1989), Shirihai *et al.* (in prep.).

Some Poorly Known Phylloscopus *Warblers*

Where and When Hume's Warbler *P. humei* and Mountain Chiffchaff *P. sindianus* appear quite regularly in W Palearctic, where probably the least-known of the genus. Hume's is very closely related to (or conspecific with) Yellow-browed Warbler *P. inornatus*, which is the most regular Siberian vagrant (annual W, N and C Europe and Near East); Hume's much scarcer. Both recorded chiefly in autumn (a few winter and spring records). Mountain Chiffchaff (of distinctive race *lorenzii*) breeds only at high levels in NE Turkey and S Russia, including Caucasus-Transcaucasia; very closely related to, and often treated as conspecific with, Chiffchaff *P. collybita*, which it replaces altitudinally (or apparently partly sympatric, without hybridising). Race *lorenzii* is a summer visitor; passage and wintering areas not fully understood (mainly vertical migration possible).

Hume's and Yellow-browed Warblers

Hume's differs from Yellow-browed as follows. **1** VOICE Call usually distinctly di-syllabic, likened to that of Greenish Warbler *P. trochiloides*, rather short, high-pitched but loose, e.g. 'tsuee-eep', or somewhat sparrow-like and flat 'sweelou', 'chwee' and 'ch'leep', with downward inflection on second syllable; Yellow-browed has strident 'tseeweest' or 'tsweest' with distinct upward inflection, sometimes likened to Coal Tit's *Parus ater*.

Hume's song is excited repetition of 'sesou', usually followed by thin, falling, nasal, rasping and drawn-out 'zweeeeeeeeee' somewhat like flight call of Redwing *Turdus iliacus*; Yellow-browed's is very high-pitched and thin, 'tsew-tsee-o-wee . . . tseee' or 'tsitsitsui itsui-it see'. **2** GENERAL COLORATION (Fresh) Upperparts paler and greyer, more brownish-grey (pale individuals), lacking distinct greenish-yellow tinge of Yellow-browed; brightest Hume's, however, show some buffish-green suffusion, chiefly on mantle and rump. Underparts dirtier white than on Yellow-browed, normally lack yellowish pigments, but some (brightest) show slight yellowish-buff on flanks. **3** WINGS Both have two wingbars when fresh. On Hume's, upper bar (on median coverts) generally reduced (tip of each covert contrasts less with surroundings and therefore indistinct) and both bars off-white or buffy-white, yellow being reduced or largely absent. Yellow-browed always shows some yellow (variable) in wingbar. Hume's shows narrow buffy-green edges to remiges, and remiges and centres of greater coverts are paler, so lacks bright yellow-green wing panel and dark area between wingbars which make Yellow-browed much more attractively patterned. Outer edge of longest tertial of (most) Hume's is whitish (green on most Yellow-browed). **4** SUPERCILIUM AND EAR-COVERTS Hume's has rather plain buffish-white and only slightly mottled ear-coverts (darker and

Autumn Yellow-browed Warbler. Yellow plumage tones including wingbars and tertial edges, giving strong pattern. Mottled ear-coverts and strong yellow supercilium. Pale base to lower mandible. Pale legs.

Dull autumn Hume's Warbler. Grey, usually with little or no yellow, wingbars whitish, wing lacking strong contrast.

Voice the best distinction, see text.

Ear-coverts plain, cream supercilium, reduced before eye. Bill mostly dark.

Autumn Hume's Warbler, a bright individual. Median-covert wingbar often reduced, and wing lacks strong contrast of Yellow-browed Warbler.

Worn spring Yellow-browed Warbler. Much greyer than autumn, usually still with some yellow. Some indistinguishable from worn Hume's Warbler (right). Spring Hume's Warblers are greyer and whiter with wear, median-covert bar often worn off. Legs usually darker than Yellow-browed Warbler.

strongly mottled on Yellow-browed) and less prominent (often very inconspicuous) dark eye-stripe, as well as narrower, reduced supercilium in front of eye (unlike Yellow-browed), and supercilium normally pale buffish (yellowish on Yellow-browed). **5 BARE PARTS** Hume's bill averages slightly broader/ shorter, with restricted pale base to lower mandible (difficult to see even at close range), and appears darker overall; Yellow-browed's is finer, often longer, with extensive pale base readily visible. A very few Hume's, however, show rather large pale area on bill base, and on some Yellow-browed in spring summer pale base greatly reduced. Hume's legs are normally darker (dark/blackish-brown) than Yellow-browed's (fleshy-brown or greyish-brown with some pale brown and yellowish on lower tibia and feet). **Worn Plumages** From midwinter both are greyer and whiter, and slight plumage differences even more difficult to assess; wingbars

and pale tertial fringes become progressively narrower and more whitish (median bar often worn away). Some initially bright(est) Hume's are, when worn (in spring), inseparable from equally worn Yellow-browed unless voice heard and bare parts seen. Individual variation, however, also quite strongly age-related, as 1st-winter/spring and rather heavily bleached Yellow-browed will often appear paler/greyer (but very worn), approaching adult Hume's at same time (but latter only moderately worn). **Other Confusion Risks** There is risk of confusion with the 'Greenish group' (*P. plumbeitarsus, P. trochiloides*). Latter, however, are larger and lack Hume's and Yellow-browed's distinct pale edges/dark centres to tertials (indistinct when worn!) and Yellow-browed's dark area (greater-covert centres) between wingbars; thus appear generally more uniform, with weaker wingbars.

Mountain Chiffchaff

Following refers to race *lorenzii* of Mountain Chiffchaff. This should be distinguished from Siberian race *tristis* of Chiffchaff and other forms of latter by combination of following most significant characters. **1** GENERAL COLORATION Upperparts warm grey-brown or dark slaty-brown, including rump (i.e. lacks greenish tinge to rump present to varying degree on all Chiffchaff forms, though worn *tristis* almost identical in this respect), and breast, flanks and undertail-coverts variably brownish/dull fulvous, slightly paler than upperparts. General slightly warmer brown tone remains even on worn birds, so never becomes so grey as *tristis*, *fulvescens* and many *abietinus* Chiffchaffs. **2** REMIGES AND RECTRICES Base colour distinctly darker, and completely lacking olive-green edges, instead having very thin hint of paler buffish-sandy, olive-brown or golden-brown fringes (*tristis* and by implication other Chiffchaff races are progressively greener in these parts). Tertials rather uniform (indistinct edges) owing to broad diffuse fringes, on some almost imperceptible. **3** HEAD Supercilium (and eyering) whitish or light buff, and long, usually wider, brightest and more prominent between bill and eye; on most Chiffchaffs (except some *tristis* and *abietinus*) supercilium shorter and reduced in front of eye. Lores and eye-stripe dark brown or blackish and very contrasting, forming broad stripe from bill to rear ear-coverts; ear-coverts slightly paler than crown and more mottled with buff, also generally look darker than on most Chiffchaffs. Whitish eye-ring thicker, upper half concolorous with broad supercilium, but lower half conspicuous against surrounding ear-coverts. All this gives more strikingly contrasted head pattern than Chiffchaff. **4** BARE PARTS Bill looks

Autumn Chiffchaff of the race 'tristis'. Pale brown-grey above, whitish below, slight green suffusion to rump and remiges only. Often a diffuse wingbar on greater coverts.

Autumn Chiffchaff of the race 'abietinus'. Note strong green suffusion.

Worn summer Mountain Chiffchaff. Dark, warmish brown, lacking all green even on rump and wings; dark underparts. Bill with clear pale base.

Autumn Mountain Chiffchaff. Supercilium whitish, widest between eye and bill; strong dark eye-stripe and lores. Tertials nearly uniform.

somewhat shorter, sharper and finer than on most Chiffchaff races; upper mandible brownish-black, lower yellowy-brown, usually with clear yellow base (most Chiffchaffs show restricted pale area on bill, mainly confined to cutting edges and base of lower mandible). Legs dark brown or black with contrasting deep yellow soles. **5** SIZE AND STRUCTURE Similar to Chiffchaff in size, but a little more delicate and slightly shorter-winged; primary projection shorter than Chiffchaff's (in this also differs from anomalously brownish Willow Warbler *P. trochilus*: see below). **6** VOICE Song clearly of Chiffchaff group: in pitch, accent and tones differs slightly from nominate *collybita* and *abietinus*, but to human ear usually inseparable if individual variation taken into account. Call a soft 'psew' or higher

'tiss-yip', closely similar to *tristis* Chiffchaff. **Likelihood of Confusion** There is slight risk of confusion between *lorenzii* and Dusky Warbler *P. fuscatus*: latter has pale mandible base, stronger supercilium, pale pinkish-brown legs, also outermost rectrix more often has thin pale fringe and tip (when fresh) and supercilium and underparts washed pale rufous-buff; call and action also very different. Confusable also with some brownish Willow Warblers (*acredula*, but mainly *yakutensis*), but latter larger, with much longer primary projection, pale legs and whiter underparts (some yellowish on *acredula*).

References Alström & Olsson (1988), Beaman (1994), Shirihai (1987a), Shirihai & Madge (1993), Svensson (1992), Ticehurst (1938), Williamson (1967b).

West Palearctic Black-and-white Flycatchers

Where and When Three species occur in the region. Pied Flycatcher *Ficedula hypoleuca* breeds rather widely from British Isles and Scandinavia east to SW Siberia and south through most of Europe to NW Africa; Collared Flycatcher *F. albicollis* is widespread but local in C and SE Europe and from Baltic and W Russia east to Ukraine; and Semi-collared Flycatcher *F. semitorquata* is confined to SC Eurasia from Balkans to Transcaucasia and SW Transcaspia/NW Iran. All frequent woodland with some deciduous element, in parks and gardens and in more remote forest, Semi-collared generally in more open montane forest, and all winter in Africa. On passage, Pied occurs in varying numbers throughout; the others have more restricted routes, with Collared only a vagrant in north and westernmost areas and Semi-collared recorded west only to Italy/Malta. Good numbers of all pass through Levant in spring. **General Remarks** Identifying breeding males generally straightforward, but beware hybrid Pied x Collared (males resemble Semi-collared). Also, Iberian and N African races of Pied (*iberiae* and *speculigera*) differ from nominate, having mixed characters of Collared and

Semi-collared, and are very like Pied x Collared hybrids. Problems are compounded by plumage (age) variation: e.g. male Semi-collared is sometimes overlooked as Pied. Separation of female-type birds (including in autumn) considerably more difficult, and observers should accept that many individuals are impossible to separate in field on plumage alone; only those showing all features suggesting one of the species should be identified.

Breeding males

Classic Males Collared is easily separated from nominate Pied by its marked white neck band, larger white forehead and primary patches (but vary, usually with age), usually rather obvious whitish rump/lower back and nearly all-black tail, Pied having white forehead patch smaller and usually divided into two spots, smaller primary patch and moderate white in outer tail feathers. Beware, however, that 1st-summer Collared (1st-summers of all aged by worn brownish primaries, primary coverts, alula and usually some outermost greater coverts contrasting with blackish upperparts) has much smaller primary

FLYCATCHERS

Spring ♂ Collared Flycatcher. Note white collar, large forehead patch. Large white patch on primaries, pale rump. Typically no white in tail.

Spring ♂ Semi-collared Flycatcher. Note large primary patch and median-covert bar. Forehead patch midway between Pied and Collared Flycatcher patterns. Largest amount of white in tail.

Typical undersides of tails of ♂ Pied (right) and Semi-collared Flycatchers (left).

Spring ♂ Pied Flycatcher. Small white patches on forehead and primaries.

Brown ♂ Pied Flycatcher in spring. Note ♂-like tertials

Spring ♂ Pied Flycatcher of race 'speculigera'. Large white forehead and primary patches, all black tail.

Adult ♀ Pied Flycatcher in spring. Upperparts brown, white primary base very small or absent.

Hybrid ♂ Pied × Collared Flycatcher shows mixed characteristics.

Typical tertial and outer-tail patterns of spring ♀ Flycatchers.

Pied   Collared   Semi-collared

Spring ♀ Collared Flycatcher. Grey above, large white primary patch, pale rump and collar. Blackish uppertail-coverts.

Spring ♀ Semi-collared Flycatcher. Grey above, narrow white tertial fringes, white-tipped median coverts.

patch than adult, as small as or even smaller than adult Pied (1st-summer Pied often lacks patch). Although adult Semi-collared is intermediate between the other two (sharing Pied's smallish white forehead patch and Collared's jet-black upperparts, whitish rump and relatively large primary patch), it is rather easily distinguished by its second wingbar (formed by white-tipped median coverts), its half-collar (to neck) and distinctly greater amount of white on outer rectrices. Note that some Semi-collared can have less obvious half-collar (with more black on neck sides) or a less obvious median-covert bar (as white tips merge into greater coverts) and can look like Pied, but other features (e.g. amount of white in tail and primary patch) should separate this species.

'Tricky' Males Races *iberiae* and, especially, *speculigera* of Pied differ from nominate in many respects (large forehead and primary patches, all-black tail, sometimes slightly whiter rump, and some are half-collared), and are almost identical to Collared, though always lack full white collar. Could easily be mistaken for Semi-collared, but lack latter's white-tipped median coverts and large white area in tail feathers and also have large white forehead patch. Most likely confusion, however, is between these races of Pied and some hybrid males of nominate Pied x Collared. Mixed pairs of last two (regular in some areas of sympatry) produce hybrids (males often fertile) with obvious intermediate characters, distinguishable as such. Majority, however, tend towards one of parent species: Collared-like hybrids usually told from pure Collared by having more dark on neck (even more than 1st-summer male, which has diffuse greyish tinge on mid neck creating broken collar), and Pied-like hybrids normally differ from pure nominate Pied in having larger white forehead and primary patches and more black in tail. Many individuals very close to one of the parent species are easily overlooked as either Pied or Collared, as well as being mistaken for Semi-collared, but, except in rare cases, lack latter's white median-covert tips and distinctive white in tail.

Female-type plumages

Sexing and Ageing Although some of the main features separating the three species are to varying degree useful for all female-type plumages, they vary greatly (and often show some overlap) within and between age/sex classes. Identifying an individual's age (and sex) is therefore an essential starting point, so that comparison can be made between these very similar forms in equivalent plumage. In *spring/summer* (i.e. breeding plumage) caution is urged, since 1st-summer females (aged by more worn/browner primaries, primary coverts and often some outer greater and median coverts, alula and sometimes rectrices) often have reduced white primary patch. It is not rare for 1st-summer female Collared to have a primary patch as small as adult Pied (but many 1st-summer Pied have very small or no patch). In *autumn*, ageing extremely important before attempting identification. For example, on 1st-winters (aged by having central tertials with step-like extension at tip of outer web, and greater coverts with large wedge-/step-like whitish tips), tertial and primary-patch features are of less use owing to high degree of overlap. On adult (more evenly and narrowly tipped tertials and greater coverts), tertial and primary patch are often valid as in spring/summer, but usually rather highly influenced by variation between sexes (though sexing normally impossible!). Remember that an individual's age can explain atypical tertial and primary-patch (and other plumage) features which may otherwise be confusing or lead to misidentification.

Breeding Pied and Collared Females Once age/sex determined, following differences, in combination, should in most cases enable specific identification. **1 WHITE PRIMARY PATCH** Considerably larger and more rectangular in shape on Collared (on Pied, usually much smaller and narrower, bar-like, directed downwards along border of primary coverts), and reaches farther down towards wing edge, as well as far beyond tips of longest primary coverts (usually at most to longest primary-

FLYCATCHERS

Adult autumn Pied Flycatcher. Note very small white primary patch. Brown wings.

Upperparts of all three species browner in autumn, and variable.

Ageing characteristics common to all three species, and essential first step to identification. Note central-tertial pattern of adult (left) and 1st-winter (right).

1st-winter Pied Flycatcher. Brown wings and tail. Very small or absent primary patch. Diffuse second wingbar sometimes present.

Adult ♂ Semi-collared Flycatcher in autumn. Tends to be greyish. Black wings, uppertail-coverts and tail. Medium-sized white primary patch, second pale wingbar.

Tail with much white.

Adult ♀ Semi-collared Flycatcher in autumn. Blackish wings, medium-sized white primary patch and second wingbar. Thin edges to tertials.

Adult ♂ Collared Flycatcher in autumn. Tends to be greyer on rump and neck. Black wings and tail, large white primary patch. Tail with little white.

1st-winter Semi-collared Flycatcher. Typically dark brown wings, medium-small white primary patch, thin tertial edges, second wingbar.
1st-winter Collared Flycatcher (below) very similar. Larger white primary patch, second wingbar indistinct or lacking.

Adult ♀ Collared Flycatcher in autumn. Dark wings and medium white primary patch.

covert tips on Pied). Beware, however, that shape and size of patch vary greatly in both species: some Pied (usually 1st-summer) show no visible patch, while some extreme adult Pied may have patch larger than many 1st-summer Collared (which have relatively small patch); moreover, *iberiae* and *speculigera* Pied often have rather large primary patch, only slightly smaller than average Collared. An additional confusion risk (fortunately, rare) involves male Pied showing full female appearance and which sometimes have similar large white primary patch to that of average Collared (see below). 2 WHITE TERTIAL EDGES Average narrower on Collared (forming slightly smaller and more broken tertial panel) than on Pied. 3 UPPERPART COLORATION Most Collared have colder and slightly paler brown-grey ground colour, variable hint of diffuse pale greyish collar at neck sides, and paler (and larger) rump patch; most Pied have warmer dirty brown colour, indistinct hint of paler neck-side collar, and usually brownish rump (only occasionally slightly paler than rest of upperparts). On both, however, upperpart features vary individually and can be confusingly similar. 4 OTHER DIFFERENCES Some (chiefly adult) female Collared have diffuse whitish forehead patch (never shown by nominate Pied, but commonly present on adult *iberiae* and *speculigera*), and more commonly have blackish short and long uppertail-coverts than same-age Pied (but much overlap in these features). Comparing equivalent-age individuals, most Collared are darker brownish-black on primaries, rectrices and primary coverts, which contrast with greyish upperparts (browner with less contrast on most Pied), and have marginally larger and whiter wing patch (narrow white tips to greater coverts and white bases to secondaries), but this very difficult to judge in field. The whiter wing patch combined with greyer upperparts and darker remiges/rectrices gives Collared a more contrasty appearance.
Breeding Semi-collared Female Generally approaches Collared, having greyish upperparts, distinct pale rump and larger white primary patch than most Pied, almost as on Collared. Many have diagnostic second wing-bar created by broad white median-covert tips (but bar often incomplete or diffuse) and narrower white outer tertial edges, forming well-broken tertial panel with separated edges (almost even in width right to base) and virtually no (or no basal) tertial patch; some Semi-collared (and a few Collared) lack white edges to shortest tertial. Most also show paler ground colour to dark areas of primaries and rectrices, as well as tertials and upperwing-coverts, giving less contrast between pale and dark areas on upperparts and wings, especially compared with Collared (often obvious also in comparison with Pied). This always gives Semi-collared a rather greyer and duller appearance. Further, and possibly detectable when tail fanned, the pale edge on outer web of outermost rectrix of Semi-collared continues broadly around tip and up along inner web (usually lacking or very indistinct on other two species); and Semi-collared never has blackish uppertail-coverts rather frequently shown by the other two.

Cautionary note Presence of an upper wingbar does not on its own identify Semi-collared, since a few females of Pied and Collared may also show pale-tipped median coverts. On Semi-collared, however, the tips are usually broader and purer white (as well as having more obvious 'steps/wedges'), and usually more coverts are tipped white (appearing as an unbroken row) than on any birds of the other two species. Although Semi-collared is typically rather dull and more uniform (lacking any contrasting blackish feather tracts), colour tones are always difficult to judge in field and different light conditions easily create a multiplicity of tones, while some female Pied and Collared (chiefly 1st-summers) are more uniform than typical individuals owing to less dark remiges and rectrices. In particular, dull Collared can be very like Semi-collared, though normally lack white-tipped median coverts and have different tail and tertial patterns. Although Semi-collared's primary patch is rather similar to that of Collared, on a few (chiefly 1st-summers) it is as small as Pied's; such Semi-collared also often have narrower and more diffuse white median-covert tips than typical adults. Some female Semi-collared may, therefore, be extremely difficult to separate from Pied, and especially from dull Collared with small primary patches. Unless pattern of median coverts and tertials strongly indicates Semi-collared, such birds are often impossible to identify in the field.

Further Areas of Possible Confusion in Breeding Plumages Existence of female-looking male Pied, chiefly among 1st-summer individuals, adds further complication and calls for extra caution. Many are partly grey/brown-and-black or all brown-grey, but have white forehead patch, much white on greater coverts and black and white tertials, and are easily separated from females. Some, however, unless singing, are very difficult to sex (these are more prevalent in E European/Siberian populations). In particular, those with pure-female appearance could also be mistaken for female Collared. 1st-summer Collared is greatest confusion risk (adults should show considerably larger and differently shaped primary patch), but tertial pattern is as on typical female Pied and primary patch is normally too small even for most 1st-summer female Collared. Female-like male Pied usually have darker tail and remiges than 1st-summer female Collared. Female-type hybrids (Collared x Pied) are extremely difficult to recognise (both in autumn and in spring): majority are so close to one or other of parent species that they are impossible to separate.

Adults in Autumn First refer to Sexing and Ageing (above). All three species are basically female-like, but males of Collared and Semi-collared are predominantly black on remiges, rectrices, outer wing-coverts and uppertail-coverts (only indistinctly on Pied), these black/contrasting features being useful identification aids against the much browner and uniform-looking autumn Pied (all plumages); also, unlike male Pied, both often appear to have diffuse suggestion of forehead patch.

Otherwise all three are rather similar, being warm brown (most tonal differences apparent in female-type plumages in spring are obsolete or less valid), and can be identified by same features as for breeding females. White-tipped median coverts combined with medium-sized primary patch and narrow regular tertial edges with indistinct basal tertial patch of typical Semi-collared should eliminate most/all Pied and Collared. Adult Pied's generally small and differently shaped primary patch (short rounded blob at base of inner primaries or short tapering dagger-like bar/line never projecting beyond longest primary coverts, or even non-existent) should readily eliminate most Collared and Semi-collared in corresponding plumage. Almost all female Collared in autumn have broad primary patch projecting beyond longest primary coverts and virtually to leading edge of wing, forming flask- or rectangular-shaped mark bulging on middle primaries (not inner primaries as on Pied), and with other features usually favouring Collared, such as more contrast in overall plumage and less white in tertials, this species should be identifiable.

1st-winters Identification generally based on same criteria as for adults, but allocating each to species is even more difficult owing to higher degree of overlap and frequent intermediates. Using primary patch demands even greater caution: only birds showing extreme typical features suggesting one of the species should be identified, and most must be left indeterminate (in W Europe, where both Collared and Semi-collared are vagrants, field identification of either at this age is fraught with danger!). In this age class white-tipped median coverts are not exclusive to Semi-collared, since many Collared and Pied also have a second wingbar; these pale tips are usually on juvenile feathers (narrowly and often diffusely tipped, sometimes buff-fringed) and tend to be sparser or more widely spaced along the row. Moulted (i.e. 1st-winter) medians of Semi-collared are whiter and broadly tipped (normally greyish and narrower on Collared and Pied), so birds with such new median coverts are more likely to be Semi-collared. Typical Semi-collared should also show medium-sized primary patch and tendency for more evenly narrower tertial edges and reduced basal tertial patch (but much overlap), and also pale tips to outer rectrices (but may overlap with Pied). Many 1st-winter Collared and Semi-collared have well-developed primary patch (more extensive on males) of slightly different shape, and can thereby be separated from Pied (see details above).

Voice

Pied has rather powerful and fast, melodious and sprightly song with rhythmic phrases (slightly reminiscent of Redstart *Phoenicurus*

phoenicurus), e.g. 'psi-tschu-tschi-tschu-tschi'; call a repeated short metallic 'peek', on passage often 'huee-peek'. Collared's song contains slower drawn-out squeaky notes, but with characteristic higher-pitched notes, e.g. 'siu-tree-see-tree-see-seep' or 'siip-tsi-tsi-siu'; call louder, shrill, squeezed and penetrating 'heeep', often repeated (unlike Pied's but more as Semi-collared's, often included in song). Semi-collared's song recalls Collared's but faster, less drawn-out and less high (weaker); call rather like Collared's but less sharp/loud and high-pitched, 'hueep'. All have rather similar tongue-clicking 'tett'.

References Cramp & Perrins (1993), Mild (1993, 1994a,b, 1995), Mild & Shirihai (1994), Svensson (1992).

Choughs

Where and When Alpine Chough *Pyrrhocorax graculus* frequents the highest mountains and alps, regularly to 4000 m, coming slightly lower in winter, to valleys and around villages and high-lying ski stations; breeds Atlas, Sierra Nevada, Pyrenees, Alps, Apennines, Balkans, Caucasus and its extensions, the high mountains of Turkey and in Lebanon. Red-billed Chough *P. pyrrhocorax* lives at lower levels of rocky mountains in southern parts of region, also along rocky coasts of W Europe. The two meet, mainly in winter, in some southern areas (e.g. Pyrenees).

On Ground *Adults* Instantly separable by bill: on Red-billed, long, scarlet-red and strongly decurved (especially upper mandible, making whole bill appear downcurved); Alpine has much shorter bill with fairly straight lower but clearly decurved upper mandible (appears much less downcurved), pale yellow in colour (looks whitish), and usually feathering extends further onto upper mandible than onto lower (about equal on Red-billed). Both have pinkish-red legs. Alpine's plumage often shows less obvious blue-purple gloss than Red-billed's, can at times even appear rather brownish, especially around head. Useful distinction at longer ranges is tail length: on Red-billed, tail shorter

than or equal to wingtips; on Alpine, projects well beyond wings. *Juveniles* Juvenile plumage of both duller, brown-tinged, less glossy. On Alpine, bill duller than adult's (but still yellowish) and legs duller, brownish-red. Juvenile Red-billed's bill shorter than adult's and rather pale pinky-brown or orange-brown (but always slightly longer than Alpine's and without yellow colour).

In Flight The two are very similar and differences in silhouette are in most cases very subtle; voice often the best (or only) safe way of separating them (see below). Red-billed has proportionately slightly broader wings (as broad as tail length) than Alpine (wings narrower than tail length), tends to give impression of short arm but long hand (reverse on Alpine) and normally shows 6 well-spaced, deeply fingered primaries (frequently only 5, shorter and less obvious fingers on Alpine), but beware effects of wing moult when counting primaries. Also has slightly broader and shorter tail which, when closed, looks more square-ended than closed tail of Alpine (differences impossible to judge when tails fanned), and appears somewhat larger-headed. All these features, however, require some real field experience of both species to be used safely, and many

Alpine Chough. Tail longer and rounder, wings slimmer and less fingered.

Alpine Chough

Jackdaw. Blunt-winged.

The relationship between wingtip and tail tip separates distant perched birds.

Alpine Chough.

Juvenile Red-billed Chough.

Adult Red-billed Chough.

Red-billed Chough. Broad deep-fingered wings, shorter, squarer tail. Such differences very difficult to judge in the field.

Red-billed Chough.

individuals cannot be distinguished by these alone. If bill can be seen, problems disappear. **Voice** Some overlap, but generally Red-billed's calls lower in pitch. Typical of Red-billed is loud, throaty 'kyaach' (recalls Jackdaw *Corvus monedula* but much hoarser and coarse-voiced). Typical of Alpine are a very sharp, piercing 'tsi' coupled with characteristic whining 'eeh' ('tsi-eeh') and a trilling 'shrrrree' or 'krrrrree' (likened to sound of a stone thrown across ice).
Separation from Jackdaw Both choughs are very dark-plumaged. In flight they differ from somewhat smaller Jackdaw in having prominently fingered wingtips, narrower-based and slightly longer tail, and smaller and narrower head; in certain lights, under-wing-coverts appear obviously darker than flight feathers (underwing uniform dark grey on Jackdaw). Although Jackdaw is a skilful flier and can perform aerobatics, it lacks choughs' incredible diving and soaring abilities, though can still be impressive.
References Madge & Burn (1994a,b).

Brown-necked Raven

Where and When Brown-necked Raven *Corvus ruficollis* is resident in desert and semi-desert regions across the Sahara and Middle East. It overlaps only marginally in range with Common Raven *C. corax*.
Identification The two species are very similar and not easy to separate in the field, especially without (as usually happens) direct comparison, when Brown-necked's slightly smaller size is impossible to judge. Given some experience, the following tendencies should enable their separation, but in most instances voice remains the easiest distinction.

On Ground Brown-necked looks somewhat less robust, with neck and head slimmer and bill slightly less stout, and generally lacks the obvious shaggy-throated appearance and prominent nostril feathering of Common (but calling or agitated Brown-necked can certainly show 'untidy throat'). Folded wings fall about level with tail tip (usually shorter on Common). At close range or in certain lights, bronzy-brown tinge to nape may perhaps be seen (but note that Common can show brownish on nape, especially when worn).

Brown-necked Raven in flight. Slighter than Common Raven, tail rounder. Under-remiges contrast with underwing-coverts.

Brown-necked Raven. Sleeker and less robust, wingtips reach tail tip.

Brown neck rarely shows.

Brown-necked Raven. Shaggy beard shows only when calling or agitated.

Common Raven. Note heavy head, shaggy throat, wedge-shaped tail.

Common Raven Shaggy beard, obviously feathered nostrils.

In Flight Brown-necked appears slighter than Common, with less heavy head/neck area; wing marginally narrower, with generally more tapered hand (fingers shorter, less splayed, with noticeably shorter 5th primary), and tail less wedge-shaped and less full, with narrower base (and can show slight projection of central feathers). In good light, worn birds often show contrast between flight feathers and coverts on underwing. A surprisingly useful clue is Brown-necked's frequent habit of holding its bill slightly drooping in flight.

Calls Brown-necked has a rising 'kraa-kraa-kraa', and also a sharp but soft croak very like that of Carrion Crow *C. corone*, altogether lacking the deep resonance and rolling quality of Common Raven's wooden croak.

References Cramp & Perrins (1994a), Madge & Burn (1994b).

Spotless Starling

Where and When Spotless Starling *Sturnus unicolor* is largely resident in NW Africa and Iberia, very locally in SW France, and in Corsica, Sardinia and Sicily, replacing Common Starling *S. vulgaris* as a breeder (minimal overlap, in NE Spain/SW France). In winter, however, migrant Common occur throughout the range of Spotless.

Identification At all times, adult Spotless has noticeably longer, shaggier throat (and often nape) feathers than Common, and duller and more uniform greyish-purple gloss (may from certain angles show hint of greenish gloss); adult Common has obvious pale wing-feather edges and shows strong purple and green lustre (green gloss obvious on mantle/back and upperwing-coverts). Difference in gloss colour partly obscured by pale tips in winter (and also less marked in eastern races of Common). **Breeding** In spring and summer, Spotless Starling lacks all pale spots (females and 1st-summers may retain a few minute spots on vent and undertail-coverts) and lacks pale edges to wing feathers. Common normally shows a few small pale spots on upperparts (especially females and 1st-sum-

Adult ♂ Spotless Starling in spring. All plumage glossed greyish-purple, nape and throat very shaggy. No spots or cream edging anywhere. Legs often purer pink.

1st-winter ♀ Spotless Starling, the 'spottiest' plumage. Overall 'dusty' looking with silvery sheen. Fine cream edging to secondaries worn off by midwinter.

♂ Common Starling in summer, at its least 'spotty'. Note strong green sheen, all wing with cream edging.

mers, which may also have spots on breast sides and lower underparts) and has narrow creamy edges to wing (and tail) feathers. Legs of Spotless may appear brighter, purer pink. *Non-breeding* Adult winter Spotless appears much darker than Common, having no spots (most males) or only very small pale tips to body feathers (females), and only narrow pale fringes to wing feathers (pale tips and edges worn off by around midwinter); at distance looks rather dark with slight greyish cast. Winter Common Starling is boldly spotted above (including on crown, which generally unspotted on Spotless) and especially below, and has broader and more prominent pale fringes to wing feathers (at distance looks much paler than Spotless); female Common has larger pale tips than male, appearing more heavily spotted at any season. *1st-winters* As winter adults, but duller, less

glossy, and generally more 'spotty'. 1st-winter Spotless has pale feather tips on mantle and underparts, largest and most extensive on females (but still smaller than on winter Common), but crown usually unspotted (unlike most winter-plumaged Common); looks 'dusty' with a silvery sheen. 1st-winter Common has even larger, more rounded pale spots than adult, often joining to form solid pale buff patch on forehead and white patch on chin. *Juveniles* Juveniles of both rather uniform brown and very similar, perhaps inseparable in field, though Spotless may appear darker, almost blackish-brown.

Voice Little difference. Song of Spotless perhaps simpler, with less mimicry, drier-sounding trills and sharper whistle sounds.

References Cramp & Perrins (1994a), Svensson (1992).

Female Sparrows

Where and When House Sparrow *Passer domesticus* is widespread and abundant, especially around human habitations. Spanish Sparrow *P. hispaniolensis* breeds locally from N Atlantic islands through Mediterranean region and eastwards (partial migrant), requiring some tree cover near open cultivation. The two hybridise occasionally in overlap areas, while 'Italian Sparrow' '*P. italiae*' probably represents a variably stabilised hybrid (divided into 'hybrid form x *italiae*' and 'hybrid form x *maltae*') occurring locally around Mediterranean, including S Switzerland, Italy, Crete, Malta, Corsica and NW Africa. Dead Sea Sparrow *P. moabiticus* is partial migrant breeding patchily in Levant, Tigris-Euphrates region and Iran/Afghanistan (expanding westwards?).

Spanish and House Sparrows

Females of these two are extremely difficult to separate, especially when seen singly or without males, and field experience often needed to determine atypical individuals; even in hand identification not always possible. Problem further complicated by hybridisation and by existence of 'Italian Sparrow', and great caution required. Combination of following differences most reliable. **1** STRUCTURE Generally similar. Spanish's bill

averages slightly longer and broader-based, with cutting edge of upper mandible more curved than on House Sparrow; forehead to crown centre more elongated but a little rounded towards rear crown, producing slightly less square head profile with steeper-sloping forehead than House; gape point roughly level with fore edge of eye (ends slightly before eye on most House), but on both this varies with stage of wear of surrounding feathers and with other factors, e.g. after drinking, when calling, etc. Primary projection of Spanish about two-thirds exposed-tertial length (about half on most House), but often hard to determine or possibly overlaps, and its proportionately slightly longer primaries may produce (minimally) shorter-looking tail. **2** HEAD PATTERN Spanish tends to have broader, longer and clear supercilium, usually paler or more

♀ House Sparrow in fresh plumage. Sandy mantle lines, sandy-grey supercilium. Markings overall less distinct and contrasting than in Spanish Sparrow.

♀ House Sparrow in worn plumage. Smaller bill than Spanish Sparrow. Underparts uniform, mantle lines indistinct or absent.

♀ Spanish Sparrow in fresh plumage. Bold mantle lines and supercilium. Underparts dappled.

♀ Dead Sea Sparrow. Small, neat. Wide sandy supercilium, pale throat.

♀ Spanish Sparrow in worn (summer) plumage. Note strong bill, gape running to below eye, strong cream supercilium and bold pale mantle lines. Underparts show dark shaft streaks.

cream (warm grey-brown on House) and restricted to behind eye, but often narrowly also in front of eye where emphasised by darker grey lores (fore supercilium more concolorous with lores or lacking on most House); ear-coverts normally darker grey, contrasting less with darker grey-brown eye-stripe behind eye (most House show greater contrast, with paler sand-grey or brown ear-coverts). Most Spanish have faint hint of darker shaft streaks on crown (paler, more uniform on House). 3 UPPERPARTS AND UPPERWING Variable on both, in most aspects highly similar, but Spanish normally shows much better-pronounced, paler (whiter) tramlines on mantle sides and upper scapulars (less pronounced and/or discontinuous on most House); uppertail-covert/rump area normally with faint dark-ish shaft streaks (rare on House). Tertial fringes of Spanish paler, more sandy-grey (less rufous-brown), and merging slightly more with less blackish centres; remiges normally appear paler buffy-grey at base and fringed less rufous, giving indistinct paler/sandier-brown wing panel (warm brown on House). Also, most Spanish show diffuse olive-brown inner webs and buffy outer webs to lower scapulars, generally with little contrast between them (House has largely blackish-brown inner webs contrasting with buff-sandy outers), and median-covert tips often appear strikingly whiter in field. 4 UNDERPARTS Spanish relatively paler, with variable hint of faint darkish streaks and dots across breast and (becoming more diffuse) onto flanks; worn late-summer House with 'ravaged' plumage can show darkish pencil-streaks on flanks/breast, but still lacks 'dappled' appearance of Spanish (but not all Spanish are so clearly marked). Spanish's undertail-coverts have more diffuse greyish centres (on House, tend to be narrow, often almost restricted to shaft area, and darkish).

'Italian Sparrow', intermediates and hybrids

Typical female 'Italian' tends to share char-

acters of both Spanish and House, but often closely approaches or is inseparable from either; commonly resembles either one in head pattern but Spanish in mantle tramlines, while lacking latter's darker underpart markings. All such intermediates/hybrids subject to confusion and, in case of 'Italian', usually not safely separable outside known range, while in all contact and overlap areas where hybrids known or suspected caution is demanded when identifying Spanish/House, especially when faced with odd-looking females.

Dead Sea Sparrow

Clearly smaller and more compact than preceding species, small-billed and short-winged; primary projection less than half tertial length, with 3 tips visible and sometimes hint of fourth just behind tertials (4-5 on other species). More nervous, clumsy and faster in movements. Differs in having very distinct buffish-grey/sandy supercilium above and behind eye, broadening rearwards; paler sandy-grey above, with more regular and fine dark streaking on mantle (generally sharper, and both webs 'well fringed'); paler and rather uniform/plain greyish-white below, often with faint yellow suffusion on throat sides and buffish on flanks. On 1st-winter/summer females, median coverts have more rounded and browner centres less sharply demarcated from buffish/whitish tips (more boldly patterned blackish-brown and white on Spanish and House), these becoming progressively black and orange-rufous respectively from 2nd winter onwards.

Voice

All calls of House and Spanish similar, a variety of chirps varying in pitch: House's basic 'chrip' or 'chirrup' generally deeper or richer than Spanish's more metallic 'chirp' or 'chirrip' (or even higher-pitched 'chweeng'); both have monosyllabic 'siep' or soft 'swee', less drawn-out from Spanish, which also gives typical squeaky and far-carrying 'chee-chee-chee' or 'chiree'. Excitement rattle of

House, 'churr-r-r-r-it-it', is shorter and deeper, with softer 'ch' sounds. Dead Sea Sparrow's voice recalls typical chirping of Spanish but sharper, deeper and more liquid, 'tchrelp' and repeated disyllabic 'chp-chew' or 'tcheep-tcheep'; rattle call nearer Spanish but higher-pitched.

Reference Harris (1990).

Arctic Redpoll

Where and When Arctic Redpoll *Carduelis hornemanni* breeds in the northernmost Holarctic, moving somewhat south to winter; numbers reaching southern Baltic and NW Europe (mainly Britain) vary annually. Its range is overlapped fully by that of Redpoll *C. flammea*, which also breeds further south (to British Isles and C Europe) and in winter occurs throughout N and C Palearctic. No significant differences in habitat choice, and Arctic are often found in flocks of Redpoll.

Taxonomy and Races The taxonomy of these species has long been disputed; some suggest that the two are conspecific, others that they should be split into three or four species, while the affiliations of the various races have also been questioned. The current view is as follows. Arctic Redpoll occurs in two races, *exilipes* occupying entire range apart from NE Canada and Greenland, where nominate *hornemanni* breeds. Redpoll is distributed in three to four races: nominate 'Mealy Redpoll' *flammea* (including 'holboellii') of northern parts, wintering Russia with varying numbers in W and C Europe; *cabaret* of S Scandinavia to W and C Europe; *rostrata* of Greenland and Baffin Island; and a little-studied darkish population in Iceland (possi-

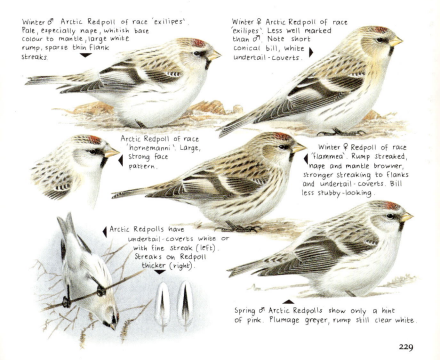

Winter ♂ Arctic Redpoll of race 'exilipes'. Pale, especially nape, whitish base colour to mantle, large white rump, sparse thin flank streaks.

Winter ♀ Arctic Redpoll of race 'exilipes'. Less well marked than ♂. Note short conical bill, white undertail-coverts.

Arctic Redpoll of race 'hornemanni'. Large, strong face pattern.

Winter ♀ Redpoll of race 'flammea'. Rump streaked, nape and mantle browner, stronger streaking to flanks and undertail-coverts. Bill less stubby-looking.

Arctic Redpolls have undertail-coverts white or with fine streak (left). Streaks on Redpoll thicker (right).

Spring ♂ Arctic Redpolls show only a hint of pink. Plumage greyer, rump still clear white.

bly part of *rostrata*, possibly a separate form '*islandica*'). The position of pale redpolls also breeding in Iceland is unclear; they may be Redpolls, or perhaps an unnamed population of Arctic.

Identification

'Classic' Arctic, very pale and unstriped, is the exception: the species varies considerably in plumage, from very pale, almost unstreaked adult males to dark, heavily streaked 1st-years very close to pale Redpolls (also very variable). Specific identification often requires experience of the plumage variation of both. While extremes of the two should not cause major problems, overlap exists in all features and some individuals are best left unidentified.

General Variation Adults (especially males) are less streaked than 1st-winters. Adult males have variable amount of pink (Arctic) or pinkish-red (Redpoll) on breast, flanks and rump, partly concealed by pale tips when fresh; female (and some immature male) Arctic lack pink, but some female Redpolls are very close to male. ***Effects of wear*** Adults moult (complete) once a year, in summer; post-juvenile moult partial (body, a variable number of wing-coverts, rarely a few tertials or rectrices). The species are most easily separable in autumn and winter, when relatively fresh. Later, as pale fringes abrade, dark feather centres produce a darker, more streaked, more contrasty plumage (e.g. Arctic can show fine streaking down whole length of white rump, whereas fresh Arctic only very rarely lack unstreaked area in white rump).

Racial Variation Nominate Arctic (occasional vagrant from Greenland) is very pale, with much white (on head, wingbars, tertials and tail) and little streaking; clearly bigger and larger-billed than both *exilipes* Arctic and *flammea* Redpoll, it should not cause any real problems. Large *rostrata* Redpoll is also fairly straightforward: very dark (almost as *cabaret*), with a heavy bill with strongly curved culmen. Race *cabaret* of Redpoll, the smallest and darkest, should always be easy to distinguish. Main problem is separating *exilipes* Arctic

from the pale and less streaked northern race *flammea* of Redpoll, but beware also that a pale *flammea* among a flock of dark *cabaret* can look so pale by comparison that it is easily mistaken for Arctic by the unwary. (Remember also that large and pale birds from Iceland, breeding alongside very large and dark *rostrata*-like individuals, may reach N Britain in winter and could lead to perhaps insoluble identification problems in the field.)

Separating *exilipes* Arctic from *flammea* Redpoll

Following text concentrates on separating these two in non-breeding season, when the observer is most likely to encounter the problem. Typical adult male Arctic should stand out among a flock of Redpolls by its pale overall coloration and poor streaking, but darker, more strongly streaked individuals are very similar to nominate Redpoll (though may perhaps be picked out by their ochre-yellowish face/breast, relatively uniform head pattern, and paler flanks with weaker streaking); closer examination should be focused on coloration and pattern of rump and undertail-coverts (the most useful features). Always remember, however, that wide variation in both species leads to overlap in all characters, and some birds must still be left unidentified in the field.

Size and General Appearance Although race *exilipes* of Arctic is about the same size as most Redpolls (but larger than *cabaret*), its plumage normally looks softer, more fluffy, and is often ruffled, making it look plump, broad-headed and almost neckless (rounded, pale and 'snowball-like'). Some Redpolls can, however, match Arctic in general appearance. **Most Useful Distinguishing Features** The following tendencies should, in combination and given reasonable views, enable most individuals to be identified specifically. 1 RUMP Fresh-plumaged Arctic normally shows about 1-2 cm of unstreaked white (sometimes faintly tinged greyish/yellowish) on rump, 1st-winters occasionally showing less, but with wear the darker feather centres produce slight streaking (late spring onwards). Redpoll usually has greyer or yellow-buff rump fully and diffusely streaked (some adult males can show variably large unstreaked area), but occasional Redpolls show whitish ground colour to rump and can resemble some extremely well-streaked Arctic. 2 LONGEST UNDERTAIL-COVERTS Often a surprisingly useful feature (e.g. when birds hanging on twigs), but be sure to examine the correct, i.e. longest, coverts. On Arctic, these are either all white and unmarked or have very narrow (mostly 1-3 mm broad) greyish shaft streaks; on Redpoll, streaks generally broader and almost blackish. Some variation and overlap exists, however, and occasional adult male Redpolls can show plain white/whitish undertail-coverts. 3 HEAD PATTERN On Arctic more uniform, less contrasty, and in fresh plumage with creamy ground colour to head sides (extending to throat and breast); ear-coverts usually pale and unstreaked (or with fine greyish streaks, though can look spotted), contrasting little with broad supercilium (barely streaked) and pale nape (weakly and thinly streaked); often has greyish rear eye-stripe extending around rear ear-coverts. Redpoll often has pale yellow-brown ground colour to face (becoming darker on breast), with contrast between more heavily streaked (or more solidly dark) ear-coverts, pale supercilium (narrow and more strongly streaked behind eye) and heavily streaked dark nape. 4 BILL On Arctic averages shorter and deeper-based, with straight culmen (on Redpoll slightly convex, especially towards tip), in fresh plumage looking even shorter owing to longer, denser blackish feathering at bill base and nostrils. Although extremes of the two species differ clearly, most individuals are intermediate in length and shape of bill, so this feature of limited use. 5 UNDERPARTS On fresh Arctic, ground colour to throat and breast and sometimes upper flanks usually creamy to ochre-yellowish (on some, especially 1st-winters, very indistinct and more pale greyish), becoming whitish-grey with wear; streaking varies greatly, on adult males often restricted to breast sides, whereas most

heavily streaked individuals (mostly 1st-winters) are very close to Redpoll, but 'average' Arctic shows paler, thinner and sparser streaking (generally most distinct on breast sides) than Redpoll, and streaks do not merge to form stripes. Redpoll usually has more brownish ground colour to throat and breast, paling on lower flanks (but occasional individuals virtually identical to Arctic), and streaks extend to lower flanks, average broader, darker and longer and tend to form more continuous stripes on flanks (note that adult males often have reduced streaking on breast and upper flanks, as on Arctic, though usually still show prominent streaks on lower flanks). 6 UPPERPARTS On fresh Arctic, ground colour averages paler (pale creamy-grey/tawny-brown) than on Redpolls of same age, sex and feather condition, which are darker and browner, though darkest/brownest Arctic can be extremely similar to pale Redpolls; feather centres on mantle and back quite narrow and darkish grey-brown (on Redpoll average larger and blackish, on well-marked individuals forming stripes), and pale edges of central mantle and back feathers often broadly white or pale yellowish and form very broad, well-demarcated lines which are generally more conspicuous than on most Redpolls. (Note that, for both species, coloration and pattern vary with age, sex and degree of wear: adults are paler and have weaker and finer streaking than immatures, and males are paler than females; with wear and fading of pale fringes, both species become darker and more streaky in spring and summer than in winter.) 7 WINGS Pale tips/fringes to wing-coverts, tertials and remiges average broader and whiter on Arctic (more prominent greater-covert bar), rather narrower and more brownish on Redpoll, though these tendencies soon obscured by bleaching and wear. 8 SUBSIDIARY FEATURES Arctic's pale edges to rectrices average whiter, broader and more contrasting (especially on inner webs, visible from below) than on Redpoll in equivalent plumage. Shortest uppertail-coverts on Arctic often white or pale creamy (usually brownish on Redpoll), and pale edges to longest coverts often broader and contrastingly greyish-white or creamy (usually brownish on Redpoll).

Calls Differences very slight and subtle: Arctic's flight call is a little higher and slower, its call when perched perhaps rather hesitant and hoarse and falling at end (against Redpoll's purer rising whistle), and foraging Arctic may give a more sparrow-like chirp than Redpoll's sharp 'chit-chit-chit'. Picking out an Arctic among a noisy Redpoll flock is, however, impossible!

Spring Birds Adult male Arctic in spring shows only subdued pale pink flush on breast and rump, whereas Redpoll has extensive pinkish-red on breast and variable amount on flanks, rump and head sides. Those Redpolls with most red on underparts and rump tend to be the least streaked (extremes can be as unstreaked as Arctic, but are identifiable by intense and extensive red on breast and rump).

References Jännes (1995), Lansdown *et al.* (1991), Molau (1985).

Pine Bunting

Where and When Pine Bunting *Emberiza leucocephalos* breeds at open woodland and forest edge in Siberia and west to Urals. Largely migratory, winters west to Middle East (regular N and C Israel); vagrant elsewhere, mainly late autumn/winter. Overlaps in both breeding and non-breeding seasons with Yellowhammer *E. citrinella* (hybridises): in winter mixed parties found in lightly wooded country, often farmland with deciduous growth, including orchards with interspersed pine woods or open bushy areas; prefers higher elevations than Yellowhammer.

General Features In structure, behaviour and voice Pine Bunting and Yellowhammer appear almost identical (even to experienced observers). Adult and 1st-year males of Pine show unmistakable chestnut, white and black head pattern and rufous on breast. Females of both have virtually identical pattern and coloration, though most Yellowhammers show variable amount of yellow at least on central belly, crown and supercilium (Pine lacks all yellow). Main problem is separating female Pine from 'non-yellow' female Yellowhammers (regionally not uncommon): at close range most individuals of both exhibit combination of constant differences, but a degree of overlap exists and a few are so alike as to be inseparable. Adult and 1st-year females are largely similar (latter have more pointed and worn primaries and rectrices, and more worn unmoulted tertials), but most 'non-yellow' Yellowhammers are apparently 1st-years.

Identifying Females In the field and even in the hand, the only constant differences of female Pine compared with 'non-yellow' Yellowhammer are as follows. **1** REMEX FRINGES White or whitish-buff, never any yellow pigment as Yellowhammer. **2** HEAD-TOP Crown streaks generally more marked on individual feathers, creating total crown pattern, on average blacker and narrower, more often almost confined to feather shafts, with slightly more pointed end (browner on Yellowhammer, averaging wider and with less/no point). Streaks more restricted to lateral crown, with far fewer on central crown (can appear as paler crown-stripe), this pattern added to by deeper supercilium (often giving apparent darker lateral crown-stripe); Yellowhammer normally (not always) shows more evenly streaked crown and narrower supercilium. Otherwise, female Pine shows striking contrast between lateral crown area and paler and almost unstreaked supercilium (but sometimes whitish with very thin faint streaks), whereas Yellowhammer shows less contrast owing to greyer supercilium; most (not all) tend to have conspicuous brownish patch on rear lateral crown area/side of upper neck created by slightly denser streaking with more brown/rufous fringes (patch reduced or lacking on most Yellowhammers). **3** SIDE OF HEAD Pine's apparently broad supercilium is also result of its extension to almost half eye level (on most 'non-yellow' Yellowhammers,

Winter ♀ Yellowhammer. Yellow to head and underparts.

♀ Yellowhammer lacking yellow pigments. All streaking more diffuse

♀ Yellowhammers occur apparently without yellow. Close inspection should reveal yellow-edged primaries, less sharply defined crown streaks.

Winter ♀ Pine Bunting. Head pattern a diffuse copy of ♂, lateral crown-stripe extends down nape. Greyish above, rufous in underparts, white edges to primaries.

Winter ♀ Pine Bunting. Pale, fine streaked crown, pale wide supercilium and wider area of malar streaking.

reaches only just below top of eye). Its deeper supercilium (well apparent in front of eye) is almost concolorous with (broader) paler loral area but contrasts greatly with (smaller) ear-covert area; Yellowhammer's darker loral area is more concolorous with (wider) ear-covert area, together producing less contrast with greyer (whitish on Pine) supercilium. Pine's whitish eye-ring averages narrower than Yellowhammer's. **4 NAPE COLOUR** Grey area on sides of neck, nape and hindneck is slightly suffused with and/or faintly streaked brown (on Yellowhammer purer and cleaner grey, and from most angles covers smaller area than on most Pine). **5 UNDERPARTS** Apart from Pine's moustachial stripe tending to appear more prominent, it also tends to have stronger/better-defined malar stripe composed of 3–4 rows of blackish blotches, rather than Yellowhammer's generally weaker stripe of 2–3 rows of blackish-brown blotches (but can appear as conspicuous as on Pine). Pine in general tends to have fine spots/streaks over wider area of throat, often

quite evenly and extending from lower throat up towards bill, whereas Yellowhammer's throat shows fewer markings (often extending just to lower or central throat). Pine's entire underparts are whiter apart from buff suffusion on chest, and upper-breast streaking is more blackish, fading (and with intermixed rufous-orange markings) towards breast sides and flanks. Rather comparable pattern occurs in Yellowhammer, but it lacks Pine's diagnostic fine blackish marks on upper breast. Pine's undertail-coverts are on average more finely and faintly streaked than Yellowhammer's, or even unstreaked (unlike latter species), but can rarely be quite heavily streaked. **6 LESS OBVIOUS DIFFERENCES** These include Yellowhammer's diagnostic yellowish underwing-coverts (sometimes inconspicuous). Pine tends to have more intense rufous pigment to fringes of lowest row of scapulars, and lesser upperwing-coverts more uniform grey-brown (less grey than on Yellowhammer). Pine's head often appears more square-shaped, peaking at rear

233

crown, and small crest slightly erected when nervous (indistinct on Yellowhammer). Primary projection about same on both (sometimes somewhat longer on Pine) and both show 2 closely spaced primary tips at wingtip as well as one shorter primary tip, but only Pine shows (not always) a 4th tip (or tertial tip falls roughly level with or rarely slightly conceals this 4th tip). A few 'very adult' female Pine show indication of non-adult-male pattern, with at least some rufous on chest and even a whitish patch on central crown and more chestnut on head.

References Bradshaw & Gray (1993), Byers *et al* (1995), Lewington (1990), Svensson (1992).

Near Eastern Bunting Specialities

Where and When Ortolan *Emberiza hortulana*, Cretzschmar's *E. caesia*, Grey-necked *E. buchanani* and Cinereous Buntings *E. cineracea* are all closely related. Their occurrence together is unique to Levant and other Middle East areas. Ortolan breeds most of Europe south to Mediterranean region and east to about the Kirghiz steppes and SW Siberia, migrating (chiefly mid August to mid October, April-May) mainly to Africa; inhabits open country with bushes and trees, but in south of range usually above 1300 m and up to 2300 m (slight overlap with Cretzschmar's). Cretzschmar's is restricted to barren and stony slopes (below 1300 m) with sparse, scrubby Mediterranean vegetation, from Balkans east to S and W Turkey and south to C Israel; migrates (chiefly mid August to mid September, mid February to April) to winter mainly NE Africa. Grey-necked breeds on dry rocky foothill and mountain slopes with scattered shrubs, mostly at 2000-2800 m (well above most Ortolans), from E Turkey east to W China/Mongolia; migrates (chiefly August-September, March-April) to main winter quarters in W and C India. Cinereous breeds discontinuously in W and S Turkey and EC Iran, migrating (chiefly August-September, March-April) to NE Africa and SW Arabia; in scrub on arid rocky slopes, also sheltered valleys, sharing habitat/elevation with preceding three species (mainly first two).

Identification Adult males (from 1st-summer) easily distinguished at all seasons. Ortolan has greenish olive-grey head, malar stripe and chest band, but yellow throat and submoustachial stripe and yellow-brown rump. Cretzschmar's has head and chest mostly lead-grey, throat and submoustachial stripe rufous-buff and rump basically rufous. Grey-necked has Cretzschmar's grey head, but breast to belly largely rufous (no grey chest band) and often (mainly when fresh) mottled with whitish feather tips; throat and submoustachial stripe whitish-buff and rump pale greyish-brown, but (unlike other three species) lacks any real blackish-centred mantle feathers. Cinereous distinctively different, showing yellow face, unstreaked greenish-grey (nominate) or yellowish-grey (race *semenowi*) crown and nape, lacking or having indistinct malar stripe and chest band, and having greyish-white (nominate) or variably intense yellowish (*semenowi*) breast to belly; rump grey, unstreaked. Adult females (from 1st-summer, mainly older) of all four often show hint of male coloration and pattern and can be very like 1st-summer males (apart from latter's slightly more worn and pointed rectrices, more worn and bleached primaries, and retained juvenile tertials and wing-coverts), thus facilitating identification. Main problems are with juveniles and 1st-winters of both sexes and with 1st-summer females, and following discussion focuses on these.

Separating Ortolan and Cretzschmar's

Helpful Structural Features Cretzschmar's bill averages shorter and always appears smaller/delicate with less heavy base, but slightly more conical with steeper culmen ridge (slightly more pointed with longer and less steep ridge on Ortolan), and cutting edge is stronger and drops steeply down at base (more gradual, shallower drop on Ortolan), though experience required to determine this. Its primary projection is shorter, usually showing one primary tip (two on Ortolan) beside bunched and very closely spaced tips of wingpoint, but sometimes tertials fall approximately on (rarely, even very slightly short of) next inner primary tip and then appears as Ortolan (but exposed primary tip still never widely spaced as on Ortolan). Tertial spacing also useful (but judgement requires care and experience) when feathers not worn: on most (not all) Cretzschmar's, greater space between shortest and middle feathers than between middle and longest, whereas most Ortolan have equal spacing between the three tips (but beware differing age/wear of feathers, or those not fully grown, which can mislead).

Spring Females 2nd-summer or older Ortolan (but also at least some 1st-summers) show crown and breast tinged with varying amount of olive-green and faint tinge of yellow on throat, whereas Cretzschmar's show at least some ash-grey on breast and crown and buffy-brown throat, lacking any trace of greenish or yellow. Individuals lacking this diagnostic coloration (mostly 1st-summers) are often difficult and require careful examination of following characters. 1 HEAD PATTERN Cretzschmar's shows finer and browner crown streaks, together producing a few well-defined crown-stripes, rather than blacker, fairly narrow streaks of Ortolan, which appears more heavily/fully streaked and normally not regularly striped but with blackish feather centres often merging with/surrounded by brown (Cretzschmar's crown feathers mostly plain grey-brown, centres never merge into fringes). Cretzschmar's ear-coverts show indistinct contrast with rest of head; Ortolan's are slightly darker (often suffused with olive-brown), often accentuate paler supercilium (always lacking on Cretzschmar's) and are always obviously darker than crown. Pale area before eye usually larger on Cretzschmar's, and throat and submoustachial stripe dirty white buff-white (on Ortolan, whitish-yellow/sandy) and malar stripe weaker/narrower, composed largely of one row of brown blotches and generally without dark spots extending towards central throat (Ortolan has prominent, well-defined malar, often of 2-3 rows of blacker blotches which often extend as a few small dark spots towards central throat). Cretzschmar's eye-ring is whitish or pure white; Ortolan's always has a degree of faint yellowish, though on pale (chiefly worn) females can in many lights appear just whitish. Both have pinkish/reddish-orange bill, but Cretzschmar's is slightly paler and upper mandible has on average larger blackish area than on most Ortolan. 2 UNDERPARTS 1st-summers (most lack diagnostic coloration) show some important differences. On Cretzschmar's, slightly narrower brownish streaks virtually restricted to central upper breast, and only very indistinct/fine streaks extend to upper flanks, whereas Ortolan shows much heavier and broader blackish streaks (fading to brown on lower breast) extending well onto breast sides and more often distinct on flanks. Cretzschmar's also looks more buff-rufous below (most Ortolan largely pale orange-chestnut with yellowish-buff hue, especially rearwards), this colour extending well onto vent and undertail-coverts (unlike Ortolan's yellowish-buff, which gives pale undertail-covert contrast). Folded tail feathers usually reveal differences in visibility/shape of dark bases on both sides of undertail-coverts: rather prominent and almost straight-ended on Cretzschmar's, while Ortolan's strongly tapered dark bases largely concealed by undertail-coverts. 3 UPPERPARTS AND WINGS Much individual variation (particularly in Ortolan) prevents definitive states. Cretzschmar's tend, however, to have sandy-grey ground colour above with more obviously contrasting chestnut uppertail-coverts, narrower and browner feather centres (streaks) largely restricted to mantle and normally strongly reduced or even lacking on lower back and rump, and scapulars with narrower and sharper (pointed) dark centres, and inner visible remiges always show same greyish-buff colour to fringes as outers. Ortolan has more olive-grey/buff ground colour

BUNTINGS

1st-summer ♀ Ortolan Bunting. Olive and yellow tones to head, bold streaking to malar area, breast and often onto yellow-orange flanks. Uppertail-coverts olive, undertail-coverts cream.

1st-winter ♀ Ortolan Bunting. Strong malar stripe.

Ortolan Bunting. Bill larger than Cretzschmar's Bunting, with straighter culmen.

1st-summer ♀ Cretzschmar's Bunting. Like Ortolan Bunting, but head greyer. underparts rufous-brick extending onto undertail-coverts. Fine streaking to crown, breast and upperparts. Uppertail-coverts warmer, bill weaker and paler than Ortolan Bunting.

Juvenile Ortolan Bunting. Heavily streaked above and below.

1st-winter ♀ Cretzschmar's Bunting. Note weak malar stripe.

1st-summer Grey-necked Bunting. Poorly streaked above, cold rufous below, extending up throat.

Juvenile Grey-necked Bunting. Cinnamon underparts, broadly fringed paler. Tertials without broad 'stepped' blackish bases as on Ortolan and Cretzschmar's Buntings.

Juvenile Cretzschmar's Bunting. Weaker streaking than Ortolan Bunting, warm cinnamon tinge below.

Juvenile Cinereous Bunting. Note grey bill, dusky breast, pale belly, neat thin streaks above and below, rump greyish.

and indistinct contrast with largely olive-brown uppertail-coverts, and generally the broader and blacker centres (streaks) continue from mantle/scapulars to rump, scapular centres are normally not pointed, and most have some olive or greenish-yellow pigment to inner remex fringes. These differences not reliable on heavily worn birds. Diagnostic feature is Cretzschmar's rufous-tinged whitish axillaries (pale yellowish-white on Ortolan), but largely indiscernible.

Autumn Birds As in spring, 2nd-year and older females distinguishable by coloration suggestive of respective adult male. 1st-winter male Cretzschmar's also to variable degree recalls adult, but 1st-winter Ortolan does not. Main problem in autumn is with 1st-winter female Cretzschmar's and 1st-winter Ortolan of both sexes, but all should be separable in same way as for 1st-summers, as well as by some structural features (see above). Many 1st-winters, chiefly of Ortolan, moult a very few juvenile wing-coverts, head and breast feathers before migration, resulting in wide individual variation between juvenile and 1st-winters (see also below for those with many retained juvenile feathers).

Juveniles Both species show more extensive and triangular streaks below, on Cretzschmar's browner and concentrated more on central upper breast (less obvious on breast sides, very few on upper fore flanks and normally none on rear flanks); Cretzschmar's also tend to have warmer (but pale) cinnamon on lower breast to undertail-coverts, contrasting with much paler whitish-rufous-buff upper breast, throat and submoustachial stripe, and malar stripe far stronger than on 1st-winter female, being 2-3 rows of blotches, though still relatively weak and browner. Ortolan has broad blackish-brown streaks covering whole chest and well down to rear flanks (becoming browner), with ground colour almost invariably pale gingery-yellow quite evenly from throat to undertail-coverts, but exceptionally shows slightly warmer lower throat and belly; malar appears thicker, especially on lower part, giving prominent malar patch and gorget of 3-4 rows of profuse blackish blotches, which together with rest of underparts recalls Tree Pipit *Anthus trivialis*. Juvenile Cretzschmar's has warmer brownish-grey mantle and more rusty tone to rump and uppertail-coverts (never Ortolan's olive brown-grey), with mantle and scapulars more finely and much less heavily streaked. Otherwise, head and wing differences as for 1st-year females.

Grey-necked Bunting

Unlike preceding species, sexual plumage dimorphism inconspicuous (many cannot be sexed), though females marginally paler/duller than males, with varying amount of blackish-brown spots and streaks on breast; wide range of intermediates exists. After post-juvenile moult (August-October) many 1st-winters, but chiefly males, well advanced towards adult. Problem thus reduced to separating juvenile or 1st-winters (mainly females) from those of Ortolan and Cretzschmar's. In those plumages differs from both in being inconspicuously and finely streaked above, where lacks bold blackish-brown scapular and mantle streaks of Ortolan, though streaks only slightly more narrow than Cretzschmar's (but lacks latter's rufous tinge to ventral region and uppertail-coverts, which are instead brownish-grey and indistinctly streaked); as a rule, has less well-defined and rather straight tertial centres (on Ortolan and Cretzschmar's, centres sharply defined and outer webs with L shape), and paler and browner remiges (never dark or blackish) with indistinct sandier edges; malar and breast streaks less developed. Less striking differences include broad, diffuse greyish-buff greater-covert fringes (always well-defined bold blackish centres on other two species), and slightly longer, pointed and slender-based bill which normally lacks any dark on upper mandible. Differs from Cretzschmar's also in pale buff (not rufous-buff) undertail-coverts, and from Ortolan in lacking pale yellow pigments in eye-ring, chin/throat, submoustachial stripe and axillaries. Primary projection and spacing nearer Ortolan, but tertial spacing as Cretzschmar's.

Cinereous Bunting

In all plumages identification should be straightforward, but in Middle East juveniles and 1st-year females have been confused with above congeners. Diagnostically has bluish/horn-grey bill (but darker on upper part of upper mandible), never reddish or pink as preceding species; dusky ash-brown breast and flanks contrast with paler belly (normally uniform and warmer on others), and is mostly greyish olive-brown above, with neat streaks on crown and finely streaked on mantle, scapulars and underparts. Malar-submoustachial pattern much weaker, malar largely one row of narrow/small blackish blotches or virtually absent. In addition, juvenile and 1st-year females of Ortolan and Grey-necked have, respectively, olive-brown and greyish-brown rump and uppertail-coverts (rufous-brown on Cretzschmar's), while Cinereous also lacks Ortolan's obvious rump streaking.

Voice

Common flight or contact calls as follows. Ortolan: 'pslee-e-chu' and dry 'plit' or 'chieep' and shrill 'tseeip', in characteristic regular alternating pattern. Cretzschmar's: 'tjitt' or 'tchitt-let', also 'tchipp' or 'spit' (very like Ortolan's but harder and sharper, more metallic). Grey-necked: 'chep' or 'tsip', slightly higher-pitched than preceding. Cinereous: short metallic 'kjip' or quite hard 'tshri' or 'kleup' or 'tsik'.

References Cramp & Perrins (1994), de Knijff (1991), Hollom *et al.* (1988), Small (1992), Svensson (1992).

Female and Autumn Rustic Bunting

Where and When Rustic Bunting *Emberiza rustica* breeds in damp forests from SE Norway across N Palearctic, overlapping from N Fennoscandia eastwards with Little Bunting *E. pusilla*. Both winter mainly in SE Asia, but are regular vagrants (and occasional in winter) through much of W Palearctic.

General Spring males highly distinctive and unlikely to be misidentified. Female and all autumn Rustic (most appear female-like, and ageing and sexing in field impracticable) need to be told from Little but especially from the widespread Reed Bunting *E. schoeniclus*. Look for the following main features.

Size and Structure Rustic appears almost as big as Reed but larger than Little, with (as Little) proportionately shorter tail than Reed; head rather angular, usually with ragged crest. Both Rustic and Little have more pointed, conical bill (lower mandible pinkish) than Reed, whose stubbier (more uniformly coloured) bill and more rounded head give less angular-looking head, but Rustic's is also quite long (Little's shorter bill can have slightly concave culmen, can appear almost 'snub-nosed'). Both also have more evenly spaced primary tips than Reed.

Plumage 1 CROWN AND NAPE Rustic has thin whitish or pale buff central crown-stripe, broadening at rear to form variable pale spot above rusty-tinged hindneck, and dark lateral crown-stripes (on Little, lateral stripes similar but central stripe chestnut/buff and usually no obvious pale spot on greyish rear neck); Reed usually lacks distinct central crown-stripe, but note that crown sides can be brighter than centre (immatures) or blackish (late-winter males). 2 FACE Rustic has bolder facial pattern than Little or Reed (though all three well patterned), with broad creamy-buff to white supercilium most striking behind eye and curving down nape side, broad submoustachial stripe concolorous with supercilium and bending back below ear-coverts, bordered by dark moustachial and malar stripes which extend to bill; ear-coverts brownish, variably mottled, and with darker border with usually distinct pale spot at rear. Reed similar, with less prominent pale stripes, but malar stripe stronger and more triangular, and never shows clear pale ear-covert spot. Little has much brighter plain chestnut ear-coverts with blackish border (often pale buff spot at rear), but supercilium less obvious

Winter ♀ Rustic Bunting. Peaked rear crown pale, lower nape warm rust, conspicuous pale supercilium and ear-covert surround, pale ear-covert spot. Breast with rufous marks diffuse, extending to flanks. Rump rufous, two wingbars.

Summer ♀ Rustic Bunting. Strong white supercilium, submoustachial stripe, and crown and ear-covert spots.

Winter ♂ Rustic Bunting. Strong head pattern, rufous pectoral band distinct.

Winter ♀ Reed Bunting. No rufous on nape or breast, no clear-cut pale ear-covert spot.

Winter Little Bunting. Distinctive face pattern, malar and moustachial stripes not reaching bill. Pale eye-ring. Greyish nape, two wingbars.

Summer ♀ Reed Bunting. Dark ear-coverts, lores and moustachial stripe. Stout, stubby bill. Rump grey-brown, no wingbars.

(almost absent before eye) and often tinged chestnut, submoustachial stripe paler than supercilium, and moustachial (often lacking) and malar stripes thinner and not meeting bill. Unlike Little, Rustic shows no significant eye-ring. **3** UNDERPARTS Rustic is white below (throat tinged buffy-yellow) with very broad, diffuse rufous-chestnut streaks/blotches from breast (often form pectoral band) extending well down flanks (Reed whitish, with dusky or light buffish throat and flanks, and with broad brown streaks; Little also white, but has pale throat often tinged rufous, and breast and flank streaking thinner, better defined and blackish). **4** WING-BARS Rustic and Little almost always show distinct bars formed by whitish tips to greater and especially median coverts (bars indistinct or lacking on Reed). **5** RUMP Rufous on Rustic (grey-brown on Reed, grey-brown to red-

brown on Little). **6** LESSER COVERTS Chestnut on Rustic and Reed (grey-brown on Little), but normally not visible in field.

Call and Behaviour Rustic gives sharp 'tzik' or 'tic', sometimes softer 'tzip', similar to calls of Little but quite unlike Reed's distinctive drawn-out 'tseeu' or (mainly autumn migrants) buzzing 'bzee'. Both Rustic and Little tend to feed on ground close to cover (on passage also in more open situations but often skulk), with frequent wing-flicking and tail-spreading (Reed spreads and flicks tail but does not flick wings). When flushed, Rustic has strong, direct flight, looking bigger and more purposeful than Little, and both species lack long-tailed appearance and rather jerky and hesitant flight action of Reed. *References* Bradshaw (1991), Cramp & Perrins (1994b), Svensson (1992).

Black-headed and Red-headed Buntings

Where and When Black-headed Bunting *Emberiza melanocephala* is a summer visitor to SE Europe (west to Italy, Bulgaria, Romania) east through Near East to about Caspian, there meeting (and hybridising with) Red-headed *E. bruniceps*, which also extends east-

Adult ♀ Red-headed Bunting. Adult rump colour is olivy-yellow. Upperparts olive-grey, fine streaking to head, wing fringes buffy.

Old ♀ Black-headed Bunting. Both species tend towards male plumage as they get older.

Adult ♀ Black-headed Bunting. Rump with rufous, back and mantle also. Head streaking often prominent, wing fringes whitish. Bill usually bigger than Red-headed Bunting's.

1st-winter Red-headed Bunting. Most inseparable from 1st-winter Black-headed Bunting. Marginal differences may separate some birds: Red-headed may appear longer-tailed, small billed, shorter primary projection, colder upperparts, less yellow beneath.

1st-winter Black-headed Bunting. May have clearer crown streaking, paler face, more yellow beneath, larger bill.

wards. Both winter chiefly in Indian subcontinent. Small numbers of Black-headed are recorded on passage in parts of S Europe and Levant outside breeding areas; otherwise most records of both species refer to vagrants (though most Red-headed have been considered escapes). In summer both favour open lowland grassland or scrub, and mountain slopes and semi-arid areas with open forest/maquis and undergrowth, also orchards and other cultivation; at other times recorded also in more open areas such as semi-deserts.

General Features Although no bigger than Yellowhammer *E. citrinella*, both appear larger and in particular more robust, with heavy head and bill; also differ greatly in plumage from other W Palearctic buntings, lacking conspicuous tail pattern and appearing rather uniform. Adult males (1st summer onwards) unmistakable: Black-headed is chestnut above and yellow below, with black crown and head sides; Red-headed chestnut-brown from face to upper breast, rest of body greenish or yellow. In winter, patterns partly concealed by broad grey-buff and whitish feather tips, but still largely discernible. 1st-winter and female plumages, however, present major problems and some individuals, especially lone vagrants in W Europe, must be left unidentified; some females (apparently mainly 2nd-years) show trace of male colours and are easier to identify.

Identifying Females and 1st-winters No one feature will clinch identification in field. A combination of following is essential, but it should be stressed that a degree of overlap occurs. 1 SIZE AND STRUCTURE Red-headed's bill averages slightly shorter and deeper, and its primary projection is marginally shorter, with 4 (infrequently 5) exposed tips beyond longest tertial (5, rarely 6, on Black-headed). Red-headed's relatively shorter wing may make its tail appear slightly longer, and it averages smaller and a little less heavy-bodied, but very hard to assess without direct comparison. While both species are large for W Palearctic buntings, Black-headed appears longer, heavier, and in general a bigger bird with a longer bill. 2 HEAD PATTERN Most Red-headed have indistinct (fainter) crown streaks (hardly any on forehead/forecrown) and head appears more uniform overall, largely lacking darker ear-covert area of most Black-headed (which on average has more, and more prominent, crown streaks). 3 UPPERPARTS Typical Red-headed tends to have paler and greyer olive-brown ground colour, lacking rufous tinge, whereas Black-headed tends to show chestnut tint on both mantle and rump (can be absent, or confined to mantle); but this difference of very little value for 1st-winters (when both show buffy greenish-yellow/sandy suffusion above) or worn birds. With spring birds and autumn adults, combination of more greyish-tinged upperparts with better-defined blacker streaks points to Red-headed, against Black-headed's browner and more diffuse streaks with varying degree of chestnut pigmentation above. 1st-winters of the two are very similar in coloration and pattern, but again Red-headed is slightly greyer and has slightly darker and blacker (less brown) streaks. 4 UNDERPARTS In all plumages, Red-headed tends to have paler-throat/darker-breast effect, and overall less yellow, especially on undertail-coverts, and broader streaking than Black-headed in corresponding plumage. Some spring female Red-headed are even uniform dusky buff-grey with almost no yellow or streaking, as opposed to Black-headed's more obvious yellow and variable streaking. 5 WINGS Comparison of typical adults (spring and autumn) of the two provides rather constant differences. Red-headed has buffy or sandy-brown (often quite ginger-looking) fringes to coverts and remiges (fringes whitish on Black-headed, producing distinctive wingbar pattern and even central wing panel), but note that Red-headed's fringes may wear to whitish. In 1st-winter plumage, both show largely similar whitish to sandy-white fringes. *Male-type females* Some adult female Red-headed (chiefly in spring) have some chestnut on forecrown, face, even down to breast centre, reflecting male pattern, and female Black-headed can have rather a lot of black on crown and forehead and darkish ear-coverts, looking quite darkish-headed.

Call Commonest call of Black-headed a rather hard, deep 'tchup' or 'plütt', less often 'tzik'. Red-headed's calls are a little thinner or more metallic, to human ear probably inseparable. *Reference* Shirihai & Gantlett (1993).

References

Alström, P., Barthel, P.H., & Schmidt, C. (1989) Die Bestimmung von Weißbürzel- *Calidris fuscicollis* und Bairdstrandläufer *C. bairdii. Limicola* 3: 49-61.

Alström, P., Colston, P., & Lewington, I. (1991a) *A Field Guide to the Rare Birds of Britain and Europe.* Jersey.

Alström, P., Colston, P., & Round, P.D. (1994) Bestimmung der kleinen fernöstlichen Rohrsänger *Acrocephalus. Limicola* 8: 121-31.

Alström, P., Mild, K., & Zetterström, D. (1991b) Identification of Lesser Short-toed Lark. *Birding World* 4: 422-7.

Alström, P., & Olsson, U. (1988) Taxonomy of Yellow-browed Warblers. *Brit. Birds* 81: 656-7.

Alström, P., & Olsson, U. (1989) The identification of juvenile Red-necked and Long-toed Stints. *Brit. Birds* 82: 360-72.

Barthel, P.H. (1993) Bemerkungen zur Bestimmung von Nachtigall *Luscinia megarhynchos* und Sprosser *L. luscinia. Limicola* 7: 57-76.

Barthel, P.H. (1994) Die Bestimmung der Fischmöwe *Larus ichthyaetus. Limicola* 8: 64-76.

Barthel, P.H., & Königstedt, D.G.W. (1993) Die Kennzeichen der Dünnschnabelmöwe *Larus genei. Limicola* 7: 165-77.

Beaman, M. (1994) *Palearctic Birds. A checklist of the birds of Europe, North Africa and Asia north of the foothills of the Himalayas.* Harrier Publications, Lancashire.

Becker, P., & Schmidt, C. (1990) Kennzeichen und Kleider der europäischen kleinen Rallen und Sumpfhühner *Rallus* und *Porzana. Limicola* 4: 93-144.

Bradshaw, C. (1991) Identification of Little and Rustic Buntings. *Birding World* 4: 309-13.

Bradshaw, C. (1993) Separating juvenile Little and Baillon's Crakes in the field. *Brit. Birds* 86: 303-11.

Bradshaw, C., & Gray, M. (1993) Identification of female Pine Buntings. *Brit. Birds* 86: 378-86.

Brooke, R.K., Grobler, J.H., Irwin, M.P.S., & Steyn, P. (1972) A study of migratory eagles *Aquila nipalensis* and *A. pomarina* (Aves: Accipitridae) in southern Africa, with comparative notes on other large raptors. *Occ. Pap. Nat. Mus. Rhodesia* B5: 61-114.

Byers, C. (1992) Scops Owls and Striated Scops Owls. *Birding World* 5: 107-10.

Byers, C., Olsson, U., & Curson, J. (1995) *Buntings and (North American) Sparrows.* Mountford.

Carey, G., & Olsson, U. (1995) Field identification of Common, Wilson's Pintail and Swinhoe's Snipes. *Birding World* 8: 179-90.

Chandler, R.J (1989) *North Atlantic Shorebirds.* London.

Clark, W.S., Frumkin, R., & Shirihai, H. (1990) Field identification of Sooty Falcon. *Brit. Birds* 83: 47-54.

Clark, W.S., & Shirihai, H. (1995) Identification of Barbary Falcon. *Birding World* 8: 336-43.

Clark, W.S. (1992) The taxonomy of Steppe and Tawny Eagles, with criteria for separation of museum specimens and live eagles. *Bull. BOC* 112: 150-6.

Clement, P. (1987) Field identification of West Palearctic wheatears. *Brit. Birds* 80: 137-57, 187-238.

Cramp, S. (*et al.*) (1977-94) *The Birds of the Western Palearctic.* 9 vols. Oxford.

de Knijff, P. (1991) Little-known West Palearctic birds: Cinereous Bunting. *Birding World* 4: 384-91.

Delin, H., & Svensson, L. (1988) *Photographic Guide to the Birds of Britain and Europe.* London.

Dennis, R.H., & Wallace, D.I.M. (1980) Field identification of Short-toed and Lesser Short-toed Larks. In Sharrock, J.T.R. (ed.), *The Frontiers of Bird Identification.* London.

Doherty, P. (1991) Identification of juvenile Long-toed Stint and Least Sandpiper. *Birding World* 4: 279-81.

Dowsett-Lemaire, F., & Dowsett, R.J. (1979) European Reed and Marsh Warblers identification. *Brit. Birds* 72: 190-1.

Dubois, P.J., & Yésou, P. (1995) Identification of Western Reef Egrets and dark Little Egrets. *Brit. Birds* 88: 307-19.

Flint, P. (1995) Separation of Cyprus Pied Wheatear from Pied Wheatear. *Brit. Birds* 88: 230-41.

Forsman, D. (1984) *Rovfågelsguiden*. Helsinki.

Forsman, D. (1991a) Aspects of identification of Crested Coot. *Dutch Birding* 13: 121-5.

Forsman, D. (1991b) Die Bestimmung von Schell- *Aquila clanga*, Schrei- *A. pomarina* und Steppenadler *A. nipalensis. Limicola* 5: 145-85.

Forsman, D. (1993a) Identification of large falcons. *Birding World* 6: 67-72.

Forsman, D. (1993b) Hybridising harriers. *Birding World* 6: 313.

Forsman, D. (1995a) Tunnistatko punajalkahaukan. *Alula* 1: 8-13.

Forsman, D. (1995b) Field identification of female and juvenile Pallid Harrier and Montagu's Harrier. *Dutch Birding*.

Forsman, D. (in press) *Photographic Handbook to the Field Identification of West Palearctic Raptors*. London.

Forsman, D., & Shirihai, H. (in press) Identification, ageing and sexing of Eurasian Honey Buzzards. *Dutch Birding*.

Forsman, D., & Shirihai, H. (in prep.) Field identification of spotted, Steppe and Tawny Eagles. *Brit. Birds*.

Fry, C.H. (1990) Foraging behaviour and identification of Upcher's Warbler. *Brit. Birds* 83: 217-21.

Gantlett, S., & Millington, R. (1992) Identification forum: large falcons. *Birding World* 5: 101-6.

Gargallo, G. (1991) Identificacio del Busquerat Coallarga (*Sylvia sarda balearcia*). *An. Orn., Deles balears*.

Garner, M.S. (1991) Mystery photographs 173. Barrow's Goldeneye. *Brit. Birds* 84: 543-6.

Gillon, K., & Stringer, G. (1994) Elsie II - the next generation of hybrid Lesser Crested x Sandwich Terns. *Birding World* 7: 312-15.

Glutz von Blotzheim, U.N., & Bauer, K.M. (1991) *Handbuch der Vögel Mitteleuropas. Band 12/I*. Wiesbaden.

Grant, P.J. (1980) Identification of two first-winter Marsh Warblers. *Brit. Birds* 73: 168-89.

Grant, P.J. (1986a) *Gulls: a guide to identification*. Berkhamsted.

Grant, P.J. (1986b) Four probem stints. *Brit. Birds* 79: 609-21.

Grant, P.J. (1987) Notes on Armenian Herring Gull. *International Bird Identification, Proc. 4th Internat. Identification Meeting, Eilat*: 43.

Hancock, J. (1984) Field identification of West Palearctic white herons and egrets. *Brit. Birds* 77: 451-7.

Harrap, S. (1988) Identification of Icterine and Melodious Warblers/Identification of Olivaceous and Booted Warblers. *Birding World* 1: 273-7, 312-15.

Harrap, S. (1989) The difficulties of Reed, Marsh and Blyth's Reed Warblers identification. *Birding World* 2: 318-24.

Harris, A. (1988) Identification of adult Sooty and Bridled Terns. *Brit. Birds* 81: 525-30.

Harris, A. (1990) Mystery photographs 153. Spanish Sparrow. *Brit. Birds* 83: 163-5.

Harris, A., Tucker, L., & Vinicombe, K. (1989) *The Macmillan Field Guide to Bird Identification*. London.

Harrison, P. 1983. *Seabirds: an identification guide*. Beckenham.

Harvey, W.G., & Porter, R.F. (1984) Field identification of Blyth's Reed Warbler. *Brit. Birds* 77: 393-411.

Hayman, P., Marchant, A.J., & Prater, A. H. (1986) *Shorebirds: an identification guide to the waders of the world*. London.

Hirschfeld, E. (1991) Further comments on the identification of sand plovers. *Birding World* 4: 394.

Hirschfeld, E. (1992) Identification of Rufous Turtle Dove. *Birding World* 5: 52-7.

Hirschfeld, E., & Svensson, L. (1985) Fältbestämning av större turturduva *Streptopelia orientalis*. *Vår Fågelvärld* 44: 145-52.

Hollom, P.A.D., Porter, R.F., Christensen, S., & Willis, I. (1988) *Birds of the Middle East and North Africa*. Calton.

Hume, R.A. (1992) Identification pitfalls and assessment problems. 11. Little Egret. *Brit. Birds* 85: 21-4.

Jännes, H. (1987) Kenttäkerttusen lajinnääritykesentö ja esiiutymisestä. *Lintumies* 22: 166-9.

Jännes, H. (1995) Die Bestimmung des Polarbirkenzeisigs *Carduelis hornemanni*. *Limicola* 9: 49-71.

Jonsson, L. (1992) *Birds of Europe with North Africa and the Middle East*. London.

Jonsson, L., & Grant, P.J. (1984) Identification of stints and peeps. *Brit. Birds* 77: 293-315.

Kennerley, P.R., & Leader, P.L. (1992) The identification, status and distribution of small *Acrocephalus* warblers in Eastern China. *Hong Kong Bird Report* 1991: 143-87.

Knox, A.G. (1988) Taxonomy of the Rock/Water Pipit superspecies *Anthus petrosus, spinoletta* and *rubescens*. *Brit. Birds* 81: 206-11.

Laird, W.L. (1992) Plumage variation of Clamorous Reed Warblers in Israel. *Brit. Birds* 85: 83-5.

Laird, W., & Gencz, A. (1993) Field identification of Long-billed Pipit in the West Palearctic. *Brit. Birds* 86: 6-15.

Lansdown, P., Riddiford, N., & Knox, A. (1991) Identification of Arctic Redpoll *Carduelis hornemanni exilipes*. *Brit. Birds* 84: 41-56.

Lewington, I. (1990) Identification of female Pine Bunting. *Birding World* 3: 89-90.

Lontkowski, J., & Skakuj, M. (1995) Die Unterscheidung von Korn- *Circus cyaneus*, Wiesen- *C. pygargus* und Steppenweihe *C. macrourus*. *Limicola* 9: 233-75.

Madge, S. (1991) Mystery photographs 167. Pink-backed Pelican. *Brit. Birds* 84: 218-19.

Madge, S. (1992) Identification of Moustached Warbler. *Birding World* 5: 299-303.

Madge, S., & Burn, H. 1988. *Wildfowl: an identification guide to the ducks, geese and swans of the world*. Bromley.

Madge, S., & Burn, H. 1994a. Identification of jackdaws and choughs. *Brit. Birds* 87: 99-105.

Madge, S., & Burn, H. 1994b. *Crows and Jays: a guide to the crows, jays and magpies of the world*. London.

Malling Olsen, K., & Larsson, H. (1995) *Terns of Europe and North America*. London.

Marchant, J.H. (1984) Identification of Slender-billed Curlew. *Brit. Birds* 77: 135-40.

Marchant, J. (1985) Mystery photographs 107. Baird's Sandpiper. *Brit. Birds* 78: 589-90.

Mild, K. (1990) Bird Songs of Israel and the Middle East. 2 cassettes and booklet. Stockholm.

Mild, K. (1993) Die Bestimmung der europäischen schwarzweißen Fliegenschnäpper *Ficedula*. *Limicola* 7: 221-76.

Mild, K. (1994a) Field identification of Pied, Collared and Semi-collared Flycatchers. Part 1: males in breeding plumage. *Birding World* 7: 139-51.

Mild, K. (1994b) Field identification of Pied, Collared and Semi-collared Flycatchers. Part 3: first-winters and non-breeding adults. *Birding World* 7: 325-34.

Mild, K. (1995) The identification of some problem flycatchers. *Birding World* 8: 271-7.

Mild, K., & Shirihai, H. (1994) Field identification of Pied, Collared and Semi-collared Flycatchers. Part 2: females in breeding plumage. *Birding World* 7: 231-40.

Molau, U. (1985) Gråsiskkomplexet i Sverige. *Vår Fågelvärld* 44: 5-20.

Parmenter, T., & Byers, C. (1991) *A Guide to the Warblers of the Western Palearctic*. Uxbridge.

Pearson, D.J. (1981) Identification of first-winter Marsh and Reed Warblers. *Brit. Birds* 74: 445-6.

Pearson, D.J. (1989) The separation of Reed Warbler *Acrocephalus scirpaceus* and Marsh Warbler *A. palustris* in East Africa. *Scopus* 13: 81-9.

Pearson, D.J., & Backhurst, G.C. (1988) Characters and taxonomic position of Basra Reed Warbler. *Brit. Birds* 81: 171-8.

Porter, R. (1984) Mystery photographs 96. Slender-billed Curlew. *Brit. Birds* 77: 581-6.

Porter, R.F., Willis, I., Christensen, S., & Nielsen, B.P. (1981) *Flight identification of European Raptors.* Berkhamsted.

Robertson, I. (1989) Mystery photographs 146. Crested Lark. *Brit. Birds* 82: 346-8.

Rogers, M.S. (1982) Greater and Lesser Sand Plovers. *Brit. Birds* 75: 96.

Schulze-Hagen, K., & Barthel, P.H (1993) Die Bestimmung der europäischen ungestreiften Rohrsänger *Acrocephalus. Limicola* 7: 1-34.

Serra, L., Baccetti, N., & Zenatello, M. (1995) Slender-billed Curlews wintering in Italy in 1995. *Birding World* 8: 295-9.

Shirihai, H. (1986) Identification of Oriental Skylark. *Brit. Birds* 79: 186-97.

Shirihai, H. (1987a) Field characters of Mountain Chiffchaff. *International Bird Identification, Proc. 4th Internat. Identification Meeting, Eilat*: 60-3.

Shirihai, H. (1987b) Identification of Upcher's Warbler. *Brit. Birds* 80: 217-21.

Shirihai, H. (1988) Pintail Snipe in Israel in November 1984 and its identification. *Dutch Birding* 10: 1-11.

Shirihai, H. (1989) Identification of Arabian Warbler. *Brit. Birds* 82: 97-113.

Shirihai, H. (1993) Separation of Striated Scops Owl from Eurasian Scops Owl. *Brit. Birds* 86: 286-7.

Shirihai, H. (1994a) Separation of Tawny Eagle from Steppe Eagle in Israel. *Brit. Birds* 87: 396-7.

Shirihai, H. (1994b) Field identification of Dunn's, Bar-tailed Desert and Desert Larks. *Dutch Birding* 16: 1-9.

Shirihai, H., & Christie, D.A. (1992) Raptor migration at Eilat. *Brit. Birds* 85: 141-86.

Shirihai, H., Christie, D.A., & Harris, A. (in press) The identification of *Hippolais* warblers. *Brit. Birds*.

Shirihai, H., & Colston, P.R. (1987) Siberian Water Pipit in Israel. *Dutch Birding* 9: 8-12.

Shirihai, H., & Doherty, P. (1990) Steppe Buzzard plumages. *Birding World* 3: 10-14.

Shirihai, H., & Forsman, D. (1991) Steppe Buzzard morphs on migration and their separation from Long-legged Buzzard. *Dutch Birding* 13: 197-209.

Shirihai, H., & Forsman, D. (in press) A review of field identification of large falcons in the Western Palearctic. *Brit. Birds*.

Shirihai, H., & Gantlett, S. (1993) Identification of female and immature Black-headed Buntings. *Birding World* 6: 194-7.

Shirihai, H., Harris, A., & Cottridge, D. (1991) Identification of Spectacled Warbler.*Brit. Birds* 84: 423-40.

Shirihai, H., Harris, A., & Cottridge, D. (in prep.) *The Sylvia Warblers.* London.

Shirihai, H., & Madge, S. (1993) Identification of Hume's Yellow-browed warblers. *Birding World* 6: 439-43.

Shirihai, H., Madge, S., Hoogendoorn, T., & Christie, D.A. (in prep.) The large gull complex in the Near and Middle East. *Brit. Birds*.

Shirihai, H., Mullarney, K., & Grant, P. (1990) Identification of Dunn's, Bar-tailed and Desert Larks. *Birding World* 3: 15-21.

Shirihai, H., Roselaar, C.S., Helbig, A.J., Barthel, P.H., & van Loon, A.J. (in press) Identification and taxonomy of large *Acrocephalus* warblers. *Dutch Birding*.

Skakuj, M. (1990) Die Bestimmung der Eiderenten-Arten *Somateria mollissima, spectabilis, fischeri* und *Polysticta. Limicola* 4: 285-306.

Small, B (1992) Ageing and sexing Ortolan and Cretzschmar's Buntings in the field. *Birding World* 5: 223-8.

REFERENCES

Small, B.J. (1994) Separation of Pied Wheatear and Cyprus Pied Wheatear. *Dutch Birding* 16: 177-85.

Small, B. (1995) Field identification of Red-footed Falcon. *Brit. Birds* 88: 181-9.

Svensson, L. (1971) Stäpphök *Circus macrourus* och ängshök *C. pygargus* - problemet att skilja dem åt. *Vår Fågelvärld* 30: 106-22.

Svensson, L. (1975) Större skrikörn *Aquila clanga* och mindre skrikörn *A. pomarina* - problemet att artbestämma dem. *Vår Fågelvärld* 34: 1-36.

Svensson, L. (1981) Om bestämning i fält av bivråk *Pernis apivorus* - art, ålder och kön - samt jämförelser med ormvråk *Buteo buteo*. *Vår Fågelvärld* 40: 1-12.

Svensson, L. (1987) Underwing pattern of Steppe, Spotted and Lesser Spotted Eagles. *International Bird Identification, Proc. 4th Internat. Identification Meeting, Eilat*: 12-14.

Svensson, L. (1992) *Identification of European Passerines*. 4th edn. Stockholm.

Swash, A., & Cleere, N. (1989) Identification of Egyptian and Nubian Nightjars. *Birding World* 2: 163-5.

Taylor, P.B. (1982/83) Field identification of sand plovers. *Dutch Birding* 4: 113-30; 5: 37-66.

Taylor, P.B. (1984) Field identification of Pintail Snipe and recent records in Kenya. *Dutch Birding* 6: 77-90.

Taylor, P.B. (1987) Field identification of Greater and Lesser Sand Plovers. *International Bird Identification. Proc. 4th Int. Ident. Meeting 1986*: 47-8.

Ticehurst, C.B. (1938) *A Systematic review of the Genus Phylloscopus*. Brit. Mus., London.

Ullman, M. (1989) Identification of Upcher's and Olivaceous Warbler. *Birding World* 2: 167-70.

Ullman, M. (1990) Bill shape of Calandra and Bimaculated Larks. *Dutch Birding* 12: 82-4.

Ullman, M. (1994) Crested and Thekla Larks in Morocco. *Dutch Birding* 16: 19-20.

van den Berg, A.B. (1987) Bill shape of Bimaculated Lark in Turkey. *Dutch Birding* 9: 172-4.

van den Berg, A.B. (1990) Habitat of Slender-billed Curlews in Morocco. *Brit. Birds* 83: 1-7.

van den Berg, A.B., *et al.* (1988) Striated Scops Owl in Turkey. *Dutch Birding* 10: 161-6.

van den Berg, A.B., & Symens, P. (1992) Occurrence and identification of Basra Reed Warbler in Saudi Arabia. *Dutch Birding* 14: 41-8.

Wallace, D.I.M. (1964) Field identification of *Hippolais* warblers. *Brit. Birds* 57: 282-301.

Wallace, D.I.M. (1976) Sora Rail in Scilly and the identification of immature small crakes. *Brit. Birds* 69: 443-7.

Wallace, D.I.M. (1984) Mystery photographs 91. Crested Lark. *Brit. Birds* 77: 289-91.

Wilkinson, P.J. (1991) Mystery photographs 168. Chukar x Red-legged Partridge. *Brit. Birds* 84: 264-5.

Williamson, K. (1967a) *Identification for Ringers 1. The genera Cettia, Locustella, Acrocephalus and Hippolais*. 3rd, revised edn. BTO Guide No. 7. Oxford.

Williamson, K. (1967b) *Identification for Ringers 2. The genus Phylloscopus*. 2nd, revised edn. BTO Guide No. 8. Oxford.

Williamson, K. (1967c) *Identification for Ringers 3. The genus Sylvia*. 2nd, revised edn. BTO Guide No. 9. Oxford.

Index of vernacular names

Figures in *italic* refer to illustrations; those in **bold** to main entries within articles.

Two Points to Remember

(1) Moustachial, Submoustachial and Malar Stripes: Do not confuse these terms. The moustachial stripe is the dark line from the bill below the eye, along the lower border of the ear-coverts. The pale line below this is the submoustachial, and the dark line below that, down the sides of the chin and throat, is the malar. (Many observers confuse the moustachial and malar stripes.) **(2)** Tertials These are the elongated innermost secondaries that cloak the primaries at rest (the secondaries are often hidden or mostly hidden).